AF505595

Public Policies for Human Development

Public Policies for Human Development

Achieving the Millennium Development Goals in Latin America

Edited By

Marco V. Sánchez

Rob Vos

Enrique Ganuza

Hans Lofgren

and

Carolina Díaz-Bonilla

In Association with
UNDP
UN-DESA
The World Bank

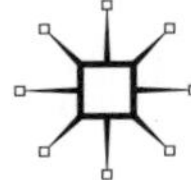

First published 2010 by
PALGRAVE MACMILLAN

Palgrave Macmillan in the UK is an imprint of Macmillan Publishers Limited, registered in England, company number 785998, of Houndmills, Basingstoke, Hampshire RG21 6XS.

Palgrave Macmillan in the US is a division of St Martin's Press LLC, 175 Fifth Avenue, New York, NY 10010.

Palgrave Macmillan is the global academic imprint of the above companies and has companies and representatives throughout the world.

Palgrave® and Macmillan® are registered trademarks in the United States, the United Kingdom, Europe and other countries

ISBN 978–0–230–24776–5   hardback

This book is printed on paper suitable for recycling and made from fully managed and sustained forest sources. Logging, pulping and manufacturing processes are expected to conform to the environmental regulations of the country of origin.

A catalogue record for this book is available from the British Library.

A catalog record for this book is available from the Library of Congress.

10 9 8 7 6 5 4 3 2 1
19 18 17 16 15 14 13 12 11 10

Printed and bound in Great Britain by
CPI Antony Rowe, Chippenham and Eastbourne

Contents

List of tables and figures

Tables

Figures

Preface

Over the past ten years, the United Nations Development Programme (UNDP) has coordinated a number of comparative studies on the macroeconomic performance, poverty and inequality in Latin America and the Caribbean. Completed projects include macroeconomic policies and poverty during the 1980s and 1990s,[1] the impact of balance-of-payments liberalization on income distribution and poverty,[2] and the impact of trade liberalization and free trade agreements on distribution and poverty.[3] These studies were all collaborative efforts involving other UN agencies (including the Economic Commission for Latin America and the Caribbean, UN-ECLAC, and the United Nations Department of Economic and Social Affairs, UN-DESA), as well as renowned international research institutes (including the International Food Policy Research Institute, IFPRI, in Washington D.C., and the Institute of Social Studies, ISS, in The Hague) and the multilateral development banks (World Bank and the Inter-American Development Bank). Most importantly, however, the studies brought together high-level researchers and policymakers from most (that is, 16 or more) countries in the region in order to obtain the best possible insights in country-specific conditions and the reasons for success or failure in reducing poverty and improving human development. The studies clearly revealed that while countries fairly uniformly engaged in Washington-consensus style economic reform measures, the outcomes in terms of growth, income inequality and poverty have been quite diverse because of different institutional settings, economic structures and human resource endowments. The more common finding, though, was that the market-oriented reforms did not yield the progress towards higher and sustained growth and substantial poverty reduction promised by the advocates of the reforms. Furthermore, inequality remains unchanged at very high levels.

Rather than evaluating the performance of past policies, the present book takes a more forward looking approach. It assesses what feasible financing strategies policymakers in the region would be advised to follow in pursuance of the United Nations' millennium development goals (MDGs) and their achievement in 2015. The studies relate to similar concerns as those of the previous projects, though: how to make macroeconomic policies more conducive to support sustained growth and reduce the still widespread poverty and inequality in the region. In addition, the present study also addresses the question how such policies could ensure sufficient levels of public spending in support of improvements in human development in terms of ensuring that all children complete at least primary education, that child and maternal mortality rates are brought down substantially and that all of the region's population has adequate access to basic sanitation. In doing so, the study keeps an economy-wide perspective as progress on human development and increased resources allocated towards social services will affect the composition of the labour supply, change relative prices, and may exercise financing constraints in different parts of the economy. This provides great value added over more sector-based needs assessments for achieving the MDGs as the analysis shows that the macroeconomic repercussions strongly influence the cost estimates of the resources needed to achieve the goals in education, health and sanitation. The model-based approach of the study also enables policymakers to get a better sense of whether their country is "on track" or "off track" towards the achievement of the MDGs. Standard assessments of that kind typically make linear projections based on past performance. The analyses in the present study simulate whether with a continuation of existing policies the goals can be reached or whether greater efforts are needed and, if so, how the additionally required resources can best be mobilized. While the region has made much human progress, severe deficits remain and achievement of the MDGs clearly will require important additional efforts. The study concludes these are affordable for all countries, but it will require that some hard choices in favour of social development and, in most countries, at the expense of higher taxes will have to be made.

As in the previous projects, also this study was a collaborative endeavour. The study was initiated by UNDP's Regional Bureau for Latin America and the Caribbean, which also organized the funding for the project. The World Bank also provided financial support and, importantly, the core modelling framework— the MAquette for MDG Simulations (MAMS)— which was applied and further developed in the country studies conducted for this project. UN-DESA and the ISS provided expertise in helping adapt the MAMS framework to the Latin American context, the methodologies for the social sector analysis and the microsimulations. ECLAC and the Inter-American Development Bank provided institutional and financial support to facilitate the implementation of several of the country studies.

In order to obtain answers as close as possible to country realities, the project conducted the investigation in collaboration with teams of local researchers and policymakers in nineteen countries in the region. Combining country expert knowledge with a common, rigorous modelling methodology to assess feasible financing strategies to achieve the MDGs ensured both a high degree of realism and policy relevance in the analysis and maximum comparability. Without the input of the country experts, most appearing as chapter authors in this volume, this undertaking would not have been possible. The investigation took place over a period of two and a half years, during which four workshops were held at which the research methodology was agreed and refined and intermediate results were discussed and compared. UNDP country offices in Uruguay, Venezuela, Guatemala, and Chile offered invaluable support in making these events happen.

Samuel Morley of IFPRI provided crucial ideas and impetus to the conceptualization of the project and at various project workshops he helped place the sophisticated modelling exercises back into the reality of Latin American development. We also thank Hans Timmer and Jaime Saavedra at the World Bank for their support throughout the project and their suggestions for the project's design.

The coordinators of the project received invaluable research support from Martín Cicowiecz, research fellow at *Centro de Estudios Distributivos, Laborales y Sociales* (CEDLAS) of *Universidad Nacional de La Plata*. He was instrumental in the further development of the modelling techniques and their application in each of the countries. Furthermore, his enthusiasm and dedication to the project helped create the right kind of team spirit among all country teams and he managed to solve an infinite number of problems for the country teams and get their models running. The country experts from the Research Centre of the *Universidad del Pacífico* (CIUP), Peru, besides preparing their own country study also provided support in the analysis of determinants of MDG achievements to the country team of Guatemala. Sherman Robinson of the University of Sussex gave most valuable methodological advice during several of the project's workshops. We are also grateful to Cornelia Kaldewei of UN-DESA who assisted in making sense out of the mass of country-specific results while providing support to the comparative country analysis as presented in Chapter 2.

Maria Isabel Bruna provided excellent editorial support for chapters 4-8 and 10-12 that were originally written in Spanish. Kathy Ogle took care of the translation of those chapters to English.

The Swedish International Development Agency (SIDA) and the Spanish Agency for International Development Co-operation (AECID) provided generous support to the project.

The authors are most grateful to the hosting agencies, UNDP, UN-DESA, and the World Bank. These agencies provided all the institutional support required, while leaving all the intellectual freedom needed to conduct this research on issues so central to the well being of the populations in the countries of the region. It goes without saying that the opinions expressed in this volume are exclusively those of the authors.

Marco V. Sánchez
Rob Vos
Enrique Ganuza
Hans Lofgren   *New York, Santiago de Chile, and Washington D.C.*
Carolina Díaz-Bonilla   *October 2009*

Notes

1   See Enrique Ganuza, Lance Taylor and Samuel Morley, eds. (1998). *Política macroeconómica y pobreza en América Latina y el Caribe*, Madrid: Ediciones Mundi-Prensa (for UNDP).
2   See Enrique Ganuza, Ricardo Paes de Barros, Lance Taylor and Rob Vos, eds. (2001). *Liberalización, desigualdad y pobreza: América Latina y el Caribe en los 90*, Buenos Aires: EUDEBA (for UNDP); and Rob Vos, Lance Taylor and Ricardo Paes de Barros, eds. (2002). *Economic Liberalization, Distribution and Poverty. Latin America in the 1990s*, Cheltenham (UK) and Northampton, MA: Edward Elgar Publishers.
3   See Rob Vos, Enrique Ganuza, Samuel Morley and Sherman Robinson, eds. (2006). *Who Gains from Free Trade? Export-led Growth, Inequality and Poverty in Latin America*, London, New York: Routledge; and Enrique Ganuza, Samuel Morley, Sherman Robinson and Rob Vos, eds. (2004). *Quién se beneficia del libre comercio? Promoción de exportaciones y pobreza en América Latina y el Caribe en los 90*, Bogotá: Alfaomega.

About the editors

Marco V. Sánchez is economic affairs officer at the Department of Economic and Social Affairs of the United Nations (UN-DESA), New York, and was previously associated with the Sub-Regional Office in Mexico City of the UN Economic Commission for Latin America and the Caribbean.

Rob Vos is director of the Development Policy and Analysis Division at the Department of Economic and Social Affairs of the United Nations (UN-DESA), New York, and Professor of Finance and Development at the Institute of Social Studies, The Hague.

Enrique Ganuza is resident representative of the United Nations in Santiago de Chile and was chief economist for Latin America and the Caribbean of the United Nations Development Programme (UNDP) at the initiation of the project leading to the present publication.

Hans Lofgren is senior economist of the Development Economics Prospects Group (DECPG) of the World Bank. Prior to joining the Bank he was senior research fellow at the International Food Policy Research Institute (IFPRI).

Carolina Díaz-Bonilla is currently economist in the Poverty and Gender Unit of the Latin America and Caribbean Region (LCSPP) of the World Bank, working on issues of poverty, income distribution, and labour market performance. Previously, during most of the project's duration, she was an economist in the Development Economics Prospects Group (DECPG) of the World Bank.

About other contributors

Maurizio Bussolo is a senior economist at the World Bank in the Development Economics Prospects Group (DECPG). His main line of research is in studying the links between trade, growth and poverty.

Gustavo Canavire is an economist and PhD candidate at Georgia State University and previously did advisory work for the Bolivian government and the World Bank.

Juan F. Castro is lecturer and researcher at the Economics Department of the Pacific University, Lima, Peru.

Martín Cicowiez is lecturer at the *Universidad Nacional de La Plata* and research fellow at the *Centro de Estudios Distributivos, Laborales y Sociales* (CEDLAS) of the university. He is also associated with the International Economics Centre of the Ministry of Foreign Affairs of Argentina.

Luciano Di Gresia is lecturer and researcher at the *Universidad Nacional de La Plata*. Presently, he is Under-secretary of Finance of the Province of Buenos Aires.

Leonardo Gasparini is professor of economics at the *Universidad Nacional de La Plata* and director of the *Centro de Estudios Distributivos, Laborales y Sociales* (CEDLAS) of the university.

Wilson Jiménez is director of the National Institute for Statistics (INE) of Bolivia. At the time of writing he was a consultant for UNDP-Bolivia.

Cornelia Kaldewei is economic affairs officer at the Department of Economic and Social Affairs of the United Nations (UN-DESA).

Camilo Lagos is researcher at the Institute of Public Affairs of the Universidad de Chile.

Mauricio León is Vice-Minister Inclusive Economic and Social Development of Ecuador. Previously, he was coordinator of the Integrated System of Social indicators of Ecuador (SIISE).

Mirna Mariscal is economist at the Unit for Economic and Social Policy Analysis (UDAPE) in Bolivia.

Denis Medvedev is an economist with the Development Prospects Group at the World Bank. His research interests focus on the impact of macro policies (trade policy, fiscal policy, adaptation to climate change) on economic development and income distribution.

Carlos de Miguel is environmental affairs officer of the Sustainable Development and Human Settlements Division at UN-ECLAC, Santiago, Chile. When the project started, he was economic affairs officer at the Office of the Deputy Executive Secretary in the same institution.

Araceli Ortega is currently chief advisor to the Undersecretary for Secondary Education, Ministry of Education, Mexico. Previously, she was chief advisor of the Undersecretary for Planning and Evaluation at the Ministry of Social Development, Mexico.

Raúl O'Ryan is associate professor at the Industrial Engineering Department of the Universidad de Chile. His main field of research is in environmental economics. He has been an adviser to Chile's Environmental Commission and several ministries and a consultant for international agencies, including the World Bank

José Rosero is Vice-Minister in the Ministry of Coordination of Social Development in Ecuador. Previously, he worked as an economist for the Integrated System of Social indicators of Ecuador (SIISE).

Miguel Székely is currently Undersecretary for Secondary Education of Mexico. Previously, he was the Undersecretary for Planning and Evaluation at the Ministry of Social Development, Mexico.

Gustavo Yamada is lecturer and researcher at the Economics Department of the Pacific University, Lima, Peru. Previous functions include Undersecretary of Social Advancement in Peru, fiscal economist at the International Monetary Fund, and senior economist of the Inter-American Development Bank.

1
Overview

Rob Vos, Marco V. Sánchez and Enrique Ganuza

Progress towards the human development goals in Latin America

Poverty in Latin America and the Caribbean tends to be lower than in most other developing country regions. The region also scores better in terms of education and health achievements. Social indicators reveal substantial progress in terms of human development in recent decades. Nonetheless, on several counts progress has been slower than in other parts of the developing world. In terms of the Millennium Development Goals (MDGs), agreed upon by all countries in the world in the framework of the 2000 Millennium Declaration of the United Nations, increased efforts will be needed to meet the established targets by 2015. Regarding access to primary education and reducing child mortality, the countries in Latin America and the Caribbean have been able to keep pace with fast growing East Asia, for instance. However, where it comes to reducing extreme poverty, the region has made very little progress since 1990, with the share of the population living on less than one dollar a day barely falling (see Figure 1.1). In contrast, fast and sustained economic growth in many of the countries in East Asia has contributed to a substantial decline in poverty in that part of the world. Also progress in expanding the coverage of drinking water and basic sanitation has been relatively slow on average in the Latin America and the Caribbean.

Per capita income growth in the region reached a meagre 1.8 per cent per annum between 1990 and 2008, well below the average welfare improvements witnessed in the 1960s and 1970s and also underachieving compared with other parts of the developing world. Growth in the region also tends to show substantially higher volatility than elsewhere (United Nations, 2008). Stronger recent growth performance in the region since 2003 was greatly helped by a buoyant world economy and favourable commodity prices, but has not been enough to overcome the discontent with the outcomes of the drastic economic reform measures introduced by most countries of the region since the late 1980s. The

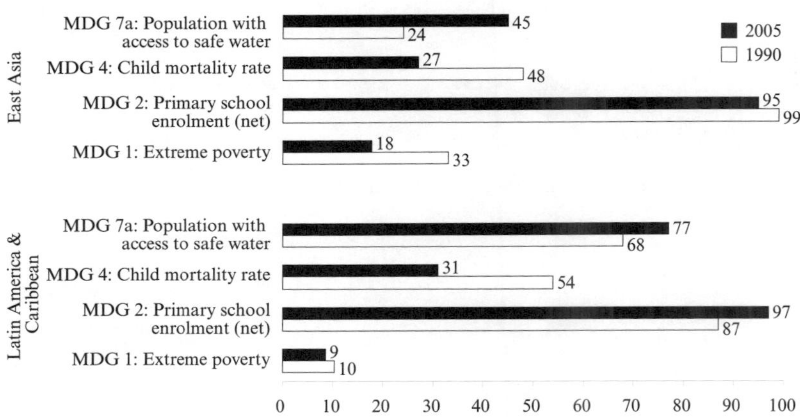

Figure 1.1 Progress towards the MDGs in East Asia and Latin America and the Caribbean, 1990-2005[a]

Source: United Nations (2007).

[a] All indicators are in per cent, except MDG 4 which defines under-five mortality per 1,000 live births.

far-reaching liberalization of trade, capital flows, financial sectors and domestic markets for goods and services in the countries of the region, among others, formed the showcase of the Washington Consensus, but failed to yield high sustainable growth. Volatility in capital flows and world commodity markets exercised an even stronger influence on stop-go economic cycles in the countries of the region and economic opening seems to have done little in support of reducing poverty and pervasive income inequality, as predecessor studies to the present volume have pointed out (see Vos and others, 2002, 2006). Those earlier studies emphasized that insufficient human development, manifested among other things through constraints in the supply of skilled workers, is one element in explaining the limited capacity of the countries in the region to take greater advantage of potential gains from opening borders to international trade and investment. Those studies also concluded that existing income inequality would hamper more of economic growth trickling down to the poor, thereby also limiting the resources for the poor to invest in education and better health.

The MDG agenda adopted under the auspices of the Millennium Declaration should provide the impetus to reinvigorate efforts to invest in human development which had been pretty much undervalued by the Washington Consensus. The MDG framework is foremost an advocacy tool for putting poverty reduction, improvement in primary education, child and maternal mortality, gender equality and a sustainable environment to the forefront of priority setting in public policies. As such, it does not identify specific sets of policies that would need to be put in place to achieve the targets that are to be achieved by 2015. Such policies need to be defined at the country level and embedded in broader national development strategies. Hence to assess the different dimensions of development strategies and policies oriented at the achievement of the MDGs, there are at least three crucial questions that must be answered. First, what is the trajectory that the country will follow under current policies and investments, and what is the likelihood of achieving the goals (or a subset of them) in those circumstances? If projections based on a continuation of existing policies suggest important departures from the desired outcomes, then the second question is: What changes in development strategy, institutions, policies, and investments may be needed to achieve the goals? To answer the second question requires analysis of the links between policy choices and economic outcomes—the subject matter of much of development economics. A related third question is: What are the costs of different strategies, policies, and investment alternatives, including the macroeconomic adjustment costs of alternative financing options?

By seeking answers to these questions, the present study analyzes the feasibility of timely reaching goals in 18 countries in Latin America and the Caribbean, covering practically all of the region's population and GDP.[1]

For a variety of reasons, the most important being insufficient data availability, this study will not cover all MDGs and the related specific targets but will explicitly consider the following goals and specific targets which countries will be attempting to reach by the year 2015:

- MDG 1 – Eradicate extreme poverty and hunger: Halve, between 1990 and 2015, the proportion of people whose income is less than one dollar a day.[2]
- MDG 2 – Achieve universal primary education: Ensure that, by 2015, children everywhere, boys and girls alike, will be able to complete a full course of primary schooling.
- MDG 3 – Promote gender equality: Eliminate gender disparity in primary and secondary education, preferably by 2005, and in all levels of education no later than 2015.
- MDG 4 – Reduce child mortality: Reduce by two-thirds, between 1990 and 2015, the under-five mortality rate.
- MDG 5 – Improve maternal health: Reduce by three quarters, between 1990 and 2015, the maternal mortality rate.
- MDG 7 – Ensure environmental sustainability: Halve, by 2015, the proportion of people without sustainable access to safe drinking water and basic sanitation.

An integrated analytical framework for assessing MDG strategies

The process of selecting the best policy interventions and estimating their costs is particularly difficult because there are likely trade-offs and synergies among MDGs as well as economy-wide effects that need to be taken into account.

Investing in children's nutritional status and health (MDGs 1 and 4) will result in better performance at school (MDG 2). This is an example of synergy. Governments with limited resources and wishing to prioritize spending on education and health services may find little fiscal revenue left for maintaining and investing in general physical infrastructure. The result could be that there is an improvement in education and health outcomes (MDGs 2, 4, and 5) but at the cost of lower output growth and income poverty reduction (MDG 1). Poorly maintained road and transportation infrastructure also could limit the accessibility of schools and health centres and thereby limit the effectiveness of public expenditures in these areas. These are examples of possible trade-offs in priority setting in public spending and outcomes for the various goals. If achieving the education and health goals implies hiring of additional teachers and health workers in large amounts, their wages, and with it the cost of the policy intervention, are likely to go up since such skills are not in unlimited supply. If, to finance the required increase in spending on education, health and basic sanitation, taxes will have to increase this may also affect disposable incomes of the poor and this then may indirectly affect the achievement of the MDGs. If financing involves more foreign aid or external borrowing, the real exchange rate might appreciate hurting output and employment in export sectors. These are examples of undesirable economy-wide, general-equilibrium effects. At the same time, of course, countries with a better educated and healthier work force likely are able to sustain stronger productivity growth supporting higher welfare in the long run. This likely entails an intertemporal trade-off, as there may be growth costs associated with enhanced investment in the human capital of the younger population now to obtain those future welfare gains.

Ideally policy makers should possess a tool for MDG analysis which helps identify the determinants and the costs of MDG achievement which would capture all synergies, trade-offs, input-output linkages, and economy-wide effects. At the same time, it should be transparent, easy to understand and adaptable, compatible with expenditure planning processes in line ministries, implementable even in a context with severe data limitations, and capable of simulating impact of policies in specific country settings.

Unfortunately, in real life no such tool exists. In practice, policymakers, academics and international organizations have used a variety of approaches to estimate the potential effects and costs of policy interventions to achieve the MDGs, including needs assessments and other sectoral approaches and macro approaches ranging from relatively simple poverty-growth elasticity estimates to more complex multi-sector general equilibrium models.

Needs assessments and other sector approaches

The "needs assessment" approach has been applied in an increasing number of countries. Many of these assessments have been supported by the work developed through the United Nation's Millennium Project (United Nations Millennium Project, 2005). The approach tries to identify which interventions are needed in any specific context and estimate the related resource needs in terms of finance, infrastructure and trained personnel. This analysis is subsequently used to calculate the magnitude by which public expenditures need to be "scaled up" in order to reach the MDGs. When fit into the broader public sector budget framework of a nation, it may also serve to identify financing gaps. As such, it may provide inputs for negotiations with donors and multilateral financial institutions in order to ensure adequate resource mobilization. In essence, the approach does no more than one would minimally expect governments to undertake when trying to match budgets with plans for enhancing performance in education, health or water and sanitation. In practice, however, many developing countries show weak capacity to engage in such result-oriented budgeting as critical assessments of poverty reduction strategy papers have indicated (see, for example, ODI, 2003). The needs assessments have helped fill such lacunae in many instances.

Analytically, the needs assessment approach is best compared with cost-effectiveness studies for social sectors. Such studies seek to assess with greater quantitative precision which are the determinants of access to and/or outcomes in education, health and so on. A version of the human capital model derived from economic theory typically underlies the related microeconometric analysis (see, for example, Glewwe, 2002). Using micro and sector data sets, the analysis seeks to quantify the relative impact of each determinant on expected outcomes. For example, by how much should school subsidies or the supply of trained teachers increase to achieve a one-percent increase in school enrolment. After subsequent use of information about unit costs an idea can be obtained of the most cost-effective interventions. While similar in approach, in practice needs assessments more typically focus entirely on "supply side effects" (for example, the need for more school infrastructure, teachers, textbooks, and so on) without considering "demand factors" (such as household income, parent's education, child's health and other socio-economic characteristics of households and individuals). Consistent with the human capital approach, demand factors feature more prominent in cost-effectiveness analyses, but studies with complete specifications more typically consider both supply and demand-side determinants. Other shortcomings of the needs assessments, as conducted in practice, include the lack of consideration of the synergy effects, of the existence of possible non-linearities in the effectiveness of policy interventions, and of macroeconomic trade-offs of the kinds suggested above. Further, the needs assessments also do not consider the impact of scaled-up public expenditures on education, health, water and sanitation on income poverty.

Macro approaches

Income poverty is the main focus of the so-called "poverty-growth elasticity approach". In its most rudimentary form, it builds on an extension of the Harrod-Domar growth model to calculate the required investments that will be needed in order to reach a target growth rate.[3] To estimate the costs of achieving the goal of halving extreme poverty, assumed or estimated parameter values are added for the country's poverty-growth elasticity, which measures the amount of poverty reduction for each per cent of per capita output growth, and the incremental capital-output ratio (ICOR), which is a broad measure of the productivity of investment. The approach then can be used for calculating how much investment is needed for a country to halve poverty by 2015. This approach may be combined with a broader macroeconomic framework, as currently being implemented in several Asian countries (Seth and Kathiwada, 2007), adding a role for required investments in education and health, national savings, and domestic and external sources of finance.

While adding a link to income poverty and a link to macroeconomic variables, this approach also has important weaknesses. In particular, assuming a constant poverty-growth elasticity and ICOR over a prolonged period of time seems far from realistic. By definition, the poverty-growth elasticity will change as mean incomes rise or the poverty incidence falls.[4] Also, one may expect an MDG-oriented public investment strategy to affect income distribution, which in turn will affect the poverty-growth elasticity. The macroeconomic framework, as applied, assumes constant-price projections of required public investment outlays, which along with a constant ICOR and generally Keynesian model features under excess supply capacity, may well lead to optimistic projections of growth and hence of poverty reduction, under the given assumptions.

Agénor and others (2005) combine a macro model with an MDG module in a framework that requires relatively little data, but does use econometrically estimated parameters. On the other hand, the macro model is highly aggregated: it has only one production sector and it does not include intermediate inputs, factor markets, or factor wages (rents). These considerations limit its ability to analyze key aspects of MDG strategies such as how the direct exchange rate and labour market repercussions of scaled-up government programmes differ depending on whether the programme emphasizes, for example, education or infrastructure. Also, its high level of government and labour market aggregation makes it less informative for fiscal analysis.

The links between growth, service delivery, MDG achievements and financing outlined above demonstrate that a more sophisticated and coherent framework is needed. The analysis must consider macroeconomic factors and trade-offs between objectives. For example, increases in foreign aid (borrowing or grants, although the latter is less common in most of the countries in Latin America and the Caribbean) lead to concerns over the possibility of "Dutch disease" effects, characterized by real exchange rate appreciation and a structural erosion of the capacity to produce tradables (for exports or the domestic market); a capacity that may be needed in the future. If, on the other hand, the MDG strategy is financed via increases in taxes or domestic borrowing, then private sector growth, investment, and consumption are all likely to be affected negatively. This could offset some of the gains the MDG strategy is trying to achieve. It may imply less progress on poverty reduction and, indirectly, towards the achievement of other MDGs because of effects on household incomes and consumption. A related critical issue is the pace at which large programmes should be scaled up. Rapid initial expansion may drive up costs more quickly and could be more expensive in real present value terms. On the other hand, given time lags, especially in education, expanding investment too slowly may make it impossible to achieve the MDGs by 2015.

Such limitations do not turn such studies into meaningless exercises. Any modelling exercise is bound by its assumptions and the amount of realism those contain. They may well serve contexts with severe data limitations which leave the application of fairly simple frameworks as a second-best option.

An integrated macro-micro framework

In the present volume, we take a somewhat more ambitious approach. The analysis is based on a comparative economy-wide model framework that accounts for both the microeconomic determinants of needs satisfaction in education, health and drinking water and basic sanitation and macroeconomic trade-offs in the financing of public spending options directed at satisfying those needs. The analysis further considers synergies between degrees of progress towards education, health, access to drinking water and basic sanitation, and poverty reduction goals. As explained in detail in Chapters 2 and 3, an integrated framework building on three sets of methodologies has been used in all country studies in this volume.

First, microeconomic and sector analyses of determinants of outcomes for MDGs 2, 4, 5 and 7 are undertaken along the lines of the aforementioned cost-effectiveness studies and needs assessments. Human capital models were estimated to identify the influence of both supply and demand factors on outcomes in education, health and drinking water and sanitation. Regarding MDG 2, the demand for primary and other levels of schooling is a function of student behaviour (enrolment, repetition, graduation). Student behaviour, in turn, depends on the quality of education (identified by variables such as classroom availability and student-teacher ratios), the income incentives (the expected wage premium from education), the under-five mortality rate (a proxy for the health status of the student population), household consumption per capita (a proxy for the capacity to pay for education and opportunity costs) and the level of public infrastructure (a proxy for the effective distance to school). Regarding

MDGs 4 and 5, under-five and maternal mortality are considered to be determined by the availability of public and private health services, household consumption per capita, the level of public infrastructure (a proxy for the effective distance to health centres and hospitals), and the coverage of water and sanitation services. Access to drinking water and basic sanitation was modelled as a function of household consumption per capita, the provision of such services by public or private providers and the level of public infrastructure. Country-specific conditions were considered in the case studies through adding additional explanatory and control variables.

Second, the findings of the analysis of MDG determinants are subsequently inserted into an economy-wide framework, as recently developed at the World Bank as an analytical tool to help countries think through the requirements and implications of scaling up resources to achieve the MDGs. The framework is labelled MAMS (*Maquette* for **MDG** **S**imulation) and was originally presented in Lofgren (2004). It has been extended and applied in the context of the present study covering 18 countries in Latin America and the Caribbean. Chapter 3 provides a detailed description of the version of MAMS applied to these country cases. MAMS has been built from a fairly standard computable general equilibrium (CGE) framework with dynamic-recursive features but incorporates a special module which specifies the main determinants of MDG achievement and the direct impact of enhanced public expenditures on MDG-related infrastructure and services. MAMS has been designed to help analysts and policymakers perform policy experiments (such as alternative financing scenarios) that consider the economy-wide implications of scaling up public expenditures in order to reach the MDGs.

Third, the achievement of the goal for reducing income poverty is defined in the integrated macro-micro framework as a function of the overall general equilibrium effects from dynamic adjustments in production, employment, wages and other relative prices, as well as changes in the quality of human capital through MDG-related expenditures. The final outcome for income poverty can be estimated by looking at the outcomes for per capita household income and consumption for different household groups. However, CGE models can typically only specify a limited number of representative households, which results in insufficient detail regarding changes in the distribution in order to be able to make robust statements regarding the poverty outcomes. In consequence, the CGE analysis is supplemented by a method of microsimulations that takes the labour market outcomes (unemployment, employment structure, relative remunerations, and skill composition) from the CGE for different types of workers and applies them to a micro data set (such as a household survey) to obtain the required details about income distribution for the poverty analysis. Chapter 2 details this approach which fits a recent tradition of combining economy-wide modelling instruments with micro level data of the full income distribution.[5]

Main findings

The integrated macro-micro framework allows to assess what would be required to achieve the MDGs, including what type of actions to be undertaken at the sector level, realistic estimates of the macroeconomic costs, and how macroeconomic trade-offs of alternative financing strategies might be dealt with. The framework also provides policy makers with a more appropriate tool to establish whether the country is "on track" or not towards the goals. Existing studies often try to establish this by looking at past trends and projecting those trends forward in linear fashion. The past need not be a good predictor of the future and what may be more important is to establish what resources and mechanisms are currently in place in support of the achievement of the MDGs and take into consideration possibly decreasing marginal returns in the effectiveness of social spending in achieving the MDG. In MAMS, this situation is identified through a "business-as-usual" scenario of trends under continued existing policies and given exogenous circumstances. If this baseline scenario does not meet the given MDG targets, countries are said to be "off track" in this framework and the effectiveness of additional or alternative policies can be readily measured against this benchmark. In the "MDG scenarios", public expenditures are scaled up to the level required to reach the targets set for MDGs 2, 4, 5 and 7 and the economy-wide implications are assessed by comparing the MDG scenario results with what would be the simulated outcome of "business-as-usual".

Against this analytical backdrop, the selected country studies presented in Chapters 4 to 12 and the comparative analysis of Chapter 2 demonstrate that achieving the MDGs is within reach for most Latin American and Caribbean countries. Additional efforts to those currently undertaken will be needed. The country analyses also show that in most cases the cost of the additional public spending are low to moderate in macroeconomic terms. Even so, alternative financing mechanisms to cover those costs need to be assessed carefully as these tend to generate macroeconomic trade-offs. These findings can be detailed in four points.

First, the poverty reduction target is within reach, even with unchanged policies, in six countries of the region, including the most populous ones, Mexico and Brazil. This results under the assumptions of a baseline scenario which would reflect continued good economic performance from around 2003. For 12 of the 18 countries, however, baseline output and employment growth would not suffice to meet MDG 1. The goals for safe drinking water and basic sanitation (MDG 7) are more uniformly achievable with continued existing efforts in most countries of the region. The region is also making good progress in improving primary school enrolment, but keeping all children in primary school until graduation remains a big challenge in nearly all of the countries of the region, with the exception of Cuba, and, possibly, Chile, Costa Rica and Mexico. All countries have made significant progress in reducing child mortality, but efforts will need to be stepped up in most countries in order to reduce early childhood deaths by two thirds by 2015. Only Chile and Cuba appear to be "on track" for this goal. Estimates of maternal mortality are subject to measurement errors, but the best available evidence for the region suggests very little progress and, again, only Chile and Cuba seem to be "on track" for this related target.

Second, these findings indicate that additional efforts have to be made to achieve the MDGs for education, health and drinking water and basic sanitation. The country studies estimate the required additional public spending on MDG-related services in the order ranging from about 1–1.5 per cent of GDP per annum in the cases of Peru, Costa Rica, Ecuador, and Jamaica to an annual additional cost of 4–6 per cent of GDP in Mexico, Nicaragua, Honduras, and Guatemala. Only for Cuba and Chile, which are the countries that should be able to achieve the goals under 'business-as-usual' policies, no additional costs would need to be incurred. For most countries, however, the additional cost would be less than 3 per cent of GDP, which seems moderate in macroeconomic terms, although it would imply substantial increases (sometimes a doubling) from base-year levels.

The additional resources would have to be spent effectively on improving the availability and quality of educational services, health care delivery systems and basic sanitation provisioning. What this entails precisely for sector policies will vary from country to country depending on initial conditions and institutional settings, but typically it would imply a focus on improving school inputs and enhancing teacher quality, as well as increased access to health services, and enhanced coverage of vaccination programmes and basic sanitation. Further, improving general infrastructure (including roads and energy supply) are found to help improve the accessibility and functioning of health and education services, thereby supporting the achievement of the goals indirectly. However, meeting the MDGs is not only a matter of expanding social spending in these directions. The country studies show strong effects from improved socio-economic conditions at the household level, as better education helps improve health outcomes and vice versa, and improved income situations of households generally also contribute to enhancing access to health and education. The latter implies that reducing income poverty should also help achieve the other MDGs.

This brings us to the third main finding, which is that a public spending strategy in pursuance of MDGs 2, 4, 5 and 7 is not sufficient to achieve the target for poverty reduction. The model-based analyses did not consider specific interventions to reduce income poverty, but rather assumed poverty outcomes to result from the employment and income effects generated throughout the economy under the business-as-usual and MDG strategy scenarios.

The aggregate demand injections through the simulated increases in required public spending on education and health services and on drinking water and sanitation infrastructure in most cases does not induce sufficiently strong employment and income distribution effects to make adequate progress towards the targeted poverty reduction. In most country cases, moderate to high average GDP growth under both the business-as-usual and MDG scenarios would generate rather modest employment growth. In fact, in only four country cases, namely Brazil, Guatemala, Honduras and Nicaragua, would the MDG strategy induce a significantly stronger decrease in income poverty as compared with the scenario of unchanged trends and policies.

High income inequality remains an obstacle for more aggregate growth to trickle down to the poor in Latin America and the Caribbean. As one may expect, the country studies show that the MDG strategy generally reduces the supply of unskilled workers as more and more boys and girls complete primary education and also more tend to continue into secondary-level education. Over time, the supply of skilled workers increases. Also the demand for better educated workers tends to increase with the expansion of skill-intensive social services. In many of the country cases, the net effect is a shift in real wages in favour of unskilled workers, but overall, the impact on income inequality at the household level is rather weak, at least over the time period up to 2015.

Consequently, without additional policy interventions, most of the poverty reduction effects of the MDG strategy depend on the aggregate effects on employment and mean incomes. It may be argued that improved education and health of the working population will facilitate faster productivity growth and this could accelerate poverty reduction. Such gains will take time to mature, though, among others because of the length of schooling cycles, and most likely will kick in after 2015.

Fourth, the financing strategy matters. Assessing strategies to finance the increase public spending for the MDGs, the country studies generally find that foreign financing is less costly –in terms of required increases in public spending– than domestic borrowing or increased taxation. This is so because domestic resource mobilization by the government tends to crowd out disposable incomes or private investment to some degree, and this in turn would reduce private spending on MDG related services and require the government to step in more in order to reach the goals. There are, however, important macroeconomic trade-offs to consider in the case of an MDG strategy financed through external borrowing or foreign grants. Foreign financing tends to generate a stronger appreciation of the real exchange rate and weaker export growth than in the case of a strategy based on domestic resource mobilization. Furthermore, a strategy based on external borrowing would lift public debt to unsustainable levels in virtually all country cases. Such limitations to foreign financing put the burden on domestic resource mobilization. Domestic government borrowing, however, appears to generate a rather strong crowding-out of private spending and would also lift total public debt to unsustainable levels in most country cases. As a result, increasing the tax burden seems the core option for countries to consider. Effective tax burdens in most countries of the region are low by any standard, suggesting ample scope for a tax-financed MDG strategy. This probably should be a priority in all countries, but as the studies in this volume make clear, the nature and extent of a feasible tax reform needs careful assessment from case to case.

Impact of the global economic crisis

A substantial slowdown in the progress towards the Millennium Development Goals (MDGs) should be expected as a consequence of the global economic crisis that emerged in 2008. At the time the country studies for this report were undertaken, Latin American countries along with other parts of the developing world enjoyed robust rates of income growth. The outlook has become much less bright with the intensification of the financial crisis in the United States in mid-2008 which quickly spread to become a global economic crisis that is also hitting hard on Latin American economies. Rising unemployment and underemployment, drops in per capita incomes and less government revenue will also affect both public and private spending and no doubt imply significant setbacks in the progress made towards the MDGs. The precise magnitude of the setback is difficult to estimate at this point and will vary from country to country according to existing fiscal policy space and institutional capacity to respond to the crisis.

The framework presented in this volume can also be applied to make an ex-ante assessment of the possible impact of the crisis on the MDGs and reassess the costs and macroeconomic implications of putting countries back on track towards achievement of the goals by 2015. A recent study by Sánchez and Vos (2009) using the model framework used in this volume's country studies but applied only to six of the countries (Bolivia, Brazil, Chile, Costa Rica, Honduras and Nicaragua) addressed the following questions in this context: (i) to what extent will the global economic crisis affect MDG achievement? (ii) how much additional public spending will be needed to achieve the MDGs by 2015 owing to the negative impact of the crisis? (iii) will governments still be able to find sustainable funding for their MDG strategies? and (iv) to what extent will increased MDG spending operate as an effective counter-cyclical response for economic recovery?

For this analysis a new baseline scenario was generated projecting a prolonged recession in all countries during 2009-2010 and a slow but gradual recovery towards pre-crisis growth levels by 2015. The region's low-income countries (Bolivia, Honduras and Nicaragua) would fall substantially further off track towards the MDGs for primary school completion, child and maternal mortality, and access to drinking water and basic sanitation. Brazil, Chile and Costa Rica seemed well on track towards achieving most of the goals by 2015, would fall short in meeting several targets because of the crisis.

Reassessment of the MDG costs suggest that the governments of Bolivia, Honduras and Nicaragua would need to spend an extra 1.5 to 2.0 per cent of GDP per year on education, health and basic services between 2010 and 2015 to achieve the MDGs, as compared with the pre-crisis scenario. This would come on top of an additional required annual social spending of 2 per cent of GDP in Bolivia, 5 per cent in Nicaragua, and 7 per cent in Honduras, in absence of the crisis as reported in this volume.[6] For Brazil, Chile, and Costa Rica, the required additional spending caused by the expected impact of the crisis would be between 0.5 and 1.5 per cent of GDP per annum. Clearly, additional costs of this magnitude further stretch government finances and in most of these cases (with the exception of Chile and Costa Rica) would lead to unsustainable increases in public debt if financed through external or domestic borrowing and, consequently, could become a source of macroeconomic instability in the future if recovery and sustained growth do not set in swiftly. Tax financing would also become much less feasible in most of these cases (again with the exception of Chile and, possibly, Costa Rica) given that the tax burden would need to be increased substantially further, which in turn could delay recovery as it would depress recovery of domestic demand.

These financing concerns are further corroborated by the relatively mild impact on growth of the additional increases in social spending in the short run. While exerting a counter-cyclical effect, the immediate gain in aggregate demand growth is estimated to be less than the cost to the government as a share of GDP. As a result, the fiscal stimulus provided by the MDG scenario may not be sufficient for these economies to return to pre-crisis levels of economic growth and employment as spending on MDG-related services represents relatively low shares of aggregate demand in these countries. Stronger growth effects are likely to emerge over time as improved education and health outcomes underpin stronger productivity growth. The counter-cyclical response becomes much stronger if the MDG strategy is complemented by needed investments in public infrastructure. For a full recovery, however, other factors need to contribute as well, especially the resumption of external demand. This will require globally concerted stimulus measures to take effect. In the meantime, the low-income countries would need additional external financial support in the form of aid and/or debt relief in order to create the required additional fiscal space and avoid an insurmountable rise in external debt. A main conclusion of the pre-crisis scenarios as analyzed in this volume holds even more strongly in the crisis situation and the road to recovery, namely that careful macroeconomic management will be required to avoid growth costs elsewhere in the economy—especially a loss of competitiveness in export sectors owing to appreciation of the real exchange. The upshot is that counter-cyclical macroeconomic policies can be feasibly aligned with long-term development objectives if carefully managed and supported by the international community.

Concluding remarks

Bearing the above in mind, achievement of the MDGs remains within reach for countries in Latin America and the Caribbean. The analyses in this volume make clear that this implies much more than priority setting in social spending or finding the additional resources to finance the costs of the MDG strategy. Equally important is to ensure careful management and integration of macroeconomic and social sector policies. The study also makes clear that enhanced spending on MDG-related services and further progress towards the education, health, and drinking water and basic sanitation goals by themselves do not guarantee that income inequality will be reduced or poverty reduction targets will be met. Additional policies will need to be put in place to foster structural change in Latin American economies conducive of stronger employment growth and greater absorption over time of an increasingly educated labour force. The analysis of this volume aims at providing practical and country-specific frameworks for assessing policy options and trade-offs when addressing the challenge of reaching sustained and equitable growth.

Notes

1   The analysis was also undertaken for Venezuela, but the case study could not be fully completed on time to be included in this volume. The 18 countries included are Argentina, Bolivia, Brazil, Chile, Colombia, Costa Rica, Cuba, Dominican Republic, Ecuador, El Salvador, Guatemala, Honduras, Jamaica, Mexico, Nicaragua, Paraguay, Peru and Uruguay.
2   This poverty line was used to estimate income poverty as part of the internationally comparable set of MDG indicators of the United Nations until 2007. In 2008, new estimates by the World Bank led to establishing the international threshold for extreme poverty at $1.25 per day per person valued at purchasing power parity (PPP). The present study uses the previous poverty line as the country studies were completed in 2007.
3   See Devarajan and others (2002) and Kakwani and Sun (2006).
4   The elasticity is defined as $\varepsilon_P = (\partial P/\partial y) \cdot (y/P)$, where P is the poverty incidence and y stands for mean per capita income. Hence, a higher mean per capita income or a lower poverty incidence will increase the elasticity and less economic growth would be needed to reduce poverty.
5   See Bourguignon and others (2002), Ganuza and others (2002) and Vos and others (2006) for a discussion of parametric and non-parametric microsimulations methods and their application in conjunction with CGE model analysis. Appendix A2.1 of Chapter 2 of this volume spells out the non-parametric microsimulation method as applied to the 18 country cases in Latin America and the Caribbean.
6   Chapters 2 and 9 report for the case of Honduras that the additional required annual social spending would be between 4.3 and 5.1 per cent of GDP per annum—depending

on the financing strategy—in order to achieve the MDGs, rather than the 7 per cent as reported in Sánchez and Vos (2009). This difference is explained by the fact that, unlike Sánchez and Vos, the authors of Honduras' country study (Chapter 9) included the positive impact of increased investment in public infrastructure on MDG achievement and economic growth as part of the country's simulated MDG strategy.

References

Agénor, Pierre-Richard, Nihal Bayraktar, Emmanuel Pinto Moreira and Karim El Aynaoui (2005). "Achieving the Millennium Development Goals in Sub-Saharan Africa: A Macroeconomic Monitoring Framework", *Policy Research Working Paper*, 3750. World Bank, Washington, D.C.

Bourguignon, François, Anne-Sophie Robilliard and Sherman Robinson (2002). "Representative versus real households in the macro-economic modeling of inequality", Washington, D.C.: World Bank and IFPRI (mimeo).

Devarajan S., M. Miller and E. Swanson (2002). "Goals for development: history, prospects and costs", Policy Research Working Paper No. 2819, Washington D.C.: The World Bank.

Ganuza, Enrique, Ricardo Paes de Barros and Rob Vos (2002). "Labour Market Adjustment, Poverty and Inequality during Liberalisation". In: *Economic Liberalisation, Distribution and Poverty: Latin America in the 1990s*, Rob Vos, Lance Taylor, and Ricardo Paes de Barros, eds. Cheltenham (UK) and Northampton (US): Edward Elgar Publishers, pp. 54-88.

Glewwe, Paul (2002). "Schools and skills in developing countries: education policies and socioeconomic outcomes", *Journal of Economic Literature*, Vol. XL (June): 436-482.

Kakwani, Nanuk, and Hyun H. Sun (2006). "How costly is it to achieve the millennium development goal of halving poverty between 1990 and 2015?", International Poverty Centre Working Paper No. 19, Brasilia: UNDP International Poverty Centre (May).

Löfgren, Hans (2004). "MAMS: An economy wide model for analysis of MDG country strategies". World Bank, Development Prospects Group, Washington, D.C. (processed).

ODI (2003). "Results-oriented budgeting: will it reduce poverty?", Briefing Paper, Overseas Development Institute, London.

Sánchez, Marco V., and Rob Vos (2009). 'Impact of the global crisis on the achievement of the MDGs in Latin America', DESA Working Paper No. 74, New York: United Nations Department of Economic and Social Affairs (http://www.un.org/esa/desa/papers/2009/wp74_2009.pdf).

Seth, Anuradha, and Yuba Raj Khatiwada (2007). "MDG-consistent macroeconomic frameworks: an analytical approach", MDG Development Goals Initiative Working Paper No. 1, Colombo: UNDP Regional Centre in Colombo (May).

United Nations (2007). *The Millennium Development Goals Report 2007*, New York: United Nations.

United Nations (2008). *World Economic and Social Survey 2008: Overcoming Economic Insecurity*, New York: United Nations.

United Nations Millennium Project (2005). *Investing in Development: A Practical Plan to Achieve the Millennium Development Goals*, London: Earthscan.

Vos, Rob, Lance Taylor and Ricardo Paes de Barros, eds. (2002). *Economic Liberalisation, Distribution and Poverty: Latin America in the 1990s*, Cheltenham (UK) and Northampton (US): Edward Elgar Publishers.

Vos, Rob, Enrique Ganuza, Samuel Morley and Sherman Robinson, eds. (2006). *Who gains from Free Trade? Export-led Growth, Income Distribution and Poverty in Latin America*, London: Routledge.

2

Latin America and the Caribbean's challenge to reach the MDGs: financing options and trade-offs

Rob Vos, Marco V. Sánchez and Cornelia Kaldewei

Introduction

Leaders from all countries have agreed to pursue the Millennium Development Goals (MDGs) and to reach them by 2015 with a view to securing a world with less poverty, hunger and disease, with better-educated children, more gender equality, greater survival prospects for infants and mothers, and a healthier environment. With less than ten years to the time horizon, the challenges ahead are still staggering, though there are some signs of progress. In most developing countries, providing every child with primary school education appears to be within our grasp. In the developing world as a whole, income poverty has been on the decline and there have been important gains in assisted child delivery and coverage of vaccination programmes, which have contributed to declining child and maternal mortality.[1] Progress has been uneven, however. Most of the gains in declining income poverty have been concentrated in much of Asia. Sub-Saharan Africa tends to lag far behind for most of the MDG indicators. Child mortality has been on the decline globally, but again with the least relative progress in Africa. Disparities in progress are also vast within countries and many of the poorest tend to be left behind, particularly in rural areas.

In Latin America and the Caribbean (LAC), poverty indicators tend to be lower on average than in most other regions of the developing world. By and large, the region also scores better on education and health performance indicators. At the same time, however, progress on many of these indicators has been slower than in many parts of East and South Asia. Yet it is safe to argue that countries in the LAC region have made important progress on average towards the MDGs (see figure 2.1). According to the United Nations MDG report (United Nations, 2007), with unchanged trends in past achievement, the region should be able to attain the goals regarding net enrolment in primary education, gender equality in education, coverage of sanitation and drinking water, and possibly also that of child mortality. The speed of progress for achieving

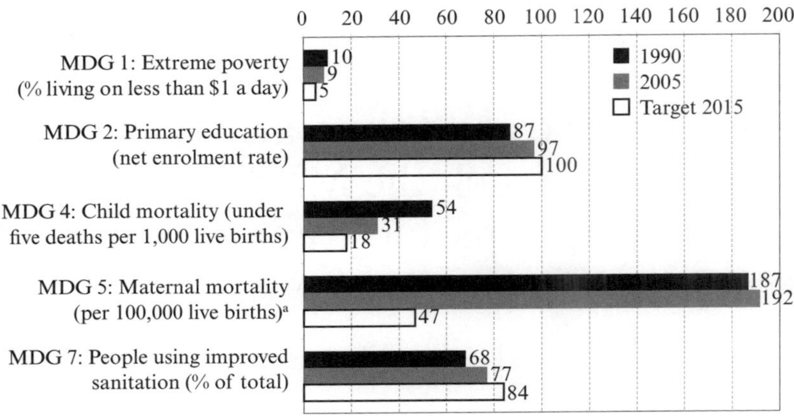

Figure 2.1 Progress towards the MDGs in Latin America and the Caribbean[a]

Source: United Nations, *The Millennium Development Goals Report, 2007*; and United Nations, MDG database.

[a] In the case of MDG 5, data for 2005 refers to 2000 (latest year available).

the goals for extreme poverty reduction and decreasing maternal mortality seems to be insufficient.[2] The region as a whole would thus seem to be "off track" for those two goals and "on track" for the former set of goals, under the assumption that progress towards the goals will continue linearly according to the observed trend since 1990.

There can be no reason for complacency, however, since such linear projections should be taken with extreme caution. First, the path towards the goals need not follow a linear pattern. For instance, once child mortality rates have been lowered substantially, reducing them even further may require other, possibly more costly, interventions. Second, a "business-as-usual" (BAU) scenario would need to be defined more appropriately as policies may have changed since 1990, and new policies in place may make it more—or even less—likely to achieve the goals. Using a model-based analysis of the economy-wide implications of a continuation of BAU policies, we find that, in the case of child mortality, for instance, LAC as a region does not appear to be on track, contrary to what a linear projection based on the data in figure 2.1 would suggest. In contrast, the region would be on track for meeting the poverty-reduction target as defined by the BAU scenario, owing mainly to the projected performance of the region's larger economies, including Brazil and Mexico. Third, caution is also needed when looking more precisely at how the goals are defined. In the case of education, for instance, good progress is being made in terms of net enrolment, but the outlook is much less bright for primary school completion rates. Persistently high repetition and drop-out rates in primary education continue to pose a major challenge, and only four out of the 18 countries of the LAC region in the study (Chile, Costa Rica, Cuba and Mexico) are expected to achieve the goal of 100 per cent primary school completion by 2015 with unchanged policies. Of course, the above picture only represents regional averages and disguises important differences between countries, as well as disparities in human development within the countries of the region.

The MDG agenda reflects awareness of such differences and of the challenges ahead, faced predominantly by the world's poorest countries. In this context, many donor countries have made explicit commitments to "scale up" aid over the medium term to meet the development goals. This focus on aid and on the poorest countries is understandable, as the challenges in reaching the MDGs are greatest in sub-Saharan Africa and other least developed countries, many of which lack the necessary resources for financing the substantial increase in public spending that would be required to meet the goals.[3] Therefore, much of the financing would be expected to come from increased aid flows. This situation in turn has spurred a debate about the trade-offs that would be associated with a "scaling-up" of aid by such magnitudes. The effectiveness of such a financing strategy has been questioned on several grounds (see, for example, Heller, 2005; Bourguignon and Sundberg, 2006), such as a lack of good governance or sufficient absorptive and managerial capacity to efficiently utilize substantial aid flows for investment in MDG-related action; the potential cost of an appreciating real exchange rate (RER) and the consequent undermining of export competitiveness (often labelled "Dutch disease"); and constraints on managing macroeconomic policy, both fiscal and monetary, owing to an increased reliance on multiple and volatile external sources of financing, as aid flows are typically provided by many donors subject to annual allocation processes.

Such issues are highly relevant for the poorest countries and require careful examination before embarking on strategies of massive foreign assistance. At the same time, this should not divert attention from what could be done in terms of domestic resource mobilization, which—next to increased and more effective aid—is another pillar of the Monterrey Consensus on Financing for Development (United Nations, 2002, annex), but one that has been less at the forefront of the current debate on MDG financing strategies. Domestic resource mobilization will be central to most middle-income developing countries, including those in LAC, which—except for Bolivia, Guyana, Honduras and Nicaragua— are not eligible for increased aid flows and enhanced debt relief under the Heavily Indebted Poor Countries (HIPC) Initiative. While middle-income countries are closer to achieving the MDGs, it is nonetheless true that about 40 per cent of the world's moderate poor live in these countries.[4] Moderate ($2 a day) and extreme poverty ($1 a day) also remain pervasive in LAC as they affect 40 per cent and 10 per cent of the population of the region, respectively. In addition, the inequalities in levels of human development and the income distribution within these countries, as pointed out earlier, add to the tremendous challenges in this part of the developing world.

While the less poor countries may have greater access to (private) foreign borrowing, it is not entirely clear that Governments would wish to use much of these sources for public investments in social sectors and in poverty-reduction programmes. On the other hand, greater reliance on domestic resources may imply stronger redistributive effects within the economy, which could impose political constraints on this kind of financing strategy. In addition, the issues faced by aid-recipient countries when shifting budgets to MDG-related programmes—including the associated relative price and resource shifts—may equally apply to countries relying on domestic financing strategies.

In this chapter, we will focus on a number of such trade-offs and financing constraints and provide a comparative analysis for 18 LAC countries, based on the case studies prepared by experts from each of those countries. Nine of these studies are included in this volume. In the following section, we will review the main issues at stake and the policy options for addressing related challenges. The third section outlines the contours of a modelling framework designed to analyse the trade-offs empirically—which is presented in detail in Chapter 3 of this volume. The comparative analysis of feasible financing strategies to achieve the MDGs in LAC is provided in the subsequent section. The final section summarizes the main findings and presents the policy lessons that can be learned from the comparative analysis.

Constraints to financing MDG-oriented development strategies

The Monterrey Consensus emphasizes that ensuring conditions to enable the mobilization of domestic and external resources is essential for development. This would entail, among other things, good governance that is responsive to the people's needs and sound macroeconomic policies aimed at sustaining high growth rates, full employment, stability and poverty eradication. This should be supported by sustainable debt financing and debt relief and sufficient and effective provisioning of official development assistance (ODA).

Against this backdrop, financing for achieving the MDGs may face several constraints, particularly in the short run. Below we discuss some key macroeconomic policy areas and related trade-offs associated with different financing strategies for the achievement of the MDGs in LAC. Without attempting to be comprehensive, these include: limited policy space for prudent and counter-cyclical macroeconomic management for growth and employment generation; competitiveness and RER constraints associated with both domestic and external financing strategies; the creation of fiscal space and maintenance of fiscal sustainability; and, labour-market constraints.

Countercyclical macroeconomic policies

Economic growth is an essential ingredient for generating domestic resources to address development needs, including human development. But it is likely that, at any given growth rate, a higher degree of volatility limits the ability of Governments to mobilize a steady stream of resources for different purposes. For instance, extended periods of booms and busts over recent decades did not allow Latin American economies enough time to recover or to draw on stable tax revenues.

More generally, macroeconomic stability strongly influences the long-term growth performance of an economy. In turn, the capacity to conduct countercyclical policies is a necessary condition to reduce volatility and increase a Government's degree of freedom in times of possible crisis, and to enable it to have enough resources to protect the socially vulnerable and prevent further regress in poverty reduction. Against this backdrop, countercyclical policies may therefore be seen as a prerequisite for preventing the MDG-related achievements of developing countries from regressing during times of macroeconomic instability and crises. History has shown, however, that the fiscal policy stance in both African and Latin American countries has been highly pro-cyclical on average since the 1960s, whereas in East Asia it has more typically been either neutral or countercyclical (United Nations, 2006b; Ocampo and Vos, 2008). It further shows that a pro-cyclical macroeconomic policy stance has been generally detrimental to long-term growth by exacerbating the short-run volatility in the economy and increasing perceived investment risks and uncertainty. The boom-bust economic cycles in Latin America during the 1990s closely followed the trend of capital flows. The upward and downward swings in the economy were typically exacerbated by pro-cyclical macroeconomic policy responses (Ocampo, 2005; Ocampo and Vos, 2006).

Social expenditures also have been found to be pro-cyclical in many developing countries, sometimes even more so than total public expenditures, especially in Latin America (see, for example, Martner and Aldunate, 2006). This was very much a characteristic of fiscal policy during the 1990s, but more recently policymakers seem to have managed to protect social spending better. This is evidenced by a study of the United Nations Economic Commission for Latin America and the Caribbean (ECLAC, 2005) which showed that, during the period 1991-97, the variation in overall social spending was almost three times higher than the variation in GDP, implying significant overshooting of social spending in both directions during cyclical up- and downswings. Between 1998 and 2003, this relationship weakened as the fluctuations in social spending were actually lower than those in GDP. According to the ECLAC study, most social spending sub-categories in the region became less volatile, except for health spending, which showed increased volatility and pro-cyclicality from 1998-2003.

In summary, improvements in human development require adequate and sustained levels of public spending. For many developing country Governments, however, the space for conducting countercyclical macroeconomic policies is limited, as the available fiscal and foreign-exchange resources tend to be small relative to the size of the external shocks these countries face. Against this backdrop, mobilizing and committing fiscal resources for MDG achievement on a sustained basis for the medium-to-long run could in itself help attenuate the pro-cyclicality of fiscal spending and support more growth-oriented macroeconomic policies.

Competitiveness and real exchange-rate constraints

While sustained growth is important to ease the path towards MDG achievement, in most countries much greater priority will need to be given to public spending to meet infrastructure needs and improve the quality and coverage of basic social services. Public spending injections for these purposes may, however, put upward pressure on the RER. One way to define the RER is to see it as the price of "tradables" relative to "non-tradables". Government services, including education, health, and infrastructure are typically seen as "non-tradable commodities" and many MDG-related activities are therefore considered non-tradables.[5] Consequently, a large shift in domestic spending towards MDG-related goods and services will push up demand for non-tradables. As a result, the price and cost of MDG-related services is likely to increase, since the Government will, among other things, try to hire more teachers and medical personnel, and may have to increase their wages if such workers are in short supply.[6] Rising costs of non-tradable services will in principle shift the relative price against tradables, thus inducing an RER appreciation as defined above.

Financing MDG-related spending through aid flows or foreign borrowing will likely exacerbate the appreciation of the RER, as it will increase the supply of foreign exchange in the economy.[7] In any case, the appreciation of the RER results in a loss of competitiveness of exports and import-competing firms. This may have important implications for long-term growth, as the export sector in many developing countries is an important contributor to aggregate growth and has potential dynamic spillover effects for the economy at large. RER appreciation may result in what is often labelled Dutch disease when it leads to a resource allocation away from export industries, resulting in an undesirable structural change away from dynamic production activities—a shift that is typically difficult and time-consuming to reverse.

The actual impact on the RER and competitiveness will, however, depend on many factors, including the import intensity of aggregate demand and of MDG-related expenditures in particular, and on the existing slack in production capacity (see for example, Vos, Sánchez and Inoue, 2007). The impact on competitiveness will also depend on how greater achievement of the MDGs will affect the economy over time. Better infrastructure and a better-educated and healthier labour force may have important externalities in the form of productivity growth, attract foreign investors and thereby have a dynamic impact on economic growth. This presents an inter-temporal trade-off, as the RER appreciation would erode export competitiveness in the short run, while productivity gains and faster economic growth from increased MDG achievement would pay off only in the medium-to-long run. The question then is whether the negative short-run effects can be contained so as not to limit the resources available for long-term investments in human capital.

The empirical literature on Dutch disease shows a wide range of RER adjustments in response to strong increases in aid flows or private capital inflows, with the extent of the effects depending largely on the relative demand and supply effects across sectors, and thus on country-specific circumstances (Bevan, 2005; Heller, 2005; Bourguignon and Sundberg, 2006; Gupta, Powell and Yang, 2006). Similarly, the degree to which increased taxation or domestic government borrowing changes the composition of domestic demand will depend on how private investors respond to higher public indebtedness and, possibly, higher domestic interest rates, and on which parts of the population have to carry the extra tax burden, and so on.

In summary, the risk of a loss of export competitiveness due to larger MDG expenditures is clear and present both in the case of external and of domestic financing. Nonetheless, one cannot say *a priori* that a poverty reduction strategy aimed at increased public expenditures for the MDGs would be harmful for growth or export capacity.

Creating fiscal space for MDG investment

Tax reform

Taxation should be central to any strategy for domestic resource mobilization aimed at enhancing public expenditures for social development. In most Latin American and Caribbean countries, there appears to be ample scope for increasing fiscal space through an expansion of the tax base and an increase in tax rates. The average level of tax revenues in LAC amounted to only 17 per cent of GDP around 2005 (see figure 2.2); less than half of the average for the Organization for Economic Cooperation and Development (OECD). Only Argentina (including provincial governments), Brazil, Jamaica and Uruguay had tax revenues above 23 per cent of GDP (Martner and Aldunate, 2006).

An important caveat with regard to increasing taxation as a means of financing MDG-related spending is the impact on domestic demand, as consumers will have less disposable income and investors may foresee lower net profits and therefore choose to reduce investments. Moreover, reduced disposable income and profits are likely to constrain private savings for investment financing. The

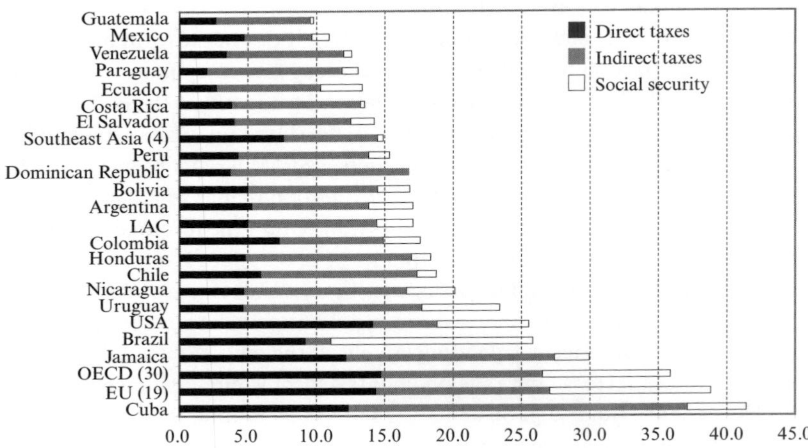

Figure 2.2 Average tax revenues of central Governments in Latin America
and the Caribbean and selected other countries and country groups, around 2005[a]
(percentage of GDP)

Sources: For Latin America and the Caribbean (LAC): ILPES-CEPAL on the basis of official
country data; for OECD, EU and USA: OECD Revenue Statistics 1965-2005; for Southeast Asia and
Jamaica: IMF Government Finance Statistics and IMF, International Financial Statistics, various issues.
[a] General government for OECD, European Union (EU) and United States (USA); 2002 for
Southeast Asia (4); 2004 for OECD, EU, USA, Brazil and Bolivia; 2003 for Cuba.
Southeast Asia (4) includes Indonesia, Malaysia, Singapore and Thailand.

domestic demand effect will also depend on who is to carry the additional tax
burden. If indirect taxes have a greater effect on low-income households, reforms pushing for increases in the value-added tax (VAT) and other indirect
taxes could offset some of the welfare gains the poor would receive from enhanced MDG expenditures. Even if increased tax efforts are more distribution-
neutral, they could affect the poor through lower economic growth in the short
run as private domestic demand would fall. Increased public expenditures
would compensate for this, but the long-run growth gains would depend on the
efficiency of these expenditures.

Another important caveat relates to possible limits on how much additional tax
revenue can be generated through tax reforms. If the experience of tax reforms
of recent decades is indicative, one should not be overly optimistic in this regard.
Latin American countries have been able to increase tax revenue (excluding social security contributions) since 1990 by about 2 percentage points of GDP on
average (see for example, Tanzi, 2000; Martner and Aldunate, 2006). While there
is quite some variation across countries, the upper bound in the increases would
be between 3 and 4 percentage points, though typically taking about a decade
to achieve such increases. Studies for other developing countries also suggest
that significant increases in tax revenue are not easy and are time-consuming

to achieve (McKinley, 2007; Thirsk, 1997). In other words, while there seems to be clear scope for significant tax reform in Latin America, in practice the actual gains in mobilizing the necessary revenue for MDG-related spending may well be limited in the time span leading up to 2015. Another, potentially more promising, way to increase fiscal space for MDG-related public spending would therefore be an increase in efficiency in budget allocations.

More efficient budget allocation

There are at least three mechanisms for more efficient budget allocation through which one could seek to create more fiscal space for MDG spending. First, there may be scope for redefining priorities across budget items. This could entail readjustments across government sectors or ministries (for example, from defence spending to education and health), or across subsectors within ministries or programmes (for example, from higher education to primary and secondary education).

Second, there may be scope for improving efficiency in the delivery of services. The quality and efficiency with which public services are provided will differ from country to country, and inefficiencies can emerge for a variety of reasons. In some cases, there may be blatant inefficiencies, such as absenteeism among teaching and medical personnel, which, if addressed, could generate important fiscal savings and social benefits. For instance, primary school teacher absence rates have been found to be as high as 27 per cent in Uganda, 25 per cent in India, 19 per cent in Indonesia and 14 per cent in Ecuador (see Rogers and others, 2004). In the case of Ecuador, for example, it has been estimated that reducing primary school teacher absenteeism by half could "save" about 2 per cent of the overall budget for the education sector. In the health care sector, a shortage of medical personnel may not be the only, or even the main, problem for improving the coverage of health services. For instance, doctors and nurses tend to be present mostly in Ecuador's main urban centres, leaving the rest of the country uncovered (see, for example, Vos and others, 2004; World Bank, 2004). Problems such as these and many others suggest that with a more efficient delivery of services the same amount of resources could yield much higher outcomes in education and health.

Third, even without such inefficiencies in delivery systems, MDG-related spending could be made more cost-effective by ensuring that within programmes and subsectors, resources are prioritized towards those "inputs" and activities which produce the greater outcome per dollar spent. For instance, a cost-effectiveness analysis of the actions needed to meet the target of universal primary education in Ecuador suggested that with a more efficient allocation of resources it would be possible to achieve the education MDG at an annual extra cost of 0.2 per cent of GDP (Vos and Ponce, 2004). Specifically, a more cost-effective allocation of resources would entail focusing incremental budget resources on hiring better-trained teachers, expanding a conditional cash transfer programme to stimulate school attendance by the poor and improving the availability of rural schooling infrastructure.

Public borrowing and fiscal sustainability

In the short run, overall fiscal revenues and expenditure decisions determine an important part of the resources available for social development. However, in the medium- and long-run, what happens "below the line" of fiscal accounts (that is, the financing of deficits) will determine the sustainability of fiscal resources. Therefore, while public borrowing may be used as a source of financing for MDG-related public spending, this will have to be subject to medium- and long-term debt sustainability considerations.

While it is difficult to establish any standardized benchmark for sustainable public debt levels, assessments by Governments in consultation with the IMF and the World Bank suggest that public debt distress in LAC decreased substantially during the 1990s, and even more so in recent years (see table 2.1). More prudent fiscal policies (albeit sometimes at the expense of social spending and public infrastructure investment) and substantial debt relief in the HIPC countries have contributed to this trend, as well as to improved economic performance in a number of cases. As seen in the assessments of debt sustainability reported in table 2.1, most economies in the region have sailed away from acute debt distress. Nonetheless, it also holds for most countries that sustainability problems could easily return when faced with a growth slowdown, terms-of-trade shocks or exchange-rate pressures. Hence, while for most countries there would at present appear to be scope for financing an MDG strategy through domestic or external borrowing, such measures would have to be cautiously assessed in the light of the country's ability to maintain enhanced MDG spending alongside sustained economic growth.

Borrowing on domestic capital markets may be limited in some countries of the region as they have rather poorly developed markets for long-term government and corporate bonds denominated in local currency. A deficient domestic bond market makes it more difficult to finance long-term public infrastructure investments and major private modernization projects (see United Nations, 2006b; Ocampo and Vos 2006, 2008). A poorly developed bond market in conjunction with a relatively low level of financial savings in the economy may further imply that government demand for domestic financing of its deficits would have rather strong upward effects on domestic interest rates and limit financing available for private investment. Under such circumstances, heavy reliance on domestic borrowing to finance the MDG strategy could lead to a quickly rising domestic debt-service burden. As mentioned above, rising interest rates will also increase the cost of borrowing for private investors and hence domestically financed MDG investments could crowd out private investments and lower economic growth.

Table 2.1 Public debt-to-GDP ratio and debt sustainability in Latin America and the Caribbean, 1990-2006

	Average 1990-2000	Average 2001-2006	Around mid-point[a]	Debt sustainability[b]
Argentina	36.3	100.1	138.2	Sustainable over medium term, some risks in near term; sensitivity to growth performance and real exchange rate (Art. IV, 2005)
Bolivia	56.3	74.5	60.7	Sustainable; some sensitivity only to significantly lower oil prices (Art. IV, 2007)
Brazil	24	32.9	34	Improved sustainability (Art. IV, 2006)
Chile	23	11.1	13	Sustainable (Art. IV, 2006)
Colombia	18.7	47.2	50.3	Sustainable, as long as primary fiscal surplus does not decrease significantly below 1 per cent of GDP (Art. IV, 2006)
Costa Rica	40.2	40.1	43.6	Sustainable, assuming fiscal reforms; without reforms, sensitivity to growth performance, real exchange rate shock or contingent liability shock (Art. IV, 2006)
Cuba[c]	49.3	40	38.4	
Dominican Republic	..	20.5	21.2	Improved sustainability; further fiscal prudence (primary surplus!) needed to reach more manageable levels over time (Art. IV, 2005)
Ecuador	67.6	43.4	56.9	Improved sustainability; further fiscal prudence (primary surplus!) needed to reach more manageable levels over time (Art. IV, 2005)
El Salvador	26.2	36.1	35.2	Improved public debt situation; further decrease in public debt levels (through fiscal consolidation) needed to achieve sustainability, since current debt levels imply vulnerability to growth and real interest rate shocks (Art. IV, 2006)
Guatemala	18.2	20.5	20.2	Sustainable (Art. IV, 2005)
Honduras	66.3	59.8	70.1	Improved sustainability, moderate risk of distress; severe exogenous and endogenous shocks could lead to distress, fiscal discipline is needed to reduce the risk of distress in the medium-to-long term (WB/IMF joint DSA, 2006)
Jamaica[d]	100.7	140	111	High risk of distress; reduction of public debt levels must be a policy priority (Art. IV, 2007)

Table 2.1   (cont'd)

	Average 1990-2000	Average 2001-2006	Around mid-point[a]	Debt sustainability[b]
Mexico	31.6	23.2	24.2	Sustainable; only a severe oil shock in both quantity and prices could imply a risk of distress (Art. IV, 2006)
Nicaragua	189	107.5	113	Improved sustainability, moderate risk of distress; exogenous and endogenous shocks could lead to distress, further debt relief and fiscal discipline are needed to reduce the risk of distress in the medium-to-long term (Art. IV, 2005)
Paraguay	16.8	39.8	41.1	Low risk of distress; exchange-rate shocks and a return to primary fiscal deficits of about 1.6 per cent of GDP (historical average) could lead to distress (Art. IV, 2004)
Peru	54.2	41.3	41.8	Moderate risk of distress; especially a non-interest current-account shock and a contingent liabilities shock could trigger distress (Art. IV, 2007)
Uruguay	24.8	72.6	67	Improved sustainability, but public debt remains highly vulnerable to interest rate, exchange rate, and rollover risks; also, continued fiscal prudence (target: primary surplus of 4 per cent of GDP) is needed to maintain downward trend of public debt ratio in baseline scenario without shocks (Art. IV, 2006)

Source: ECLAC (for debt-to-GDP ratios). See notes for additional sources.

[a] Mid-point of the MDG-relevant period 1990-2015. The selected year varies between countries and is defined in accordance with the base year of the period for which MDG achievement is modelled for the relevant country (see table 2.3).

[b] Based on World Bank and IMF debt sustainability assessment in most recent year available.

[c] Data for Cuba are taken from the Economist Intelligence Unit (EIU).

[d] Data for Jamaica are taken from the World Bank's World Development Indicators database (WDI). The latest available figure is for 2005.

Labour-market constraints

For low-income countries, large-scale investments for the achievement of the MDGs could meet severe skilled-labour constraints in the short-to-medium run. Public expenditures centred on meeting the MDGs in the form of expanding basic social services in health and education would put intense pressure on a pool of teachers, doctors and other trained workers that is likely to be limited. Constraints on skilled labour could then lead to upward pressure on the skill premium for such workers, which in turn would increase the overall labour costs for the public sector and the cost of achieving the MDGs. Bourguignon and Sundberg (2006) suggest that, for reasons such as these, a sequenced approach to expanding MDG-related social services may be needed in order to avoid disruptive pressures on labour costs owing to skill bottlenecks. Investing in specialized education and training for teachers and medical personnel should then precede or move in parallel with the expansion of the services themselves.

Such constraints may also exist in LAC, but they are likely to be less severe as most countries in the region rank as middle-income with, on average, higher initial educational levels. Trying to achieve the MDGs in the region may induce other labour-market constraints over time, however. As the MDG target for primary education is reached and more students are also likely to complete higher levels, the supply of skilled workers in the labour market will gradually increase. If the economy's structure does not adjust commensurately to absorb the increased supply of better-educated workers, the skill premium will likely fall. While this, in turn, may lower the cost of achieving the MDGs, it is also likely to provide a disincentive to invest in education. Most empirical studies of the determinants of access to education indicate that expected private returns to education are not the sole determinant by far, but an important one nonetheless (Glewwe, 2002). Hence, insufficient creation of skilled jobs in the economy could jeopardize the achievement of the education MDG. While this could be counteracted by additional efforts by the Government to stimulate school attendance, the real problem would be how to improve the environment for stimulating a structural change in the economy towards technologies and activities that can absorb larger amounts of skilled labour.

How the indicated trade-offs present themselves will depend further on the functioning of the labour market, that is to say, on the degree of labour-market segmentation and the flexibility in real wage adjustment. Labour markets in developing countries are typically segmented owing to many factors that prevent certain workers from finding a job in some sectors (Agénor, 1996). High barriers to entry into MDG-related sectors may prevent the real wage from adjusting in a flexible way. For example, skill requirements may be very high in some MDG-related sectors, particularly in activities that are relatively advanced from a technological point of view (for example, hospital services). This may prevent certain types of workers who have a higher education but do not possess the required skills from having full access to jobs in MDG-related sectors. If skilled but not highly-skilled, workers may end up seeking employment in non-MDG-related sectors where, as a consequence, the real wage will probably fall. Should the real wage adjustment be insufficient to clear the labour market, unemployment and, most likely, underemployment will emerge, resulting in negative repercussions in terms of rising income inequality and poverty.

These changing patterns in the demand for labour could limit the degree to which aggregate income growth translates into poverty reduction. A strategy based on increased public spending for MDG-related services could alter the employment-growth pattern by increasing the skilled labour supply and, at least in the short run, expanding employment in non-tradable services. What this means in terms of reducing poverty will depend on country-specific conditions and will be discussed in more detail in the fourth section.

Such labour-market concerns and their implications for inequality and poverty are particularly pressing against the backdrop of recent labour-market developments in LAC. In most countries of the region, employment creation just about kept pace with GDP growth during the 1990s and early 2000s, indicating employment generation with little to no productivity growth. For half of the countries, employment growth has been less than labour-force growth, as reflected in the negative "net" employment growth rates in figure 2.3. More atypically, Colombia and Jamaica witnessed the strongest net job creation rates at about 0.3 per cent per year between 1990 and 2005, even as their per capita GDP growth remained relatively modest. Among the faster-growing economies of the region since 1990, Cuba and the Dominican Republic managed to sustain a relatively

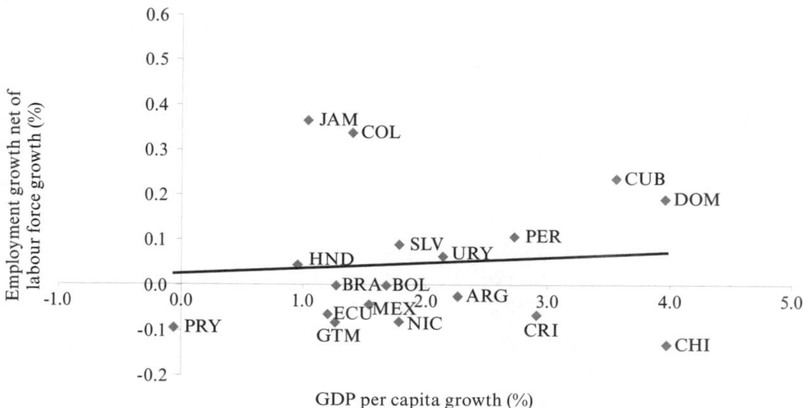

Figure 2.3 Net employment and GDP growth in Latin America and the Caribbean, 1991-2006 (annual average growth rates)

Source: ILO, Key Indicators of the Labour Market (KILM) and the World Bank, World Development Indicators database.

labour-intensive growth pattern, whereas in Chile and Costa Rica productivity growth has implied insufficient employment generation for these countries' growing labour forces. Overall, employment growth has been rather limited in all countries. In addition, especially in the countries with slower growth, much of the job creation has been in the informal sector (ECLAC, 2005).

An economy-wide framework to assess feasible financing strategies for achieving the MDGs

An economy-wide framework is required to examine the capacity and financing constraints to achieving the MDGs and the trade-offs discussed in the previous section. The existence of a wide range of interaction effects is the rationale for the use of a computable general equilibrium (CGE) model. As discussed above, the pursuit of a strategy towards the achievement of the MDGs will likely have strong effects throughout the economy. It will undoubtedly affect the demand for and supply of different types of goods and services, labour and capital, and foreign exchange, and the related adjustments may imply important trade-offs throughout the period for achieving the MDGs. The general equilibrium framework also takes into consideration the possible synergies between the different MDGs. Such synergies may influence the required expansion of services (for example, greater coverage of drinking water supply may reduce the need for health service expansion) or the speed at which the various MDGs are achieved. Studies that take all of these general equilibrium and synergy effects into account may generate substantially different outcomes than studies that focus exclusively on sector analyses.

The outcomes will also depend to an important extent on the way in which the strategy is financed. Foreign financing may induce RER effects of the type discussed above, while financing through domestic taxes could reduce private consumption demand, among other things, and domestic borrowing could crowd out credit resources for private investment. Policymakers thus may face important trade-offs. No doubt increased public spending is essential for achieving the MDGs, but adjustments in the RER, real wages and other relative prices may increase the unit costs for achieving the MDGs along with the costs for other sectors, or discourage exports, thereby widening the external deficit that needs to be financed, and so on. The productivity gains from greater MDG achievement will take some time to materialize and are thus unlikely to impact growth visibly in the short and medium terms. Therefore, it is critical that short-run trade-offs not offset potential economic and social gains in the longer run.

Dynamic CGE models for the simulation of policies aimed at human development goals have been developed before in studies during the 1970s and 1980s, especially in those providing analytical depth to the so-called basic needs approach to development (see, for example, Kouwenaar, 1986; Hopkins and van der Hoeven, 1982). At the time, such exercises were very time-consuming and costly because of data and computational limitations. Later, the shift away from concerns about employment, income distribution and poverty towards macroeconomic stability and structural adjustment in mainstream development policies also de-emphasized the need for such modelling efforts. More recently, work undertaken at the World Bank has revived the approach in the context of the ongoing debate about scaling up resources to achieve the MDGs. This newly developed framework has been labelled MAMS (**_Ma_**quette for **M**DG **S**imulation) and was originally presented in Lofgren (2004). A version with more limiting assumptions can be found in Bourguignon and others (2004). The framework was originally designed to deal in particular with low-income country contexts and the trade-offs associated with the scaling-up of aid inflows for MDG-related expenditures. It has been extended and applied in the context of the present study covering 18 Latin American and Caribbean countries. Chapter 3 of this volume provides a detailed description of the version of MAMS applied to these country cases. Here, we only highlight some of the main features relevant for the subsequent discussion.

The MAMS framework has been built from a fairly standard CGE framework with dynamic-recursive features but incorporates a special module which specifies the main determinants of MDG achievement and the direct impact of enhanced public expenditures on MDG-related infrastructure and services. MAMS considers specific targets for the MDGs of poverty reduction (MDG 1), achieving universal primary education (MDG 2), reducing under-five and maternal mortality (MDGs 4 and 5) and increasing access to safe water and basic sanitation (MDGs 7a and 7b). In the case of MDG 2, the demand for primary and other levels of schooling is a function of student behaviour (enrolment, repetition, graduation). Student behaviour, in turn, depends on the quality of education (identified by variables such as classroom availability and student-teacher ratios), income incentives (the expected wage premium from education), the under-five mortality rate (a proxy for the health status of the potential student population), household consumption per capita (a proxy for the capacity to pay for education and for opportunity costs) and the level of public infrastructure (a proxy for the effective distance to school). Under-five and maternal mortality are considered to be determined by the availability of public and private health services, household consumption per capita, the level of public infrastructure (a proxy for the effective distance to health centres and hospitals), and the coverage of water and sanitation services. Access to water and sanitation, on the other hand, is modelled as a function of household consumption per capita, the provision of such services by public or private providers and the level of public infrastructure. Achievements in the reduction of income poverty are measured as the outcome of the overall general equilibrium effects from dynamic adjustments in production, employment, wages and other relative prices, as well as changes in the quality of human capital through MDG-related expenditures.

The final outcome for income poverty can be estimated by looking at the outcomes for per capita household income and consumption for different household groups. However, CGE models can typically only specify a limited number of representative households, resulting in insufficient detail regarding changes in the distribution for making robust statements regarding the poverty outcomes. As a consequence, the CGE analysis needs to be supplemented by certain assumptions (such as fixed within-group distributions) or, as has been done for the empirical analysis reported here, by a method of microsimulations that takes the labour-market outcomes (unemployment, employment structure, relative remunerations and skill composition) from the CGE for different types of workers and applies them to a micro data set (such as a household survey) to obtain the required detail about income distribution for the poverty analysis. See Bourguignon, Robilliard and Robinson (2002) and Vos and others (2006) for a discussion and application of such methods in conjunction with CGE model analysis. The appendix gives further details of the method as applied to the 18 country studies covered in the present study.

MAMS includes a relatively detailed specification of social services related to the MDGs, spelling out different levels of education, different health sectors, sectors for drinking water and sanitation, and other public infrastructure. According to the model's specifications, these services may be provided publicly or privately. Nonetheless, it is only new government investment and current expenditures that will lead to a policy-driven increase in the supply of MDG-related services and public infrastructure. For this to take place, the Government has to mobilize sufficient domestic or foreign resources to finance those new investments and expenditures.

The average skill level of the labour force will increase over time as more better-educated graduates leave the schooling system. This will in turn enhance productivity growth, with subsequent wage- and income-distribution effects. Output growth may be fostered as a result of those productivity gains, potentially triggering economy-wide effects which in turn will affect MDG achievement.[8] Achievements in drinking water and sanitation supply also help to improve health conditions, and improved health status may in turn impact positively on education outcomes along with other determinants.

Per capita household consumption responds positively to the Government's increasing the supply of MDG-related services, and this may have further favourable implications for MDG achievement. However, since MAMS is an economy-wide model, per capita household consumption can also change as a result of relative price changes or could be affected by increased taxes to finance the additional MDG-related spending. Furthermore, all domestic income changes affect the economy's capacity to generate savings. The macroeconomic viability of financing the new MDG-sector investment will depend on the macroeconomic constraints of the country, the initial debt burden, the source of financing, and the productivity of public investments towards the MDGs, among other factors.

MDG financing strategies for LAC: a comparative country analysis

In this section, the outcomes of the MAMS-based analyses for 18 countries in the LAC region are scrutinized and compared. The following key questions guide the discussion:

- Will the countries of the region be able to achieve the MDGs with essentially unchanged public spending and financing strategies?
- How much additional resources would be needed, if any?[9] Are there important cost-saving effects from the synergies among the various MDGs? Are there decreasing returns to MDG spending; that is to say, as one gets closer to achieving the MDGs, do the marginal costs of the policy interventions in education, health and sanitation increase?
- Which financing strategy seems to be the most feasible in each context? Which macroeconomic trade-offs are the most important when comparing financing of the MDG strategy through increased aid flows, taxation, domestic borrowing or external borrowing?
- Is there a trade-off between trying to achieve the MDGs for education, health and sanitation and the achievement of the MDG for income poverty?

The country studies referred to in this chapter have tried to answer these questions by running and analysing a number of alternative policy scenarios with the country-specific application of MAMS. These policy scenarios are compared to a baseline or BAU scenario, which aims to replicate observed performance and policy stance in each country case. The common denominator in each of these policy scenarios is that—unlike in the baseline—MDG spending is scaled up in such a way that MDGs 2, 4, 5 and 7 are achieved by 2015. There are two kinds of policy scenarios: one simulates the achievement of each MDG target separately (or two simultaneously, as in the case of the health and the sanitation goals), whereas in the other, public spending is scaled up as much as required to ensure the simultaneous achievement of all MDG targets—excluding that of poverty reduction. All these MDG scenarios are performed under alternative financing rules, that is to say, the required increase in public spending is financed through, alternatively, increased foreign grant aid, foreign borrowing, domestic borrowing or direct taxation. These scenarios allow us to assess synergy effects among the MDGs (by comparing the "individual" with the "simultaneous" MDG-achievement scenarios) as well as the MDG-related spending requirements and macroeconomic trade-offs under different financing settings.

Is "business as usual" good enough for MDG achievement?

The BAU scenarios have been tailored to each country context, assuming in all cases what are considered to be realistic rates of economic growth and levels of public spending under a scenario of unchanged policies and absence of external shocks.

Table 2.2 gives an overview of the regional and country achievement of the MDGs by 2015 under the BAU scenarios. The regional aggregates are computed by using weighted averages following the same methodology used in United Nations (2007). However, the present study uses a different definition of whether the countries and the region are on or off track in achieving the MDGs. In the absence of a better measure, the aforementioned publication (like many other studies) simply assumes the linear continuation of past trends in order to project whether any particular MDG would be achieved by 2015. In contrast, the BAU scenarios present better benchmarks for assessing whether countries are on or off track towards the MDGs, because the scenarios identify the currently expected growth scenario and assume continuation of current public spending policies; moreover, the MAMS model duly considers non-linearities in the effectiveness of social spending in achieving the targets.

Taking these factors into consideration, we find that, on average, the region appears to be on track to achieve MDG 1—to halve, between 1990 and 2015, the percentage of the population living on less than a dollar a day—under the BAU scenario. By the mid-point of the timeline from 1990 until 2015 (around 2002-03),[10] the region had already achieved about 75 per cent of the target, as can be derived from Appendix A2.2, table A2.1). However, this is almost entirely on account of progress in poverty reduction in Brazil and Mexico, the region's most populous countries. Eleven of the eighteen countries considered appear to be off track under the BAU scenario. Next to Brazil and Mexico, Chile, Colombia, Guatemala, Jamaica and Peru also appear to be on track, whereas the remaining countries would have to undertake additional efforts to reach the income poverty target. It is important to note, however, that extreme poverty, as measured using the poverty line of one dollar per person a day, is already very low in a number of the countries that are identified here as presumably being off track, such as Argentina, Costa Rica, Cuba and Uruguay, whose extreme poverty incidence was below 3 per cent at around the mid-point of the trajectory to 2015. National poverty lines in LAC are generally more in the order of two dollars a day, and thus define a poverty challenge of much larger magnitude in the region. The present analysis concentrates on the international target for reasons of comparability; most country studies, however, assess the challenges for both moderate and extreme poverty measured with national poverty lines.[11]

This analysis suggests, contrary to other reports, that the region is off track in achieving the education target. The region has made considerable progress in improving net enrolment rates and by this standard the region might be on track,

Table 2.2   Achievement of MDGs by 2015 under the BAU scenario in Latin America and the Caribbean[a]

	MDG 1	MDG 2	MDG 4	MDG 5	MDG 7a	MDG 7b
Argentina				--		
Bolivia						
Brazil				--	✓	✓
Chile	✓	✓	✓	✓	✓	✓
Colombia	✓				✓	✓
Costa Rica		✓			✓	✓
Cuba		✓	✓	✓	✓	✓
Dominican Republic					✓	✓
Ecuador					✓	
El Salvador						✓
Guatemala	✓					
Honduras						
Jamaica	✓					
Mexico	✓	✓			✓	✓
Nicaragua						
Paraguay						
Peru	✓			--		
Uruguay				--	✓	✓
LAC[b]	✓	--			✓	✓

Sources: Authors, based on country studies referred to in this chapter, and UN-DESA Population Division (World Population Prospects: The 2006 Revision Database) and United Nations (2007) for the construction of weighted regional averages.

Legend: ✓ = YES; blank = NO; and -- = not analysed.

[a] The achievement of MDGs by 2015 is defined with respect to the situation in 1990, the base year of the MDG timeline, and is indicated in the table by including a checkmark. Due to data limitations, for some countries MDG achievement is seen starting from the nearest available year to 1990.

[b] Weighted averages are used for the region as a whole. These are calculated using the same aggregation methods as applied in United Nations (2007). The weights used are total population for MDG 1, 7a and 7b; population under five for MDG 4; and number of births for MDG 5. For MDG 2, no regional average was computed because the age cohorts corresponding to the primary cycle differ across countries.

as reported elsewhere (for example, United Nations, 2007). However, all country studies considered here use 100 per cent primary school completion rates as the target for MDG 2.[12] The approach illustrates that the main challenge for the region is to keep children in school and to improve the internal efficiency of the primary schooling system by reducing both repetition and drop-out rates. This is also important in order to ensure sufficient transition of students into secondary education, thereby helping to reduce existing deficiencies in the supply of skilled labour, which has been identified as a bottleneck for the ability of the region's economies to adapt to the technological demands emanating from their increased exposure to global markets (see, for example, Vos and others, 2006).

Only four countries in the region (Chile, Costa Rica, Cuba and Mexico) meet the target under the BAU scenario, and only one of these (Mexico) and two others (Peru and Nicaragua) have been able to achieve 50 per cent or more of the target for primary completion by mid-point (see table 2.2).[13] A continuation of existing policies does not seem to ensure further progress in Nicaragua, and this may also prove problematic in Guatemala. In all other countries, economic conditions like those simulated in the BAU scenario would produce substantial improvements in primary school completion rates by the year 2015, but not enough to meet the established target.

The region also appears to be off track for the health goals for reducing child mortality and improving maternal health (see table 2.2). Child mortality rates have declined substantially throughout the region over the past decades. By mid-point, 14 out of the 18 countries had achieved 50 per cent or more of the targeted reduction in child mortality.[14] Observed trends in Jamaica, Uruguay, Costa Rica and Colombia suggest less progress in these countries. Projected trends in health spending and progress on other determinants of reductions in child mortality (such as improved education and higher real consumption levels) are expected to produce further important reductions in child mortality in most countries, though to a lesser extent in Honduras, Peru, Guatemala and El Salvador. Only Chile, and most likely Cuba (the country with the lowest child mortality rate in the region), would be able to meet the target under the conditions of the BAU scenario. All other countries would fall short of the target. It should be noted, however, that child mortality rates are already quite low in some of these countries (such as in Argentina, Chile, Costa Rica, Cuba and Uruguay) and that further reductions will have relatively high marginal costs.

Progress in terms of maternal mortality has been much less and, on average, the countries of the region had achieved just one third of the required progress towards the target by mid-point (see table 2.2).[15] Only two countries (Cuba and Chile) would achieve the goal on time under the BAU scenario.

A more optimistic picture emerges concerning the achievement of goals 7a and 7b, the provision of access to safe drinking water and basic sanitation. The region as a whole is on track, and many countries already achieved the international goals around mid-point (see table 2.2). More precisely, 10 out of the 18 countries had already achieved more than 50 per cent of MDG 7a by around the mid-point. Six of these countries (Brazil, Chile, Costa Rica, Cuba, Mexico and Uruguay) have already achieved the internationally defined target for MDG 7a and have set more ambitious national targets, which they would also achieve on time under the BAU scenario. Several countries, however, would remain far-removed from achieving the international goal under the BAU scenario, including El Salvador, Guatemala, Paraguay and Peru.

Six countries (Brazil, Chile, Costa Rica, Cuba, the Dominican Republic and Uruguay) had already achieved the international goal of halving the percentage of the population without sustainable access to basic sanitation by mid-point. These countries and some others that have not yet achieved the international goal (Colombia, Ecuador, Honduras and Peru) have set more ambitious national goals. Under the BAU scenario, the region on average is on track towards the internationally defined target for MDG 7b, but would be off track when considering the more ambitious goals that some countries have established. One country (Costa Rica) would achieve its more ambitious national goal well in advance under the BAU scenario and six others (Brazil, Cuba, Chile, Colombia, the Dominican Republic and Uruguay) are on track. Mexico is on track to achieve the less ambitious international goal. Argentina, Bolivia, Ecuador, Guatemala, Honduras, Nicaragua, Paraguay and Peru are among the countries that require substantial additional efforts to meet this goal.

In summary, the region as a whole seems on track (as more appropriately defined) for the targets for income poverty reduction (MDG 1) and off track for the targets for reducing child and maternal mortality (MDGs 4 and 5). While by and large on track for meeting universal access to primary education as measured by net enrolment rates, the region is off track when it comes to ensuring school completion on time by all that enrol in primary education. The (international) targets for water and basic sanitation appear to be achievable under existing policies in 9 of the 18 countries. Since these include Brazil and Mexico, the regional average suggests adequate progress towards these goals in the LAC region, although increased efforts will be needed in half of the countries.

How much will it cost to achieve the MDGs?

As discussed above, the MDG scenarios analysed with MAMS delineate a path towards the full achievement of the targets for goals 2, 4, 5 and 7a and 7b, as defined above (see notes to table 2.2). In these scenarios, the MAMS model allows an estimation of the required additional public spending based on what were found to be core determinants of primary school completion rates, child and maternal mortality and access to drinking water supply and basic sanitation. Apart from overall general equilibrium effects, the model considers three important factors which may influence these cost estimates considerably.

First, the complementarities or synergies among the various development goals, for instance, extra public spending on primary schooling leading to better educational outcomes may positively influence health behaviour and thus simultaneously help reduce child mortality. Such synergy effects can be captured by comparing the cost estimates for the scenarios under which the Government aims to achieve each of the MDGs separately with those for meeting them simultaneously.

Second, the source of financing for the additional public spending could influence the required cost of achieving the MDGs. For instance, when additional MDG-related public spending is financed through direct taxes, disposable household incomes may be affected and hence also private spending on education, health and sanitation, which in turn may require the Government to step in with additional efforts in order to achieve the MDGs. In the event that increased domestic borrowing by the Government crowds out private investment, future GDP growth would be affected, thus impacting the cost estimate of MDG-related spending relative to GDP.

Third, the MAMS model assumes that there are increasing marginal costs for achieving each of the development goals. This is captured through (logistic) functions calibrated with parameters that in most cases were estimated on the basis of country-specific sector analyses. It is thus possible that the required additional public spending for countries that are already close to achieving the goals may still be substantial because of the higher marginal costs.

Below, we analyse the required additional MDG spending for the 18 LAC countries, where "additional MDG-related public spending" is defined as the difference between the estimate for total spending on MDG-related services under the MDG scenarios and that under the BAU scenario for each country model. In the cases of Cuba and Chile, in particular, the MDGs can be achieved at no additional cost. The model analysis for these two countries suggests that MDGs 2, 4, 5 and 7 will be achieved under the BAU scenario (see table 2.2). For the other 16 countries, additional MDG-related public spending ranges from 0.9 per cent of GDP on average per year between the base year and 2015 for Peru, to 6.1 per cent of GDP per year for Guatemala (see table 2.3).

Synergies among MDGs yield cost savings

Progress on all MDGs creates cost-saving synergies. Such synergies are observed for all countries needing to increase MDG-related spending in order to reach the goals, except for Honduras and Uruguay. The synergy effect can amount to more than 1 per cent of GDP per annum, as in the case of Guatemala (see table 2.3). Significant cost savings of more than 0.5 percentage points of GDP per annum originating from positive interaction effects between education, health and sanitation are also estimated for Bolivia, Brazil, Colombia, Nicaragua and Paraguay, although not for all financing scenarios discussed below. In any case, the existence of such synergy effects is a strong argument— including from the point of view of the efficiency of public spending—for a simultaneous, rather than a phased, achievement of the MDGs.

The financing strategy matters for MDG cost estimates

In seven countries (Argentina, Colombia, Costa Rica, Ecuador, Jamaica, Paraguay and Peru), the additional costs are 2 per cent of GDP per annum or less regardless of the financing scenario (see table 2.3). The cost would be of a similar magnitude for Bolivia, if that country were able to finance the MDG strategy fully with foreign financing (grants or borrowing), and for Brazil, if financed

Table 2.3   Required additional MDG-related public spending for achieving all MDGs simultaneously under alternative financing scenarios in Latin America and the Caribbean, 2000-2015 (percentage of GDP)

Country	Base year	BY	MDGs scenario with foreign grants			MDGs scenario with foreign borrowing			MDGs scenario with domestic borrowing			MDGs scenario with income taxes		
			AS[a]	IS[b]	SE[c]	AS[a]	IS[b]	SE[c]	AS[a]	IS[b]	SE[c]	AS[a]	IS[b]	SE[c]
Argentina	2003	3.8				1.3	0.4	0.3	1.6	0.6	0.2	1.4	0.4	0.2
Bolivia	2000	4.8	1.7	0.0	0.7	2.0	0.0	0.3	2.8	0.6	0.2	2.8	0.6	0.3
Brazil	2003	9.5				1.7	0.0	0.6	2.2	0.1	0.0	2.2	0.1	0.0
Chile	2003	5.0				0.0	0.0	0.0	0.0	0.0	0.0	0.0	0.0	0.0
Colombia	2002	7.3				1.4	0.9	0.1	1.6	1.0	0.5	1.7	1.1	0.0
Costa Rica	2002	9.6				1.1	0.0	0.1	1.4	0.0	0.1	1.4	0.0	0.0
Cuba	2002	13.8	0.0	0.0	0.0	0.0	0.0	0.0						
Dominican Republic	2004	2.7				3.3	1.1	0.1	4.1	1.7	0.0	3.7	1.3	0.0
Ecuador	2001	3.6				1.3	1.1	0.3	1.4	1.2	0.3	1.5	1.2	0.2
El Salvador	2002	5.3	2.6	0.2	0.3	2.6	0.2	0.3	2.8	0.2	0.2	2.8	0.2	0.2
Guatemala	2001	3.3	4.8	1.9	1.1	4.8	1.9	1.1	6.1	3.1	1.3	6.1	3.1	1.3
Honduras	2004	2.7	4.3	1.0	0.0	4.3	1.0	0.0	5.1	1.5	0.0	4.6	1.1	-0.5
Jamaica	2000	5.4				1.3	1.3	0.2	1.5	1.9	0.2	1.4	1.6	0.2
Mexico	2003	3.3				2.9	1.4	0.3	5.5	3.3	0.0	5.5	3.3	0.0
Nicaragua	2000	5.6	3.6	1.3	0.8	3.6	1.3	0.8	4.4	2.0	0.9	4.7	1.4	0.3
Paraguay	2001	5.3				2.0	0.6	0.9				2.1	0.7	0.9
Peru	2004	1.3	0.9	0.5	0.4	0.9	0.5	0.4	0.9	0.5	0.4	0.9	0.5	0.4
Uruguay	2005	5.4				2.5	0.4	0.0	3.3	0.5	0.0	3.3	0.5	0.0

Source: MAMS country model simulation results reported in country studies.

Abbreviations: BY = Base-year MDG-related public spending; AS = Additional MDG-related public spending; IS = Incremental MDG-related public spending; SE = Synergy effect on MDG-related public spending

[a] Annual average MDG-related public spending (in percentage points of GDP) under the respective MDGs financing scenario minus the annual average MDG-related public spending (in percentage points of GDP) under the BAU scenario.

[b] Annual average additional MDG-related public spending (in percentage points of GDP) during the period 2010-15 minus the annual average additional MDG-related public spending (in percentage points of GDP) during the entire simulation period.

[c] Annual average additional MDG-related public spending saved (in percentage points of GDP) when achieving the MDGs jointly instead of separately.

through external borrowing. The MDG scenario is more costly for these two countries when the additional spending is financed through domestic resource mobilization. Guatemala, Honduras and Nicaragua require the largest extra public spending effort (more than 3.5 per cent of GDP per year), regardless of the financing scenario. The Dominican Republic and Mexico also fall into this category, but only if the MDG strategy is financed through domestic resource mobilization; for these countries, external financing would be a cheaper option.

These results illustrate that the financing strategy has an important bearing on the cost estimates. The required additional MDG-related public spending is generally lower when financed from abroad, since both sources of domestic finance come at a price. As indicated above, domestic borrowing may crowd out private investment. Not only does this have implications for GDP growth, it also hurts the private provisioning of MDG-related services, and the Government would have to spend more to achieve the MDGs. On the other hand, an increase in income taxes may affect disposable household income, which could also affect private investment through lower private savings; more importantly, it causes a "consumption-compression effect" which results in a decrease of private demand for MDG-related services compared to the other financing scenarios. Again, in order to achieve the MDGs, the Government needs to compensate the reduction in private demand for MDG-related services by further increasing MDG-related public spending.

For a large number of the country cases analysed, the estimated cost of the required additional MDG-related public spending is lower under the tax financing scenario than under that of domestic borrowing (see table 2.3). In Colombia, Ecuador and Nicaragua, however, the "consumption-compression" effect of higher taxation is relatively strong, making taxation the more expensive financing strategy. Raising income taxes is unambiguously more costly than mobilizing resources from abroad but, as discussed below, this does not necessarily mean that domestic resource mobilization could not be the better financing option, as countries may face external borrowing constraints, as well as other macroeconomic trade-offs which also need to be considered.

MDG costs rise as countries get closer to the target

The average additional annual MDG-related public spending during the last five years (2010-15) is larger than during the entire simulation period (that is to say, from the base year to 2015) in 13 countries out of 16 (see table 2.3). This difference—or "incremental MDG-related public spending"—is the result of a rise in the marginal public spending that is necessary to achieve the MDGs towards the end of the period, as the goals are already closer to being achieved.

The "incremental MDG-related public spending" tends to be higher when resources are mobilized domestically because the crowding-out and consumption-compression effects magnify over time. Incremental spending is substantial in some countries. It is estimated at about or above 1 per cent of GDP per year in eight countries (Colombia, Dominican Republic, Ecuador, Guatemala, Honduras, Jamaica, Mexico and Nicaragua), regardless of the MDG financing strategy, and even slightly above 3 per cent of GDP per annum in two countries (Guatemala and Mexico) in the case of domestically mobilized resources. This evidence should be seen as a reminder to Governments that sustained higher public spending efforts will still be required when the MDGs are (close to being) achieved.

"Feasible" financing scenarios

In order to establish the "optimal" financing strategy for the increased MDG-related public spending, a number of factors must be considered. One possible criterion for assessing the desirability of certain financing options is the effect that these will have on the estimated costs of delivering MDG services, as discussed above. There are other important considerations, however. As discussed in the second section, borrowing strategies will need to take into account the implications for public debt sustainability over time. Foreign aid financing may not be a feasible option for most of the middle-income countries of the region, and those that do have access to this financing source will need to consider consistency of policy conditionality with the MDG strategy and the desirability of prolonged aid dependency. Each of the financing strategies will need to take into account possible macroeconomic trade-offs, such as RER appreciation and possible erosion of export competitiveness, which are likely to be stronger in the case of external borrowing or foreign aid financing. Meanwhile, domestic financing strategies risk the crowding-out of private consumption and investment.

There are no absolute benchmarks for rigorously establishing the feasibility or optimality of the various financing strategies. For instance, the critical level of public indebtedness will vary from one country context to another. Furthermore, the degree to which Governments will be able to raise tax revenues to the required levels will depend on the initial levels of tax burden and, no less importantly, on political economy considerations. Hence, in the analysis below, the choice of financing strategy recommended by the country studies is used as the initial reference, and is then reassessed in the light of the macroeconomic trade-offs and political economy considerations.

One caveat here is that the analysis of the financing scenarios only allows the comparison of situations in which the additional MDG-related spending is fully financed through one of the four options considered. While this has the advantage of helping to understand the merits of one financing option vis-à-vis another, it has the disadvantage of not giving explicit consideration to possible "mixed" financing strategies which might avoid or mitigate certain undesirable trade-offs. The question of the feasibility of mixed strategies will be addressed below.

Table 2.4 summarizes some key results of the country studies regarding the assessment of financing strategies. Upon initial inspection, three main findings stand out. First, most country studies recommend financing the MDG strategy through increased taxation. This is the case for all but five countries: Bolivia and Honduras recommend aid financing, in line with the poverty-reduction strategy framework they adopted in the context of the HIPC Initiative. Despite a high public debt overhang, the authors of the Jamaican study see external borrowing as the more desirable financing strategy, since the alternative of tax financing is considered to be less feasible in the light of an already high tax burden and recent increases in rates. The authors of the studies for Guatemala and Uruguay do not rank any single financing option superior to another.

Second, while tax financing appears the most favoured option, external borrowing or aid financing is in all cases cheaper in terms of the required additional public spending on MDG-related services. The country studies, nonetheless, typically prefer tax financing, as further external borrowing is considered to lift public debt beyond a critical level of sustainability and/or entails other important trade-offs, such as significant declines in export competitiveness.

Third, no country study recommends a strategy exclusively based on domestic government borrowing. Not only would domestic borrowing generally be more costly in terms of the required extra spending, as indicated above, but in many cases it would also raise the total public debt burden to unsustainable levels. In the cases of Colombia, Ecuador and Nicaragua, where this financing strategy would be (slightly) less costly than increasing taxes (see table 2.3), the weakly developed domestic bond market and the possible consequences for levels of total public indebtedness (should the Government indeed be able to borrow domestically) would render such a strategy untenable.

Given these recommendations, the question remains: How "feasible" are those "recommended" financing strategies and what would be the alternatives?

The scope for tax financing

As discussed in the second section, most LAC countries have comparatively low tax burdens, suggesting ample space to increase some of that burden in favour of achieving the MDGs. As shown in table 2.4, the required increase in tax revenues may differ from the estimated increase in MDG spending because of general equilibrium effects; in other words, the increased public spending may affect output and employment differently across sectors and this may have a bearing on overall tax revenue.[16] In a number of cases (6 out of 13) reported in table 2.4—including Guatemala and Uruguay for which the respective country studies did not recommend any preferred financing strategy—tax revenue would have to increase by about 0.4 per cent of GDP more than the estimated MDG costs.[17] This is due to a resource shift towards activities that on average tend to be taxed less (such as services which are produced in large parts by the

Table 2.4   MDG financing strategies and required increases in tax or public debt burdens in Latin America and the Caribbean[a]

Country	Recommended financing strategy[b]			Least costly financing strategy[c]			Memo items (% of GDP)			
								Total Public debt (2015)		
	Strategy	AS[d]	AB[e]	Strategy	AS[d]	AB[e]	Base-year tax revenue	Base year	BAU scenario	Foreign borrowing scenario
Argentina	Taxes	1.4	1.7	Foreign borrowing	1.3	3.3	23.9	128.2	70.3	87.5
Brazil	Taxes	2.2	2.0	Foreign borrowing	1.7	4.5	34.0	57.5	50.7	76.1
Colombia	Taxes	1.7	2.3	Foreign borrowing	1.4	2.8	18.5	60.6	67.8	91.4
Costa Rica	Taxes	1.4	1.6	Foreign borrowing	1.1	0.9	14.2	48.2	51.8	66.5
Dominican Republic	Taxes	3.7	2.8	Foreign borrowing	3.3	5.8	14.9	52.2	37.5	62.5
Ecuador	Taxes	1.5	1.7	Foreign borrowing	1.3	4	14.0	67.0	51.1	70.5
El Salvador	Taxes	2.8	3.2	Foreign borrowing	2.6	5.1	10.2	44.6	47.3	90.4
				Foreign grants	2.6	3.1				
Mexico	Taxes	5.5	6.0	Foreign borrowing	2.9	9.8	15.7	25.6	24.1	65.3
Nicaragua	Taxes	4.7	4.4	Foreign borrowing	3.6	3	14.8	130.6	127.8	158.3
				Foreign grants	3.6	3.5				
Paraguay	Taxes	2.1	2.1	Foreign borrowing	2.0	4	12.6	36.4	50.6	76.1
Peru	Taxes	0.9	1.3	Foreign borrowing	0.9	2.6	13.5	47.2	38.6	49.6
				Foreign grants	0.9	1.1				
Bolivia	Foreign grants	1.7	3.1	Foreign grants	1.7	3.1	17.8	73.0	52.4	95.6
Honduras	Foreign grants	4.3	7.7	Foreign borrowing	4.3	16.3	15.8	94.5	46.0	113.6
				Foreign grants	4.3	7.5				
Jamaica	Foreign borrowing	1.3	5.3	Foreign borrowing	1.3	5.3	31.9	102.3	103.5	115.1
Guatemala	None	6.1[g]	12.7[g]	Foreign borrowing	4.8	18.1	9.8	23.0	22.3	137.5
				Foreign grants	4.8	9.6				
Uruguay	None	3.3[g]	4.1[g]	Foreign borrowing	2.5	5.1	28.3	80.7	80.8	109.9

Sources: MAMS country model simulation results and analysis from country studies.

Abbreviations: AS = Additional MDG-related public spending (per cent of GDP); AB = Additional burden (per cent of GDP).

[a] Chile and Cuba are not considered in this section as they do not need to finance any additional public spending to achieve the MDGs.

[b] Refers to financing strategies as recommended by the authors of country studies.

[c] Least costly strategy in terms of additional MDG-related public spending.

[d] Difference (in percentage points of GDP) between MDG-related public spending under the BAU scenario and corresponding MDGs scenario.

[e] Average increase (in percentage points of GDP) in tax revenue, foreign borrowing or foreign grant aid, compared with the BAU scenario.

[f] No financing strategy is suggested in the country study, but the results for the tax financing scenario are included for informative purposes.

Government itself or by the informal sector). In Brazil, the Dominican Republic and Nicaragua, the tax burden needs to rise by less because of opposite resource shifts, whereas in Paraguay the tax burden would need to rise in proportion to the estimated additional MDG-related spending.

Having said this, among those countries for which the tax-financing strategy is recommended in the respective country studies, the required additional tax burden would range between 1.3 per cent of GDP in Peru to 6.0 per cent in the case of Mexico. For seven countries (Argentina, Brazil, Colombia, Costa Rica, Ecuador, Paraguay and Peru), the required increase in tax revenue would be between 1.0 per cent and 2.5 per cent of GDP. This seems to be a feasible range of effective tax revenue increase, which countries conducting tax reforms have been able to achieve on average over more or less a decade, as discussed in the second section. Beyond this, admittedly arbitrary, upper bound of the indicated range, tax reform should be expected to be much more demanding for a variety of reasons, not least owing to political economy concerns. Such is the case for the Dominican Republic, El Salvador, Guatemala, Mexico, Nicaragua and Uruguay. This is not to suggest that these countries should not pursue tax reform for the MDG financing strategy, but they will have to give cautious consideration to how far out they can effectively push the tax revenue curve. For all countries, it is probably the case that increasing tax revenue, even by a few percentage points of GDP, may not be something that can be achieved overnight, but may take years to effectuate. In the meantime, this would require some kind of mixed financing strategy as discussed below.

More aid?

The possibility of financing the MDG strategy through increased grant aid is considered in the modelling of a few of the country cases only, since most countries in the region lack significant access to this type of funding. Where this applies (that is, in the cases of Bolivia, El Salvador, Honduras, Nicaragua and Peru), aid financing is least costly in terms of required additional public spending (see table 2.4).[18] Only Bolivia, Honduras and Nicaragua are eligible for debt relief, however, and have already received, to varying degrees, significant amounts of development assistance under the HIPC initiative. In order to finance the required additional public MDG-related spending, aid flows to these countries would have to increase by 3.1, 7.7 and 3.5 percentage points of GDP on average per year, respectively. In the case of Honduras, current levels of aid inflows are about 8 per cent of GDP and, hence, would almost need to double. Such an increase may be difficult to negotiate with donors. Dutch disease effects explain why the required aid inflows for this country (16.3 per cent of GDP per annum) are so much higher than the required additional public spending (4.3 per cent of GDP per annum): the average rate of RER appreciation under the aid-financing scenario would be about 7.5 per cent compared to the BAU scenario, causing the exports-to-GDP ratio to drop by more than 5 percentage points and the trade deficit to widen (see figure 2.4).

This effect is also present in Bolivia, but to a much lesser extent, and appears to be absent in Nicaragua. In the case of Nicaragua, however, aid dependence is already quite high (ODA amounted to more than 18 per cent of GDP on average during 2000-05), which is why the country authors recommend a tax financing strategy rather than proposing a further increase in aid dependence. However, given the rather substantial required increase in the tax burden (4.4 per cent of GDP) that is estimated for Nicaragua, it may be more realistic to pursue a combination of a tax increase and, at least in the short run, additional foreign aid. On the other hand, aid flows to Bolivia currently average about 8 per cent of GDP per year and the required increase of 3.1 per cent to achieve the MDGs would be substantial, though perhaps negotiable, and could be replaced by higher tax revenues over time.

More public borrowing?

While foreign borrowing is typically least costly in terms of required additional spending, it also seems to entail substantial trade-offs in the form of RER appreciation and a loss in export revenue. This explains much of the difference between columns (5) and (6) in table 2.4. Such trade-offs are much less substantial

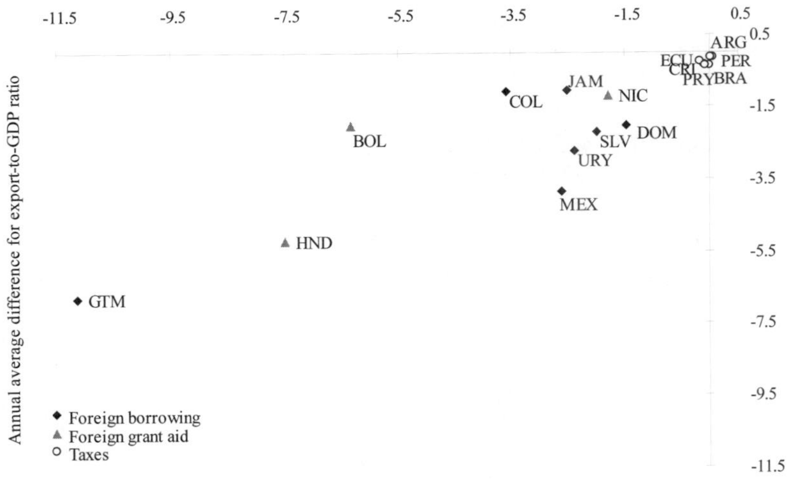

Figure 2.4 Annual average difference of the RER and the export-to-GDP ratio under the "feasible" MDGs financing scenario relative to the BAU scenario in Latin America and the Caribbean[a]

Source: MAMS country model simulation results and analysis from country studies.
[a] The "feasible" MDGs financing scenario is indicated in table 2.5.

under the tax financing scenarios, for example (see figure 2.4). In addition, in all country cases (with the exception of Peru), total public debt would rise to 65 per cent of GDP or (much) more under both the foreign borrowing (table 2.4) and the domestic borrowing scenarios. This would put public indebtedness beyond critical levels of sustainability in all countries (except perhaps Peru) based on the information in table 2.1 above.[19] The country studies confirm this, concluding that financing the MDG strategy fully through either internal or external government borrowing is not feasible, with the possible exception of Jamaica for the reasons indicated above.

"Feasible" financing strategies

The policy scenario analysis of the MAMS framework involved assessing alternative single financing options for the MDG strategies. Based on our further assessment of these options, however, it appears that only in a few countries would a "one-legged" financing strategy seem feasible, as summarized in table 2.5. For Bolivia, aid financing would seem a feasible option, provided that donors are willing to support it. Of course, it would remain advisable for the Government of Bolivia to consider enhancing domestic resource mobilization also, especially through tax reform, in order to reduce aid dependency over time.

Tax financing would seem a feasible strategy for Argentina, Brazil, Costa Rica, Ecuador, Paraguay, Peru, and possibly also Dominican Republic—if combined with foreign borrowing, as will be explained below—given the degree of tax revenue increase that would be required as well as the milder macroeconomic trade-offs generated by tax increases compared to alternative financing scenarios. Costa Rica, Dominican Republic and Peru have manageable baseline levels of public indebtedness and hence would have space to distribute the financing burden by combining tax revenue increases and foreign borrowing.

In the other country cases, a mixed financing strategy would also seem the most realistic. For Honduras and Nicaragua, this could consist of a combination of initiating tax reform and seeking more foreign aid. As already discussed, in the case of Nicaragua, tax financing (as recommended in the country study) would require a rather substantial increase in government revenue (4.4 per cent per annum), more than any tax reform is likely to accomplish in the short-to-medium run. For Honduras, foreign aid financing is recommended in the country study, but considering the presumably strong erosion of export earnings this would generate, a "two-legged" strategy of tax-cum-aid financing might be better suited to mitigating the trade-offs.

All other country cases would probably need to seek a combination of tax reform, very limited public borrowing, and a change in public spending priorities and/or increases in the efficiency of MDG-related spending. In those cases (Colombia, El Salvador, Guatemala, Jamaica, Mexico and Uruguay), either the required tax increase would be too high in relation to what a well-executed tax

Table 2.5   "Feasible" financing strategies for the achievement of the MDGs in Latin America and the Caribbean[a]

	Foreign aid	Tax increase	Tax increase combined with foreign aid	Tax increase combined with foreign borrowing	Tax increase with public expenditure reform and more efficient service delivery
Argentina		✓			
Bolivia	✓				
Brazil		✓			
Colombia					✓
Costa Rica		✓✓		✓	
Dominican Republic				✓	
Ecuador		✓			
El Salvador					✓
Honduras			✓		
Jamaica					✓
Guatemala					✓
Mexico					✓
Nicaragua			✓		
Paraguay		✓			
Peru		✓✓		✓	
Uruguay					✓

Sources: MAMS country model simulations, country studies and analysis in text. The cases of Cuba and Chile are not considered here, as they are expected to meet MDGs 2, 4, 5 and 7 under the BAU scenario.

[a] Two checkmarks indicate that the main emphasis in the financing strategy should be on taxation, where more than one option is indicated.

reform might be able to achieve, or levels of public indebtedness are already close to or above critical points of sustainability—or both.

A mixed financing strategy should possibly be recommended for all 18 countries in order to minimize detrimental macroeconomic trade-offs. Even so, our comparative analysis makes it clear that in most countries the emphasis should be on increasing tax revenue. For many countries, however, this will most likely not be sufficient, and they would need to supplement this strategy with some (limited) degree of foreign financing and/or improved efficiency in MDG-related expenditures.

Poverty reduction (MDG 1), inequality and growth

As discussed above, the MAMS scenario analysis treats the results for MDG 1 as endogenous to economy-wide adjustments as manifested in labour-market shifts that are then translated into expected outcomes for poverty and inequality at the household level, using the microsimulation methodology described in the appendix. Using this approach, we find that the income poverty reduction target is expected to be met under the BAU scenario in Brazil, Chile, Colombia, Guatemala, Jamaica, Mexico and Peru (see tables 2.2 and A2.1). The inclusion of Brazil and Mexico sets the region at large on track for the goal. BAU does lead to poverty reduction for the other countries,[20] but not by enough of a margin to meet the target.

The question is, then, whether a strategy of increased public spending for the achievement of the MDGs in education, child and maternal health, and water and sanitation will also help reduce income poverty beyond what is achieved under the BAU scenario. Results for the poverty incidence of those living on less than one dollar a day show that in 10 countries, the "feasible" MDG strategy—as defined in table 2.5 for each country—would lead to further poverty reduction compared to the BAU scenario, but only Honduras is expected to join the countries that are anticipated to meet the target for MDG 1 by 2015 (see tables 2.6 and A2.1). Substantial reductions in extreme poverty by 2015 are also expected in Ecuador, Guatemala, Nicaragua and Paraguay, but this would largely also be achieved under the BAU scenario, and whatever further poverty reduction may be expected under the MDG scenario would not be sufficient to meet the target for MDG 1 in these countries. For most countries, the degree of poverty reduction under the MDG scenario is either the same as or greater than under BAU. Only in the cases of Paraguay, Peru and Uruguay would there actually be slight losses in poverty reduction, mostly explained by relatively small changes in income distributions triggered by the MDG strategy.

The results of the microsimulations suggest that most of the progress towards MDG 1 is explained by average income and employment growth under both the BAU and MDG scenarios. In fact, employment and GDP growth tend to move together. Figure 2.5 shows that this pattern is more or less the same under the BAU and the MDG scenarios (using the "feasible" financing scenario for the latter). Only in the cases of Guatemala and Honduras would the implied employment-output elasticity fall significantly under the MDG scenario (by 47 per cent and 23 per cent, respectively), apparently because of the lower labour intensity of MDG-related services sectors compared to the average for tradable sectors. In the other country cases, the implied employment-output elasticity is more or less the same under both scenarios and ranges from a low of 0.2 for Uruguay to a high of 0.9 for Nicaragua, with a regional average of about 0.5.

Countries with above-average employment-output elasticities (Bolivia, Brazil, Guatemala, Honduras, Nicaragua and Paraguay) are also the ones which would see greater absolute changes in poverty reduction (see figure 2.6). Other countries with employment elasticities above the regional average, like Argentina, Dominican Republic and Mexico have low base-year values for income poverty and show only limited further poverty reduction.

Table 2.6   Labour market, inequality and poverty indicators

| | Annual average growth rate | | | | | | | | Absolute change from the base year | | | |
| | Employment | | U/S[a] | | RW | | U/S[a] | | Inequality (GC) | | Poverty[b] | |
	BS	MS[c]	BS	MS[c]	BS	MS[c]	BS	MS[c]	BS	MS[c]	BS	MS[c]
Argentina	1.8	2.0	-0.9	-1.2	2.1	2.3	0.3	0.1	-0.01	-0.01	-1.3	-1.4
Bolivia	2.2	2.2	-0.1	-0.4	1.4	1.9	0.1	0.2	0.00	0.00	-2.4	-3.0
Brazil	2.5	2.7	-1.6	-1.9	0.9	1.0	1.6	1.5	-0.12	-0.12	-4.7	-6.9
Colombia	2.4	2.4	-1.2	-1.4	2.4	2.6	1.3	1.2	-0.03	-0.03	-2.0	-2.0
Costa Rica	1.8	1.8	-3.0	-3.0	1.1	1.6	1.0	1.1	-0.02	-0.02	-0.3	-0.3
Dominican Republic	3.3	3.4	-1.0	-1.9	2.1	2.9	1.0	0.7	-0.04	-0.04	-1.9	-2.1
Ecuador	1.4	1.4	-3.0	-3.1	2.2	2.3	0.3	0.2	-0.07	-0.07	-7.6	-7.8
El Salvador	1.0	1.2	0.2	0.1	1.9	2.1	-0.2	-0.4	0.00	0.00	-0.5	-0.9
Guatemala	1.4	0.9	2.0	1.3	3.3	7.0	-3.4	-5.5	-0.04	-0.05	-8.6	-11.0
Honduras	2.6	2.6	-0.1	-0.5	1.7	3.3	-0.7	-1.5	0.01	0.01	-5.5	-7.4
Jamaica	1.3	1.3	-0.2	-0.2	1.7	2.0	0.1	-0.1	-0.01	-0.01	-3.8	-3.8
Mexico	3.4	3.5	-1.5	-2.0	2.2	3.2	1.5	0.8	-0.03	-0.03	-1.4	-1.6
Nicaragua	2.7	2.7	-3.3	-3.7	1.4	1.6	2.8	3.2	-0.05	-0.02	-10.7	-12.3
Paraguay	2.4	2.4	-1.0	-1.1	1.1	1.1	0.1	0.1	-0.07	-0.06	-12.9	-12.4
Peru	1.9	1.9	0.0	0.0	2.7	2.8	0.3	-0.4	0.02	0.03	-1.0	-0.8
Uruguay	0.4	0.4	-1.9	-2.0	2.6	2.9	2.5	1.5	-0.02	-0.01	-0.8	-0.7

Sources: MAMS country model simulation results and analysis from country studies. No results for the MDG scenario are shown for Cuba and Chile as these countries reach the MDGs in the BAU scenario.

Abbreviations: U/S = Unskilled/skilled employment ratio; RW = Real wage per worker; GC = Gini coefficient of per capita household income; BS = BAU scenario; MS = MDG scenario.

[a] Unskilled labour includes workers who have less than a complete secondary education, whereas skilled labour includes workers who have completed secondary education or above.

[b] Refers to the percentage of the population living on less than a dollar a day.

[c] The reported results are for the MDG strategy under the "feasible" financing scenario as defined in table 2.5 for each country. Simulation results are for the foreign borrowing scenario for those countries with no single feasible financing scenario indicated in table 2.5.

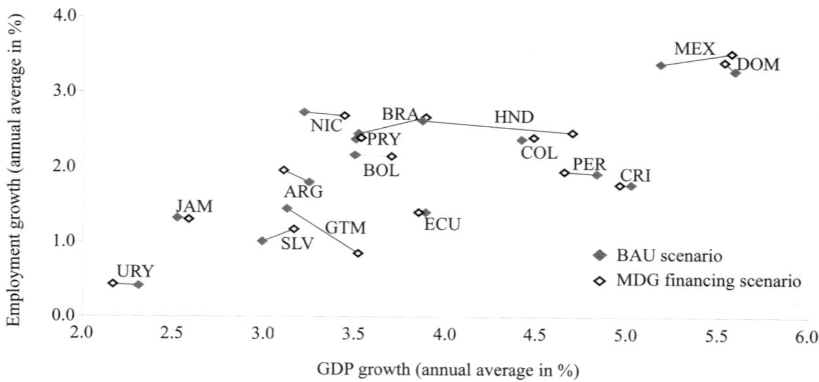

Figure 2.5 Employment-output nexus under the BAU scenario and the "feasible" MDG financing scenarios in Latin America and the Caribbean[a]

Sources: MAMS country model simulation results and analysis as reported in the country studies.
[a] The MDG financing scenarios are considered "feasible" as defined in table 2.5. for each country. Simulation results are for the foreign borrowing scenario for those countries with no single feasible financing scenario indicated in table 2.5.

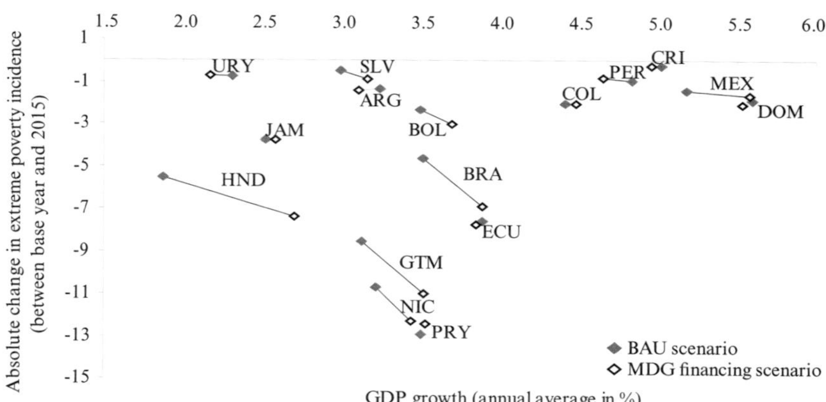

Figure 2.6 Change in income poverty and per capita GDP growth under the BAU scenario and the 'feasible' MDG financing scenarios in LAC[a]

Source: MAMS country model simulation results and analysis as reported in the country studies.
[a] The MDG financing scenarios are considered "feasible" as defined in Table 2.5 for each country. Simulation results are for the foreign-borrowing scenario for those countries with no single feasible financing scenario indicated in Table 2.5.

Initial poverty levels and income distribution patterns would also seem relevant in explaining why countries like Colombia, Costa Rica, Dominican Republic, Mexico and Peru show relatively little absolute poverty reduction while sustaining relatively high growth rates under both the BAU and MDG scenarios. On the other hand, Bolivia, Brazil, Guatemala, Honduras, Nicaragua and Paraguay show more visible absolute poverty reduction (5 percentage points or more) at moderate per capita GDP growth rates (between 0.7 per cent and 2.5 per cent per annum). In those cases where the MDG scenario yields greater poverty reduction than the BAU scenario, the former also yields a higher growth rate than the latter, and vice versa.

The predominance of employment and average income effects in explaining changes in poverty suggests that income redistribution effects under both the BAU and the MDG scenarios tend to be weak. This is confirmed by the results for the changes in the Gini coefficient of per capita household income (see table 2.6). During the simulation period to 2015, little income redistribution is generally achieved under either the BAU or the MDG scenario. As a general finding, this might be surprising, as the MDG scenario, in particular, should help raise education levels and labour-market opportunities for all, with most of the gains benefiting the poor who currently tend to have a lower education level. The MDG strategy, as discussed in section 2.2, should be expected to raise both the demand for and supply of skilled workers. One should, however, also expect a timing disparity: the demand for skilled workers in MDG-related services will go up first, whereas the increase in the supply of skilled workers would materialize with a lag, given the time it will take before the better-educated school graduates enter the labour market—most likely beyond the time horizon of the present analysis. However, in the case of the LAC countries, much progress was already made in improving access to education during the 1990s, and hence skilled labour-supply growth may already be relatively strong without the MDG strategy. Shifts in the skilled-unskilled composition of labour demand will depend further on changes in sectoral labour demand induced by general equilibrium effects of the MDG strategy.

The results shown in table 2.6 indicate that in nearly all countries the demand for unskilled labour falls relative to that for skilled labour, and in most cases this shift is more predominant under the MDG scenario, confirming the hypothesis outlined above.[21] In the presence of a time lag, this shift towards greater employment opportunities for skilled workers would likely push up income inequality. However, as table 2.6 also indicates, in most cases this inequality-increasing employment shift tends to be offset (more than proportionately in most cases) by increasing relative labour incomes for unskilled workers. This reflects the fact that, indeed, in most countries, the growth of the supply of skilled workers is already outpacing that of unskilled workers, while production technologies in most sectors of the LAC economies remain fairly intensive in the use of unskilled labour. In other words, their economies are not yet able to absorb fully the growing numbers of skilled workers; this in turn is putting downward pressure on the wage premiums for education and, on balance, reduces the wage gap between skilled and unskilled workers in most country cases.

These opposing shifts in the skill composition of employment and in the unskilled-skilled wage ratios explain the minimal effects on income distribution. Both labour and per capita household income inequality tend to fall in most country cases, but by small margins only. The only real exception is Brazil, which shows stronger income redistribution effects; these are, however, expected to occur under both the BAU and MDG scenarios where income poverty falls remarkably (see table 2.6). Income distribution in Brazil appears to be particularly sensitive to changes in the mean wage and in the wage of a large population of unskilled workers relative to skilled workers. Only in a few countries do very small changes in inequality weigh substantially enough to offset partially the income-poverty reduction of the BAU scenario. As mentioned above, in Paraguay, Peru and Uruguay, poverty reduction in the MDG scenario is lower relative to that in the BAU scenario. Income distribution in these countries would actually be slightly more unequal under the MDG scenario than under the BAU scenario.

Conclusions and policy recommendations

The results from the country studies referred to in this chapter demonstrate that achieving the MDGs in LAC is within reach for most countries, but BAU alone is inadequate; even if it comes at a modest cost, the financing of an MDG strategy will require careful macroeconomic management. The main findings and policy conclusions of the present analysis can be grouped under four headings.

Business as usual is, for the most part, not good enough

The region is on track for MDGs 1 and 7 (poverty reduction and access to safe drinking water and basic sanitation), but appears to be off track for the education (MDG 2) and health goals (MDGs 4 and 5). "On track" and "off track" have been defined more appropriately here than elsewhere, where progress towards the goals is usually projected linearly, based on the trend observed since 1990. The present analysis is instead based on a benchmark or baseline scenario which allows an assessment of whether the MDGs are likely to be achieved assuming unchanged policies (BAU) and taking into account non-linearities in the progress towards the outcomes for education, health, and water and sanitation.

Considerable differences across countries are evident. The poverty-reduction target is within reach for LAC as a whole, essentially because the baseline scenario for the region reflects continued good economic performance and policies in Brazil and Mexico; but existing growth performance and policies would not suffice to meet this goal for 11 out of the 18 countries. The goals for safe drinking water and basic sanitation are more uniformly achievable with the continuance of existing efforts in most countries of the region. The region is also making good progress in improving access to education, but—as highlighted in the present study—keeping all children in primary school until timely graduation remains a big challenge in nearly all of the countries of the region. Most countries are relatively off track in terms of meeting the ambitious target of 100 per cent completion rate, with the exception of Cuba, and, possibly, Chile, Costa Rica and Mexico. All countries have made significant progress in reducing child mortality, but efforts will need to be stepped up in most countries in order to reduce early childhood deaths by two-thirds by 2015. Only Chile and Cuba appear to be on track for this goal. Estimates of maternal mortality are subject to measurement errors, but the available evidence for the region suggests very little progress and, again, only Chile and Cuba seem to be on track for the target.

The analyses conducted in the country studies assume that additional resources are spent effectively on improving the availability and quality of education services, health care delivery systems and basic sanitation and water provisioning. Precisely what this entails for sector-level policies at the country level varies (depending on initial conditions), but it would typically imply a focus on improving school inputs and enhancing teacher quality, as well as providing increased access to health services and enhanced coverage of vaccination programmes and basic sanitation. The studies also find that improving general infrastructure (including roads and energy supply) would improve the accessibility of health and education services and hence help support the achievement of the goals indirectly. However, meeting the MDGs is clearly not only a matter of expanding social spending in these directions. The country studies show strong effects from improved socio-economic conditions at the household level, as better education helps improve health outcomes and vice versa, and improved income situations of households generally also contribute to enhancing access to health and education. The latter implies that reducing income poverty should also help achieve the other MDGs.

MDG 1 requires stronger employment growth and less income inequality

In most countries, additional policies will be required to meet the target for MDG 1. The present analysis does not consider specific interventions to reduce income poverty, but rather assumes poverty outcomes to result from the employment and income effects generated throughout the economy under the BAU and MDG strategy scenarios. It appears that the MDG strategy, through increased public spending on education and health services, and on water and sanitation, does not induce sufficiently strong employment and income-distribution effects to make adequate progress towards the required level of poverty reduction in more than half of the countries of the region. Moderate-to-high average GDP growth under both the BAU and MDG scenarios only leads to modest employment growth effects. Only in a few countries, such as Brazil, Guatemala, Honduras and Nicaragua would the MDG strategy lead to significantly stronger aggregate demand growth and a larger decrease in poverty levels than under the BAU scenario. In the case of Honduras, this additional growth effect would enable the country to reach the target of halving extreme poverty by 2015. Brazil and Guatemala would already reach it under the BAU scenario, whereas the additional output and employment growth would not be sufficient for Nicaragua to achieve MDG 1.

High income inequality remains an obstacle to the trickling down of stronger aggregate growth to the poor in the LAC countries. As the country studies show, and as expected, the MDG strategy generally reduces the supply of unskilled workers as boys and girls at primary-school age enrol in the education system. It further raises the relative demand for skilled workers, owing to the expansion of skill-intensive social services. In some cases, the net effect is a shift in real wages in favour of unskilled workers, but where the increase in the demand for skilled workers is relatively strong, the reverse distributional shift may take place. Overall, the impact on income inequality at the household level is rather weak, at least over the time period under consideration.

Consequently, without additional policy interventions, most of the poverty-reduction effects of the MDG strategy depend on the aggregate effects on employment and mean incomes. However, macroeconomic trade-offs, such as the compression of private consumption and investment or slower export growth, weaken the aggregate demand effects of the growth in MDG-related public spending. Hence, as discussed further below, careful management of the financing of the MDG strategy is required. Some of the poverty-reduction gains may be felt more at a later date as improved education and health of the working population produce greater externalities in the form of total factor productivity growth. Arguably, however, most of these effects will manifest themselves only after 2015, bearing in mind, in particular, the length of schooling cycles.

To sum up, in order to make more progress towards a timely achievement of MDG 1, most countries would require complementary policies to strengthen employment growth and income opportunities for the poor.

MDG strategies will require sustained increases in social spending

The costs in terms of required additional spending on MDG-related services range from about 1 per cent to 6 per cent of GDP per year, except for Chile and Cuba, which should be able to achieve the goals under BAU policies. For most countries, however, the additional cost would be less than 3 per cent of GDP, which seems moderate in macroeconomic terms, although it would imply substantial increases (in some cases a doubling) from base-year levels. For the Dominican Republic, Guatemala, Honduras, Mexico, Nicaragua and Uruguay, the estimated additional cost would be higher than 3 per cent of GDP per annum. For nearly all countries, synergies between greater needs satisfaction in terms of primary education, child and maternal health, and water and sanitation entail cost savings when striving to achieve all goals simultaneously. Such notional savings could range from 0.1 per cent to about 1 per cent of GDP per annum compared to the (higher) estimated cost under a phased strategy for achieving the MDGs separately or under a purely sectoral approach to assessing MDG costs. The country analyses also suggest that the required MDG-related spending tends to increase as the targets approach achievement. This might imply that increased levels of social spending need to be sustained not only up to 2015 but also beyond that milestone, in order to avoid slippage from the achieved levels of human development.

Tax and spend

The financing of the additional social spending may involve important macroeconomic trade-offs and influence the MDG cost estimates. The country studies suggest that foreign financing (either through more borrowing or grants) would generally be cheaper in terms of the required additional public spending. However, foreign financing would generate other important trade-offs as it would engender significantly stronger RER appreciation and deceleration of export growth than under the scenarios of domestic resource mobilization. Furthermore, a financing strategy based solely on foreign borrowing would lift public debt to unsustainable levels in virtually all country cases. The appreciation pressure on the RER could be manageable to the extent that countries have the necessary policy space to keep their exchange rates competitive, but in many cases this space may be limited in circumstances of rapidly increasing foreign debt and could cause currency mismatches in public finances and the financial sector (for a discussion, see, for example, Ocampo and Vos, 2006). Financing the strategy through foreign aid is not a realistic alternative for most countries, except for Bolivia, Honduras and Nicaragua; in the case of Honduras, however, foreign aid financing appears to generate rather strong Dutch disease effects, raising the need for foreign financing well beyond the increased fiscal needs; in Nicaragua, aid dependency is already quite high and increasing it further may therefore not be desirable.

These limitations to foreign financing put more weight on the role of domestic resource mobilization. Domestic government borrowing, however, appears to generate a relatively strong crowding-out of private spending and would also lift public debt to unsustainable levels in most country cases. The crowding-out effect is essentially "model driven", of course, but is likely a realistic approximation of insufficiently developed domestic bond markets in the countries of the region, making it difficult and costly for Governments to borrow from the private sector. Consequently, increased taxation is left as the core option for countries to consider. Effective tax burdens in LAC are low by any standard, suggesting ample scope for a tax-financed MDG strategy. This should probably be a priority in all countries, but a number of associated caveats deserve consideration.

First, tax financing generally raises the required additional social spending as it compresses private spending, including that on MDG-related services, and hence the Government would have to step in more forcefully. Governments could try to avoid this by ensuring that tax increases are mainly paid for by higher income groups. This may not be easy given the existing scope for tax evasion, but the objective of keeping the MDG strategy affordable would make closing such loopholes even more imperative.

Second, tax reforms take time to become effective and the scope for significantly raising government revenue may be limited. In the present analysis, we suggest that over the period remaining between now and 2015, it might be possible to increase tax revenue at best by 2.5 percentage points of GDP—relative to the base year of the analysis—with a successful and swiftly implemented tax reform. If such a move on tax reform can be made politically acceptable, then tax financing would seem a feasible option for financing the MDG strategy in Argentina, Brazil, Colombia, Costa Rica, Ecuador, Paraguay and Peru. For other countries, this would likely remain a tall order, and those countries may have to employ mixed financing strategies after weighing the different trade-offs.

Most likely, a combination of financing sources will have to be considered in all cases. Measured foreign borrowing could be considered in an initial period during which a tax reform is to be implemented. Furthermore, all countries should assess the scope for creating more fiscal space by enhancing the efficiency of public spending and tax collection. The model analyses assume that the additional fiscal allocations for achieving the MDGs are targeted towards effective interventions. Even so, there may be scope for improving efficiency where existing resources for education, health, and water and sanitation are underutilized, as discussed in the second section. The country models do not assess the scope for such efficiency gains, as this would require further in-depth sector analysis in each of the countries, nor do they gauge efficiency in tax collection; however, it is generally assumed that there is ample space for improvement on this front in most countries of the region.

Bearing these caveats in mind, achieving the MDGs is within reach and clearly affordable for all LAC countries in the study. It is clearly more than a matter of priority-setting or finding the additional resources, however; it also entails carefully managing and integrating macroeconomic and social-sector policies. It is also clear that enhanced spending on MDG-related services and the progress towards the education, health, and water and sanitation goals do not guarantee strong income redistribution and poverty reduction results in the short-to-medium run. Most countries will have to make additional efforts in this direction. What is more, for most countries it appears that the improved educational performance in recent decades is already accelerating the supply of skilled workers, but their economies have not sufficiently adjusted to accommodate the changing composition of the labour force and they are therefore not reaping the potential benefits in terms of productivity improvements. This shows that further economic reforms are needed to adjust to higher levels of human development for the population of the region. It also suggests that while upholding the promise of achieving the MDGs, policymakers also need to stretch their horizons well beyond these goals.

Appendix A2.1

Microsimulation methodology

The computable general equilibrium (CGE) model used for generating the BAU and MDG scenarios (MAMS) provides only relatively aggregate outcomes for employment and wages by labour category. Similarly, the model typically only distinguishes between a few groups of households for assessing the impact of alternative policy scenarios on per capita household consumption and income. CGE simulations therefore only allow us to draw conclusions about the differences in impact for these aggregate labour and household groups—thus ignoring income distribution changes within those groups. Hence, we revert to a microsimulation methodology to take account of the full income distribution. In line with recent practice of methodologies studying the economy-wide effects of economic policies, we adopt a top-down approach. That is to say, we take the CGE simulation results and apply them to the full distribution as given by a micro data set (that is, the household survey) and assume there are no further feedback effects.

The top-down causal chain works from policy changes or exogenous shocks through the operation of factor and product markets yielding prices, wages and employment, and finally to household income and expenditure. A crucial part of analysing and modelling distributional outcomes at the household level is the specification of the various sources of income at that level and of how those sources are linked to the operation of factor and product markets.

For current purposes, we focus on the labour market as the main transmission channel of the modelled impact of the simulated scenarios on poverty and income distribution. To go from the counterfactual labour-market effects simulated with the CGE model to poverty and income distribution at the household level, we need to deal with two methodological issues. First, how can both between- and within-group effects be incorporated into the distribution analysis? That is to say, how can we account for the full distribution and thus for the heterogeneity of the population within households when assessing the poverty and inequality effects? Second, people may change position in the labour market (and hence also affect household income) due to external shocks, trade reforms, or other policy changes such as the MDG strategies examined in this study. Workers may shift from one sector to another, change occupation or lose their jobs. The methodological issue is to find a procedure that can account for such labour-market shifts and identify which individuals are most likely to shift position in order to be able to simulate a new, counterfactual income distribution.

Various microsimulation methodologies have been proposed in the literature to deal with these problems.[22] We note two types that attempt to answer the type of questions raised in this study. The first involves the estimation of a microeconomic, partial-equilibrium household income generation model through a system of equations that determine occupational choice, returns to labour and human capital, consumer prices and other household (individual) income components (see, for instance, Bourguignon, Fournier and Gurgand, 2001; Bourguignon, Ferreira and Lustig, 2001). Combining this methodology in "top-down" fashion with a CGE model has been probed by Bourguignon, Robilliard and Robinson (2002) for the case of Indonesia.

A second microsimulation approach of less modelling intensity assumes that occupational shifts may be proxied by a random selection procedure within a segmented labour-market structure. This procedure allows the imposition of counterfactual changes in key labour-market parameters (participation rate, unemployment, employment composition by sector, wage structure, and so on) on a given distribution derived from household survey data, and the estimation of the impact of each change on poverty and income distribution at the household level. This is the approach used here, based on the methodology developed in Ganuza, Paes de Barros and Vos (2002) and more widely applied in Vos and others (2006). The basic intuition behind this approach is as follows.

Total per capita household income is defined as:

$$ypc_h = \frac{1}{n_h}\left[\sum_{i=1}^{n_h} yp_{hi} + yq_h \right] \tag{1}$$

where n_h is the size of household h, yp_{hi} the labour income of member i of household h, and yq_h the sum of all non-labour incomes of the household, defined as:

$$yq_h = \left[\sum_{i=1}^{n_h} yqp_{hi} + yqt_h \right] \tag{2}$$

In equation (2), yqp_{hi} equals individual non-labour income of member i of household h and yqt_h equals other household incomes. In the simulations, yp_{hi} is altered for some individuals i of household h as a result of changes in the labour-market parameters. Ganuza, Paes de Barros and Vos (2002) define the labour-market structure in terms of rates of economic participation P_j and unemployment U_j among different groups j of the population at working age (defined according to sex and skill), the structure of employment (defined according to sector of activity S and occupational category O) and remuneration W_1, as well as overall level of remuneration W_2. The skill composition of the employed population is represented by variable M. The labour-market structure can be written as $\pi = \pi(P,U,S,O,W_1,W_2,M)$. In the application of the methodology in the country studies referred to in this chapter, the labour-market structure was defined in a somewhat more limited fashion as $\pi = \pi(U,S,W_1,W_2,M)$, as changes in participation rates P are not explicitly modelled in MAMS and the labour factor was not classified by occupational group O.

For all types of individuals, the unemployment rates determine part of the labour-market structure. The latter is further determined by the structure of employment. The employed workforce is classified according to segment k, defined on the basis of sector of activity. For the three skill groups (unskilled, semi-skilled and skilled workers) within segments k in the labour market, the average remuneration is calculated and these averages are expressed as a ratio of the overall average. The effect of altering each of the parameters of the labour-market structure on poverty and inequality can then be analysed using the accounting identities of equations (1) and (2). The impact of changes in the labour market can be analysed both separately and sequentially.

The Ganuza-Paes de Barros-Vos approach introduces a number of important assumptions about the labour market. First, as indicated, for lack of a full model of the labour market, a randomized process is applied to simulate the effects of changes in the labour-market structure. That is to say, random numbers are used to determine which persons at working age change their labour force status; who will change occupational category; which employed persons obtain a different level of education; and how new mean labour incomes are assigned to individuals in the sample.[23] Hence, the assumption is that, on average, the effect of the random changes correctly reflects the impact of the actual changes in the labour market. Because of the introduction of a process of random assignation, the microsimulations are repeated a large number of times in Monte Carlo fashion.[24] This allows constructing 95 per cent confidence intervals for the indices of inequality and poverty, except in the case of the simulations of the effect of change in the structure and level of remuneration, which do not involve random numbers. In each simulation, a number of poverty and inequality measures are calculated.

The approach outlined above is fairly straightforward when applied with static CGE models; in other words, when generating just one change from a given base year which is also (close to) the base year of a household survey. The present analysis, however, covers a simulation period that runs from the country-specific base year to 2015, the point at which the MDGs are expected to have been achieved. Therefore, the application of the microsimulation method needs to be situated in a dynamic setting.

For the application of the methodology in a dynamic setting, we follow the procedure spelled out in Sánchez (2004) and Sánchez and Vos (2005 and 2006). As indicated in these studies, a number of additional, restrictive assumptions are required, as observed survey data may only be available for the base year and perhaps a few years beyond that, but not for the entire projected forward period. In the microsimulations beyond the base year of the household survey data and for lack of additional modelling of demographic shifts and labour participation, it is assumed that no changes in the population structure (such as migration or population ageing) take place during the simulation period. This is an obvious limitation of the methodology, but justifiable to the extent that the CGE model does not consider such demographic changes either.

Table A2.1   MDG indicators in 1990, mid-point (around 2002-2003), and 2015[a]

Country	MDG 1					MDG 2				MDG 4			
	1990[b]	MP	B	MS[c]	T	1990[b]	M	B	T	1990[b]	M	B	T
Argentina	4.3	5.2	2.8	2.7	2.2	80.2	81.7	86.1	100.0	29.6	19.1	12.6	9.9
Bolivia	29.0	27.0	21.4	20.8	14.5	52.0	70.0	93.4	100.0	89.0	54.0	40.3	29.7
Brazil	14.0	7.5	2.7	0.5	7.0	16.8	53.8	78.3	100.0	54.0	32.3	22.3	18.0
Chile	3.5	2.3	0.8	n.a.	1.7	84.5	81.6	98.9	100.0	19.3	9.6	5.0	6.4
Colombia	5.4	4.5	2.5	2.5	2.7	29.0	41.4	91.5	100.0	37.4	28.2	20.1	17.0
Costa Rica	3.4	2.8	2.5	2.5	1.7	80.3	89.4	99.1	100.0	18.0	13.0	7.0	6.0
Cuba	0.6	1.8	1.7	n.a.	0.3	98.6	98.8	100.0	100.0	13.2	7.7	5.0	4.4
Dominican Republic	2.6	3.3	1.5	1.3	1.3	22.0	53.0	87.5	100.0	58.0	38.0	25.3	19.3
Ecuador	15.5	17.0	9.4	9.2	7.7	67.4	71.9	95.4	100.0	42.3	24.8	15.7	14.1
El Salvador	27.0	18.6	21.6	21.2	13.5	25.0	30.5	87.9	100.0	52.0	31.0	24.9	17.3
Guatemala	20.0	16.0	7.3	4.9	10.0	43.7	65.1	52.5	100.0	110.0	53.0	45.0	36.7
Honduras	38.0	26.3	20.7	18.8	19.0	64.7	75.9	91.1	100.0	58.0	30.5	29.4	24.0
Jamaica	16.0	3.8	0.2	0.2	8.0	75.0	76.0	90.4	95.0	28.5	26.6	14.5	9.5
Mexico	10.8	4.1	2.7	2.5	5.4	70.1	89.3	98.2	100.0	44.2	25.0	16.0	14.7
Nicaragua	44.0	39.4	32.3	30.7	22.0	44.3	73.1	71.9	100.0	68.0	38.0	24.3	22.7
Paraguay	35.0	34.8	21.9	22.4	17.5	43.0	50.0	87.5	100.0	40.0	25.0	14.9	13.3
Peru	6.6	4.0	3.0	3.2	3.3	22.7	56.8	65.6	71.4	81.0	34.0	32.0	27.0
Uruguay	0.4	1.4	0.7	0.8	0.2	69.4	69.2	90.3	100.0	20.6	15.3	9.9	6.9
LAC[f]	11.8	7.4	4.1	3.3	5.9	n.a.	n.a.	n.a.	n.a.	50.3	29.3	20.7	17.1

Table A2.1   (cont'd)

Country	MDG 5				MDG 7a					MDG 7b				
	1990[b]	MP	B	T	1990[b]	MP	B	IT[d]	NT[e]	1990[b]	MP	B	IT[d]	NT[e]
Argentina	n.a.	n.a.	n.a.	n.a.	65.1	78.4	79.9	82.5		33.6	42.5	51.4	66.8	
Bolivia	416.0	230.0	158.9	104.0	57.0	70.0	76.1	78.5		28.0	40.0	57.1	64.0	
Brazil	n.a.	n.a.	n.a.	n.a.	75.9	90.4	99.9	88.0	100.0	85.8	94.7	99.9	92.9	100.0
Chile	40.0	19.0	10.0	10.0	97.4	98.0	99.4	98.7	99.0	82.6	94.4	98.9	91.3	97.2
Colombia	100.0	99.0	57.4	45.0	92.0	92.0	99.6	96.0	99.4	82.0	86.0	98.1	91.0	97.6
Costa Rica	33.0	41.0	25.4	20.0	50.0	79.5	80.5	75.0	79.5	75.8	93.5	93.5	87.9	93.5
Cuba	42.0	38.5	10.1	10.5	81.6	95.6	99.0	90.8	97.6	88.7	95.0	98.9	94.4	97.1
Dominican Republic	229.0	178.0	91.7	57.3	83.0	86.0	91.4	91.5		60.0	90.0	91.5	80.0	91.5
Ecuador	117.2	96.9	36.0	29.3	60.8	77.0	83.6	80.4	89.0	37.1	44.9	60.9	68.6	73.0
El Salvador	158.0	120.0	80.9	39.5	40.0	60.0	63.4	70.0		74.0	85.7	86.2	87.0	
Guatemala	248.0	121.0	95.9	62.0	68.0	75.0	76.1	84.0	82.0	35.0	47.0	50.6	67.5	66.0
Honduras	280.0	108.0	101.7	70.0	73.0	82.2	84.0	86.5	95.0	66.0	76.7	79.4	83.0	95.0
Jamaica	106.2	106.2	48.8	26.6	92.0	93.0	94.9	96.0		75.0	80.0	86.0	87.5	
Mexico	89.0	65.2	25.7	22.3	75.4	89.4	96.1	87.7	94.7	58.1	77.3	79.7	79.1	
Nicaragua	160.0	230.0	48.9	40.0	70.0	76.0	83.3	85.0		45.0	46.3	65.4	72.5	
Paraguay	150.0	160.0	57.2	37.5	25.4	52.5	58.7	62.7		7.2	9.2	28.1	53.6	
Peru	n.a.	n.a.	n.a.	n.a.	63.0	75.0	75.8	81.5	88.0	54.0	56.0	57.8	77.0	78.0
Uruguay	n.a.	n.a.	n.a.	n.a.	89.5	96.1	100.0	94.8	100.0	85.2	93.1	100.0	92.6	100.0
LAC[f]	115.6	87.7	43.1	32.5	74.7	86.8	93.3	87.3	94.4	68.3	79.0	84.9	84.2	88.2

Source: Country studies.

Abbreviations: MP = Mid-point; B = BAU scenario (2015); MS = MDG scenario (2015); T = Target; IT = International target; NT = National target

[a] For the MDG scenario, the 2015 indicator is only presented for MDG 1 as this is the only goal that might not necessarily be achieved by 2015.

[b] For some countries, data are for the nearest available year.

[c] The simulation results are for the MDG financing scenario considered "feasible", as defined in table 2.5 for each country.

[d] International goal consisting of halving the related percentage of people from 1990 (or nearest available year) to 2015.

[e] National goal set in some country studies.

[f] A regional average, weighted by each country's relevant population group is presented for LAC for all MDGs except MDG 2, owing to the use of varying indicators by country.

Acknowledgements

We are grateful to Carolina Díaz-Bonilla, Enrique Ganuza, Hans Lofgren and Martín Cicowiez for helpful comments and suggestions to a first draft of this chapter and to all country case authors for country-specific inputs.

Notes

1   See United Nations (2007) for a recent update on progress towards the MDGs.
2   The present analysis addresses MDGs 1, 2, 4, 5 and 7, reflecting the main focus of the 18 country studies carried out in the LAC region, whose results are discussed in this chapter.
3   According to estimates of the UN Millennium Project, in order to achieve the MDGs, the required additional public expenditures per year for a typical low-income country with an average per capita income of $300 could amount to 10 per cent-20 per cent of its gross national product (GNP) (United Nations Millennium Project, 2005). If these figures are accurate, it would be hard to imagine that those countries would be in a position to finance the required additional spending through increased taxation or domestic borrowing.
4   Moderate poor are defined here as the population living on less than $2 a day. The middle-income country group refers to 86 developing countries with per-capita incomes of between $826 and $10,000 (2004 data). This group comprises just under half of the world's population. For more details, see World Bank (2006).
5   The production of some of these services, such as telecommunications, may nonetheless have a high import content.
6   While a shortage of this nature may put upward pressure on wages for skilled workers of this kind, arguably such a wage adjustment need not immediately eliminate the labour shortage, since the "generation" of new teachers, nurses and doctors will take several years of training.
7   MDG-related spending includes all expenditures that are directly related to the achievement of the MDGs, such as spending on primary education, on health care aimed at reducing child and maternal mortality and combating major diseases like malaria, tuberculosis and HIV/AIDS, and on the provision of basic sanitation infrastructure and services.
8   A productivity parameter for each MDG-related sector can also allow the simulation of efficiency improvements in the delivery of such services. While the MAMS framework in principle allows the capture of such efficiency gains, the key problem is to obtain quantitative estimates for such externalities. This would require further country-level investigation. The MAMS-based country analyses discussed in the fourth section do not consider such productivity gains and therefore, potentially, may underestimate the possible welfare gains from the MDG strategy. It could be argued, however, that because of the time lags involved between MDG investments today and enhanced productivity of workers tomorrow, most gains are likely to become effective after 2015, assuming that with better access to education, most children will remain in the schooling system for ten years or more.
9   The country studies also answer a related question: what social sectors would require the most additional spending?
10   The mid-point, 2002-03, also roughly corresponds to the base year for most of the country models (see table 2.3).

11   Fifteen country studies also report poverty outcomes for one or more nationally defined poverty line (those with more than one include a national poverty line for "extreme" poverty and one for "moderate" poverty). The three countries reporting international poverty lines only are Brazil and Ecuador (one dollar per day only) and Cuba (one dollar per day and two dollars per day). Results for the BAU scenario appear consistent for all poverty lines in terms of the direction and relative extent of poverty reduction and in terms of whether the target for MDG 1 is likely to be attained. The exceptions are Costa Rica and El Salvador (where MDG 1 would be achieved using national poverty lines but not when using the one dollar per day poverty line) and Colombia and Mexico (where MDG 1 would be achieved under the BAU scenario for the international poverty line but not for the national one).

12   It should be noted that completion rates are defined in a strict sense in the country studies: that is to say, completion on time, without repetition, for the relevant country-specific age cohort for primary school. Please note that a less ambitious national goal is being used for Peru and Jamaica (that is, 71.4 per cent and 95 per cent, respectively). Chile, Costa Rica and Mexico essentially meet the target (that is, their projected primary school completion rates for 2015 are 98.9 per cent, 99.1 per cent and 98.2 per cent, respectively, and thus these would be very difficult to be reduced further).

13   In the country studies of Chile, Costa Rica and Mexico, the authors argue that the target for MDG 2 will not be achieved, as the primary completion rates in 2015 level off at 98.9 per cent, 99.1 per cent and 92.2 per cent, respectively. In this chapter, however, MDG 2 is considered to be achievable in practical terms in view of the relatively small margin by which these figures fall short of 100 per cent and the difficulty in further reducing this margin.

14   For Bolivia, the analysis refers to the infant (under-one) mortality rate. Cuba essentially achieves the national target of 4.4 deaths per 1,000 live births. Cuba's under-five mortality rate levels off at 5 deaths per 1,000 live births by 2015, which is the lowest in the region and for that very reason difficult to reduce much further.

15   Argentina, Brazil, Peru and Uruguay are not included because MDG 5 is not analysed in their respective country studies. It should be noted, however, that data on maternal mortality generally suffer from major deficiencies. The country studies which did include maternal mortality in the analysis made an effort to ensure that the best possible data were used. In addition, a less ambitious, national target is being used for Costa Rica (that is, 20 deaths per 100,000 live births).

16   If tax revenue ultimately falls short of financing all—and not only MDG-related—public spending, then direct taxes will tend to increase beyond what is strictly required to finance new MDG-related spending in order to keep a fiscal deficit from emerging. This in turn leads to an added tax burden to finance the additional MDG-related spending.

17   In the case of Guatemala, this difference is found to be substantially larger than anywhere else. According to the country case study, an increase in income taxes to finance MDG achievement would greatly reduce household incomes. Consequently, the resulting "compression effect" on private spending on MDG-related services is also strong, lowering aggregate demand and the tax base of the economy. This then requires rather significant increases in the direct tax rate to be able to finance the large additional public spending needed to meet the MDGs, including the spending needed to offset the drop in private spending. The magnitude of this outcome for Guatemala is, of course, driven by the specific parameter values used in the country model.

18   It should be noted, however, that at present Peru and El Salvador receive rather small amounts of official development assistance (ODA). In 2005, net ODA receipts by these

two countries amounted to 0.5 per cent and 1.2 per cent of gross national income, respectively. In the other countries, especially Bolivia, Nicaragua and Honduras, ODA receipts, historically and in recent years, have been much more substantial, in part owing to their HIPC status.

19   Chile and Cuba are not considered here, as these two countries are expected to reach the MDGs under their respective BAU scenarios.

20   The only exception is El Salvador, where observed extreme poverty in 2005 is lower compared with that in the BAU scenario in 2015. This setback is depicted in table A2.1 and, according to the study for this country, is due to the fact that labour income distribution deteriorates for informal and underemployed workers and for workers that are paid below the minimum wage.

21   Only in El Salvador and Guatemala under both the BAU and the MDG scenarios does growth in the demand for unskilled workers outpace that for skilled workers.

22   See Bourguignon, Pereira da Silva and Stern (2002) for an overview of related methods. It should be noted that the approach is relatively new in its application to the developing country context, but that combinations of macro or CGE policy models and microsimulations, for instance to assess distributional effects of tax reforms, are quite common in applications in developed countries.

23   Mean incomes per decile are calculated in the simulations. These means are subsequently assigned to newly employed or to already-employed persons who changed sector of employment, occupational category or moved from one educational group to another. In principle, to assess the impact of changes in the labour-market structure, one would have to calibrate the database prior to simulating the effect of said changes—that is to say, to replace the original labour incomes by mean incomes per decile. A test showed that neither the direction of change nor the magnitude of the effect altered when using the original values of the labour incomes instead of calibrated values.

24   Experiments with the methodology for several household survey data sets show that about 30 iterations are sufficient. Further iterations do not alter the results.

References

Agénor, Pierre-Richard (1996). "The Labor Market and Economic Adjustment", *IMF Staff Papers* 43(2): 261-335.

Bevan, David (2005). An analytical overview of aid absorption: Recognizing and avoiding macroeconomic hazards. Paper for the Seminar on "Foreign Aid and Macroeconomic Management", March 14-15, Maputo, Mozambique. In Macroeconomic Management of Foreign Aid: Opportunities and Pitfalls, Peter Isard, Leslie Lipschitz, Alexandros Mourmouras, and Peter Heller, eds. Forthcoming, International Monetary Fund: Washington, D.C.

Bourguignon, François, Maurizio Bussolo, Luiz Pereira da Silva, Hans Timmer, and Dominique van der Mensbrugghe (2004). "MAMS: Maquette for MDG simulations". March, World Bank: Washington, D.C. (processed).

Bourguignon, François, Anne-Sophie Robilliard and Sherman Robinson (2002). "Representative versus real households in the macro-economic modeling of inequality", Washington, D.C.: World Bank and IFPRI (Mimeo).

Bourguignon, François, and Mark Sundberg (2006). "Constraints to achieving the MDGs with scaled-up aid", DESA Working Paper No. 15, New York: United Nations Department of Economic and Social Affairs (ST/ESA/DWP/15).

Bourguignon, François, Francisco Ferreira and Nora Lustig (2001). "MIDD: the microeconomics of income distribution dynamics. A comparative analysis of selected developing countries", Paper presented at the Latin American Meeting of the Econometric Society, Buenos Aires (July) (Mimeo).

Bourguignon, François, M. Fournier and M. Gurgand (2001). "Fast development with stable income distribution: Taiwan, 1979-1994", *Review of Income and Wealth*, 43(3): 139-164.

Bourguignon, François, Luis Pereira da Silva and Nicholas Stern (2002). "Evaluating the poverty impact of economic policies: Some analytical challenges", Washington, D.C.: The World Bank (Mimeo).

ECLAC (Economic Commission for Latin America and the Caribbean) (2005). *Panorama Social de América Latina y el Caribe 2005*, ECLAC, United Nations, Santiago.

__________ (2002). "La modernización de los sistemas nacionales de inversión pública: análisis crítico y perspectivas," *Serie manuales no. 23*, December 2002, (ILPES/CEPAL, Santiago).

__________ (2001). *Una Década de Luces y Sombras: América Latina y el Caribe en los Años Noventa*, Alfaomega and ECLAC, Bogotá and Santiago: United Nations.

Escaith, Hubert, and Keiji Inoue (2001). "Small Economies' Tariff and Subsidy Policies in the Face of Trade Liberalization in the Americas," *Integration and Trade*, no. 14, vol. 5, May- August, 2001 (INTAL/IADB, Buenos Aires).

Ganuza, Enrique, Ricardo Paes de Barros and Rob Vos (2002). "Labour Market Adjustment, Poverty and Inequality during Liberalisation". In: *Economic Liberalisation, Distribution and Poverty: Latin America in the 1990s*, Rob Vos, Lance Taylor and Ricardo Paes de Barros, eds. Cheltenham (UK) and Northampton (US): Edward Elgar Publishers, pp. 54-88.

Glewwe, Paul (2002). "Schools and skills in developing countries: education policies and socioeconomic outcomes", *Journal of Economic Literature*. Vol. XL (June): 436-482.

Gupta, Sanjeev, Robert Powell and Yongzheng Yang (2006). *Macroeconomic challenges of scaling up aid to Africa. A checklist for practitioners*, Washington, D.C.: International Monetary Fund.

Heller, Peter S. (2005). "Pity the finance minister: Managing a substantial scaling-up of aid flows", Fiscal Affairs Department, Washington, D.C.: International Monetary Fund (processed).

Hopkins, Michael, and Rolph van der Hoeven (1982). "Policy analysis in a socio-economic model of basic needs applied to four countries", *Journal of Policy Modeling*, 4 (3): 425-55.

Kaminsky, Graciela, Carmen M. Reinhart and Carlos A. Végh (2004). "When it rains, it pours: procyclical capital flows and macroeconomic policies", NBER Working Paper, No. 10780. Cambridge, Massachusetts: National Bureau of Economic Research. September.

Kouwenaar, Arend (1986). *A Basic Needs Policy Model*, Amsterdam: North-Holland.

Lofgren, Hans (2004). "MAMS: An economy wide model for analysis of MDG country strategies", World Bank, Development Prospects Group, Washington, D.C. (processed).

Martner, Ricardo, and Eduardo Aldunate (2006). "Política Fiscal y Protección Social," *Serie Gestión Pública no. 53*, January 2006, ILPES/CEPAL: Santiago.

McKinley, Terry (2007). "Why have tax reforms hampered MDG financing?", International Poverty Centre, *One Pager* No. 42 (September), Brasilia: UNDP International Poverty Centre.

Ocampo, José Antonio (2005). "A Broad View of Macroeconomic Stability," *DESA Working Paper No.1*, October, United Nations: New York.

__________ (2002). "Developing Countries' Anti-cyclical Policies in a Globalized World," in *Development Economics and Structuralist Macroeconomics: Essays in Honor of Lance Taylor*, Dutt, Amitava Krishna and Jaime Ros, eds. Edward Elgar, (Aldershot, 2003).

__________, and Stephany Griffith-Jones (2006). "A counter-cyclical framework for a development-friendly international financial architecture", Paper presented at the IDRC workshop on "International Financial Architecture, Macroeconomic Volatility and Institutions", New York, 17 and 18 April 2006.

__________, and Rob Vos (2006). "Policy space and the changing paradigm in conducting macroeconomic policies in developing countries", Paper presented at the FONDAD-UN/DESA seminar on "Policy Space for Developing Countries in a Globalized World", New York, 7 and 8 December 2006.

__________, and Rob Vos (2008). *Uneven Economic Development*, New York, London, Hyderabad and Penang: Oriental Longman, Zed Books and Third World Network (forthcoming).

ODI (2003). "Results-oriented budgeting: will it reduce poverty?", Briefing Paper, Overseas Development Institute, London.

Rodriguez, Francisco (2007). "Have collapses in infrastructure spending led to cross-country divergence in per capita GDP?", in: José Antonio Ocampo, Jomo K.S. and Rob Vos (eds) *Growth Divergences: Explaining Differences in Economic Performance*, Hyderabad, London, New York: Oriental Longman, Zed Books and TWN.

Rogers, F. Halsey, José López-Calix, Nazmul Chaudury, Jeffrey Hammer, Nancy Córdova, Michael Kremer and Karthik Muralidharan (2004). "Teacher absence and incentives in primary education", in: World Bank and Inter-American Development Bank, *Ecuador: Creating Fiscal Space for Poverty Reductio*n, Volume II, Washington, D.C.: World Bank and IDB (Report No. 28911-EC).

Sánchez, Marco V. (2004). *Rising inequality and falling poverty in Costa Rica's agriculture during trade reform. A macro-micro general equilibrium analysis,* Maastricht: Shaker.

__________, and Rob Vos (2005). "Impacto del Tratado de Libre Comercio con Estados Unidos en el crecimiento, la pobreza y la desigualdad en Panamá: Una evaluación ex ante usando un modelo de equilibrio general computable dinámico", Project Report prepared for the Government of Panama, The Hague, Mexico and Panama City: Institute of Social Studies, Sub-regional Office of ECLAC in Mexico and UNDP (August, mimeo).

__________, and Rob Vos (2006). "Impacto del CAFTA en el crecimiento, la pobreza y la desigualdad en Nicaragua". Managua: Ministerio de Fomento a la Industria y el Comercio and UNDP.

Tanzi, Vito (2000). "Taxation in Latin America in the last decade", Center for Research on Economic Development and Policy Reform, Working Paper No. 76, Stanford (CA): Stanford University.

Thirsk, Wayne, ed. (1997). *Tax Reform in Developing Countries*, World Bank Regional and Sectoral Studies, Washington D.C.: The World Bank.

United Nations Millennium Project (2005). *Investing in Development: A Practical Plan to Achieving the Millennium Development Goals*, London: Earthscan.

United Nations (2007). *The Millennium Development Goals Report, 2007*, New York: United Nations.

__________ (2006a). *The Millennium Development Goals Report, 2006*, New York: United Nations.

__________ (2006b). *World Economic and Social Survey 2006: Diverging Growth and Development*, United Nations (New York).

__________ (2006c). "Follow-up to and implementation of the outcome of the International Conference on Financing for Development," Report of the Secretary-General, submitted to the General Assembly on its sixty-first session, (A/61/253). 8 August 2006, New York.

__________ (2006d). "Recent developments in external debt," Report of the Secretary-General, submitted to the General Assembly on its sixty-first session, (A/61/152). 16 July 2006, New York.

__________ (2005). "The Millennium Development Goals: A Latin American and Caribbean Perspective", Document prepared by the United Nations Economic Commission for Latin America and the Caribbean. August 2005, Santiago de Chile.

__________ (2004). *World Economic and Social Survey 2004*, Part I, United Nations (New York, 2004).

__________ (2003). *World Economic and Social Survey 2003*, United Nations (New York, 2003).

__________ (2002). *Report of the International Conference on Financing for Development, Monterrey, Mexico, 18-22 March 2002*. Sales No. E.02.II.A.7.

Vos, Rob, Marco V. Sánchez and Keiji Inoue (2007). "Constraints to achieving the MDGs through domestic resource mobilization", UN-DESA Working Paper Series No. 36, New York: United Nations Department of Economic and Social Affairs.

Vos, Rob, Enrique Ganuza, Samuel Morley and Sherman Robinson, eds. (2006). *Who gains from Free Trade? Export-led Growth, Income Distribution and Poverty in Latin Americ*a, London: Routledge.

Vos, Rob, and Maritza Cabezas (2006). *Illusions and disillusions with pro-poor growth*, SIDA Studies No. 17, Stockholm: Swedish International Development Cooperation Agency.

Vos, Rob, José Cuesta, Ruth Lucio, Mauricio León and José Rosero (2004). "Health", in: World Bank and Inter-American Development Bank, *Ecuador: Creating Fiscal Space for Poverty Reductio*n, Volume II, Washington, D.C.: World Bank and IDB (Report No. 28911-EC).

Vos, Rob, and Juan Ponce (2004). "Education", in: World Bank and Inter-American Development Bank, *Ecuador: Creating Fiscal Space for Poverty Reductio*n, Volume II, Washington, D.C.: World Bank and IDB (Report No. 28911-EC).

World Bank (2004). *World Development Report 2004: Making Services work for Poor People*, New York: Oxford University Press (for the World Bank).

__________ (2006). "The World Bank's Support to Middle-Income Countries: An Independent Evaluation Group Review, Approach Paper", World Bank: Washington, D.C. (available from: http://www.worldbank.org/ieg/mic/docs/mic_approach_paper.pdf).

__________ and Inter-American Development Bank (2004). *Ecuador: Creating Fiscal Space for Poverty Reduction*, Vol. I, Washington, D.C.: World Bank and IDB (Report No. 28911-EC).

3

MAMS: an economy-wide model for analysis of MDG country strategies— an application to Latin America and the Caribbean

Hans Lofgren and Carolina Díaz-Bonilla

Introduction

This chapter documents MAMS (*Maquette* for **MDG S**imulation), the underlying methodological framework of this multi-country study for Latin America and the Caribbean (LAC), which is used to address the three development strategy questions posed in Chapter 1. MAMS is a dynamic Computable General Equilibrium (CGE) model designed to analyse strategies for achieving the Millennium Development Goals (MDGs) and, more broadly, policies for medium- and long-run growth and poverty reduction in developing countries.[1] The model is sufficiently flexible to address the key processes for MDG achievement and other development strategies in a wide range of countries, linking to country databases that capture country characteristics and may vary widely in terms of disaggregation. This chapter emphasizes model features relevant to the LAC context.

An economy-wide approach is typically needed in the analysis of development strategies whenever the outcomes of interest (for example, an MDG target) are influenced significantly not only by the direct effects of single policies, but also by indirect effects and policy interactions that feed back into the processes that determine these outcomes. For example, an increase in MDG-related government spending may have very different effects on MDG indicators depending on whether the spending increase is accompanied by an increase in foreign borrowing or domestic taxes.

Various approaches have been used both to plan or monitor progress toward achieving the MDGs and to evaluate the additional (or total) public resources needed to meet them. Clemens and others (2004) and Reddy and Heuty (2004) survey a large number of studies that forecast and cost MDGs. As emphasized by Vandemoortele and Roy (2004), however, data availability and simplifying analytical assumptions severely affect the quality of quantitative estimates of all these studies.

Four major sets of limitations affect studies on MDG achievement. First, many sector studies fail to properly account for the interdependencies that exist among different MDGs and among policies designed to reach them. Second, MDG-related policies interact with the rest of the economy by altering prices, demands, and supplies of commodities and factors (including different types of labour). Third, inter-temporal equilibrium consistency is seldom checked. Financing needs, debt accumulation, and the inter-temporal sustainability of fiscal policies need to be integrated in a complete study on strategies to achieve the MDGs. Finally, as stressed by Devarajan and others (2002), the policy and institutional environment is as important a component of success in achieving the MDGs as the availability of public resources or financial assistance.

Keeping these potential limitations in mind, we briefly report on some recent MDG studies and approaches:[2] (1) The UNDP Human Development Report (2005, pp. 39-48) covers most MDGs, projecting trends for individual countries. However, policies and linkages between MDGs are not considered, so this approach is not designed, and cannot be used, for the analysis of MDG strategies. (2) The SimSIP (Simulations for Social Indicators and Poverty) tool, developed by Wodon and co-authors (see Christiaensen and others, 2002) has a target setting module that is useful for assessing the feasibility of achieving different targets. On the other hand, the fiscal sustainability component of their method is weak, reflecting the fact that a set of independent tools cannot capture interdependencies between GDP growth, different MDG targets, programme costs (including wage changes), and alternative financing approaches. (3) The different publications of the UN Millennium Project report represent a more detailed sector approach (see, for example, United Nations Millennium Project, 2005), but this approach—while rich in detail—has typically ignored or simplified the synergies across the MDGs and has not been designed to consider increasing marginal costs and the interactions with the broader economy. (4) Recognizing the need for an economy-wide perspective, Agénor and others (2005) combine a macro model with an MDG module in a framework that requires relatively little data and draws on econometrically estimated parameters (a key strength of their approach). On the other hand, the macro model is highly aggregated: it has only one production sector and it does not include intermediate inputs, factor markets, or factor wages (rents). These considerations limit its ability to analyse key aspects of MDG strategies such as how the direct exchange rate and labour market repercussions of scaled-up government programmes differ depending on whether the programme emphasizes, for example, education or infrastructure. Also, its high level of government and labour market aggregation makes it less informative for fiscal analysis.

The links between growth, service delivery, MDG achievements and financing outlined above demonstrate that a more sophisticated and coherent framework is needed. The analysis must consider macroeconomic factors and trade-offs between objectives. For example, increases in foreign aid (borrowing or grants, although the latter is less common in the LAC region) leads to concerns over the possibility of "Dutch disease", characterized by real exchange rate appreciation and a structural erosion of the capacity to produce tradables (for exports or domestic market), a capacity that may be needed in the future. At the same time, the content of the MDG strategy (such as whether the expansion in demand is geared toward imports or non-tradables) has a decisive impact on the magnitude of any Dutch Disease effects. On the other hand, if an MDG strategy is financed via increases in taxes or domestic borrowing, then private sector growth, investment, and consumption are all likely to suffer, negatively impacting poverty reduction and, because of indirect effects, the achievement of other MDGs (which are influenced by household incomes and consumption). A related critical issue is the pace at which large programmes should be scaled up. Rapid initial expansion may drive up costs more quickly and could be more expensive in real present value terms. On the other hand, given time lags, especially in education, expanding investment too slowly may make it impossible to achieve the MDGs by 2015. By allowing the performance of policy experiments that consider these links, MAMS helps analysts and policymakers to think about the issues in a systematic manner, which helps inform the policy dialogue.

MAMS at a glance

The starting point for MAMS is the static, standard CGE model developed at the International Food Policy Research Institute (IFPRI) (Lofgren and others, 2002). MAMS is significantly extended in two key respects: the inclusion of (recursive) dynamics (that is, a time dimension) and the addition of an MDG module that endogenizes MDG and education outcomes.[3] Other extensions include the endogenization of factor productivity (which depends, in the basic specification, on economic openness and government capital stocks) and the tracking of assets (liabilities) of the different institutions (factor endowments, domestic government debts and foreign debts).

A key premise of MAMS is that it is designed to link government spending and MDG outcomes in a dynamic way, permitting several outside influences. First, it permits the returns to scale of government spending to vary with the level of service delivery. At low levels, increasing returns may prevail as network and learning effects and synergies are predominant. At high levels of service delivery, government spending may suffer from decreasing returns to scale. To exemplify, water supply, health care, and education can be relatively easily provided in densely populated areas, but become increasingly expensive as coverage expands to remote areas. Also, when mortality rates are low it becomes increasingly difficult to reduce these rates further. Similarly, if completion rates in education are already high, it is difficult to ensure that the last percentages of children complete the programme.

Second, MAMS permits the effectiveness of government spending to depend on many variables. For example, spending on education may become more effective if health conditions improve (reducing absenteeism at schools), if public infrastructure improves (facilitating access to schools), if income levels rise (making parents less inclined to keep children at home or in the labour market) or if skill premiums increase (triggering a greater incentive to finish formal education). In general terms, this means that spending on services becomes more effective if demand conditions for those services are more favourable.

Third, MAMS considers that the costs of service delivery may change with macroeconomic conditions. The services are often skill intensive and in many cases also capital intensive. The more intense the MDG effort, the stronger the impact on costs as skilled labour becomes scarcer and financial conditions become tighter. From a general budgetary perspective the impacts on costs are even larger, because changes in macroeconomic conditions do not only affect MDG-related spending, but also other, non-MDG-related government spending. The relative competitiveness of different parts of the private sector is also affected.

The first two aspects above (changing returns to scale and the impact of demand variables) are captured in the MDG functions introduced in MAMS (explained in detail in the MDG section of this chapter). The third aspect (macroeconomic interactions) is captured as the MDG functions are incorporated in a dynamic economy-wide general equilibrium framework that also includes detailed fiscal accounts (explained in more detailed terms in the core model section).

Mathematically, MAMS is divided into two modules—a core CGE module and an MDG module—both of which are integrated in a simultaneous system of linear and non-linear equations. For each time period, the core CGE module gives a comprehensive and consistent account of decisions and related payments involving production (activities producing outputs using factors and intermediate inputs), consumption (by households and the government), investment (private and government), trade (both domestic and foreign), taxation, transfers between institutions (households, government, and the rest of the world), and the distribution of factor incomes to institutions (reflecting endowments). This module also considers the constraints under which the economy operates (the budget constraints of institutions and producers; macro balances; and market constraints for factors and commodities). Lastly, in addition to these standard features of a static CGE model, the core CGE module in MAMS also updates selected parameters (including factor supplies, population, and factor productivity) on the basis of exogenous trends and past endogenous variables.

The MDG module captures the processes that determine MDG achievement in the human development area, most importantly the provision of services in the areas of education, health, and water and sanitation. The size and skill composition of the labour force is endogenized, in large measure depending on the evolution of education. The MDG module has feedback effects into the rest of the economy, primarily via the labour market.

In the model, growth depends on the accumulation of production factors (labour at different educational levels, private capital, and other factors such as land, if present) and changes in factor productivity, which is influenced by the accumulation of government capital stocks and openness to foreign trade. The structure is recursive: the decisions of economic agents depend on the past and the present, not the future; in other words, the model does not consider forward-looking behaviour.

Poverty and inequality analysis, as in other CGE models, can be performed in several ways. The simplest but least desirable method uses an elasticity calculation for poverty given changes in per-capita household consumption. Representative-household or survey-based microsimulation approaches are preferable. The former assume fixed distributions of income or consumption within each household group, providing welfare estimations directly from the CGE model results. The latter type of approach does not need to recur to the rather stringent assumption of fixed within-group income distributions. It can be either top-down, feeding CGE simulation results to a household model, or integrated, with the household model built directly into MAMS. For the purposes of this study, a survey-based, top-down microsimulation approach was used for the poverty and inequality analysis, as explained in Chapter 2, Appendix A2.1.

The disaggregation of MAMS is data-driven and flexible in most areas: subject to computer memory constraints, there is no upper limit on the number of primary factors, households, production activities and commodities. The government is disaggregated by function to include sectors for education (by cycle or level), health (in some applications further disaggregated by type of service or technology), water and sanitation, and other public infrastructure. For the purposes of the country studies and to ensure that MDG achievement in education has explicit dynamic feedback effects on labour supply, the labour force is disaggregated by educational achievement into three types: those who have completed tertiary, completed secondary, or less than completed secondary. Further disaggregation of labour categories is possible in MAMS.

The applicability of the model to specific policy issues depends in large part on the degree of disaggregation. For example, the analysis of issues related to poverty requires a relatively detailed breakdown of household income sources (from factor endowments and the production activities in which they are employed). Similarly, it is likely preferable to disaggregate non-government production into multiple sectors and commodities (that is, services), as it will provide more specific results of the sectoral employment and income effects of an MDG strategy, pursued on its own or in conjunction with other policies, such as trade reform.

Detailed description of MAMS

The basic accounting structure and much of the underlying data of MAMS, like other CGE models, is represented by a Social Accounting Matrix (SAM). The SAM for MAMS has some unconventional features, especially because of the required detailed specification of how different MDG-related services, provided by both public and private sectors, are produced and delivered. Before describing the behavioural assumptions and mathematical structure of MAMS, we first describe the particular features of the SAM and the key accounting identities of MAMS.

The Social Accounting Matrix

A SAM is a square matrix in which each account is represented by a row and a column. It provides a comprehensive picture of the economic transactions of an economy during a time period, almost invariably one year. Each cell shows the payment from the account of its column to the account of its row. Thus, the incomes of an account appear along its row and its expenditures along its column. For each account in the SAM, total revenue (row total) should be equal to total expenditure (column total). It should be noted that SAMs almost invariably are limited to flows; additional data or assumptions are needed to define stocks. In most CGE models (including MAMS), the SAM is used to define base-year values for the bulk of the parameters in the equations that generate the corresponding payments in the model.

Table 3.1 shows a stylized and aggregated version of a SAM designed for MAMS, while Table 3.2 shows the notation that is used.[4]

Starting from the top left of the SAM, the activity accounts represent the entities that carry out production, allocating sales receipts to intermediates, factors (value-added) and (indirect) taxes. The commodities are activity outputs, either exported or sold domestically, and imports. The row entries of the commodity accounts represent payments from commodity demanders. The column entries show payments to the suppliers and indirect taxes (tariffs on imports and/or a sales tax on domestic sales irrespective of whether the commodity is of foreign or domestic origin). In the country studies, the accounts for the government activity and commodity are disaggregated by function, matching the requirements for the analysis of the MDGs and the educational system. Table 3.1 shows a one-to-one mapping between activities and commodities. However, MAMS permits any activity to produce multiple commodities (for example, a dairy activity may produce the commodities cheese and milk), while any commodity may be produced by multiple activities (for example, activities for small-scale and large-scale maize production may both produce the same maize commodity).[5]

The row entries of the two factor accounts in the SAM, labour and private capital, indicate that they earn value-added from domestic production activities

Table 3.1 Stylized Macro SAM for MAMS[a]

	act-prv	act-gov	com-prv	com-gov	f-lab	f-capprv	hhd	gov	row
act-prv			output						
act-gov				output					
com-prv	intmed	intmed					cons		exports
com-gov								cons	
f-lab	va	va							
f-capprv	va								yrow
hhd					va	va		trnsfr	trnsfr
gov							trnsfr		trnsfr
row			imports			va	trnsfr	trnsfr	
taxes	taxes		taxes				taxes		
interest							introw	intdom+ introw	
cap-hhd							sav		
cap-gov								sav	
cap-row									sav
inv-prv									
inv-gov									
dstk									
total									

Table 3.1 (cont'd)

	taxes	interest	cap-hhd	cap-gov	cap-row	inv-prv	inv-gov	dtsk	total
act-prv									
act-gov									
com-prv						inv	inv	dstk	
com-gov									
f-lab									
f-capprv									
hhd		intdom							
gov	taxes								
row		introw							
taxes									
interest									
cap-hhd					bor				
cap-gov			bor		bor				
cap-row									
inv-prv			inv		inv				
inv-gov				inv					
dstk			dstk	dstk					
total									

^a See Table 3.2 for the explanation of the notation.

Table 3.2   Accounts and cell entries in Stylized Macro SAM for MAMS

Account	Explanation	Cell entry	Explanation
act-prv	activity – private production	bor	borrowing
act-gov	activity – government production	cons	consumption
com-prv	commodity – private production	dstk	stock (inventory) change
com-gov	commodity – government production	exports	exports
f-lab	factor – labour	imports	imports
f-capprv	factor – private capital	intdom	interest on domestic government debt
hhd	household	intmed	intermediate inputs
gov	government	introw	interest on foreign debt
row	rest of world	inv	investment (gross fixed capital formation)
taxes	taxes – domestic and trade	output	production
interest	interest (on domestic and foreign debt)	sav	savings
cap-hhd	capital account – household	taxes	taxes (direct and indirect)
cap-gov	capital account – government	trnsfr	transfers
cap-row	capital account – rest of world	va	value added
inv-prv	investment – private capital	yrow	factor income from RoW
inv-gov	investment – government capital		
dstk	stock (inventory) change		

and, for private capital, income from the rest of the world (this is less common for labour since it only applies to income from abroad for workers who are residents of the country of the SAM). In the factor columns, value-added is distributed to the owners of the factors.[6] In the country studies, labour is invariably disaggregated by education, typically into three segments with the following achievements: completed tertiary, completed secondary but not completed tertiary, and less than completed secondary. MAMS is designed to have a single factor (and SAM account) for private capital, which we define here as capital used in activities that are not part of the functions of the general government.[7] MAMS includes one type of government capital per government activity (that is, the activities that are part of the functions of the general government). However, typically, government capital does not earn value-added and, given this, it is not represented in the SAM.

The SAM in Table 3.1 includes three types of institutions: households, the government and the rest of world (*row*).[8] Households may be disaggregated into various types and this was done in some of the country studies for this project. Each institution has a current account (its name is a shortened version of the name of the institution) and a capital account (the current-account name of the same institution prefixed by *"cap"*) linked to investment accounts and the capital accounts of other institutions. This treatment is significantly different from the more common treatment where savings and investments are handled by a unified institutional account.

In the rows of their current accounts, the domestic institutions receive their earned shares of value added, transfers from other institutions, interest income (for households), and tax revenues (for the government), while the rest of the world receives payments for the value of goods imported by the country as well as a share of value added (profit remittances), net transfers from domestic institutions (which may be negative, for instance, reflecting workers remittances received by the country), and interest payments on foreign debt (*introw*). Along their columns, the outlays of the institutions are allocated to commodity purchases (consumption for the household and the government; and the exports of the SAM country for the rest of the world), direct taxes (for the household), interest payments (for indebted institutions), and savings. Some of the country studies also include an additional institution carrying out the functions of an NGO—receiving transfers from other institutions (typically the government and/or the rest of the world) and using these resources to purchase services related to health and/or education. The tax account (which in MAMS applications is disaggregated according to type of taxation) passes on its receipts from activities, commodities, and households (along the row) to the government (along the column).[9]

The account for interest payments (in applications disaggregated into accounts for domestic and foreign interest) passes on payment from the (net) borrowers to the (net) lenders. Note that the SAM (and MAMS) only captures interest payments (and related debts) of domestic institutions to the rest of the world and of the government to households. It does not capture interest payments and debts of linking domestic non-government institutions. In their rows, the capital accounts of the institutions record their financing sources, consisting of own savings and net borrowing from selected other institutions (for the government from the rest of the world and the household; for the household, from the rest of the world). The outlays of the institutional capital accounts include payments for fixed investments (*inv*) and changes in inventories (*dstk*) and net lending to other institutions (the counterpart of net borrowing). The payments from the capital account of the rest of the world to the private investment account refer to foreign direct investment (FDI). This structure makes it possible for MAMS to capture, in a simple way, the structure of institutional assets (different types of capital and financial claims) and liabilities (financial debt) and how the evolution of this structure differs under alternative scenarios. Other things being equal, if the database has multiple households, those with more rapid income growth will likely also have more rapid savings growth, acquiring increasing shares of private capital and government debt.

Like most other CGE models, MAMS is a "real" model in which inflation does not matter (only relative prices matter). Implicitly, in the SAM, the current account of the monetary sector is merged with service activities and commodities while its capital account is merged with the government capital account. Given this, in the merged government capital account, the cells for net government borrowing from other institutions are made up of multiple items. The cell for net borrowing by the government from the household is the sum of (a) net direct borrowing by government from household (net sales of government bonds on which the government pays interest); and (b) net increases in the claims of the household sector on the monetary sector (the differences between changes in broad money holdings and monetary sector credit to the household). In MAMS (but not in the SAM), the two items in this cell are treated separately, making it possible to consider the fact that (a) gives rise to interest payments and a debt whereas (b) is a grant to the government, providing it with "seignorage" (as the one who spends this new money first). The second cell, which shows net borrowing by government from the rest of the world, is the difference between (a) net direct borrowing by the government from the rest of the world; and (b) the increase in foreign exchange reserves. In MAMS, these two items are not treated separately.[10] While this treatment remains simple, it captures the important fact that the government, by means of money creation, appropriates part of private savings. Given the fact that the model does not consider effects of and private sector responses to high general inflation, MAMS should not be used for scenarios under which the resources obtained via the monetary sector are so large that inflation would accelerate. The assessment of what is a prudent upper limit for this type of borrowing should draw on expertise on the macroeconomics of each country; a few per cent of GDP is often a reasonable figure.

Structure of MAMS

In the below, we discuss the mathematical statement of MAMS: firstly for the core CGE module and subsequently for the MDG module. Frequently, we will refer to Tables A3.1 and A3.2 (notation and equations for the core CGE module) and Tables A3.3 and A3.4 (notation and equations for the MDG Module), which are found in Appendix A3.1. The following notational conventions apply in Appendix A3.1 and various parts of the main text: upper case Latin letters are used for variables; exogenous variables have a bar on top, endogenous variables do not. Parameters have Greek or lower-case Latin letters. Subscripts refer to set indices. A "0" superscript is used to refer to base-year variable values. Otherwise, superscripts are exponents (that is, not part of the name of the variable or parameter). In the presence of the "0" superscript, the time subscript (t)

has been suppressed. The fact that an item is a variable and not a parameter indicates that, at least under certain model assumptions, its value is endogenous. In Tables A3.2 and A3.4, the domain column, which follows the column with the equations, is an important part of the mathematical statement—it indicates the set elements to which each equation applies.[11]

The core CGE module

As shown in Table A3.2, the core CGE module is divided into blocks covering prices, production and trade, domestic institutions, investments, system constraints and macro variables, and stock updating and productivity.[12] This section will describe in more technical terms the equations in each of these blocks.

Price block

The price block (equations 1-11) defines prices that can be expressed as functions of other endogenous variables (as opposed to being free variables that perform market-clearing functions). Among these prices, it is worth noting that transactions costs (the cost of moving the commodity between the border and the demanders or suppliers, or between domestic demanders and suppliers) are accounted for in the definitions of demander (domestic-currency) import prices, supplier (domestic-currency) export prices, and demander prices for domestic output sold domestically (equations 1, 2, and 4).

Whereas the transformation of output between exports and domestic sales typically is imperfect, the model also allows for the special cases of outputs exclusively produced for foreign markets (no domestic sales; see below discussion of equation 22) and of perfect transformability with zero exports as one possible outcome. Perfect transformability is useful for commodities that are relatively homogeneous; with only small differences depending on whether the demander is domestic or foreign (like grains). This case is covered by equation 3, which has three components: (a) the constraint that domestic supplier prices are larger than or equal to export prices in local currency units (LCU); (b) the constraint that exports are larger than or equal to zero (that is, zero is a possible outcome); and (c) a complementary-slackness relationship according to which at least one of (a) and (b) has to hold as a strict equality—domestic supplier prices only exceed export prices if exports are zero or, if exports are above zero, then the two prices are equal. In terms of economics, this means that the export price is a floor price and that producers prefer to sell at the highest price that is offered. If the domestic price is above the export price, then nothing is exported. If, in the absence of exports, the price would have fallen below the export price, then exports will be positive, preventing a decline below the export price.[13]

Various aggregative prices—for composite supplies, for produced commodities, and value-added—are derived from relationships that define total revenue or costs as the sum of disaggregated receipts or payments (equations 5-7 and 9).

The price of the aggregative intermediate commodity for any activity depends on its commodity composition and the prices of the commodities involved (equation 8). The model is homogeneous of degree zero in prices, with the CPI serving as the model *numéraire* (equation 10). Alternatively, the price index for non-tradables may serve as *numéraire* (equation 11).[14]

Production and trade block

This block (equations 12-27) includes the first-order conditions for profit-maximizing production and transformation decisions as well as cost-minimizing domestic demand decisions. Given available technology and market prices (taken as given in a perfectly competitive setting), producers maximize profits.[15] The technology is defined by a nested, two-level structure. At the top, output is a Leontief aggregation of real value-added and a real aggregate intermediate (equations 12-13).[16] At the bottom, these are linked to a Constant Elasticity of Substitution (CES) aggregation of primary factors (a value-added function) and a Leontief aggregation of intermediate inputs (equations 14-16). Given that the national accounts rarely attribute value-added to government capital, the CES value-added functions for government production do not include capital factors. Typically, government value-added is limited to labour.[17]

Each activity produces one or more outputs with fixed yield coefficients (equation 17). Any commodity may be produced and marketed by more than one activity. A CES approach, assuming profit-maximizing producer behaviour, is used to aggregate market sales of any commodity from different activities (equations 18-19). Production is transformed into exports and domestic sales on the basis of a CET (Constant Elasticity of Transformation) function. The profit-maximizing, optimal ratio between the quantities of exports and domestic sales is positively related to the ratio between the corresponding supply prices (equations 20-21). A less complex relationship applies to production without exports or without domestic sales (equation 22). Government and private social services are typically non-traded, that is, they have no exports and all of the supply is from domestic producers. For any exported commodity, two alternatives are possible for export demand: (a) exogenous prices in foreign currency units (FCU) combined with an infinitely elastic demand; or (b) price-sensitive export demands (defined by constant-elasticity functions) with the FCU prices determined by domestic conditions and the exchange rate (equation 23 applies to the constant-elasticity case.) Given that, in the equations, *PWE* (the export world price) has a bar on top, we assume that (b) does not apply in this specific case (and that the set *CED* is empty).

Domestic demanders are assumed to minimize the cost of imperfectly substitutable imports and commodities from domestic production according to an *Armington* (CES aggregation) function (equations 24-25). For commodities with only one supply source, the supply from this source equals the composite supply (equation 26). The transactions (trade and transport) demand for any service commodity is the sum of demands arising from domestic sales, exports, and imports, each of which is the product of the quantity traded and a fixed input coefficient (showing the quantity of the service commodity per unit of trade; equation 27).

In the country studies, government service sectors invariably produce single outputs and have fixed coefficients for intermediate inputs and capital (typically without any value-added payment; also see discussion in the section "Investment block"). Given this, "profit-maximization" merely involves some flexibility in terms of the composition of their labour employment as they supply the quantities that are demanded.

Domestic institution block

This block (equations 28-44) accounts for the receipts and expenditures of all domestic institutions, both government and non-government (households) as well as current, non-trade payment flows to and from the rest of the world; that is, factor incomes and transfers. When they represent inflows of foreign currency, these payments tend to be fixed (in FCU). The equations are structured to accommodate databases with any number of households, one government, and one entity representing the rest of the world. The payments in this block are highly interrelated since institutions often are both at the receiving and paying ends. Transfers between any two institutions may flow in both directions; however, if so, the analyst may often find it more convenient to net these in the initial model SAM.

Turning to the equations, factor incomes are defined as a function of domestic wages (which may vary across activities) and employment levels, augmented by factor incomes from the rest of the world (equation 28) and allocated across different institutions (domestic and foreign) in value shares that depend on factor endowment shares (equations 29-30). Domestic non-government institutions: (i) earn net interest incomes, defined as the difference between net interest earnings from loans to the government and net interest payments to the rest of the world on foreign debt (equation 31); (ii) transfer fixed shares of their incomes (net of direct taxes and savings) to other institutions (domestic or foreign) (equation 32); (iii) earn total gross incomes defined as the sum of factor incomes, net interest incomes, and transfers from other institutions, where the treatment of the latter differs depending on the nature of the sending institution (government, the rest of the world, or another domestic non-government institution) and the receiving institution (household or non-household) (equation 33); (iv) pay direct taxes according to rates that are fixed unless adjusted as part of the government closure rule (equation 34; note that all right-hand-side terms are exogenous); and (v) save out of incomes net of direct taxes according to marginal (and average) rates that are endogenous, depending on changes in per-capita incomes if the elasticity of savings with respect to per-capita income is different from unity (equations 35-36). Alternatively, for any given institution, the savings and/or direct tax rate may be adjusted as part of the savings-investment and government closure rules. If direct tax rates are adjusted as part of the government closure rule, either they are scaled up/down "efficiently" by a factor (*TINSADJ*) or uniformly adjusted for selected institutions (through *DTINS*). As suggested by the absence of a bar above *DTINS*, this mathematical statement assumes that changes in direct tax payments via adjustments in *DTINS* clear the government budget. This closure was the default in the country studies. The savings rates can be adjusted through similar alternative mechanisms (through *MPSADJ* or *DMPS*) as part of the savings-investment rule.

For households, incomes net of direct taxes, savings and transfers to other institutions (defined in equation 37) are allocated across different commodities according to demand functions belonging to a Linear Expenditure System (LES), defined in per-capita form with separate equations for demands from the market and from own-production (equations 38-39). If the database explicitly considers transactions costs, then market demands include these whereas demands for own production do not.

For the remaining domestic institution, the government, current incomes come from taxes (which are disaggregated into a wide range of categories), factor endowments (the government may own non-labour factors), and transfers from other domestic institutions and the rest of the world (equation 40). The (re) current expenditures of the government are divided into consumption, transfers to domestic institutions (CPI-indexed) and the rest of the world (fixed in FCU), and interest payments on domestic and foreign debt (equations 41). For each period except the first, real government consumption, disaggregated by commodity (excluding consumption for infrastructure), is defined as the level in the previous year times a growth factor that consists of multiple terms (equation 42). In the mathematical statement, the right-hand side terms are all exogenous or lagged; in simulations with other rules for determining government consumption (including simulations targeting MDGs), one of the exogenous terms is endogenous.[18] Real government consumption of infrastructure services, also for each period except the first, is defined as the quantity of government consumption per unit of the government infrastructure capital stock times the real endowment of that capital stock by the government; that is, the size of the capital stock determines consumption (which may represent maintenance, administration, and so on) (equation 43). Finally, government savings is simply the difference between current revenues and current expenditures (equation 44).

Investment block

This block (equations 45-53) covers the determination of government and private investment (including FDI) and how these are financed.

Government investment demand by capital stock ($DKGOV$) is defined in equation 45, which consists of three parts.[19] Different treatments are applied to service capital (used in the production of government services) and infrastructure capital (which requires government support services) (equation 45a). For service capital, growth in service production is the driving force; investment demand is determined as the difference between (i) the anticipated capital demand next year (assuming that production growth will be the same as last year and using a fixed capital-input coefficient) and (ii) the capital stock that would remain if no investments were made.[20] For infrastructure capital, government investment demand is determined as the difference between (i) an exogenous growth term times the infrastructure capital stock in t (similar to equation 42) and (ii) the capital stock that would remain if no investments were made.[21] A non-negativity constraint is also imposed for government investment (equation 45b). A complementary-slackness condition (equation 45c) imposes that (i) if $DKGOV$ is positive, then equation 45a must hold as an equality; and (ii) if the right-hand side of equation 45a is negative, then $DKGOV$ will be zero and equation 45a will hold as an inequality. This treatment is used to avoid a negative investment value ($DKGOV < 0$) in the exceptional case of an anticipated production *decline* that is larger than the depreciation rate. Equation 46 transfers the value of $DKGOV$ to investment by institution, $DKINS$ (for the government), a variable that is used elsewhere in the model to represent investment across all capital stocks and institutions.

The prices of new capital stocks (disaggregated by type) depend on their composition and market prices (equation 47). The resulting fixed government investment value (defined on the basis of the price and quantity information generated in the preceding equations) is financed by some combination of government savings (net of spending on stock or inventory changes), sales of government bonds (that is, new interest-bearing borrowing), borrowing via the monetary sector, foreign borrowing and foreign capital grants (which is separate from current government transfers from the rest of the world) (equation 48). Returning to the equations, government bond sales and borrowing via the monetary system are allocated across households on the basis of their savings shares (equations 49-50).[22]

Equation 48 concludes the series of equations that summarize the government budget (see also equations 40-41 and 44). The choice of mechanism for clearing the budget (the government closure rule) is an important part of the simulations in the country studies of this project. As noted above, changes in the variable $DTINS$ (see equation 34) adjust direct tax payments sufficiently to clear the budget. The other terms in the expressions for government receipts and outlays are exogenous or determined via other mechanisms. Under the other three closures that are used, direct tax rates are exogenous while one of the following variables is endogenized to clear the budget: government bond sales ($GBORTOT_t$), government borrowing from the rest of the world ($FBOR_{gov,t}$), or government grants from the rest of the world ($FGRANT_{gov,t}$).

Each alternative closure has specific macroeconomic repercussions. Increases in government bond sales reduces the amount of financing that is available for private investment (compare equation 51) while increases in foreign grants or foreign borrowing tend to permit more rapid growth in GDP and private final demand (consumption and investment). Reliance on foreign resources also tends to bring about real exchange rate appreciation, slower export growth, and more rapid growth in imports and production for domestic markets. The strength of these effects depends on the growth impact of the expansion in government spending as well as on whether the new spending has high or low import shares. If the country later needs to reverse the switch toward production of non-tradables (for example, because of a decline in foreign grants in the future), and its structure is rigid, it may end up suffering from "Dutch Disease". Expansion in foreign borrowing is less favourable than grants since it drives up the foreign debt (which, in the absence of debt relief, eventually has to be repaid) and related interest payments (more or less burdensome depending on loan conditions). The alternative of raising direct taxes tends to be less favourable to growth in GDP and private final demand than reliance on foreign resources. However, given that most of the cut in household disposable income is born by consumption as opposed to savings and investment, the direct tax alternative is more favourable than domestic government borrowing for long-run growth in GDP and private final demand.

Equation 51 defines the fixed investment values for non-government institutions—all terms do not apply to each institution—as own savings, net of spending on stock (inventory) changes and lending to the government, and augmented by borrowing, capital grants and FDI from the rest of the world. For the latter, the fixed investment value is simply the value of FDI (fixed in FCU) times the exchange rate. (The FDI term is invariably fixed at zero for domestic institutions.) Implicitly, equation 51 shows the rule that the country studies used for ensuring that total savings and total investment are equal: given that government and households savings, government investment, and FDI all are determined by other rules, the clearing variable is private household investment ($INVVAL_{h,t}$).

For each non-government institution, real investment in different capital stocks (investment by destination) is determined by its total fixed investment values, the prices of capital goods, and exogenous value shares by capital stock; the value share is unity if the database only specifies a single private capital type (equation 52).[23]

The final equation in this block defines total investment demand by commodity source (often referred to as investment by origin). It is defined on the basis of real gross fixed capital formation (both private and government; investment by destination) and the capital composition parameter (equation 53).

Other system constraints: foreign exchange, factors and commodities

In the preceding, we discussed alternative mechanisms for clearing two of the macro constraints of the model, the government budget and the savings-investment balance. The current block (equations 54-58) includes the remaining system constraints: the balance of payments and the markets for factors and commodities.

The balance of payments (or foreign exchange constraint) (equation 54) imposes equality between foreign exchange uses (spending on imports, factor incomes and transfers to the rest of the world, and interest payments on foreign debts) and sources (export revenues, transfers, factor incomes, borrowing, capital grants, and FDI).[24] In the country studies, the (real) exchange rate (EXR_t) clears this balance. For example, other things being equal, depreciation (an increase in EXR_t) will remove a deficit by raising supplies for export relative to supplies for domestic sales while reducing domestic use of imports relative to domestic use of domestic output.

The market constraint for factors (equation 55), which applies to all factors except government capital, states that total demand for any factor (the left-hand side) equals the total endowment times the employment rate (one minus the unemployment rate). This is straightforward if the unemployment rate is exogenous—if so, in any time period, the economy-wide wage variable ($WF_{f,t}$) will clear the market by influencing the quantities demanded.

Figure 3.1 shows the functioning of factor markets with endogenous unemployment. The supply curve is upward-sloping, reflecting that, *ceteris paribus*,

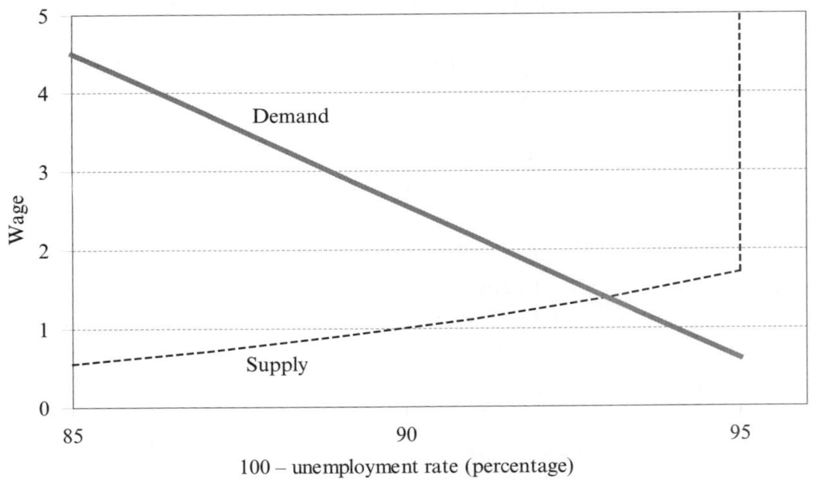

Figure 3.1 Labour market adjustment with endogenous unemployment

workers request higher wages as the labour market gets tighter. When the market reaches a state of "full employment", that is when the minimum unemployment rate is reached (which is set here at 5 per cent but varies across the country studies), the supply curve turns vertical. When the factor market is below full employment, the unemployment rate ($UERAT_{f,t}$) is the clearing variable; at full employment, the economy-wide wage ($WF_{f,t}$) clears the market. Unemployment should be seen as broadly defined, representing the degree of underutilization of the factor (and the potential for increased utilization), due to a combination of full or partial unemployment (that is, also considering underemployment).

Equations 56-57 specify our treatment of the labour market. Workers have a reservation (minimum) wage ($WFRES_{f,t}$) below which they will not work (equation 56). It is defined as a function of the economy-wide wage in the base year, and the ratios between current and base-year values for the (un)employment rate, household consumption per capita (as indicator of real living standards) and the CPI. The ratio terms are raised to elasticities that determine their importance (an elasticity of zero implies that a term has no importance). Equation 57 consists of three parts: (a) the constraint that the economy-wide wage for each factor cannot fall below the endogenous reservation wage; (b) the constraint that the unemployment rate cannot fall below an exogenous minimum (*ueratmin*);[25] and (c) a complementary slackness condition, which states that either (a) or (b) but not both are slack (non-binding). In other words: if the unemployment rate is above its minimum, then the wage must be at the reservation level; if the wage is above the reservation level, then the unemployment rate must be at its minimum.

Note that, at the activity level, the wage paid is the product of $WF_{f,t}$ and $WFDIST_{f,a,t}$ (compare equations 15 and 28). $WFDIST_{f,a,t}$, a distortion (or differential) term that typically is exogenous, reflects relative wage differences across activities. In some cases it may be desirable to impose an exogenous time path for the employment of specific factors in selected activities (drawing on other pieces of information, for example data on the expected evolution of sectors based on the exploitation of natural resources). For the factor-activity-time combination in question, the analyst only has to flex the wage distortion variable ($WFDIST_{f,a,t}$) and fix the employment variable ($QF_{f,a,t}$). Such an assumption can coexist with factor markets with or without endogenous unemployment.

For each composite commodity, the supply is set equal to the sum of demands (equation 58). As noted earlier, composite supplies stem from two sources, imports and domestic supplies to domestic markets (compare equation 24); for each commodity with both sources, demand is allocated between them on the basis of relative prices. The market-clearing variables are the quantity (QM) for imports and, for domestic output, the price (PDS for suppliers and PDD for demanders, with a wedge between the two in the presence of transactions costs).

Asset stock updating and productivity block

The equations in this block update institutional stocks of assets and liabilities, and TFP by activity (equations 59-66). Except for equations defining arguments for the definition of TFP, all equations in this block include lagged relationships. They do not apply to the first year, for which the values of the variables defined in this block are fixed.

In most country studies, MAMS has a single representative household and this is also the implicit assumption in this mathematical statement.[26] For capital, the stock of any institution (household, government and rest of world) is defined as the sum of its previous-period stock (adjusted for depreciation), new investments, and exogenous adjustments (which may reflect the impact of natural disasters or institutional changes, removing parts of the capital stock from production) (equation 59). The evolution of labour endowments is defined in equation 81. For other factors (for example, agricultural land), the growth in institutional endowments ($QFINS_{i,f,t}$) is exogenous. Except for the absence of depreciation, the relationships that hold for foreign debt (equations 60) and government bonds (equations 61) are identical to those used for capital. For foreign debt, the treatment is potentially more complex since the model allows for the possibility of non-paid interest (which is added to the debt) and debt relief.

This block includes further a set of equations used to define total factor productivity (TFP) for each activity. To simplify the algebra, equations 62-63 define real GDP at market prices and the real trade-to-GDP ratio.

In equation 64, the TFP of each activity (a variable that appears in equation 14, the CES value-added function) is defined as the product of a trend term, changes due to capital accumulation, and changes due to variations in economic openness (defined by the real trade-to-GDP ratio). The effects of capital accumulation and changes in openness depend on the values of exogenous elasticities—if they are set at zero, the effect is zero and then only the trend term matters. In the definition of the trend term (equation 65), the first of the trend growth terms, $\alpha vag_{a,t}$ invariably exogenous. The second term, $CALTFPG$, is endogenized when a certain GDP level is targeted (used in the base simulations of the country studies). In this context, the parameter *tfp01* has been used to control relative TFP growth rates across activities (with values ranging between zero and unity). However, apart from the base simulation, all right-hand terms are either exogenous or lagged while GDP is endogenous.[27] The trade-to-GDP ratio, the most common indicator of economic openness (in terms of outcome, not policy stance) is defined in real terms (to avoid the impact of nominal changes, for example due to exchange rate depreciation) and with a potential lag to avoid unrealistically large immediate productivity effects of changes in openness: in any time period, the numerator in the last term of equation 64 is a weighted average of current and past trade-to-GDP ratios. The parameter for the length of the lag is part of the country-specific database. The final equation in this block, equation 66, defines real GDP at factor cost; it is flexible unless *CALTFPG* is flexible.

The fact that the elasticity parameters in equation 64 are disaggregated (by activity for trade and by activity and function for capital) make it possible to specify different channels and magnitudes for the productivity effects of trade and different types of capital stocks. In the country studies, the productivity effects of capital are limited to infrastructure capital.[28] Depending on the degree of disaggregation of these capital stocks and activities, the productivity effects can be more or less finely targeted. For example, if irrigation and road capital stocks are singled out, these could meaningfully be linked to agriculture (especially crop activities) and transportation services, respectively; other sectors would only be influenced indirectly by these productivity changes. On the other hand, if infrastructure capital is a single capital stock, the selection of targeted sectors would have to be more general (implicitly reflecting some assumed composition of this broader spending type).

The MDG module

The MDG module (equations 67-83) specifies the mechanisms that determine the values for the indicators related to the different MDGs and educational behaviour as well as the size and disaggregation (by educational achievement) of the labour force. The rest of the economy, which was presented in the preceding sections, influences the evolution of the MDGs and the educational sector through variables related to household consumption, the provision of different types of MDG-related services, labour wages, and capital stocks in infrastructure. In its turn, the MDG module influences the rest of the economy through its impact on the size and composition of the labour force. In addition, the evolution of one set of MDGs can influence other MDGs. The notation and the equations of the MDG module are respectively presented in Tables A3.3 and A3.4.

MAMS focuses on the MDGs that typically are most costly and have the greatest interactions with the rest of the economy: universal primary school completion (MDG 2; measured by the net primary completion rate), reduced under-five and maternal mortality rates (MDGs 4 and 5), and increased access to improved water sources and basic sanitation (part of MDG 7). The poverty MDG (MDG 1) is simulated in the microsimulation model (see Chapter 2, Appendix A2.1); it is not targeted given the absence of tools (in MAMS and in most real-world, developing-country contexts) that policymakers could use to fine-tune poverty outcomes.[29]

As explained in the introductory section of this chapter, MDG outcomes depend on government and private sector provision of MDG-related services as well as demand conditions for those services. Table 3.3 lists the determinants

Table 3.3   Determinants of non-poverty MDGs

MDG	SD	HC	WI	PI	OM
2. Primary education	x	x	x	x	4
4. Under-five mortality	x	x		x	7a, 7b
5. Maternal mortality	x	x		x	7a, 7b
7a. Access to safe water	x	x		x	
7b. Access to basic sanitation	x	x		x	

Abbreviations: SD: Service delivery; HC: Household consumption per capita; WI: Wage incentives; PI: Public infrastructure; OM: Other MDGs.

that were included in a typical country study. In most cases they were identified on the basis of sector studies underpinned by econometric analysis and subject to the constraints of an economy-wide model like MAMS (including the fact that it is difficult to include finely disaggregated actions, like increasing coverage of certain types of vaccinations).[30] Beyond per-capita real service delivery (either public or a combination of public and private as is the case in most of the LAC region), the determinants include other MDGs (for example, better access to water and sanitation may improve health outcomes—MDGs 4 and 5), as well as public infrastructure, per-capita household consumption, and wage incentives (through the ratio of labour wages of different educational levels). Other potential determinants (like the impact of education on health) were not included given that their effects tend to make themselves felt only over time periods longer than the ones covered by the country simulations.

In the equations of this module, the treatment of the education MDG 2 is separate from the treatment for the remaining MDGs (4, 5, 7a, 7b) since, rather than targeting MDG 2 directly, the model defines (and may target) specific educational behavioural outcomes that jointly determine the value for MDG 2.

The first three equations define arguments that enter both education and MDG functions. Equations 67-68 define aggregate human development (HD) services (which include both MDG and education services). For each service type, equation 67 separates demand into two aggregates, government and non-government, according to who is paying for the service. Typically, services paid for by the government (non-government) are also supplied by a government (non-government) activity, but this is not necessarily the case. Equation 68 generates an economy-wide aggregate (which below is fed into the determination of MDG and education outcomes), permitting two alternative assumptions: services paid for by government and non-government are perfect substitutes (simply summed) or imperfect substitutes (according to a CES function). Equation 69 defines average real household consumption per capita ($QHPC$) as total household consumption (both marketed and home commodities) at base-year prices divided by total population.

The educational component consists of equations 70-79. It is disaggregated by cycle (with three cycles as a typical level of disaggregation). For each cycle, educational quality ($EDUQUAL$) is defined as the ratio between real services per student (aggregated services divided by total enrolment) in the current year and in the base year; that is, in the base-year, educational quality is indexed to one (equation 70). Within any cycle, the model endogenizes the following aspects of student behaviour (or outcomes):

- the shares of the enrolled that pass their current grade, drop out, or repeat the grade next year (referred to as *pass*, *dropout* and *rep*). The sum of these shares is unity—that is, during the school year, a student must either pass, drop out or become a repeater (this applies to each grade and for each cycle as a whole). Note that the term "pass" throughout this chapter and the model refers both to students who successfully complete a grade and continue to a higher grade within the cycle, and to students who successfully finish the last year of a given education cycle (and thus graduate);
- the shares among the passers from their current grade (*pass*) who graduate from their current cycle (*grdcyc*) or continue to a higher grade within this cycle (*contcyc*). In terms of shares: *grdcyc* + *contcyc* = *pass*;
- the shares among cycle graduates who exit the school system (*grdexit*) or continue to next cycle (*grdcont*). The sum of these shares is also unity. For graduates from the last cycle, the share of those who exit is unity; and
- the share of the cohort of the 1st year in primary school that enters school (*glentry*).

Drawing on the above information, we can define the number of enrolled students by cycle and year. Equation 71 defines the number of "old" enrolled students in any cycle (that is, those who were enrolled in the same cycle last year) as the sum of those who: (i) continue within the cycle after successful completion of an earlier grade; and (ii) repeat the grade they were in last year. The number of "new" enrolled students is defined in equation 72 as the sum of: (i) cohort entrants (only for the 1st grade of the primary cycle); (ii) other, non-cohort entrants entering any cycle in the educational system; and (iii) graduates from the relevant earlier cycle last year who chose to continue.[31] The total number of enrolled students in a cycle is the sum of old and new students (equation 73).

Equations 74-78 model the share variables that identify different aspects of student behaviour. For each cycle, a logistic function (equation 74) defines $SHREDU$, the shares for 1st year in-cohort entry, for graduates from the current grade, and for graduates who decide to continue to next cycle (that is, *glentry*, *pass*, and *grdcont*, the elements of the set $BLOG$). The logistic form was selected since it makes it possible to impose extreme (for education it is a maximum of one) values for the function and to incorporate extraneous information about elasticities and conditions under which target values are achieved. Another advantage is that it allows for segments of increasing and decreasing marginal returns to improvements in the determinants of educational behaviour. The only endogenous variable in the logistic function ($ZEDU$), is defined in a constant-elasticity (CE) function (equation 75) as determined by: (i) educational quality; (ii) wage incentives, defined as relative wage gains from continued schooling (that is, the relative wage gain that students can achieve if they complete a cycle that is sufficiently high to enable them to climb to the next higher level in the labour market); (iii) the under-five mortality rate (a proxy for the health status of the school population); (iv) the size of the infrastructure capital stock; and (v) household consumption per capita. Figure 3.2 illustrates the logistic functional form for education. The observed base-year value for *SHREDU* is generated at the base-year value for *ZEDU*. The parameters of the function have to be defined such that the maximum share is one, the base-year elasticities of *SHREDU* with respect to each determinants of *ZEDU* is replicated and, under values for the determinants of *ZEDU* identified in the database, a target level for *SHREDU* is realized. In terms of the algebra, the parameters in equations 74-75 are selected as follows:

- the parameter *extedu* shows the extreme (maximum) value (here unity) to which the behaviour share should converge as the value of the intermediate variable approaches infinity;
- the parameter αedu is calibrated so that, under base-year conditions, the behavioural share replicates the base-year value;
- the parameters βedu and φedu are calibrated so that the two equations: (i) replicate the base-year elasticities of the behavioural share (*SHREDU*) with respect to the arguments of the CE function; and (ii) achieve a behavioural target (for example, a share very close to one for *glentry*, the share of the relevant age cohort that enters first grade) under a set of values for the arguments of the CE function that have been identified by other studies; and

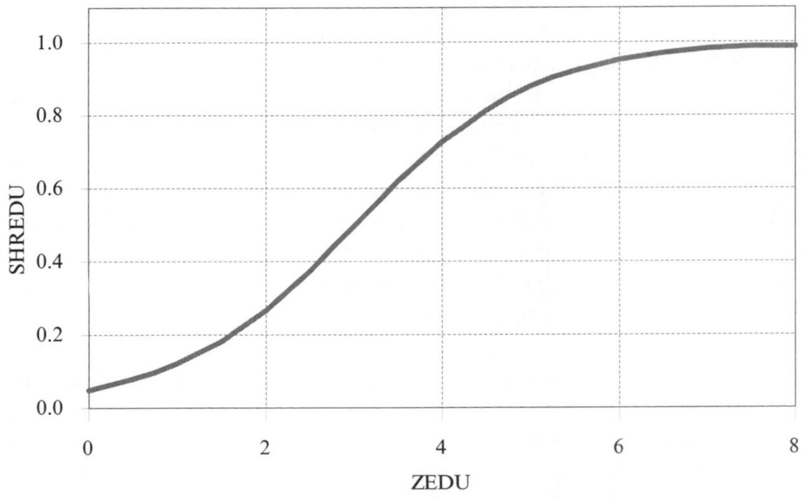

Figure 3.2 Logistic function for education

- the value of the parameter *γedu* determines how the base-year point on the logistic function is positioned relative to the inflection point (where the curve switches from increasing to decreasing marginal returns as the determinants of educational behaviour improve).

Equation 75 is calibrated so that, in the base year (under base-year conditions), $ZEDU_{b,c,t} = SHREDU^0_{b,c}$. (Note that the left-hand term enters the denominator of the second term in equation 74.)

Drawing on the shares defined in the preceding equations, the shares for repeaters, dropouts, and cycle graduates exiting from the school system (*rep*, *dropout* and *grdexit*; elements in the set *BRES*) are defined residually (equation 76). The formulation considers the fact that, as noted above, selected shares have to sum to unity. If more than one variable in *BRES* has to be adjusted in relation to one or more elements in *BLOG* (as is the case for the adjustment of shares for repeaters and dropouts in response to changes in the share of graduates), then all adjusted variables are scaled up or down by the same factor.[32] The share of graduates from a cycle (*grdcyc*) is defined as the share for the total number of passers in the cycle (*pass*) divided by the number of years in the cycle times an adjustment term (since students may not be evenly distributed across grades) whereas the residual share is assigned to graduates within a cycle (*contcyc*) (equations 77-78).

We use the net completion rate as our MDG 2 indicator. It is defined as the product of the relevant 1st-year primary school entry rate (*glentry*) and the passing rates (*pass*) over time for the cohort that graduate from primary school in the current year (equation 79).[33]

The labour force participation rate is defined as the labour force (*QFINS*) divided by the population in labour force age that is not enrolled in secondary and tertiary cycles (equation 80).[34] Institutional labour endowments (*QFINS* for labour) are defined as the sum of the following components (equation 81): (i) remaining labour from the preceding year; (ii) new labour force entrants among students who exited from the school system in the previous year (with separate terms for non-tertiary graduates, tertiary graduates, and dropouts); and (iii) new labour force entrants from the non-student population who reach the age at which they, to the extent that they seek work, become part of the labour force. Depending on their highest completed grade, the new labour force entrants are allocated to a specific labour category.

The treatment underlying MDGs 4, 5, 7a and 7b is similar but less complex. For these, a logistic function directly defines the MDG indicators as a function of an intermediate variable that is defined in a related CE function (equations 82-83). The values for the parameters *extmdg*, *αmdg*, *βmdg* and *φmdg* are defined following the same principles as the corresponding parameters in the logistic and CE functions for education. The arguments of the CE function are similar except for that the relevant service supply is expressed in per-capita form (not per enrolled student).

Overview of MAMS data needs and sources

The data needs of the core CGE module of MAMS are similar to those of other CGE models. Additional data (for the SAM and other parameters) is needed primarily for the MDG module but also to capture some other extensions, mostly related to the treatment of the government.

In an earlier section, we presented the structure of a SAM for the full (MDG) version of MAMS, as applied in the country studies. The following aspects of this SAM give rise to data requirements that go beyond what is needed for most SAMs for CGE models:[35] (i) government consumption and investment spending must be disaggregated into functions that correspond to policy tools for addressing the relevant MDGs and providing education at the three major levels (primary, secondary and tertiary); (ii) labour must be disaggregated by level of education in a manner that matches the educational system; and (iii) the SAM must include accounts for foreign and domestic interest payments. In addition, if they are important, it is also preferable to single out separate private activities and commodities in the MDG and education area; for example, the private sector may account for significant shares of the total supply of education, especially at higher levels. In other respects, the SAM is very similar to standard practice.

Other data and sources

Other than the SAM, MAMS requires data that in part coincides with those of many other models, most importantly elasticities to capture substitutability between factors in production, transformability of output between exports and domestic sales, substitutability between imports and domestic commodities in domestic demand, and responses in household consumption to income changes.

The other data requirements, specific to MAMS, are mostly due to its extensions to include MDG indicators and their determinants, an extended education module and relatively detailed government accounts. The links between labour, education and population necessitate consistent base-year data on employment (by activity and labour type), unemployment (by labour type), and enrolment (by level or cycle).[36] The model also requires projections for the total population and the population of three age groups: the cohort of entrants to primary school, the cohort of entrants to labour-force age and the broader population group in working age.

Both for education (for each of the three levels) and four of the non-education MDGs in MAMS (labelled 4, 5, 7a, and 7b), it is necessary to provide data for base-year outcomes: in education, cycle-specific rates for entry, pass, repetition and dropout; outside education, the rates that define other MDG indicators (for example, the under-five mortality rate). For these non-education MDGs, information on the situation in 1990 is needed to define the targets for 2015. To model how these outcomes change over time, two pieces of information are needed: (a) base-year elasticities (linking outcomes to determinants), preferably estimated using logit or probit models; and (b) a path for the evolution of these determinants that makes it possible to reach a set of future values (typically targets for 2015). This information is used to calibrate the functions so that they replicate base-year outcomes and elasticities, reach each MDG under specified conditions, and have the upper limits that were specified exogenously.

Finally, also for non-labour factors, it is necessary to define base-year stocks. For private capital, these may be defined on the basis of base-year data for rents, profit rates and depreciation rates.[37] For each type of government capital, the base-year stock is defined on the basis of historical data on service growth, investments, depreciation rates and the assumption that the capital stock over time has grown at the same rate as real services. For other factors such as agricultural land and natural resources, base-year stocks can typically be defined so that base-year rents are normalized to unity; data on the future stock growth is also needed—as opposed to labour and capital, growth for these factors is exogenous.

The construction of this database requires the analysts to consult existing SAMs and input-output tables, other standard databases (both country-specific and those of international organizations, covering national accounts, government budgets, and the balance of payments), surveys (of households, labour and health conditions), and relevant research on trade, production, consumption and human development, including available MDG strategies and other analyses of the determinants of MDG outcomes. Sector-focused MDG studies (in health, education, water and sanitation, and public infrastructure), public expenditure reviews and other types of country-level economic studies are often valuable sources. In the country studies for this project, it was typically necessary to complement available studies with new survey-based research to better understand the determination of MDG and education outcomes.[38]

As shown, MAMS does not replace other forms of sectoral research in human development; on the contrary, it draws extensively on and stimulates such research. Without sector studies that provide a strong empirical basis, the analysis of MDG strategies in an economy-wide framework (whether MAMS or any other) loses much of its power.

Concluding remarks

This chapter has documented MAMS, a dynamic CGE model that constitutes the central methodological framework of this study and, together with a microsimulation model complemented with sector studies, is used to answer the three development strategy questions posed in Chapter 1. MAMS is designed to analyse strategies for achieving selected MDGs and, more broadly, policies for medium- and long-run growth and poverty reduction in developing countries. The development of MAMS is and has been driven by a strongly felt need for an economy-wide approach to development strategy analysis that considers the different effects of government interventions, not only because of their resource requirement but also through their impact on human development, including the size and educational characteristics of the labour force, and public infrastructure. MAMS is sufficiently flexible to address the key processes for MDG achievement and other development strategies in a wide range of countries. The requirement is to link the model to country databases that capture country characteristics; the databases may vary widely in terms of disaggregation. The development of such a database, undertaken for the country studies in this volume, requires a considerable research effort. At the same time several aspects of MAMS were further developed to better accommodate many of the specificities of LAC countries.

In the country studies of this volume, MAMS is first used to generate a benchmark, business-as-usual scenario for a period that typically starts around 2000 and ends in 2015; as indicated by its name, the aim of this scenario is to represent a plausible projection into the future, drawing on recent trends. As a second step, MAMS is used to simulate a set of alternative scenarios under which growth in government MDG services is adjusted endogenously to achieve selected MDGs under alternative financing policies. The scenarios target different combinations of MDGs 2 (universal completion primary school), 4 (reduced under-five mortality rates), 5 (reduced maternal mortality rates) and 7 (improved access rates for water and/or sanitation). The alternative sources for the additional financing are grant aid, foreign borrowing, domestic bonds and direct taxes.

As the analysis in Chapter 2 made clear, the results vary systematically depending on the targets, the financing mechanism, the initial starting point (how far is the country from achieving the MDG) and overall macroeconomic conditions (including GDP growth under the base or business-as-usual scenario). The country analysis shows that reliance on foreign financing tends to appreciate the real exchange rate, increase import growth and reduce export growth. Real exchange rate appreciation is more significant if the spending increase primarily is directed toward non-tradables (the case for most scenarios except for those that target the water and sanitation MDGs, which tend to be relatively more investment- and import-intensive). Among the two foreign financing alternatives, grant aid differs in that it does not leave the country with a debt that requires interest payment and may be the source of sustainability problems. This form of financing of the MDG strategy does not adversely affect private consumption or private investment as is the case in taxation or domestic-borrowing strategies of increased MDG-related spending. Under the domestic financing alternatives, government expansion leaves fewer resources in the hands of households and the private sector. When a government expansion is financed via direct taxes, for example, household disposable income declines, with a stronger reduction (in value terms) for private consumption than private savings and private investment. The government will likely have to spend more to make up for a reduction in private MDG-related spending, rendering this alternative more expensive (compare Chapter 2). Other things being equal, GDP growth may suffer slightly. Poverty reduction is compromised in the short run while the medium-run results up to 2015 are very heterogeneous.

The effects of the simulations on the labour market are also systematic. For the scenarios that target MDG 2, labour force growth declines in the least educated segment and overall but expands for the more educated segments; these effects are particularly strong in countries that start out with the lowest educational achievements. Accordingly, wages grow more strongly while unemployment declines for the least educated. However, this tendency is mitigated given the fact that MDG strategies also tend to generate more rapid demand growth for more educated labour. Overall, the gains in productivity and average wages from having a more educated labour force are considerable, both for the nation and for the workers who climb the educational ladder.

Appendix A3.1

Mathematical statement of MAMS

Table A3.1   Sets, parameters, and variables for core CGE modules of MAMS model

Symbol	Explanation
<u>SETS</u>	
$a \in A$	activities
$a \in ACES\ (\subset A)$	activities with CES function between Value Added and Intermediate inputs
$a \in ALEO\ (\subset A)$	activities with Leontief function between value added and intermediate inputs
$c \in C$	commodities
$c \in CD (\subset C)$	commodities with domestic sales of domestic output
$c \in CDN (\subset C)$	commodities not in CD
$c \in CE (\subset C)$	exported commodities
$c \in CEN (\subset C)$	commodities not in CE
$c \in CECETN (\subset C)$	exported commodities without CET function
$c \in CINF (\subset C)$	infrastructure commodity
$c \in CM (\subset C)$	imported commodities
$c \in CMN (\subset C)$	commodities not in CM
$c \in CT (\subset C)$	transaction service commodities
$f, f' \in F$	factors
$f \in FCAP (\subset F)$	capital factors
$f \in FCAPGOV (\subset FCAP)$	government capital factors
$f \in FEXOG (\subset F)$	factors with exogenous growth rates
$f \in FLABN (\subset F)$	non-labour factors
$f \in FUEND (\subset F)$	factors with endogenous unemployment
$h \in H (\subset INSDNG)$	households (incl. NGOs)
$i \in INS$	institutions (domestic and rest of world)
$i \in INSD (\subset INS)$	domestic institutions
$i \in INSDNG (\subset INSD)$	domestic non-government institutions

Table A3.1   (cont'd)

Symbol	Explanation
$i \in INSNG(\subset INS)$	non-government institutions
$(f,a) \in MFA$	mapping showing that disaggregated factor f is used in activity a
$t \in T$	time periods
PARAMETERS—LATIN LETTERS	
$capcomp_{c,f}$	quantity of commodity c per unit of new capital f
$cwts_c$	weight of commodity c in the CPI
$depr_f$	depreciation rate for factor f
$dintrat_{i,t}$	interest rate on government bonds for domestic institution i
$dwts_c$	domestic sales price weights
$fdebtrelief_{i,t}$	foreign debt relief for domestic institution i
$fdi_{i,t}$	foreign direct investment by institution i (rest of world) (FCU)
$fintrat_{i,t}$	interest rate on foreign debt for domestic institution i (paid)
$fintratdue_{i,t}$	interest rate on foreign debt for domestic institution i (due)
$fprd_{f,a,t}$	productivity of factor f in activity a
$gbdist_i$	distortion factor for government borrowing from institution i
$gfcfshr_{f,i,t}$	share of gross fixed capital formation for institution i in capital factor f
$ica_{c,a}$	quantity of c as intermediate input per unit of aggregate intermediate in activity a
$icd_{c,c',t}$	trade input of c per unit of commodity c' produced & sold domestically
$ice_{c,c',t}$	trade input of c per unit of commodity c' exported
$icm_{c,c',t}$	trade input of c per unit of commodity c' imported
$ifa_{f,a}$	quantity of capital f per unit of government activity a
$igf_{c,f,t}$	quantity of gov consumption per unit of gov infrastructure capital stock f
$inta_a$	quantity of aggregate intermediate input per unit of activity a

Table A3.1 (cont'd)	
Symbol	**Explanation**
iva_a	quantity of value-added per unit of activity a
$mps01_i$	0-1 parameter with 1 for institutions with potentially flexed direct tax rates
$mpsbar_{i,t}$	Exogenous component in savings rate for domestic institution i
$poptot_t$	total population by year
$pwm_{c,t}$	import world price of c (FCU)
$pwse_{c,t}$	world price for export substitutes (FCU)
$qdst_{c,i,t}$	quantity of stock (inventory) change
$\overline{qe}_{c,t}$	export demand for c if pwe = pwse (world price for substitutes)
$qfhhtot_{f,t}$	total household stock of exogenous, non-labour factors
$qfinsadj_{i,f,t}$	exogenous factor stock adjustment
$qfpc_{i,f,t}$	per-capita quantity of exogenous-supply factor f by institution i and year t
$rqgadj_{c,c',t}$	parameter linking government consumption growth across commodities
$shii_{i,i'}$	share of net income of i' to i (i'—INSDNG)
$ta_{a,t}$	tax rate for activity a
$te_{c,t}$	export tax rate
$tf_{f,t}$	direct tax rate for factor f
$tfp01_{a,t}$	0-1 parameter for activities with endogenous TFP growth
$tfpelasqg_{a,f,t}$	elasticity of TFP for activity a with respect to government capital stock f
$tfpelastrd_a$	elasticity of TFP for a with respect to GDP trade share
$tfptrdwt_{t,t'}$	weight of period t' in tfp-trade link in t
$tgap_{t,t'}$	gap between t and t' (years used for calculation of expected growth rate for QA)
$tins01_i$	0-1 parameter with 1 for institutions with potentially flexed direct tax rates

Table A3.1 (cont'd)	
Symbol	**Explanation**
$tinsbar_{i,t}$	exogenous component in direct tax rate for domestic institution i
$tm_{c,t}$	import tariff rate
$tq_{c,t}$	rate of sales tax
$trnsfr_{i,i',t}$	Exogenous transfer from institution i' to institution i
$trnsfr_{f,i',t}$	Exogenous transfer from institution i' to factor f
$trnsfrpc_{i,i',t}$	per-capita transfers from institution i' to household institution i
$tva_{a,t}$	rate of value-added tax for activity a
PARAMETERS— GREEK LETTERS	
αac_c	shift parameter for domestic commodity aggregation function
$\alpha vag_{a,t}$	exogenous component of efficiency (TFP) for activity a
αq_c	Armington function shift parameter
αt_c	CET function shift parameter
$\beta h_{a,c,h}$	marginal share of household consumption on home commodity c from activity a
$\beta m_{c,h}$	marginal share of household consumption spending on marketed commodity c
δac_a	share parameter for domestic commodity aggregation function
δq_c	Armington function share parameter
δt_c	CET function share parameter
$\delta va_{f,a}$	CES value-added function share parameter for factor f in activity a
$\gamma h_{a,c,h}$	per capita household subsistence consumption of home commodity c from activity a
$\gamma m_{c,h}$	per capita household subsistence cons of marketed commodity c
ρac_c	domestic commodity aggregation function exponent
ρq_c	Armington function exponent

Table A3.1   (cont'd)

Symbol	Explanation
ρsav_i	elasticity of savings rate with respect to per-capita income for institution (household) h
ρt_c	CET function exponent
ρva_a	CES value-added function exponent
$\theta_{a,c}$	yield of output c per unit of activity a
VARIABLES	
$ALPHAVA_{a,t}$	efficiency parameter in the CES value-added function
$ALPHAVA2_{a,t}$	endogenous TFP trend term by a
$CALTFPG_t$	calibration factor for TFP growth
CPI_t	consumer price index
$GBORMS_{i,t}$	implicit government Central Bank borrowing (deficit monetization) from institution i
$GBORMSTOT_t$	total government Central Bank borrowing (deficit monetization)
$GBOR_{i,t}$	change in holding of government bonds for domestic institution i
$GBORTOT_t$	total change in holding of government bonds
$DKGOV_{f,t}$	gross government investment in f
$DKINS_{i,f,t}$	gross change in capital stock (investment in) f for institution i
$DMPS_t$	uniform point change in savings rate of selected domestic institutions
DPI_t	producer price index for non-traded output
$DTINS_t$	uniform point change in direct tax rate of selected domestic institutions
EG_t	government expenditures
$EH_{h,t}$	consumption spending for household
EXR_t	exchange rate (LCU per unit of FCU)
$FBOR_{i,t}$	foreign borrowing for domestic institution i
$FDEBT_{i,t}$	foreign debt for domestic inst i

Table A3.1 (cont'd)	
Symbol	**Explanation**
$FGRANT_{i,t}$	foreign grants to domestic institution i (FCU)
$GDEBT_{i,t}$	endowment of government bonds for i
$GDPREAL_t$	real GDP at market prices
$GDPREALFC_t$	real GDP at factor cost
$GSAV_t$	government savings
$INSSAV_{i,t}$	savings of domestic non-government institution i
$INVVAL_{i,t}$	investment value for institution i
$MPS_{i,t}$	marginal propensity to save for domestic non-gov institution i
$MPSADJ_t$	savings rate scaling factor
$PA_{a,t}$	activity price (unit gross revenue)
$PDD_{c,t}$	demand price for commodity c produced & sold domestically
$PDS_{c,t}$	supply price for commodity c produced & sold domestically
$PE_{c,t}$	export price (domestic currency)
$PINTA_{a,t}$	aggregate intermediate input price for activity a
$PK_{f,t}$	price of new capital stock f
$PM_{c,t}$	import price (domestic currency)
$POP_{i,t}$	population by household
$PQ_{c,t}$	composite commodity price
$PVA_{a,t}$	value-added price (factor income per unit of activity)
$PVAAVG_t$	average value-added price
$PWE_{c,t}$	export world price of c (FCU)
$PX_{c,t}$	aggregate producer price for commodity
$PXAC_{a,c,t}$	price of commodity c from activity a

Table A3.1   (cont'd)

Symbol	Explanation
$QD_{c,t}$	quantity sold domestically of domestically produced c
$QF_{f,a,t}$	quantity demanded of factor f by activity a
$QFINS_{i,f,t}$	real endowment of factor f for institution i
$QG_{c,t}$	quantity of government consumption of commodity c
$QH_{c,h,t}$	quantity consumed by household h of marketed commodity c
$QHA_{a,c,h,t}$	quantity consumed of home commodity c from act a by hhd h
$QINTA_{a,t}$	quantity of aggregate intermediate input used by activity a
$QINT_{c,a,t}$	quantity of commodity c as intermediate input to activity a
$QINV_{c,t}$	quantity of investment demand for commodity c
$QM_{c,t}$	quantity of imports of commodity c
$QQ_{c,t}$	quantity of goods supplied to domestic market (composite supply)
$QT_{c,t}$	quantity of trade and transport demand for commodity c
$QVA_{a,t}$	quantity of (aggregate) value-added
$QX_{c,t}$	aggregated quantity of domestic output of commodity
$QXAC_{a,c,t}$	quantity of output of commodity c from activity a
$QGGRW_{t}$	real government consumption growth for all c in t relative to t-1
$QGGRWC_{c,t}$	real government consumption growth of c in t relative to t-1
$SHIF_{i,f,t}$	share of institution i in income of factor f
$TINS_{i,t}$	direct tax rate for domestic non-government institution i
$TINSADJ_{t}$	direct tax scaling factor
$TRDGDP_{t}$	foreign trade as share of GDP
$TRII_{i,i',t}$	transfers from institution i' to i (both in the set INSDNG)

Table A3.1 (cont'd)	
Symbol	**Explanation**
$WF_{f,t}$	average price of factor
$WFDIST_{f,a,t}$	wage distortion factor for factor f in activity a
$WFRES_{f,t}$	reservation wage for factor f
$YF_{f,t}$	income of factor f
YG_{t}	government revenue
$YI_{i,t}$	income of domestic non-government institution
$YIF_{i,f,t}$	income to domestic institution i from factor f
$YIINT_{i,t}$	interest payment on government bonds to institution i

Table A3.2   Equations for the core CGE module of MAMS model

#	Equation	Domain
Price Block		
(1)	$PM_{c,t} = pwm_{c,t} \cdot \left(1 + tm_{c,t} \right) \cdot EXR_t + \sum_{c' \in C} \left(PQ_{c',t} \cdot icm_{c',c,t} \right)$	$c \in CM$ $t \in T$
(2)	$PE_{c,t} = \overline{PWE}_{c,t} \cdot \left(1 - te_{c,t} \right) \cdot EXR_t - \sum_{c' \in C} \left(PQ_{c',t} \cdot ice_{c',c,t} \right)$	$c \in CE$ $t \in T$
(3)	(a) $PDS_{c,t} \geq PE_{c,t}$ (b) $QE_{c,t} \geq 0$ (c) $\left(PDS_{c,t} - PE_{c,t} \right) \cdot \left(QE_{c,t} - 0 \right) = 0$ $\left[\begin{array}{l}\text{Complementary slackness relationship:} \\ \text{1. If domestic price exceeds export price then export quantity is zero.} \\ \text{2. If export quantity exceeds zero, then domestic price equals export price}\end{array}\right]$	$c \in$ $(CD \cap$ $CECETN)$ $t \in T$
(4)	$PDD_{c,t} = PDS_{c,t} + \sum_{c' \in C} \left(PQ_{c',t} \cdot icd_{c',c,t} \right)$	$c \in CD$ $t \in T$
(5)	$PQ_{c,t} \cdot \left(1 - tq_{c,t} \right) \cdot QQ_{c,t} = PDD_{c,t} \cdot QD_{c,t} + PM_{c,t} \cdot QM_{c,t}$	$c \in$ $(CD \cup CM)$ $t \in T$
(6)	$PX_{c,t} \cdot QX_{c,t} = PDS_{c,t} \cdot QD_{c,t} + PE_{c,t} \cdot QE_{c,t}$	$c \in$ $(CD \cup CE)$ $t \in T$
(7)	$PA_{a,t} = \sum_{c \in C} PXAC_{a,c,t} \cdot \theta_{a,c}$	$a \in A$ $t \in T$
(8)	$PINTA_{a,t} = \sum_{c \in C} PQ_{c,t} \cdot ica_{c,a}$	$a \in A$ $t \in T$
(9)	$PA_{a,t} \cdot (1 - ta_{a,t}) \cdot QA_{a,t} = PVA_{a,t} \cdot QVA_{a,t} + PINTA_{a,t} \cdot QINTA_{a,t}$	$a \in A$ $t \in T$
(10)	$\overline{CPI}_t = \sum_{c \in C} PQ_{c,t} \cdot cwts_c$	$t \in T$
(11)	$DPI_t = \sum_{c \in CD} PDS_{c,t} \cdot dwts_c$	$t \in T$
Production and trade block		
(12)	$QVA_{a,t} = iva_a \cdot QA_{a,t}$	$a \in ALEO$ $t \in T$
(13)	$QINTA_{a,t} = inta_a \cdot QA_{a,t}$	$a \in ALEO$ $t \in T$

Table A3.2   (cont'd)

#	Equation	Domain
(14)	$$QVA_{a,t} = ALPHAVA_{a,t} \cdot \left(\sum_{f \in F} \delta_{va\,f,a} \cdot \left(fprd_{f,a,t} \cdot QF_{f,a,t} \right)^{-\rho va_a} \right)^{-\frac{1}{\rho va_a}}$$	$a \in A$ $t \in T$
(15)	$$WF_{f,t} \cdot \overline{WFDIST}_{f,a,t} = PVA_{a,t} \cdot \left(1 - tva_{a,t} \right) \cdot QVA_{a,t} \cdot$$ $$\left(\sum_{f' \in F} \delta_{va\,f',a} \cdot \left(fprd_{f',a,t} \cdot QF_{f',a,t} \right)^{-\rho va_a} \right)^{-1} \cdot$$ $$\delta_{va\,f,a} \cdot fprd_{f,a,t}^{-\rho va_a} \cdot QF_{f,a,t}^{-\rho va_a - 1}$$	$a \in A$ $f \in F$ $t \in T$
(16)	$$QINT_{c,a,t} = ica_{c,a} \cdot QINTA_{a,t}$$	$c \in C$ $a \in A$ $t \in T$
(17)	$$QXAC_{a,c,t} + \sum_{h \in H} QHA_{a,c,h,t} = \theta_{a,c} \cdot QA_{a,t}$$	$c \in C$ $a \in A$ $t \in T$
(18)	$$QX_{c,t} = \alpha_{ac_c} \cdot \left(\sum_{a \in A} \delta_{ac\,a,c} \cdot QXAC_{a,c,t}^{-\rho ac_c} \right)^{-\frac{1}{\rho ac_c}}$$	$c \in$ $(CE \cup CD)$ $t \in T$
(19)	$$\frac{PXAC_{a,c,t}}{PX_{c,t}} = QX_{c,t} \cdot \sum_{a \in A} \left(\delta_{ac\,a,c} \cdot QXAC_{a,c,t}^{-\rho ac_c} \right)^{-1} \cdot \delta_{ac\,a,c} \cdot QXAC_{a,c,t}^{-\rho ac_c - 1}$$	$a \in A$ $c \in C$ $t \in T$
(20)	$$QX_{c,t} = \alpha_{t_c} \cdot \left(\delta_{t_c} \cdot QE_{c,t}^{\rho t_c} + (1 - \delta_{t_c}) \cdot QD_{c,t}^{\rho t_c} \right)^{\frac{1}{\rho t_c}}$$	$c \in (CD \cap$ $CECET)$ $t \in T$
(21)	$$\frac{QE_{c,t}}{QD_{c,t}} = \left(\frac{PE_{c,t}}{PDS_{c,t}} \cdot \frac{1 - \delta_{t_c}}{\delta_{t_c}} \right)^{\frac{1}{\rho t_c - 1}}$$	$c \in (CD \cap$ $CECET)$ $t \in T$
(22)	$$QX_{c,t} = QD_{c,t} + QE_{c,t}$$	$c \in$ $(CD \cap CEN) \cup$ $(CE \cap CDN) \cup$ $(CD \cap CECETN)$ $t \in T$

Table A3.2   (cont'd)

#	Equation	Domain
(23)	$$QE_{c,t} = \overline{qe}_{c,t} \cdot \left(\frac{PWE_{c,t}}{pwse_{c,t}} \right)^{\rho e_c}$$	$c \in CED$ $t \in T$
(24)	$$QQ_{c,t} = \alpha_{q_c} \cdot \left(\delta_{q_c} \cdot QM_{c,t}^{-\rho_{q_c}} + (1-\delta_{q_c}) \cdot QD_{c,t}^{-\rho_{q_c}} \right)^{-\frac{1}{\rho_{q_c}}}$$	$c \in$ $(CM \cap CD)$ $t \in T$
(25)	$$\frac{QM_{c,t}}{QD_{c,t}} = \left(\frac{PDD_{c,t}}{PM_{c,t}} \cdot \frac{\delta_{q_c}}{1-\delta_{q_c}} \right)^{\frac{1}{1+\rho_{q_c}}}$$	$c \in$ $(CM \cap CD)$ $t \in T$
(26)	$$QQ_{c,t} = QD_{c,t} + QM_{c,t}$$	$c \in$ $(CD \cap CMN) \cup$ $(CM \cap CDN)$ $t \in T$
(27)	$$QT_{c,t} = \sum_{c' \in C'} \left(icm_{c,c',t} \cdot QM_{c',t} + ice_{c,c',t} \cdot QE_{c',t} + icd_{c,c',t} \cdot QD_{c',t} \right)$$	$c \in CT$ $t \in T$

<u>Domestic institution block</u>

#	Equation	Domain
(28)	$$YF_{f,t} = \sum_{a \in A} WF_{f,t} \cdot \overline{WFDIST}_{f,a,t} \cdot QF_{f,a,t} + trnsfr_{f,row,t} \cdot EXR_t$$	$f \in F$ $t \in T$
(29)	$$SHIF_{i,f,t} = \frac{QFACINS_{i,f,t}}{\sum_{i' \in INS} QFACINS_{i',f,t}}$$	$i \in INS$ $f \in F$ $t \in T$
(30)	$$YIF_{i,f,t} = SHIF_{i,f,t} \cdot \left[\left(1 - tf_{f,t} \right) \cdot YF_{f,t} \right]$$	$i \in$ $f \in F$ $t \in T$
(31)	$$YIINT_{i,t} = gintrat_{i,t} \cdot GDEBT_{i,t} - fintrat_{i,t} \cdot FDEBT_{i,t} \cdot EXR_t$$	$i \in$ $INSDNG$ $t \in T$
(32)	$$TRII_{i,i',t} = shii_{i,i'} \cdot (1 - MPS_{i',t}) \cdot (1 - TINS_{i',t}) \cdot YI_{i',t}$$	$i \in INS$ $i' \in$ $INSDNG$ $t \in T$

Table A3.2   (cont'd)

#	Equation	Domain
(33)	$$YI_{i,t} = \sum_{f \in F} YIF_{i,f,t} + \sum_{i' \in INSDNG'} TRII_{i,i',t} + YIINT_{i,t}$$ $$+ trnsfr_{i,gov,t} \cdot \overline{CPI_t} + trnsfrpc_{i,gov,t} \cdot POP_{i,t} \cdot \overline{CPI_t}$$ $$+ trnsfr_{i,row,t} \cdot EXR_t + trnsfrpc_{i,row,t} \cdot POP_{i,t} \cdot EXR_t$$	$i \in$ $INSDNG$ $t \in T$
(34)	$$TINS_{i,t} = tinsbar_{i,t} \cdot \left(1 + \overline{TINSADJ_t} \cdot tins01_i\right) + DTINS_t \cdot tins01_i$$	$i \in$ $INSDNG$ $t \in T$
(35)	$$MPS_{i,t} = mpsbar_{i,t} \cdot \left(\frac{\left(1 - TINS_{i,t}\right) \cdot YI_{i,t}}{\overline{POP_{i,t}}}\right)^{\rho sav_i - 1}$$ $$\cdot \left(1 + \overline{MPSADJ_t} \cdot mps01_i\right) + \overline{DMPS_t} \cdot mps01_i$$	$i \in$ $INSDNG$ $t \in T$
(36)	$$INSSAV_{i,t} = MPS_{i,t} \cdot \left(1 - TINS_{i,t}\right) \cdot YI_{i,t}$$	$i \in INSDNG$
(37)	$$EH_{h,t} = \left(1 - \sum_{i \in INSDNG} shii_{i,h}\right) \cdot \left(1 - MPS_{h,t}\right) \cdot \left(1 - TINS_{h,t}\right) \cdot YI_{h,t}$$	$h \in H$ $t \in T$
(38)	$$QH_{c,h,t} = \overline{POP}_{h,t} \cdot$$ $$\left(\gamma_{m_{c,h}} + \frac{\beta_{m_{c,h}} \cdot \left(\left[\frac{EH_{h,t}}{\overline{POP}_{h,t}}\right] - \sum_{c' \in C} PQ_{c',t} \cdot \gamma_{m_{c',h}} - \sum_{a \in A} \sum_{c' \in C} PXAC_{a,c',t} \cdot \gamma_{h_{a,c',h}}\right)}{PQ_{c,t}}\right)$$	$c \in C$ $h \in H$ $t \in T$
(39)	$$QHA_{a,c,h,t} = \overline{POP}_{h,t} \cdot$$ $$\left(\gamma_{h_{a,c,h}} + \frac{\beta_{h_{a,c,h}} \cdot \left(\left[\frac{EH_{h,t}}{\overline{POP}_{h,t}}\right] - \sum_{c' \in C} PQ_{c',t} \cdot \gamma_{m_{c',h}} - \sum_{a' \in A} \sum_{c' \in C} PXAC_{a',c',t} \cdot \gamma_{h_{a',c',h}}\right)}{PXAC_{a,c,t}}\right)$$	$a \in A$ $c \in C$ $h \in H$ $t \in T$

Table A3.2   (cont'd)

#	Equation	Domain
(40)	$$YG_t = \sum_{i \in INSDNG} TINS_{i,t} \cdot YI_{i,t} + \sum_{f \in F} tf_{f,t} \cdot YF_{f,t} +$$ $$\sum_{a \in A} ta_{a,t} \cdot PA_{a,t} \cdot QA_{a,t} +$$ $$\sum_{a \in A} tva_{a,t} \cdot PVA_{a,t} \cdot QVA_{a,t} +$$ $$\sum_{c \in CM} tm_{c,t} \cdot pwm_{c,t} \cdot QM_{c,t} +$$ $$\sum_{c \in CE} te_{c,t} \cdot \overline{PWE}_{c,t} \cdot QE_{c,t} \cdot EXR_t + \sum_{c \in C} tq_{c,t} \cdot PQ_{c,t} \cdot QQ_{c,t} +$$ $$\sum_{f \in F} YIF_{gov,f,t} + \sum_{i \in INSDNG} TRII_{gov,i,t} + trnsfr_{gov,row,t} \cdot EXR_t$$	$t \in T$
(41)	$$EG_t = \sum_{c \in C} PQ_{c,t} \cdot QG_{c,t} + \sum_{i \in INSDNH} trnsfr_{i,gov,t} \cdot \overline{CPI}_t$$ $$+ \sum_{h \in H} trnsfrpc_{h,gov,t} \cdot \overline{POP}_{h,t} \cdot \overline{CPI}_t + trnsfr_{row,gov,t} \cdot EXR_t$$ $$+ \sum_{i \in INS} gintrat_{i,t} \cdot GDEBT_{i,t} + fintrat_{gov,t} \cdot FDEBT_{gov,t} \cdot EXR_t$$	$t \in T$
(42)	$$QG_{c,t} = QG_{c,t-1} \cdot \left(1 + \overline{QGGRW}_t + \sum_{c' \in C} qg01_{c,c',t} \cdot \overline{QGGRWC}_{c',t} \right)$$	$c \in C$ $c \notin CINF$ $t \in T$ $t > 1$
(43)	$$QG_{c,t} = \sum_{\substack{i \in INS \\ f \in F}} igf_{c,f,t} \cdot QFINS_{i,f,t}$$	$c \in CINF$ $t \in T$ $t > 1$
(44)	$GSAV_t = YG_t - EG_t$	$t \in T$

Table A3.2   (cont'd)

#	Equation	Domain
Investment block		

#	Equation	Domain
(45)	$(a)\ DKGOV_{f,t} \geq \displaystyle\sum_{a \in A\ \|(f,a)\in MFA} ifa_{f,a,t} \cdot QA_{a,t} \cdot EXP\left(\ln\left(\dfrac{QA_{a,t}}{QA_{a,t-1}}\right)\right)\Bigg\|_{f\,\in FCAPGOVSER}$ $+\left(\left(1+\displaystyle\sum_{c \in C} qg01_{f,c,t} \cdot \overline{QGGRWC}_{c,t}\right) \cdot QFINS_{gov,f,t}\right)\Bigg\|_{f\,\in FCAPGOVINF}$ $-QFINS_{gov,f,t} \cdot (1-depr_{f,t})$ $(b)\ DKGOV_{f,t} \geq 0$ $(c)\ \left(DKGOV_{f,t} - DKGOVDEM_{f,t}\right) \cdot \left(DKGOV_{f,t} - 0\right) = 0$ where $DKGOVDEM_{f,t}$ = right-hand of part *(a)* of Equation 45 $\left[\begin{array}{l}\textit{Complementary slackness relationship}: \\ \textit{1. If government investment exceeds its demand then this investment level is zero.} \\ \textit{2. If the government investment level is above zero, then it equals its demand.}\end{array}\right]$	$f \in$ *FCAPGOV* $t \in T$ $t > 1$
(46)	$DKINS_{gov,f,t} = DKGOV_{f,t}$	$f \in$ *FCAPGOV* $t \in T$ $t > 1$
(47)	$PK_{f,t} = \displaystyle\sum_{c \in C} capcomp_{c,f} \cdot PQ_{c,t}$	$f \in FCAP$ $t \in T$
(48)	$\displaystyle\sum_{f \in FCAPGOV} PK_{f,t} \cdot DKINS_{gov,f,t} = GSAV_t - \displaystyle\sum_{c \in C} PQ_{c,t} \cdot qdst_{c,gov,t} + \overline{GBORTOT}_t$ $+\overline{GBORMSTOT}_t + \left(\overline{FBOR}_{gov,t} + \overline{FGRANT}_{gov,t}\right) \cdot EXR_t$	$t \in T$
(49)	$GBOR_{i,t} = \dfrac{gbdist_i \cdot INSSAV_{i,t}}{\displaystyle\sum_{i' \in INSDNG'} gbdist_{i'} \cdot INSSAV_{i',t}} \cdot \overline{GBORTOT}_t$	$i \in$ *INSDNG* $t \in T$
(50)	$GBORMS_{i,t} = \dfrac{gbdist_i \cdot INSSAV_{i,t}}{\displaystyle\sum_{i' \in INSDNG'} gbdist_{i'} \cdot INSSAV_{i',t}} \cdot \overline{GBORMSTOT}_t$	$i \in$ *INSDNG* $t \in T$
(51)	$INVVAL_{i,t} = INSSAV_{i,t} - \displaystyle\sum_{c \in C} PQ_{c,t} \cdot qdst_{c,i,t} - GBOR_{i,t}$ $-GBORMS_{i,t} + \left(\overline{FBOR}_{i,t} + \overline{FGRANT}_{i,t} + fdi_{i,t}\right) \cdot EXR_t$	$i \in INSNG$ $t \in T$

Table A3.2   (cont'd)

#	Equation	Domain
Investment block		
(52)	$$PK_{f,t} \cdot DKINS_{i,f,t} = gfcfshr_{f,i,t} \cdot INVVAL_{i,t}$$	$i \in INSNG$ $f \in FCAP$ $t \in T$
(53)	$$QINV_{c,t} = \sum_{f \in FCAP} \left(capcomp_{c,f} \cdot \sum_{i \in INS} DKINS_{i,f,t} \right)$$	$c \in C$ $t \in T$
(54)	$$\sum_{c \in CM} pwm_{c,t} \cdot QM_{c,t} + \frac{\sum_{f \in F} YIF_{row,f,t}}{EXR_t} + \frac{\sum_{i \in INSDNG} TRII_{row,i,t}}{EXR_t}$$ $$+ trnsfr_{row,gov,t} + \sum_{i \in INSD} fintrat_{i,t} \cdot FDEBT_{i,t}$$ $$= \sum_{c \in CE} \overline{PWE}_{c,t} \cdot QE_{c,t} + \sum_{i \in INSDNH} trnsfr_{i,row,t} + \sum_{h \in H} trnsfrpc_{h,row,t} \cdot \overline{POP}_{h,t}$$ $$+ \sum_{f \in F} trnsfr_{f,row,t} + \sum_{i \in INSD} \left(\overline{FBOR}_{i,t} + \overline{FGRANT}_{i,t} \right) + fdi_{row,t}$$	$t \in T$
(55)	$$\sum_{a \in A} QF_{f,a,t} = \left(1 - UERAT_{f,t} \right) \cdot \sum_{i \in INS} QFINS_{i,f,t}$$	$f \in F$ $t \in T$
(56)	$$WFRES_{f,t} = WF_f^0 \cdot \left(\frac{QHPC_t}{QHPC^0} \right)^{\varphi_f^{wfqhpc}} \cdot \left(\frac{\left(1 - UERAT_{f,t} \right)}{\left(1 - UERAT_f^0 \right)} \right)^{\varphi_f^{wferat}} \cdot \left(\frac{CPI_t}{CPI^0} \right)^{\varphi_f^{wfcpi}}$$	$f \in$ $FUEND$ $t \in T$
(57)	(a) $WF_{f,t} \geq WFRES_{f,t}$ (b) $UERAT_{f,t} \geq ueratmin_{f,t}$ (c) $\left(WF_{f,t} - WFRES_{f,t} \right) \cdot \left(UERAT_{f,t} - ueratmin_{f,t} \right) = 0$ $\big[$*Complementary slackness relationship* : 1. *If wage exceeds reservation wage then unemployment rate is at its minimum.* 2. *If unemployment rate exceeds its minimum, then wage equals reservation wage.* $\big]$	$f \in$ $FUEND$ $t \in T$
Asset stock updating and productivity block		
(58)	$$QQ_{c,t} = \sum_{a \in A} QINT_{c,a,t} + \sum_{h \in H} QH_{c,h,t} + QG_{c,t} + QINV_{c,t} + \sum_{i \in INS} qdst_{c,i,t} + QT_{c,t}$$	$c \in C$ $t \in T$

Table A3.2   (cont'd)

#	Equation	Domain
(59)	$QFINS_{i,f,t} = (1 - depr_{f,t-1}) \cdot QFINS_{i,f,t-1} + DKINS_{i,f,t-1} + qfinsadj_{i,f,t-1}$	$i \in INS$ $f \in FCAP$ $t \in T$ $t > 1$
(60)	$FDEBT_{i,t} = FDEBT_{i,t-1} + FBOR_{i,t-1}$ $+ \left(fintratdue_{i,t-1} - fintrat_{i,t-1} \right) \cdot FDEBT_{i,t-1} - fdebtrelief_{i,t-1}$	$i \in INSD$ $t \in T$ $t > 1$
(61)	$GDEBT_{i,t} = GDEBT_{i,t-1} + GBOR_{i,t-1}$	$i \in$ $INSDNG$ $t \in T$ $t > 1$
(63)	$GDPREAL_t = \sum_{c \in C} \sum_{h \in H} PQ_c^0 \cdot QH_{c,h,t} + \sum_{a \in A} \sum_{c \in C} \sum_{h \in H} PXAC_{a,c}^0 \cdot QHA_{a,c,h,t}$ $+ \sum_{c \in C} PQ_c^0 \cdot QG_{c,t} + \sum_{c \in C} PQ_c^0 \cdot QINV_{c,t} + \sum_{c \in C} \sum_{i \in INS} PQ_c^0 \cdot qdst_{c,i,t}$ $+ \sum_{c \in CE} EXR^0 \cdot PWE_c^0 \cdot QE_{c,t} - \sum_{c \in CM} EXR^0 \cdot PWM_c^0 \cdot QM_{c,t}$	$t \in T$
(64)	$ALPHAVA_{a,t} = ALPHAVA2_{a,t} \cdot \prod_{f \in FCAP} \left[\dfrac{\sum_{i \in INS} QFINS_{i,f,t}}{\sum_{i \in INS} QFINS_{i,f}^0} \right]^{tfpelasqg_{a,f,t}}$ $\cdot \left(\dfrac{\sum_{t \in T} tfptrdwt_{t,t'} \cdot TRDGDP_{t'}}{TRDGDP^0} \right)^{tfpelastrd_a}$	$a \in A$ $t \in T$ $t > 1$
(65)	$ALPHAVA2_{a,t} = ALPHAVA2_{a,t-1} \cdot \left(1 + \alpha vag_{a,t} + \overline{CALTFPG}_t \cdot tfp01_{a,t} \right)$	$a \in A$ $t \in T$ $t > 1$
(66)	$GDPREALFC_t = \sum_{a \in A} PVA_a^0 \cdot \left(1 - tva_{a,t}^0 \right) \cdot QVA_{a,t}$	$t \in T$

Table A3.3   Notation for MDG module of MAMS model

Symbol	Explanation
SETS	
$a \in A$	activities
$b \in B$	student behavioural characteristics ={rep = repeater; dropout = dropout; pass = pass; grdcont = continuing graduate; grdexit = exiting graduate; glentry = entrant to grade 1; grdcyc= pass from last cycle-year; contcyc = pass within cycle}
$b \in BLOG\ (\subset B)$	student behaviour determined by logistic function ={pass, grdcont, glentry}
$b \in BRES\,(\subset B)$	student behaviour determined by residual scaling ={rep = repeater; dropout = dropout; grdexit = exiting graduate}
$c \in C$	commodities
$c \in CEDU\,(\subset C)$	education services ={c-edup = primary; c-edus = secondary; c-edut = tertiary}; can include both private and public education
$c \in CEDUT\,(\subset C)$	tertiary education services = {c-edut}
$c \in CELA$	educational cycle that corresponds to the age at which non-students would enter the labour force
$c \in CHLTH\,(\subset C)$	health services (public) ={c-hlt1g = low-tech; c-hlt2g = medium-tech; c-hlt3g = high-tech}; corresponding private health services labelled with "ng"
$cmdg \in CMDG$	aggregate MDG (non-education) service commodities = {c-hlt = aggregate health in MDG functions, not in C; c-wtsn = water-sanitation services}
$c \in CWTSN\ (\subset C)$	water-sanitation service commodities{c-wtsn = water-sanitation services}
$eduarg \in EDUARG$	arguments in CE function for educational behaviour ={edu-qual = quantity of services per student; w-prem = semiskilled-unskilled wage ratio; w-prem2 = skilled-semiskilled wage ratio; mdg4 = under-five mortality rate; fcapinf = infrastructure capital stocks; qhpc = per-capita hhd consumption}
$f \in FEXOG$	factors with exogenous growth
$f \in FLAB$	labour factors {f-labn = less than completed secondary education; f-labs = complete secondary education (without completed tertiary); f-labt = completed tertiary education
$h \in H$	households (excl. NGOs) ={h = the single household}
$i \in INSG$	government institution
$i \in INSNGAGG$	aggregate (domestic) non-government institution

Table A3.3 (cont'd)

Symbol	Explanation
$b,b' \in MBB$	mapping between b (in BRES) and b' (in BLOG): ={(rep, dropout).grd, grdexit.grdcont}
$b,b' \in MBB2$	mapping between b (in BRES) and all elements b' (also in BRES) that are related to the same element(s) in BLOG: ={rep.(rep, dropout), dropout.(rep, dropout), grdexit.grdexit}
$c,c' \in MCE$	mapping private and public education into 1 education commodity, by cycle = {c-edup.(c-edup, c-edupng)} where c-edupng is private primary;similarly for c-edus and c-edut
$c,c' \in MCHDC$	human development service c is aggregated to c'
$c,c' \in MCM$	mapping between aggregate (CMDG) and disaggregated MDG service commodities (CHLTH and CWTSN) = {c-hlt.(c-hlt1g, c-hlt2g, c-hlt3g, c-hlt1ng, c-hlt2ng, c-hlt3ng} and {c-wtsn.(c-wtsn)}
$mdg \in MDG$	selected MDG indicators ={mdg2, mdg4, mdg5, mdg7a, mdg7b}
$mcyc(c,b,t',t)$	MDG2 in t is defined as the product over selected combinations of b and t' (where $t' \in T11$) = {pass, glentry}
$mdg \in MDGSTD$	MDG indicators ={mdg4 = under-5 mortality rate; mdg5 = maternal mortality rate; mdg7a = access to safe water; mdg7b = access to basic sanitation}
$f,c \in MFC$	mapping indicating that students who have completed cycle c belong to labour type f ={f-labn.(c-edup); f-labs.(c-edus); f-labt.(c-edut)}
$mdgarg \in MDGARG$	arguments in CE function for MDGs ={cmdg = agg commodities; mdg = different MDGs; fcapinf = infrastructure capital stocks; hhdconspc = per-capita hhd consumption }
$t \in T$	time periods
$t \in T11$	time periods including preceding years for MDG2 calculation

PARAMETERS

Symbol	Explanation
$\alpha edu_{b,c}$	constant in logistic function for educational behaviour
$\alpha educe_{b,c}$	constant in CE function for educational behaviour
αmdg_{mdg}	constant in logistic function for MDG achievement
αmce_{mdg}	constant in CE function for intermediate MDG variable
αhd_{c}	efficiency term in CES aggregation function for human development
$\beta edu_{b,c}$	constant in logistic function for educational behaviour

Table A3.3   (cont'd)

Symbol	Explanation
βlog_{mdg}	constant in logistic function for MDG achievement
$\delta hd_{c,i}$	share parameter for HD CES function
$\varphi edu_{b,c,eduarg}$	elasticity of behaviour b in cycle c with respect to argument eduarg in educational CE function
$\varphi m_{mdg,mdgarg}$	elasticity of mdg with respect to argument mdgarg in CE function for MDG
$\gamma edu_{b,c}$	parameter in logistic function for education
γmdg_{mdg}	parameter in logistic function for non-education MDGs
ρhd_c	exponent in CES aggregation function for human development
$depr_{f,t}$	depreciation rate for factor f
$discrat$	discount rate
$extedu_{b,c}$	maximum share for educational behaviour b in cycle c
$extmdg_{mdg}$	maximum value for MDG 7a and 7b; minimum value for MDG 4 and 5
$grdcont01_{c,c'}$	0-1 constant showing that for c' next cycle is c
ord_t	ordinal position of t in the set T
$popg1_t$	population in age cohort entering grade 1
$poplab_t$	population of labour force age
$poplabent_t$	population in age cohort entering labour force (age at end of a model education cycle)
$poptot_t$	total population in t
$qg1entncoh_{c,t}$	number of non-cohort (non-1st-year-primary) entrants to first cycle
$shif^0_{i,f,t}$	share of domestic institution i in income of factor f
$shrdemot01_{c,c'}$	0-1 parameter showing that for dropouts from c' the highest cycle is c
$shred^0_{b,c}$	base-year share for behavioural indicator behav in cycle c
$shrgrdcyc_c$	share of graduates (passing students) graduating from cycle c in base-year

Table A3.3 (cont'd)

Symbol	Explanation
$shrlabent_{c,t}$	share of drop-outs and leavers in cycle c that enter the labour force
$shrlabent2_{f,t}$	share of labour type f of labour force entrants without education
$yrcyc_c$	years in school cycle for each education cycle c
VARIABLES	
$EDUQUAL_{c,t}$	educational quality in cycle c in year t
EG_t	government expenditures
$INVVAL_{i,t}$	investment value for institution i
$MDGVAL_{mdg,t}$	value for MDG indicator mdg in t
$PQ_{c,t}$	price of commodity c in t
$PXAC_{a,c,t}$	price of commodity c from activity a
$QENR_{c,t}$	total number of students enrolled in cycle c in year t
$QENROLD_{c,t}$	number of old students enrolled in cycle c in year t
$QENRNEW_{c,t}$	number of new students enrolled in cycle c in year t
$QFACINS_{i,f,t}$	endowment of labour type f for institution i in t
$QH_{c,h,t}$	consumption of commodity c in t by household h
$QHA_{a,c,h,t}$	quantity consumed of home commodity c from activity a by household h
$QHPC_t$	Per-capita household consumption in t
$QQ_{c,t}$	quantity of goods supplied to domestic market (composite supply)
$QXHLTH_{mdg,t}$	government and NGO provision of aggregated health services related to health MDG
$SHREDU_{b,c,t}$	share of students in cycle c with behaviour b in t
$WF_{f,t}$	economy-wide wage for factor f in t
$ZEDU_{b,c,t}$	intermediate variable for educational outcome (defined by CE function; entering logistic function)
$ZMDG_{mdg,t}$	intermediate variable for standard MDGs (4-5-7a-7b) (defined by CE function; entering logistic function)

Table A3.4   Equations for MDG module of MAMS model

#	Equation	Domain
(67)	$$QHD_{c,i,t} = \sum_{\substack{c'\in C \\ |(c,c')\in MCHDC \\ \cup\, |i\in INSG}} QGc',t + \sum_{\substack{c'\in C \\ |(c,c')\in MCHDC \\ \cup\, |i\in INSNGAGG}} \left(QQc',t - QGc',t\right)$$	$c \in C$ $i \in I$ $t \in T$
(68)	$$QHDAGG_{c,t} = \alpha_{hd_c} \cdot \sum_{i\in INS}\left(\delta_{hd_{c,i}} \cdot QHD_{c,i,t}^{-\rho_{hd_c}}\right)^{-\frac{1}{\rho_{hd_c}}}\Bigg|_{c\in CHDCES} + \sum_{i\in INS} QHDc,i,t\Bigg|_{c\in CHDPRFSUB}$$	$c \in C$ $i \in I$ $t \in T$
(69)	$$QHPC_t = \frac{\sum_{c\in C}\sum_{h\in H} PQ_c^0 \cdot QH_{c,h,t} + \sum_{a\in A}\sum_{c\in C}\sum_{h\in H} PXAC_{a,c}^0 \cdot QHA_{a,c,h,t}}{poptot_t}$$	$t \in T$
(70)	$$EDUQUAL_{c,t} = \frac{QHDAGGc,t}{QENR_{c,t}} \bigg/ \frac{QHDAGG_c^0}{QENR_c^0}$$	$c \in CEDU$ $t \in T$ $t > 1$
(71)	$$QENROLD_{c,t} = SHREDU_{contcyc,c,t-1} \cdot QENR_{c,t-1} + SHREDU_{rep,c,t-1} \cdot QENR_{c,t-1}$$	$c \in CEDU$ $t \in T$ $t > 1$
(72)	$$QENRNEW_{c,t} = SHREDU_{glentry,c,t-1} \cdot popgl_t + qglentncoh_{c,t} + \sum_{c'\in C} grdcont01_{c,c'} \cdot SHREDU_{grdcont,c,t-1} \cdot SHREDU_{grdcyc,c',t-1} \cdot QENR_{c',t-1}$$	$c \in CEDU$ $t \in T$ $t > 1$
(73)	$$QENR_{c,t} = QENROLD_{c,t} + QENRNEW_{c,t}$$	$c \in CEDU$ $t \in T$ $t > 1$
(74)	$$SHREDU_{b,c,t} = ext_{ed_{b,c}} + \frac{\alpha_{edu_{b,c}}}{1 + EXP\left(\gamma_{edu_{b,c}} + \beta_{edu_{b,c}} \cdot ZEDU_{b,c,t}\right)}$$	$b \in BLOG$ $c \in CEDU$ $t \in T$
(75)	$$ZEDU_{b,c,t} = \alpha_{educe_{b,c}} \cdot \left(EDUQUAL_{c,t}\right)^{\varphi edu_{b,c,edu-qual}} \cdot \left(\frac{WF_{f-labs,t}}{WF_{f-labn,t}}\right)^{\varphi edu_{b,c,w-prem}} \cdot \left(\frac{WF_{f-labt,t}}{WF_{f-labs,t}}\right)^{\varphi edu_{b,c,w-prem}} \cdot MDGVAL_{mdg4,t}^{\varphi edu_{b,c,mdg4}} \cdot \prod_{f\in FCAPGOVINF}\left(\sum_{i\in INS} QFINS_{i,f,t}\right)^{\varphi edu_{b,c,f}} \cdot QHPC_t^{\varphi edu_{b,c,qhpc}}$$	$b \in BLOG$ $c \in C$ $t \in T$

Table A3.4   (cont'd)

#	Equation	Domain
(76)	$$SHREDU_{b,c,t} = \left(1 - \sum_{\substack{b'\in BLOG \\ |(b,b')\in MBB}} SHREDU_{b',c,t}\right) \frac{SHREDU^0_{b,c}}{\displaystyle\sum_{\substack{b'\in BRES \\ |(b,b')\in MBB2}} SHREDU^0_{b',c}}$$	$b \in BRES$ $c \in CEDU$ $t \in T$
(77)	$$SHREDU_{grdcyc,c,t} = \frac{SHREDU_{pass,c,t}}{yrcyc_c} \cdot \left(\frac{shr_{grdcyc_c}}{\dfrac{1}{yrcyc_c}}\right)^{\frac{1-SHREDU_{pass,c,t}}{1-SHREDU^0_{pass,c}}}$$	$c \in CEDU$ $t \in T$
(78)	$$SHREDU_{contcyc,c,t} = SHREDU_{pass,c,t} - SHREDU_{grdcyc,c,t}$$	$c \in CEDU$ $t \in T$
(79)	$$MDGVAL_{mdg2,t} = \prod_{\substack{b\in B,\, t'\in T11 \\ |mcyc(c\text{-}edup1,b,t',t)}} SHREDU_{b,c\text{-}edup1,t'}$$	$t \in T$
(80)	$$LABPARTRAT_t = \frac{\displaystyle\sum_{\substack{i\in INS,\, f\in FLAB \\ |shif^0_{i,f,t}}} QFINS_{i,f,t}}{poplab_t - \displaystyle\sum_{c\in CELA} QENR_{c,t}} =$$	$t \in T$ $t > 1$ $flab \notin$ $FEXOG$
(81)	$$QFINS_{i,f,t} = shif^0_{i,f,t} \cdot \left\{\left(1 - depr_{f,t-1}\right) \cdot \sum_{i'\in INS} QFINS_{i',f,t-1}\right.$$ $$+ \sum_{\substack{c,c'\in C \\ }}\Bigg|_{\substack{(f,c)\in MFC \\ \cap c\notin CEDUT}} shrdemot01_{c,c'} \cdot shrlabent_{c,t}$$ $$\cdot SHREDU_{grdexit,c',t-1} \cdot SHREDU_{grdcyc,c,t-1} \cdot QENR_{c,t-1}$$ $$+ \sum_{c\in C}\Bigg|_{\substack{(f,c)\in MFC \\ \cap c\in CEDUT}} \left(shr_{labent_{c,t}} \cdot SHREDU_{grdcyc,c,t-1} \cdot QENR_{c,t-1}\right)$$ $$+ \sum_{c\in C}\Bigg|_{\substack{(f,c)\in MFC \\ \cap c\in CEDUT}} \left(shrlabent_{c,t} \cdot SHREDU"_{grdcyc",c,t-1} \cdot QENR_{c,t-1}\right)$$ $$\left. + shrlabent2_{f,t} \cdot \left(poplabent_t - \sum_{c\in CELA} QENRNEW_{c,t}\right)\right\}$$	$i \in INS$ $f \in FLAB$ $t \in T$ $t > 1$

Table A3.4   (cont'd)

#	Equation	Domain
(82)	$MDGVAL_{mdg,t} = extmdg_{mdg} + \dfrac{\alpha mdg_{mdg}}{1 + EXP\left(\gamma mdg_{mdg} + \beta mdg_{mdg} \cdot ZMDG_{mdg,t}\right)}$	$mdg \in$ MDGSTD $t \in T$
(83)	$ZMDG_{mdg,t} = \alpha_{mce}{}_{mdg} \cdot \left(\prod\limits_{cmdg \in CMDG}\left(\sum\limits_{\substack{c \in C \\ \|(cmdg,c) \in MCM}} \dfrac{QQ_{c,t}}{poptot_t}\right)^{\varphi m_{mdg,cmdg}}\right)$ $\cdot \prod\limits_{f \in FCAPGOVINF}\left(\sum\limits_{i \in INS} QFINS_{i,f,t}\right)^{\varphi m_{mdg,f}}$ $\cdot \left(\prod\limits_{mdg' \in MDGSTD} MDGVAL_{mdg',t}^{\varphi m_{mdg,mdg'}}\right) \cdot QHPC_t^{\varphi m_{mdg,hhdconspc}}$	$mdg \in$ MDGSTD $t \in T$

Acknowledgements

The authors would like to thank Martin Cicowiez for direct contributions to the development of MAMS and many other project participants, including the other coeditors, for valuable inputs into the adaptation of MAMS for LAC applications. Detailed comments from Rob Vos and Marco V. Sánchez on earlier versions led to significant improvements in this chapter.

Notes

1   A complementary, less comprehensive presentation of MAMS is found in Bourguignon and others (2008). Lofgren (2008) presents a simplified mathematical statement.

2   For more details, see Bourguignon and others (2008).

3   The starting point for the MDG module is the MDG model in Bourguignon and others (2004). All of these models are coded and solved in the General Algebraic Modeling System (GAMS).

4   The SAMs used in the country studies are invariably more disaggregated in three respects: (a) government activities, commodities and investment accounts are split by government function; (b) the interest account is split into two, one for interest on domestic government debt and one for interest on foreign debts; and (c) the tax account is split into separate accounts for direct, import, export, value-added, and other domestic indirect taxes (of course, in some of the applications, some of these tax types may not exist). In contexts outside this project, MAMS has also been implemented without the MDG-education module.

5   The SAM (and MAMS) may also include accounts and entries representing home consumption and transactions costs associated with the commodity marketing (of imports from the border to the demander; of exports from the producer to the border; and of

domestic output for domestic sales). For a more detailed discussion of the treatment of these aspects of the SAM, see Lofgren and others (2002, pp. 3-7).

6   In addition to the current entries, it is not uncommon that the government owns part of the capital stock and earns part of operating surplus.

7   Given this assumption, it is not necessary to model how the endowments and investments of different institutions (households, government and the rest of the world) are allocated across different private capital types (perhaps disaggregated by sector); this is a key advantage given limited knowledge of the mechanisms that determine the evolution of this distribution over time.

8   MAMS does not separate enterprises from other domestic institutions. In the SAM, these would have been linked to factors (enterprises receive factor incomes, reflecting their ownership of non-labour factors), "other" institutions (direct tax payments and transfers reflecting institutional ownership of the enterprise) and enterprise capital accounts (which spend on investments). In the country databases, these "other" institutions (primarily households) directly receive the factor transfers while assuming the savings and direct tax payments that otherwise would have been done by the enterprises. Other SAM payments are not affected.

9   The SAM and MAMS may also include direct taxes levied on factor incomes (represented by payments from factor accounts to the tax account).

10   To verify these statements and for more details, see Agénor (2004, pp. 11-22), Rao and Nallari (2001, pp. 25-32, 176 and 168), and Barth and Hemphill (2000, pp. 71-74 and 101-106).

11   For example, in Table A3.2, the domain column of equation 1 shows that this equation does not apply to all commodities; it is limited to commodities with imports.

12   Apart from the fact that variables are time-indexed, most of the core CGE module is similar to the IFPRI standard, static CGE model described in Lofgren and others (2002).

13   In GAMS, a model formulated as an MCP (mixed-complementarity programme) can handle a combination of equations that are (a) strict equalities; and (b) inequalities linked to variables with lower limits in a mixed-complementarity relationship.

14   The GAMS code permits the user to choose either the CPI or the price index for non-tradables as *numéraire*. As long as the model is homogeneous of degree zero in prices, this choice has no impact on the equilibrium values of real variables. This homogeneity condition is not met under macro closures with fixed savings or domestic borrowing for the government. In these cases, it is implicitly assumed that the fixed variables are indexed to the *numéraire*.

15   Some of the country applications include a private regulated sector (typically a utility) for which behaviour deviates from the assumption of profit-maximizing output and input demand (including capital use) given market prices and rents. Each regulated activity has its own capital stock -- otherwise, there is only one private capital stock, which is mobile across private activities. For regulated activities, output prices, investment and capital use are exogenous; production is demand-driven at fixed output prices. Their capital stocks earn an endogenous, residual share of value-added which most likely deviates from the market rent; other factors earn market wages.

16   MAMS also permits the alternative of a CES aggregation of the real aggregates of value-added and intermediates. The choice does not tend to have a major impact on results. Most country studies used the Leontief alternative.

17   Nevertheless, the model accounts for the fact that government capital stocks indeed are needed in government activities by imposing investments derived from a Leontief-relationship between government activity levels and related capital stocks, with the stocks

being defined on the basis of initial stocks, investment and depreciation (see equation 45). In the exceptional cases when the SAM indicates that government capital earns value-added, this value-added is a fixed share of the total value-added of the activity (in effect equivalent to a tax on value-added), not related to any market rent.

18 $QGGRW_t$ (a term for government consumption growth that is not commodity-specific) is flexed if the absorption share of total government consumption is fixed. $QGGRWC_{c,t}$ (a term for government consumption growth that is commodity-specific) is flexed when some target influenced by this specific government service (c) is fixed for year t. For the most straightforward case, $qg01_{c,c',t}$, a parameter for mapping one c to another, is 1 when $c = c'$ and zero otherwise. If the analyst wants one or more kinds of government consumption to grow in tandem with another, more than one c may have a value of 1 for any given c'. In either case, each c is linked to only one c'.

19 Among these, only part *(a)* is an explicit equation in the GAMS code. The non-negativity constraint on *DKGOV* is handled via a lower limit on this variable. The complementary-slackness condition is imposed by associating the first equation *(a)* to the *DKGOV* variable in the GAMS model definition.

20 In GAMS, the treatment is more general, giving the user the option to assume that the rate of expected output growth is the same as the rate of simulated output growth during the last 1, 2 or 3 years.

21 For public infrastructure, actual *QG* (government service level) is determined by the current capital stock (see equation 43). In equation 45, the exogenous growth variable $QGGRWC_{c,t}$ (which is defined over c, where the relevant c may be public infrastructure services) is mapped to the capital stock f associated with c and drives the expansion in the capital stock.

22 The savings shares are adjusted by a distortion term (*gbdisti*) that reflects deviations between household shares of government borrowing and savings. Implicitly, the burden of monetary system borrowing is felt by other agents since it extracts real purchasing power from them by reducing the value of the old money that they hold. In the absence of an explicit treatment of money in this model, this burden is allocated across households on the basis of their savings shares.

23 Typically, the model will only have one private capital stock, that is, the value of the share parameter is unity for this capital type. If the model has more than one private capital stock, the allocation between the different stocks may be endogenized, possibly deviating from the base-level allocation in response to changes in relative profit rates, a relationship that would need to be specified in one or more additional equations.

24 Implicitly, an additional system constraint, the savings-investment balance, also holds: by channelling domestic savings and the terms that make up foreign savings to investment, the model equations assure that total savings and total investment are equal.

25 The level of the base-year unemployment rate relative to the minimum unemployment rate indicates the potential for employment growth over and above the growth rate of the labour stock.

26 In applications with multiple households, it was necessary to specify how the population in each household evolves over time. Our general principle was that the household types that exist in the base-year (characterized by patterns for generation and spending of incomes) continue to exist but grow at different rates depending on the types of labour that they control. The non-labour endowments of each household type grow at the same rate as its population, scaled upwards or downwards to ensure that the total for these endowments across all households respect economy-wide constraints.

27 When developing the model base run, *CALTFPG* may be endogenous or exogenous. If it is endogenous, real GDP (at factor cost) should be fixed (growing exogenously

over time). If so, the analyst should review the resulting economy-wide growth in TFP as well as efficiency growth in different activities ($ALPHAVA_{a,t}$) and, if needed, adjust the targeted real GDP levels. On the other hand, if $CALTFPG$ is exogenous (and real GDP endogenous), the analyst should monitor overall GDP growth and, if needed, adjust either $CALTFPG$ or $avag$. The estimates of initial capital stocks and depreciation rates may also have to be revisited. For non-base runs, the determinants of trend TFP growth ($ALPHAVA2$) are typically fixed, while real GDP growth is determined by growth in factor employment and endogenous TFP changes.

28   It would also be possible to include the effects of improved health on the productivity of labour (with these effects disaggregated by labour type and activity). These were not considered in the country studies for lack of estimates of the quantitative relationship.

29   Implicitly, when MDGs 4 and 5 are achieved, the expansion in health services and other determinants may be sufficient to achieve MDG 6 (to halt and reverse the spread of HIV/AIDS, malaria and other diseases). MDG 3 (elimination of gender disparity in education and empowering women) was not addressed due to data issues. However, note that, if MDG 2 is achieved, gender equality is achieved in primary education.

30   The country studies of this volume show that the relationships between the determinants and the non-poverty MDGs in the MAMS model hold from a statistical point of view for a number of Latin American and Caribbean countries. Kamaly (2006) provides examples of the literature on health and education whose findings, although sometimes contradictory, show broad support also in sub-Saharan Africa for the inclusion of the determinants referred to in Table 3.3.

31   This category includes non-cohort entrants to the 1st primary year of primary school (who may represent a significant number during a transitional period of primary school expansion). It may also include immigrants from other countries.

32   The equation is formulated so that it works for cases with one or more than one term in any of the sums over related shares (defined by the mappings MBB and $MBB2$) in either of the sets $BRES$ and $BLOG$.

33   In other words, in order for 100 per cent of the cohort to complete the primary cycle on time, it is necessary that all of them enter at the time of their first year and that all manage to pass each year (that is, successfully complete each grade) up to the final year of the cycle. Given that we do not generate separate pass rates for students in the relevant cohort (as opposed to students outside this cohort), we assume that the rates for in-cohort students are identical to the over-all rates for students in the cycle.

34   It is assumed that, as an acceptable approximation, students in secondary and above are in labour force age. If not, this definition should be adjusted.

35   A SAM for the core (non-MDG) version of MAMS deviates from this in that may have a very aggregate treatment of sectors (activities and commodities), factors and institutions. The minimum degree of detail is two sectors (private and government); two factors (labour and private capital), three institutions (government, household and rest of world), two investment accounts (private and government capital).

36   For the 18 country studies, the base year falls within the period 2000-2005, that is, approximately at the mid-point between the starting year on the basis of which many MDG targets are defined, 1990, and the target year, 2015.

37   The following formula is used to define the base-year private capital stock: $qfcap = samrent/(netprfrat + deprrat)$ where $qfcap$ = the stock; $samrent$ = total VA to private capital in SAM; $netprfrat$ = the net profit rate (in decimal form); $deprrat$ = the depreciation rate (also in decimal form).

38   The micro-simulation approach to poverty and inequality analysis that was followed in the different country studies requires access to a recent household survey.

References

Agénor, Pierre-Richard (2004). *The Economics of Adjustment and Growth*. Second Edition. Cambridge: Harvard University Press.

__________, Nihal Bayraktar, Emmanuel Pinto Moreira and Karim El Aynaoui (2005). "Achieving the Millennium Development Goals in Sub-Saharan Africa: A Macroeconomic Monitoring Framework," *Policy Research Working Paper*, 3750. World Bank, Washington, DC.

Barth, Richard, and William Hemphill (2000). *Financial Programming and Policy: The Case of Turkey*. IMF Institute, International Monetary Fund.

Bourguignon, François, Maurizio Bussolo, Luiz A. Pereira da Silva, Hans Timmer and Dominique van der Mensbrugghe (2004). "MAMS—MAquette for MDG Simulations: a simple Macro-Micro Linkage Model for Country-Specific Modeling of the Millennium Development Goals or MDGs," Mimeo, World Bank.

__________, Carolina Diaz-Bonilla and Hans Lofgren (2008). "Aid, Service Delivery and the Millennium Development Goals in an Economywide Framework," pp. 283-315 in eds. François Bourguignon, Maurizio Bussolo, and Luiz Pereira da Silva, *The impact of Macroeconomic policies on Poverty and Income Distribution: Macro-Micro Evaluation Techniques and Tools*. Washington, D.C.: World Bank.

Christiaensen, Luc, Christopher Scott and Quentin Wodon (2002). "Development Targets and Costs," pp. 131-155 and 463-470 in ed. Jeni Klugman. *A Sourcebook for Poverty Reduction Strategies*. World Bank, Washington, D.C.

Clemens, Michael A., Charles J. Kenny and Todd J. Moss (2004). "The Trouble with the MDGs: Confronting Expectations of Aid and Development Success," Center for Global Development, Working Paper, No. 40, May, Washington, DC.

Devarajan, Shantayanan, Margaret J. Miller and Eric V. Swanson (2002). "Goals for Development: History, Prospects and Costs," World Bank Policy Research Working Paper, 2819, April.

Kamaly, Ahmed (2006). "An Econometric Analysis of the Determinants of Health and Education Outcomes in sub-Saharan Africa" Mimeo. World Bank: Washington D.C.

Lofgren, Hans (2008). "Simplified Mathematical Statement for MAMS." Mimeo. World Bank: Washington D.C.

__________, Rebecca Lee Harris and Sherman Robinson, with assistance from Moataz El-Said and Marcelle Thomas (2002). *A Standard Computable General Equilibrium (CGE) Model in GAMS*. Microcomputers in Policy Research, Vol. 5. Washington, D.C.: IFPRI (http://www.ifpri.org/pubs/microcom/micro5.htm)

Pyatt, Graham, and Jeffrey Round (1985). *Social accounting matrices: A basis for planning,* Washington, D.C.: World Bank.

Rao, M.J. Manohar, and Raj Nallari (2001). *Macroeconomic Stabilization and Adjustment*. New Delhi: Oxford University Press.

Reddy, Sanjay, and Antoine Heuty (2004). "Achieving the MDGs: A Critique and a Strategy," Harvard Center for Population and Development Studies Working Paper Series, 14(3), August.

Reinert, K. A., and D. W. Roland-Holst (1997). "Social accounting matrices," in *Applied methods for trade policy analysis: A handbook*, ed. J. F. Francois and K. A. Reinert, New York: Cambridge University Press.

United Nations Development Programme (2005). Human Development Report 2005: International Cooperation at a Crossroads: Aid, Trade and Security in an Unequal World, Oxford University Press, New York.

United Nations Millennium Project (2005). Investing in Development: A Practical Plan to Achieve the Millennium Development Goals, United Nations Development Programme, Earthscan, New York, January.

Vandemoortele, Jan, and Rathin Roy (2004). "Making Sense of MDG Costing," Poverty Group, UNDP, mimeo, August, New York. http://www.undp.org/poverty/docs/making-sense-of-mdg-costing.pdf.

4
Argentina

Martin Cicowiez, Luciano Di Gresia and Leonardo Gasparini

Introduction

When the Millennium Development Goals (MDGs) were established in the early 1990s, achieving these in Argentina seemed a doable, though challenging enterprise. The fifteen years following 1990 (the reference year for the MDG targets) were characterized by great turbulence, with periods of growth, recession and profound social crisis. As a consequence, Argentina's progress towards the goals has been far from satisfactory. The stop-go growth process did not lead to setbacks in improvements in primary education, children's health and basic sanitation, but progress in these areas has been rather modest. Progress towards MDG 1 (the eradication of extreme poverty and hunger) has been more dismal and income poverty has increased substantially since 1990. The target of halving extreme poverty between 1990 and 2015 seemed reachable in the early 1990s, but now has a low probability of being achieved.

Whether Argentina can make more rapid progress towards achieving all MDGs will depend, to a considerable extent, on public spending efforts. Resources for education, health and basic sanitation, among others, will need to be scaled up in order to achieve the MDGs. This chapter will analyze the impact of public policies of enhancing resources for the achievement of the MDGs in Argentina. The analysis revolves primarily around results generated from the use of the computable general equilibrium (CGE) model called MAMS, which is described in Chapter 3. By combining the application of MAMS with a microsimulation methodology explained in Chapter 2 (see Appendix A2.1), the impact of the expansion of basic social services on poverty and inequality is estimated. The CGE model incorporates equations that specify the determinants of MDGs achievement and links these to public expenditure. The model also makes it possible to estimate the impact that increased public spending for the MDGs will have on the rest of the economy. The modelling framework also captures the synergies that can be generated when more than one goal is reached at the same time; for example, how the reduction of under-five mortality rates (MDG 4) increases attendance in primary schools (MDG 2). All these issues are analyzed in the remainder of this chapter for the case of Argentina.

The next section describes recent socio-economic trends in Argentina. The country's prospects of reaching the MDGs in the areas of education, under-five child mortality and water and sanitation are discussed in the third section, showing the gaps between the MDG indicators and their respective targets established for 2015. The fourth section presents a brief description of how the CGE model is implemented and calibrated to Argentine data. In addition to other information, key ingredients in the estimation of the model for Argentina are the parameters that quantify the relationships between determinants and outcomes in education, health and basic sanitation. Because of the importance of these determinants in the analysis, the subsequent section is dedicated to introducing and discussing the econometric estimates of these relationships. The next two sections are the central focus of the chapter. Using the CGE model, the first analyzes a baseline scenario which determines whether or not the targets associated with MDGs 2, 4, and 7 would be reached by 2015 under "business-as-usual" assumptions for growth of the economy and public expenditures. Alternative policy scenarios are subsequently considered in order to determine the amount of public spending that would be required to achieve the goals and the various mechanisms that could be used to finance that spending. How that spending and its financing affect the economy at large is also analyzed. In the other section, the microsimulation analysis will be used to determine to what extent the general equilibrium effects of the MDG scenarios on labour market outcomes translate into sufficient progress towards the target for poverty reduction (MDG 1). Finally, the last section 4.8 summarizes the main conclusions and policy recommendations.

Argentina: a turbulent economy

Argentina's economic performance has been dismal in recent decades. Not only has the economy been unable to grow at sustained rates for any prolonged period, but it has also suffered recurring crises (see Figure 4.1). As a result, the level of per capita GDP does not differ substantially from that reached in the early 1980s. In fact, the average rate of growth between 1980 and 2004 was -0.1 per cent per year.

Indicators presented in Table 4.1 also show the high degree of volatility of the economy and lack of consistent growth trends. The 1980s, in particular, were very rocky. The first years of the decade, under de facto governments, were characterized by domestic financial crises on top of the external debt crisis of 1982. The democratic government that took power in 1983 faced a persistent fiscal deficit that caused an upward inflationary spiral, culminating in hyperinflation in 1989 and 1990. The view that the 1980s was a "lost decade" for economic

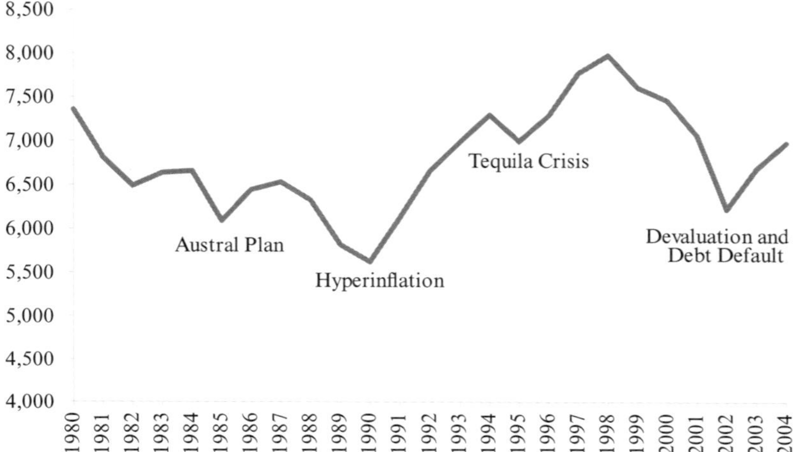

Figure 4.1 Argentina: per capita GDP at constant prices, 1980-2004
Source: International Monetary Fund (IMF).

development in Latin America applies most in particular to Argentina. While the Latin American economies shrank on average by 0.9 per cent per year (in terms of real GDP per capita), Argentina's income per capita fell by 2.6 per cent per year, according to IMF data.

During the 1990s, Argentina could benefit from a more favourable external environment and was beginning to surmount a deep crisis by implementing a series of macroeconomic and structural reforms. The reforms included the "Convertibility Law" that tied the peso to the US dollar, a large-scale privatization programme, further trade liberalization and a policy of deregulation. These measures helped to control inflation and invigorate the economy. However, the economic restructuring this induced also led to a significant reduction in the demand for unskilled labour. In the 1990s, workers with low- and medium-level skills saw their employment opportunities reduced considerably, along with reductions in job quality in terms of lower real wages, social protection and job security.

Argentina's economic vulnerability manifested itself towards the end of the decade. Fears of default on public debt payments and of exchange-rate devaluation mounted and added to existing institutional weaknesses in managing the economy. These and other factors weakened the banking system and led to a new economic crisis at the end of 2001. The year 2002 was characterized by a deep recession as per capita GDP fell by 12 per cent and poverty increased even more than during the episode of hyperinflation in the late 1980s. The new government began negotiations to restructure its debt, allowed a strong depreciation of the real exchange rate, and began a process of gradual rescue and recovery of the financial system.

Table 4.1   Argentina: key macroeconomic indicators, 1980-2004

Year	GDPpc	Cpr	Cpu	INV	TB	INFL[a] (%)	RER	UNEMP[b]
1980	7,357	65.1	12.5	24.7	-2.3	100.8	0.8	n.a.
1981	6,813	66.4	12.9	22.2	-1.6	104.5	1.1	n.a.
1982	6,489	66.8	13.2	18.3	1.6	164.8	2.1	5.3
1983	6,637	67.2	13.1	17.7	2.0	343.8	2.4	4.7
1984	6,656	68.4	13.4	16.6	1.6	626.7	2.0	4.6
1985	6,089	67.3	14.1	15.4	3.2	672.2	2.3	6.1
1986	6,442	68.8	13.5	15.9	1.7	90.1	2.2	5.6
1987	6,530	67.8	13.6	17.5	1.1	131.3	2.4	5.9
1988	6,325	66.4	13.8	17.2	2.5	343.0	2.5	6.3
1989	5,810	66.6	15.0	14.5	3.9	3.079.5	3.1	7.6
1990	5,614	67.1	15.2	12.3	5.4	2.314.0	2.2	7.5
1991	6,121	69.0	14.5	14.4	2.1	171.7	1.5	6.5
1992	6,660	70.2	14.0	17.5	-1.6	24.9	1.3	7.0
1993	6,983	69.2	13.5	19.1	-2.4	10.6	1.2	9.6
1994	7,293	69.4	12.8	20.5	-3.1	4.2	1.2	11.5
1995	6,994	68.3	13.3	18.3	-0.4	3.4	1.3	17.5
1996	7,286	68.3	12.9	18.9	-1.3	0.2	1.3	17.2
1997	7,778	68.8	12.3	20.6	-2.9	0.5	1.3	14.9
1998	7,977	68.6	12.2	21.1	-2.8	0.9	1.3	12.9
1999	7,610	69.6	13.0	19.1	-1.5	-1.2	1.1	14.3
2000	7,458	69.6	13.2	17.9	-1.2	-0.9	1.1	15.5
2001	7,059	68.7	13.5	15.8	0.9	-1.1	1.0	17.4
2002	6,217	66.0	14.4	11.3	7.3	25.9	2.3	19.7
2003	6,681	65.6	13.4	14.3	6.4	13.4	2.3	16.3
2004	6,966	65.9	12.6	17.7	4.8	4.4	2.3	13.2

Source: Ministry of the Economy, Centre for International Economics (CEI).
Abbreviations: GPDpc: Real per capita GDP (pesos); Cpr: Private consumption (% GDP); Cpu: Public consumption (% GDP); INV: Investment (% GDP); TB: Trade balance (% GDP); INFL: Inflation rate; RER: Real exchange rate (2001=1); UNEMP: Unemployment rate.
[a] Annual change in the consumer price index (CPI).
[b] Unemployed population as a percentage of the economically active population (EAP).
n.a.: data not available.

High export prices contributed to keeping the crisis from worsening and facilitated economic recovery. Nevertheless, by around 2006, public debt still amounted to about 66.7 per cent of Argentina's GDP, despite the recovery and recent debt negotiations.[1] The decline in real wages (including for public employees) following the currency devaluation was important for achieving a significant primary fiscal surplus, which helped contain inflationary expectations. The fiscal space created further allowed for the allocation of substantial public resources for the cash-transfer programme "Heads of Household" (*Programa Jefes de Hogar*) with large coverage among the population. From 2003, the economy recovered and showed robust growth till the global financial crisis of 2008.

Progress towards the MDGs in Argentina

Given the strong economic turbulence, the country has only made modest progress towards some of the Millennium Development Goals, but it has regressed with respect to others.

Rising poverty (MDG 1)

MDG 1 aims to eradicate extreme poverty and hunger. The target is to halve the percentage of the population with income under one dollar a day (valued at purchasing power parity (PPP)) between 1990 and 2015. The incidence of extreme poverty (using international or national poverty lines) is generally computed using information contained in household surveys. Poverty indicators for Argentina are calculated based on data from the Permanent Household Survey (EPH). It is important to indicate four methodological limitations when assessing poverty trends in Argentina:

- *The EPH only covers the urban population.* Hence the poverty estimates do not cover the total population, but given that 85 per cent of the Argentine population lives in urban areas, this may not be a major restriction.
- *Total household income as estimated by the EPH is not consistent with the national accounts.* Between 1992 and 2004, the annual growth rate for per capita GDP was 0.4 per cent while according to the EPH per capita household income fell by 2.9 per cent per year. This study does not settle these discrepancies, but rather coincides with Deaton (2003) and other authors who recommend the use of information as recorded in the surveys.
- *1990 is not a good year to use as a baseline for analysis.* In 1990, Argentina was immersed in one of its deepest economic crises (see Figure 4.1). Poverty was very high but started to fall soon thereafter (and to increase again later on). Thus, the prospects of reaching the goal for reducing extreme poverty in the case of Argentina changes significantly whether 1990 or some other year is used as the starting year. For instance, when using later years of greater economic stability as the reference, progress towards MDG 1 would look dramatically different. For this reason, this study uses 1992 as the starting year rather than the year of deep crisis.[2]
- *The dollar-a-day poverty line is not very relevant in the case of Argentina.* Being a middle-to-high income country, extreme poverty as measured through the international poverty line is relatively low and economic policy discussions tend to mostly address poverty measured through a poverty line of two dollars per person per day or through national (extreme and moderate) poverty lines.

Table 4.2 presents poverty trends according to four different poverty lines. The poverty incidence as measured through the two-dollars-a-day poverty line increased sharply from 4.2 per cent in 1992 to 14.2 per cent in 2004. Data from

Table 4.2   Argentina: poverty incidence according to different poverty lines, 1992-2004 (per cent of total population under given poverty line)

	1-dollar-a-day poverty line at PPP	2-dollars-a-day poverty line at PPP	National extreme poverty line	National moderate poverty line
1992	1.4	4.2	3.8	19.7
1998	3.4	9.4	8.2	30.1
2002	9.9	24.7	27.6	57.5
2004	5.2	14.2	15.0	40.2

Source: CEDLAS.

the Centre for Distributive, Labour and Social Studies (CEDLAS) of the National University of La Plata show that there has been a systematic increase in the incidence of moderate poverty (as measured through the national poverty line) since the early 1980s. This is the result of the combination of two factors: the stagnation of mean income and the increase in income inequality. As mentioned, mean per capita household income fell, on average, by 2.9 per cent per year during 1992 and 2004, according to the EPH data. Inequality increased substantially during the same period. The Gini coefficient of the distribution of per capita household income increased from 0.45 in 1992 to 0.51 in 2004; a rise in inequality unparalleled in Latin America.

Gasparini and others (2005) have determined that Argentina would have to maintain an annual rate of income growth of about 5 per cent through 2015 if it wants to half the incidence of moderate poverty from its 2004 value.[3] This would be an unprecedented performance, as Argentina's economy has never been able to sustain growth rates of 5 per cent per year for a whole decade. However, even if it could sustain this rate of growth it would not be sufficient to also reduce extreme poverty by 50 per cent as targeted through MDG 1. Income redistribution policies, therefore, may be needed to ensure meeting the target for poverty reduction, assuming such policies would not jeopardize economic growth. Politically viable income redistribution measures may not make a sufficiently large impact, however. For instance, in 2002 the government implemented one of Latin America's most ambitious cash transfer programmes, the "Heads of Household Programme", covering nearly 2 million families, but even with this programme in place, progress towards achieving the millennium goal of eradicating extreme poverty would not be enough.

Table 4.3 shows that when taking 1992 as the reference year and using the poverty line of two dollars a day, the poverty incidence would need to be reduced from 4.2 per cent to 2.1 per cent by 2015. This would not appear to be a very demanding target. In reality, however, poverty has moved in the opposite direction as by this measure it increased to 14.2 per cent in 2004. In other words, to meet the target of halving poverty between 1992 and 2015, a 12 percentage-points reduction would have to be achieved in just ten years. This

Table 4.3   Argentina: trends and targets of the MDG indicators

MDG-related Indicators	Initial Year		Base Year		Target	
	1990	**1992**	**2003**	**2004**	**2015**[a]	**2015**[b]
MDG 1: Eradicate extreme poverty						
Poverty incidence (1-dollar-a-day line at PPP)[c]	4.3	1.4	7.9	5.2	2.1	0.7
Poverty incidence (2-dollar-a-day line at PPP)[c]	11.6	4.2	23.7	14.2	5.8	2.1
MDG 2: Universal primary education						
Net enrolment rate[c]	97.5	98.0	99.3	99.2	100.0	100.0
Graduation rate (youth 15-24)[c]	95.4	95.6	96.4	96.0	100.0	100.0
Literacy rate (youth 15-24)[c]	99.1	99.1	99.3	n.a.	100.0	100.0
MDG 3: Promote gender equality						
Proportion of boys to girls in:						
gross enrolment rates for primary school	1.0	1.0	1.0	1.0	1.0	1.0
net enrolment rates for primary school	1.0	1.0	1.0	1.0	1.0	1.0
gross enrolment rates for secondary school	0.9	0.9	1.0	1.0	1.0	1.0
net enrolment rates for secondary school	0.9	0.9	1.0	1.0	1.0	1.0
MDG 4: Reduce mortality in children under five						
Under-five mortality rate (per 1,000 live births)	29.6	27.7	19.1	16.6	9.9	9.2
MDG 7: Guarantee environmental sustainability						
Goal 7a: Access to drinking water[c]						
Urban (EPH)	97.1	97.1	98.6	n.a.	98.6	98.5
National (Population Census)	92.2	92.2	92.9	92.9	96.1	96.1
National, public provisioning (Population Census)	65.1	67.3	78.4	79.7	82.5	83.7
Goal 7b: Access to basic sanitation[c,d]						
Urban (EPH)	87.8	87.8	87.7	n.a.	93.9	93.9
National (Census)	85.8	85.8	83.1	83.1	92.9	92.9
National (Census) (public system)	33.6	35.0	42.5	43.4	66.8	67.5

Source: National Population, Households and Housing Census (CNPV 1991 and 2001), PNUD (2006) and elaboration based on the EPH.
[a] With 1990 as initial year.
[b] With 1992 as initial year.
[c] Percentage of the population.
[d] Includes access to a button or chain flush toilet.

makes it unlikely that the target for MDG 1 can be met, in spite of the fact that the country has overcome the worst of the crisis of the early 2000s and gains in poverty reduction have been made since 2002.

Nearing the targets for MDG 2 and 3: education and gender equality

As Table 4.3 shows, by 2004 Argentina had already nearly met the target for MDG 2 of achieving universal primary education. Primary school attendance is nearly 100 per cent in urban areas. Only a very small group of children in poor families have not been able to access school. The graduation rates from primary school for youth between the ages of 15 and 24 are quite high (around 96 per cent) and are increasing gradually. Attendance rates did not fall significantly during the severe economic crisis of 2001-2002, which is an indication of the solidity of priority that parents give to the education of their children. Literacy rates are also at near 100 per cent levels.

Given that Argentina has practically reached the goal for universal primary education and complete literacy, education policies nowadays focus on other concerns, in particular on improving the quality of primary and secondary education and increasing access to secondary schooling and college education.

As Table 4.3 shows, the education gap for women (MDG 3) has been closed in Argentina. Most indicators suggest that the country has reached full gender equality for education, and some indicators even suggest that girls outperform boys in school attendance and performance, also at the secondary school level. This emerging gap for men is not considered a sign of discrimination, but rather the result of gender differences in opportunity costs and prospects of finding jobs in the labour market.

Slow progress towards targets in child health and basic sanitation (MDGs 4 and 7)

The child mortality rate (per 1,000 live births) has continued to decline during the past decades, despite the severe deterioration in incomes and living conditions of the poor (see Table 4.3). This result has been influenced primarily by the general progress in medicine, which has allowed substantial reductions in mortality all over the world. Greater coverage and access to potable water and sanitation services in some regions of the country have also been important factors (Galiani and others, 2005).

Under-five mortality rates dropped from 29.6 per 1,000 live births in 1990 to 16.6 in 2004. While the pattern has been positive, reducing this mortality rate further has now become more difficult since the numbers have reached relatively low levels. The target is to reduce it to 9.9 by 2015, which seems possible especially if the government is successful in providing the poorest groups with access to potable water, basic sanitation, basic health services and health education.

MDG 7, which seeks to ensure environmental sustainability, also includes targets related to basic services of potable water and sanitation. In the case of Argentina, the target is to reduce by half, between 1990 (or 1992) and 2015, the percentage of the population without access to both services (MDG 7a and 7b). A large share of the population already has access to drinking water in Argentina, in both urban and rural areas (see Table 4.3). It seems likely, therefore, that the country will reach the target for this goal by 2015, assuming past trends in expanding water and sanitation systems continue. Access to basic sanitation services (sewers) is more restricted. According to the population covered by the EPH, nearly 88 per cent of the urban population has access to a bathroom with the minimum sanitary requirements. The percentage of households connected to the public sewage system is less, however. The Population Census reports that while more than 80 per cent of the population has access to hygienic bathroom facilities, less than 50 per cent are connected to the public sewage system. Since progress in this area has been modest, achieving the target for basic sanitation is more challenging.

Social spending and the MDGs

Public social spending in Argentina has been strongly affected by the high economic volatility. Growth in social spending that has taken place since the early 1980s has been frequently interrupted, primarily by the deep economic crises (see panels (a) and (b) of Figure 4.3). Since the signing of the Millennium Declaration in 2000, the level of public social spending, both when measured as a percentage of GDP and in constant 1992 dollars, tended to fall significantly during the most recent economic crisis. The depreciation of the exchange rate, in particular, had a contractionary effect on real public social spending. Since salaries make up a large share of social spending, the drop in real wages cause by the exchange-rate adjustment explains a good part of this decline in expenditures. After 2002, social spending recovered somewhat.

Trends in real public spending on education and health are similar to that of the aggregate public social spending (see panels 'd 'and 'e' of Figure 4.2). Social welfare spending, in contrast, has increased substantially since the early 1990s and, beginning in 2002, this spending accelerated with the introduction of the "Heads of Household Programme" (see panel c of Figure 4.2).[4] Expenditures on water and sanitation, on the other hand, show large fluctuations (see panel f of Figure 4.2).

Public social spending is an important ingredient in the efforts to reach the MDGs. Yet, increasing expenditures as such may not be enough. As mentioned earlier, the increase in social welfare expenditures since the 1990s, for instance, has been sufficient to prevent a rise in poverty (see Table 4.2). At the same time, the indicators do show that the increases in spending on education and health since the early 1990s are closely correlated with the progress made towards several

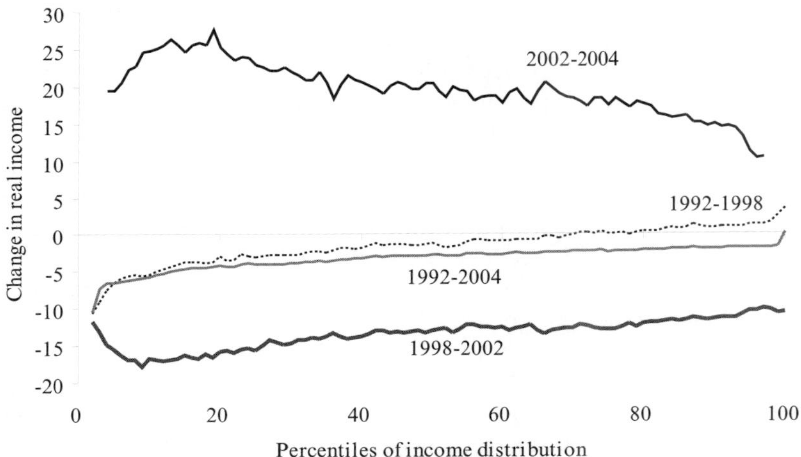

Figure 4.2 Argentina: Growth incidence curves, 1992-2004
Source: CEDLAS.

goals linked to performance in both sectors. The sharp decrease in public social spending after the 2002 devaluation has not affected either school enrolment rates or indicators in the health sector, possibly because, as indicated, the decline in spending affected mainly the wage bill rather than the delivery of the services.

Calibration of MAMS for Argentina

As explained in Chapter 3, MAMS captures the general equilibrium effects that are generated following the increase in public social spending required for reaching the targets associated with MDG 2, 4, and 7[5] and under alternative financing mechanisms. As mentioned, MDG 1 is evaluated through the micro-simulation methodology (see Appendix A2.1 of Chapter 2).

The structure of MAMS is determined by the functional forms described in Chapter 3. This section briefly describes the data sources used in the process of estimating and calibrating the model.

The accounting framework of the model is provided by a Social Accounting Matrix (SAM) for 2003, which was constructed in line with the key identity equations of MAMS.[6] The labour factor is disaggregated by level of educational attainment. Unskilled workers are those who have not finished their secondary education; semi-skilled are those who have incomplete higher education; and skilled workers are those who have completed their degrees in tertiary educa-tion. Changes in the composition of the labour supply by type of worker thus depend, in part, on the functioning of the education system. The employment data used to calibrate the model were obtained from the EPH.

The data for the MDG 2-related indicators (that is, the percentage of students that enrol in primary school and finish the cycle on time) were estimated using data from the EPH (graduation rates and repetition rates, among others) and from the administrative records of the Ministry of Education (number of students by educational level). Information on child mortality was obtained from the Ministry of Health. Data on access to potable water and basic sanitation coverage were derived from the 2001 National Census of Population, Households and Housing, and projected through the year 2003.

The elasticities that measure the links between determinants and outcomes of MDG achievement were estimated econometrically. These estimates suffer from some important limitations because of deficiencies in the data. The methodology and the results of these estimations are explained briefly in the next sub-sections on education and infant mortality. Before moving on to those issues, however, it is important to mention that the estimated elasticities were not introduced directly into MAMS, since the CGE model uses functional forms that are different from those estimated on the microeconometric data analysis and as a sensitivity analysis was conducted to find a consistent solution for MAMS.[7]

Education

Since Argentina has taken significant steps towards meeting MDG 2—namely, making primary education universal—graduation rates are also analyzed for secondary and tertiary levels. In the case of primary education, in particular, a model was estimated for analyzing the enrolment rates at the relevant age groups. Based on the extended human capital model, the decision to attend school is seen to depend on the rate of return to education, a range of individual, household and community characteristics and restrictions faced by each individual in financing his or her education.[8] In addition, probit models of the probability of graduation were estimated for each of the three levels of education. The explanatory variables used in the probit models are the same as those used for the primary education enrolment model.

The main data source for the econometric estimation was the EPH, covering 28 urban areas in Argentina for the 1997-2003 period.[9] Information on public expenditures on education and on infant mortality rates were derived from, respectively, the Office of Analysis of Public Spending and Social Programs and the Office of Health Information and Statistics of the Ministry of Health.

Infant mortality is included as an explanatory variable with the hypothesis that a better health status of children enhances the probability of school attendance and performance. This specification also makes it possible to determine whether synergies exist as different millennium goals are achieved. At the same time, the passing of each of the grades of a particular cycle—a key variable in MAMS—is modelled by using the same determinants as those used in the decision to enrol in primary school.

As observed in Table 4.4, the model for enrolment in primary school at the mandatory age was estimated using more than 5,000 observations. Based on the marginal effects of the various explanatory variables, it was found that the likelihood of enrolment is slightly higher for girls and further that enrolment rises with the level of family income and education level of parents and, conversely,

Table 4.4 Argentina: results of the probit model estimated for primary school enrolment at mandatory age

Variable	dF/dx[a]	Error	Z	P>|z|	Average	95% confidence interval	
Male	-0.012	0.009	-1.280	0.202	0.523	-0.030	0.006
Logarithm of adult-equivalent income	0.004	0.007	0.660	0.508	5.221	-0.009	0.017
Years of education of head of household	0.002	0.001	1.210	0.227	9.304	-0.001	0.005
Female head of household	-0.024	0.031	-0.860	0.389	0.117	-0.085	0.037
Single parent household	0.019	0.018	0.910	0.363	0.105	-0.016	0.055
Number of siblings	-0.002	0.003	-0.630	0.530	2.181	-0.008	0.004
Per capita income by city/year	0.000	0.000	0.090	0.932	250.484	0.000	0.000
Years of education by city/year	-0.049	0.037	-1.350	0.178	7.472	-0.122	0.024
Wage gap (skilled/semiskilled)	-0.041	0.031	-1.360	0.173	1.872	-0.102	0.019
Wage gap (semiskilled/unskilled)	-0.059	0.068	-0.870	0.382	1.309	-0.191	0.074
Infant mortality	-0.003	0.002	-1.290	0.196	17.324	-0.007	0.002
Per capita spending on basic education	0.000	0.000	-0.300	0.763	211.144	0.000	000
Observations	5,357						
Dummy variable for cities	yes						
Dummy variable for years	yes						
Pseudo R^2	0.035						

Source: Estimates based on data from EPH, the Office of Analysis of Public Spending and Social Programs and the Office of Health Information and Statistics of the Ministry of Health.
[a] In this and other tables through Table 4.8, dF/dx refers to the changes in the probability of enrolment in primary school at the mandatory age for an infinitesimal change of 0 to 1 in the independent variable, for a continuous or dummy variable, respectively. The change in probability is calculated for the average value of each one of the independent variables.

it falls with family size. The provinces with the highest infant mortality rates appear to have lower enrolment rates, suggesting a better health status positively influences access to education. The level of per capita spending on basic education was not found to be statistically significant. Most coefficients are not statistically significant, however, which may not be surprising, considering the small degree of variation observed for the dependent variable; that is, that approximately 95 per cent of Argentine children enrol in primary school at the age when they should do so.

The determinants of the model of primary school completion have greater statistical significance (see Table 4.5). Graduation rates tend to be higher for girls, at any grade of primary education and for students belonging to households with a higher income, fewer members and whose head of household has a higher level of education. Graduation also appears to be inversely related to the average years of education achieved by the population of cities and positively correlated with the wage gap between skilled and semi-skilled workers. Expenditures on basic education per capita appear to have a negative effect, though its marginal effect is close to zero.

The model for secondary school completion was estimated using a sample of more than 21,000 observations (see Table 4.6). Some of the model results seem counterintuitive. The city-specific control variables (per capita income and years of education), as well as per capita spending on basic education, seem to have a negative effect on the probability of graduation, but this could be caused by the fact the these effects are already picked up by the individual and household characteristics. Those determinants show similar results as for primary education, that is, girls and the students who belong to higher income households, with few members and whose heads of household have a higher level of education are the ones who have the greatest probability of graduating. A difference with the model for primary school graduation is that in the case of secondary education the probability of graduation decreases with the age of the students.

Finally, graduation rates fall considerably at the level of higher education. Only 50 per cent of the students at this level complete their studies. The model of completion of higher education was estimated using a sample of almost 7,000 observations (see Table 4.7). Results show that the explanatory power of the model is not very satisfactory. Few of the variables considered appear to influence the probability of graduation at this level. None of the variables that are statistically significant in the models of school completion at primary and secondary levels seem to explain graduation from higher education.

Infant mortality

MAMS assumes that changes in child mortality are determined by a number of socioeconomic conditions. Survival models are appropriate for analyzing infant or child mortality.[10] In the case of Argentina, however, it is not possible

Table 4.5   Argentina: results of the probit model estimated for primary school completion

Variable	dF/dx	Error	Z	P>|z|	Average	95% confidence interval	
Age	0.030	0.006	4.850	0.000	9.527	0.018	0.042
Age squared	-0.001	0.000	-4.720	0.000	96.063	-0.002	-0.001
Male	-0.020	0.006	-3.330	0.001	0.512	-0.032	-0.008
Logarithm of adult-equivalent income	0.018	0.004	4.420	0.000	5.172	0.010	0.026
Years of education of head of household	0.004	0.001	4.850	0.000	9.128	0.003	0.006
Female head of household	-0.008	0.017	-0.500	0.620	0.142	-0.043	0.026
Single parent household	-0.002	0.017	-0.100	0.921	0.134	-0.035	0.032
Number of siblings	-0.010	0.002	-5.250	0.000	2.399	-0.014	-0.006
Per capita income by city/year	0.000	0.000	0.540	0.587	252.047	0.000	0.000
Years of education by city/year	-0.089	0.025	-3.610	0.000	7.502	-0.137	-0.040
Wage gap (skilled/ semiskilled)	0.041	0.020	2.050	0.041	1.876	0.002	0.080
Wage gap (semiskilled/ unskilled	-0.029	0.041	-0.700	0.482	1.314	-0.109	0.051
Infant mortality	-0.001	0.001	-0.470	0.639	17.189	-0.003	0.002
Per capita spending on basic education	0.000	0.000	-2.420	0.015	212.027	-0.001	0.000
Observations	39,067						
Dummy variable for cities	yes						
Dummy variable for years	yes						
Pseudo R^2	0.039						

Source: Estimates based on data from EPH, Office of Analysis of Public Spending and Social Programs and the Office of Health Information and Statistics of the Ministry of Health.

to estimate a detailed model of this type, given the lack of adequate micro data. Instead, a simpler regression model is applied to test the significance of the determinants of infant mortality rates as specified in MAMS. While target for MDG 4 relates to reducing the child mortality rate, we use the infant mortality rate as a proxy, given that better data are available for this indicator in

Table 4.6   Argentina: results of the probit model estimated for secondary school completion

Variable	dF/dx	Error	Z	P>|z|	Average	95% confidence interval	
Age	-0.008	0.004	-1.760	0.078	15.992	-0.016	0.001
Age squared	0.000	0.000	0.640	0.520	264.466	0.000	0.000
Male	-0.067	0.010	-6.520	0.000	0.507	-0.087	-0.047
Logarithm of adult-equivalent income	0.027	0.008	3.410	0.001	5.393	0.011	0.042
Years of education of head of household	0.004	0.002	2.530	0.011	9.569	0.001	0.007
Female head of household	0.011	0.023	0.500	0.619	0.172	-0.033	0.056
Single parent household	-0.030	0.024	-1.250	0.211	0.176	-0.077	0.018
Number of siblings	-0.007	0.004	-1.850	0.064	2.044	-0.014	0.000
Per capita income by city/year	0.000	0.000	-2.080	0.038	262.960	0.000	0.000
Years of education by city/year	-0.082	0.043	-1.910	0.056	7.601	-0.167	0.002
Wage gap (skilled/ semiskilled)	-0.016	0.033	-0.500	0.620	1.883	-0.081	0.048
Wage gap (semiskilled/ unskilled)	0.072	0.064	1.130	0.261	1.317	-0.053	0.197
Infant mortality	0.000	0.002	-0.160	0.874	16.968	-0.005	0.004
Per capita spending on basic Education	-0.001	0.000	-2.460	0.014	211.326	-0.001	0.000
Observations	21,237						
Dummy variable for cities	yes						
Dummy variable for years	yes						
Pseudo R^2	0.023						

Source: Estimates based on data from EPH, Office of Analysis of Public Spending and Social Programs and the Office of Health Information and Statistics of the Ministry of Health.

Argentina.[11] We estimate a proportions model of infant mortality using panel information by province for a period of 12 years (1992-2003).

Table 4.8 shows the results of the infant mortality model. The mortality of children younger than one year of age is negatively related to the level of per capita income and the level of per capita expenditures on health in each province. Contrary to what might be expected, the percentage of households with access

Table 4.7   Argentina: results of the probit model estimated for higher education completion

Variable	dF/dx	Error	Z	P>|z|	Average	95% confidence interval	
Age	0.015	0.015	0.970	0.331	21.994	-0.015	0.045
Age squared	0.000	0.000	-1.460	0.144	495.789	-0.001	0.000
Male	-0.028	0.020	-1.370	0.170	0.418	-0.068	0.012
Logarithm of adult-equivalent income	0.008	0.016	0.490	0.621	5.996	-0.023	0.038
Years of education of head of household	0.000	0.003	0.110	0.912	11.533	-0.006	0.006
Female head of household	-0.063	0.050	-1.260	0.208	0.203	-0.160	0.035
Single parent household	0.000	0.049	-0.010	0.992	0.216	-0.097	0.096
Number of siblings	0.026	0.009	2.760	0.006	1.256	0.008	0.044
Per capita income by city/year	0.000	0.000	-0.950	0.343	288.152	-0.001	0.000
Years of education by city/year	-0.190	0.087	-2.180	0.029	7.889	-0.360	-0.019
Wage gap (skilled/semi-skilled)	-0.018	0.070	-0.250	0.799	1.888	-0.154	0.119
Wage gap (semi-skilled/unskilled)	0.060	0.117	0.510	0.610	1.321	-0.170	0.289
Infant mortality	0.002	0.005	0.340	0.737	16.351	-0.009	0.012
Public spending on higher education	0.002	0.005	0.390	0.697	18.614	-0.008	0.012
Observations	6,798						
Dummy variable for cities	yes						
Dummy variable for years	yes						
Pseudo R^2	0.015						

Source: Estimates based on data from EPH, Office of Analysis of Public Spending and Social Programs and the Office of Health Information and Statistics of the Ministry of Health.

to water does not appear to influence infant mortality.[12] However, the variable representing access to water in the estimated model refers to the presence of a source of water in the home. It is important to point out that the simple presence of water is not a necessary and sufficient condition for assuring access to water that is fit for human consumption.

The time dummies capture the presence of factors not included in the model that generate a tendency towards a decline in infant mortality rates. At the

Table 4.8   Argentina: determinants of infant mortality

Variable	Coefficient	Error	Z	P>|z|	95% confidence interval	
Log of per capita income	-3.724	1.070	-3.48	0.001	-5.831	-1.618
Per capita expenditures on health	-0.007	0.003	-2.54	0.012	-0.013	-0.002
Percentage of households with access to water	-0.011	0.100	-0.11	0.911	-0.209	0.187
Observations	270					
Dummy variable for cities	Yes					
Dummy variable for years	Yes					
Pseudo R^2	0.686					

Source: Estimates based on data from EPH, Office of Analysis of Public Spending and Social Programs and the Office of Health Information and Statistics of the Ministry of Health.

same time, the spatial variable indicates that there are significant differences in infant mortality rates across the regions of the country. In particular, the northern region of the country, both east and west, has rates that are much higher than the national rates, even after controlling for their lower levels of income, more limited access to water, and lower public expenditures on health.

Additional information for the calibration of MAMS

The variation in the indicators associated with MDG 7 (access to potable water and to basic sanitation) is also defined by a series of elasticities with respect to a series of underlying determinants. These determinants could not be estimated econometrically, however, because of a lack of relevant data. The values assumed by the corresponding elasticities were defined by validating the trajectories of the MDG 7 indicators generated by MAMS in the baseline scenario described in the following section, taking into consideration the past trends of these indicators.

MAMS also requires other information about the conditions under which the goals associated with the MDGs would be met. Specifically, a trajectory needs to be defined for scaling up per capita consumption, the provision of the relevant service (for example, health services for MDG 4) and the level of public infrastructure such that the MDGs are met by 2015. For MDG 2, projection estimates presented in Vargas de Flood (2006) were used as a reference. For MDGs 4 and 7, the information collected in PNUD (2006) about public expenditures in health and water and sanitation for 1990-2003 was used. Additionally, expert opinion was sought in sectoral matters to validate the results of the model. As mentioned in the third section, Argentina is close to meeting some of the MDG targets. As explained below, however, it is precisely because of this that large increases in public spending will be required as the marginal costs of the required interventions to meet the targets become higher.

The other elasticities of the model, which define the behaviour of the agents (producers and consumers, primarily), were obtained from a review of literature. Many parameters were taken from Díaz-Bonilla and others (2004). These authors calibrate a static model of the Argentine economy based on the CGE framework developed by Lofgren and others (2002) which, as indicated in Chapter 3, also forms a starting point for MAMS.

General equilibrium analysis

As explained in Chapter 3, MAMS is used to simulate a baseline scenario that shows how the economy would behave in the absence of economic shocks and with certain assumptions for growth of production and public spending. The MDGs are not necessarily reached in this scenario which serves as the reference for comparison with alternative policy scenarios that target the achievement of MDGs 2, 4 and 7 in a context of endogenous adjustment of growth of production and public spending. In the case of Argentina, all these scenarios are simulated for the 2003-2015 period and the results are presented in Table 4.9.

Baseline scenario: key assumptions and results

The baseline scenario assumes that GDP will grow at an annual average rate of 3.2 per cent. This pace of growth is derived from estimates of potential GDP for Argentina which in turn are based on information on factor endowments for the 1990-2001 period.[13] For 2003-2006, however, relatively higher growth rates are used with the objective of replicating the behaviour of the Argentine economy during those years.

The population growth of the country increases exogenously in the baseline scenario, at a rate consistent with the official projections of the Institute of Statistics and Censuses (INDEC). The supply of factors varies over time as the growth of the labour force depends on population growth and on the performance of the education system, while growth of the capital stock depends on the rate of investment. Both types of production factors are assumed to be perfectly mobile between sectors. Adjustment of the labour market is characterized by the existence of unemployment and downward rigidity of real wages. Full utilization of capital is assumed and the market for the factor capital clears for its price.

It is also assumed that government consumption will grow at the same rate as GDP. With respect to government financing during the entire period, it is assumed that public external debt will be reduced, that public domestic debt will grow, and that the government will not have to resort to the Central Bank to finance its deficits. As a result, the government pays interest primarily on

Table 4.9 Argentina: main results of policy simulations, 2003-2015

	2003 (values)	Baseline scenario	MDG 2 scenario			MDG 4 scenario		
			tax	fbor	dbor	tax	fbor	dbor
Macroeconomic aggregates (billions of pesos)[a]			**Annual average growth for period (%)**					
GDP at market prices	379.1	3.2	3.2	3.2	2.8	3.2	3.2	3.0
Private consumption	236.0	3.9	3.7	3.8	3.5	3.7	3.9	3.7
Public consumption	47.2	3.2	3.5	3.5	3.5	4.2	4.1	4.2
Gross capital formation	56.6	4.2	3.9	4.1	2.3	4.0	4.4	2.0
– Private	50.4	4.3	4.0	4.3	2.3	3.9	4.4	1.8
– Public	6.2	3.4	2.6	2.8	2.3	4.1	4.1	3.7
Exports	89.9	1.2	1.1	0.8	0.7	1.1	0.1	0.8
Imports	50.7	4.0	3.8	4.0	3.3	3.9	4.2	3.4
Public expenditure (% of GDP)			**Annual average for period (% of GDP)**					
Final consumption in education	2.9	2.8	3.4	3.4	3.5	2.8	2.8	2.9
– Primary cycle	1.5	1.4	2.0	2.0	2.0	1.4	1.4	1.4
Final consumption in health	1.5	1.4	1.4	1.4	1.5	2.1	2.0	2.1
Final consumption in water and sanitation	0.7	0.7	0.7	0.7	0.7	0.7	0.7	0.7
Final consumption in other government services	7.2	7.0	7.0	7.1	7.2	7.0	7.0	7.1
Investment in education	0.2	0.2	0.3	0.3	0.3	0.2	0.2	0.2
– Primary cycle	0.1	0.1	0.2	0.2	0.2	0.1	0.1	0.1
Investment in health	0.1	0.1	0.1	0.1	0.1	0.2	0.2	0.2
Investment in water and sanitation	0.0	0.0	0.0	0.0	0.0	0.0	0.0	0.0
Investment in other public infrastructure	0.5	0.6	0.5	0.6	0.5	0.5	0.6	0.5
Investment in other government services	0.7	0.7	0.7	0.7	0.7	0.7	0.7	0.7

Table 4.9   (cont'd)

	2003 (values)	Baseline scenario	MDG 2 scenario			MDG 4 scenario		
			tax	fbor	dbor	tax	fbor	dbor
Financing of MDG strategy (% of GDP)					Value in 2015			
Income tax revenue	10.0	11.2	12.2	11.2	11.3	13.6	11.3	11.3
Government domestic borrowing	1.3	1.6	1.6	1.6	3.8	1.6	1.6	4.9
Government foreign borrowing	-2.6	-1.3	-1.3	-0.3	-1.3	-1.3	1.3	-1.3
Outstanding domestic public debt	45.9	44.4	44.8	44.6	61.1	44.3	44.5	55.2
Outstanding external public debt	82.3	25.9	26.1	36.3	27.2	25.8	32.9	26.5
Real exchange rate (index, 2003=100)	100.0	91.4	91.4	90.1	91.3	91.5	87.6	91.1
Labour market					Annual average growth for period (%)			
Employment (millions of workers)	13.8	1.8	1.8	1.8	1.7	2.0	1.8	1.7
– Unskilled workers	7.5	1.4	1.4	1.3	1.2	1.5	1.3	1.2
– Semi-skilled workers	4.3	2.5	2.6	2.5	2.4	2.7	2.5	2.5
– Skilled workers	2.1	1.9	1.9	1.9	1.9	1.9	1.9	1.9
Real labour income per worker (pesos)[a]	9,279	2.1	2.2	2.2	2.1	2.1	2.3	2.2
– Unskilled workers	3,366	2.0	2.0	2.0	1.8	1.9	2.0	1.9
– Semi-skilled workers	10,497	1.4	1.4	1.4	1.3	1.3	1.4	1.4
– Skilled workers	28,039	2.2	2.4	2.4	2.2	2.6	2.6	2.5
MDG outcomes					Value in 2015			
Primary school completion rate (%)	81.7	86.1	98.0	98.0	98.0	86.0	86.3	86.1
Child mortality (per 1,000 live births)	19.1	12.6	12.8	12.6	13.1	9.9	9.9	9.9
Population with access to drinking water (%)	78.4	79.9	79.8	79.9	79.8	79.8	79.9	79.8
Population with access to basic sanitation (%)	42.5	51.4	51.3	51.3	51.0	51.3	51.4	51.1

Table 4.9   (cont'd)

	2003 (values)	Baseline scenario	MDG 7 scenario			All MDGs scenario		
			tax	fbor	dbor	tax	fbor	dbor
Macroeconomic aggregates (billions of pesos)[a]			*Annual average growth for period (%)*					
GDP at market prices	379.1	3.2	3.3	3.2	3.2	3.1	3.1	2.5
Private consumption	236.0	3.9	3.8	3.9	3.8	3.5	3.9	3.4
Public consumption	47.2	3.2	3.5	3.5	3.5	4.5	4.4	4.6
Gross capital formation (investment)	56.6	4.2	4.1	4.2	3.7	3.6	4.3	-0.6
– Private	50.4	4.3	4.2	4.3	3.7	3.7	4.4	-1.2
– Public	6.2	3.4	3.6	3.6	3.5	3.3	3.4	2.9
Exports	89.9	1.2	1.2	1.0	1.1	1.0	-0.3	0.2
Imports	50.7	4.0	4.0	4.1	3.9	3.7	4.2	2.6
Public expenditure (% of GDP)			*Annual average for period (% of GDP)*					
Final consumption in education	2.9	2.8	2.8	2.8	2.9	3.4	3.4	3.5
– Primary cycle	1.5	1.4	1.4	1.4	1.4	2.0	2.0	2.0
Final consumption in health	1.5	1.4	1.4	1.4	1.4	1.9	1.8	1.9
Final consumption in water and sanitation	0.7	0.7	0.9	0.9	0.9	0.9	0.9	0.9
Final consumption in other government services	7.2	7.0	7.0	7.0	7.0	7.1	7.1	7.2
Investment in education	0.2	0.2	0.2	0.2	0.2	0.3	0.3	0.3
– Primary cycle	0.1	0.1	0.1	0.1	0.1	0.2	0.2	0.2
Investment in health	0.1	0.1	0.1	0.1	0.1	0.1	0.1	0.1
Investment in water and sanitation	0.0	0.0	0.0	0.0	0.0	0.0	0.0	0.1
Investment in other public infrastructure	0.5	0.6	0.6	0.6	0.6	0.5	0.5	0.5
Investment in other government services	0.7	0.7	0.7	0.7	0.7	0.7	0.7	0.7

Table 4.9   (cont'd)

	2003 (values)	Baseline scenario	MDG 7 scenario			All MDGs scenario		
			tax	fbor	dbor	tax	fbor	dbor
Financing of MDG strategy (% of GDP)			**Value in 2015**					
Income tax revenue	10.0	11.2	11.7	11.2	11.2	14.7	11.3	11.5
Government domestic borrowing	1.3	1.6	1.6	1.6	2.4	1.6	1.6	7.6
Government foreign borrowing	-2.6	-1.3	-1.3	-0.7	-1.3	-1.3	2.0	-1.4
Outstanding domestic public debt	45.9	44.4	44.4	44.4	47.4	44.7	44.6	74.4
Outstanding external public debt	82.3	25.9	25.9	28.0	26.1	26.1	42.9	28.0
Real exchange rate (index, 2003=100)	100.0	91.4	91.4	90.6	91.4	91.5	86.4	91.1
Labour market			**Annual average growth for period (%)**					
Employment (millions of workers)	13.8	1.8	1.9	1.9	1.8	2.0	1.9	1.6
– Unskilled workers	7.5	1.4	1.5	1.4	1.4	1.4	1.3	1.0
– Semi-skilled workers	4.3	2.5	2.6	2.6	2.5	2.9	2.7	2.5
– Skilled workers	2.1	1.9	1.9	1.9	1.9	1.9	1.9	1.9
Real labour income per worker (pesos)[a]	9,279	2.1	2.0	2.1	2.1	2.3	2.4	2.2
– Unskilled workers	3,366	2.0	2.0	2.0	2.0	2.0	2.0	1.7
– Semi-skilled workers	10,497	1.4	1.4	1.4	1.4	1.3	1.4	1.2
– Skilled workers	28,039	2.2	2.2	2.2	2.2	2.8	2.7	2.5
MDG outcomes			**Value in 2015**					
Primary school completion rate (%)	81.7	86.1	86.1	86.2	86.1	98.0	98.0	98.0
Child mortality (per 1,000 live births)	19.1	12.6	11.7	11.6	11.7	9.9	9.9	9.9
Population with access to drinking water (%)	78.4	79.9	82.5	82.5	82.5	82.5	82.5	82.5
Population with access to basic sanitation (%)	42.5	51.4	67.7	67.6	67.7	67.8	67.6	67.9

Source: MAMS for Argentina.

[a] In real terms at base-year prices.

its domestic debt. These assumptions are justified for the Argentine economy based on MECON (2005). Additionally, an exogenous reduction of public debt is introduced in 2005, as a result of the debt swap the government conducted in that year. At the same time, it is assumed that transfers between institutions will grow exogenously at the same rate as GDP.

Chapter 3 explains how the macroeconomic closure rules are defined in MAMS for all country applications in this volume. Basically, the fiscal balance is assumed fixed following a closure rule whereby the direct tax rate is allowed to vary to ensure the government generates enough revenue to finance its capital outlays. The real exchange rate adjusts to balance the external account, while foreign savings are assumed to be exogenous. Finally, private investment is assumed to adjust proportionally to total domestic absorption, while private savings adjust endogenously to finance private investment.

The results in Table 4.9 show that real wages increase in all scenarios over the simulation period, benefiting primarily the labour categories with lower supply growth. The supply of semi-skilled workers is growing faster than that of other types of workers due to an increase in the number of students and higher rates of secondary school completion.[14] Consequently, the wage gap between skilled and unskilled workers narrows somewhat over time. Employment also increases for the three types of labour and the overall unemployment rate falls. As explained in the following section, the reduction in unemployment and the increase in real wages contribute to poverty reduction.

The MDG indicators improve in the baseline scenario, but not sufficiently to meet the given targets (see Table 4.9 and Figure 4.3). The percentage of students that enrol in primary school and complete it as scheduled increases from 82 per cent in the base year to 86 per cent in 2015, but falls short of the 100 per cent target. The reduction in the under-five child mortality rate replicates its observed change in the 2003-2006 period, to drop further by three points in the remaining period until 2015. In the baseline scenario, the share of the population with access to potable water increases, but falls 3 percentage points short of the target by 2015. The percentage of the population with access to basic sanitation also increases in the baseline, but falls short of the 2015 target by 15 percentage points. Since none of the desired goals are met, public spending in social services associated with the MDGs must increase in order to meet the established targets.

MDG scenarios

A total of 16 scenarios in which MDG targets are met were simulated, and these were divided into four sets. The first three sets target the achievement of, respectively, MDG 2, MDG 4 and MDG 7. In the fourth set, simultaneous achievement of all those MDGs is targeted. In all cases, MDG 1 is not targeted as explained in the sixth section. These scenarios generate results for the

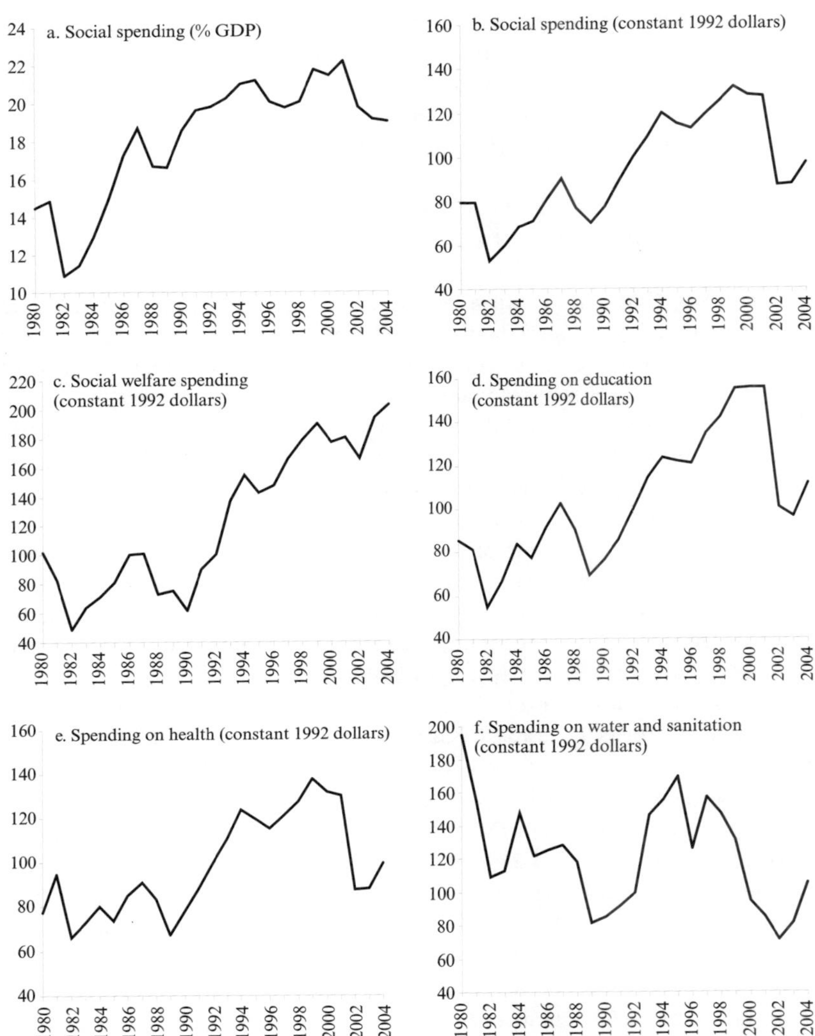

Figure 4.3   Argentina: trends in public social spending, 1980-2004
Source: Own elaboration using data from the Office of Analysis of Public Spending and Social
Programs.

required additional public spending to achieve the given targets under four alternative financing options: increasing the income tax rate (tax), domestic borrowing (dbor), foreign borrowing (fbor) or foreign grants. The latter financing strategy is not considered relevant for Argentina and, therefore, its results are not discussed here. If new public spending is not financed through taxes, the macroeconomic closure rules of the baseline scenario must be modified. For example, in the foreign-borrowing scenario, foreign savings are "endogenized" in order to finance the MDG strategy, while fixing direct tax rates at the same time. Direct tax rates are also kept fixed, when the government uses the option of domestic borrowing. This way, it is possible for the government's financing strategy to have repercussions on the growth rate of the economy, through different mechanisms discussed in the below.

Achieving the goal for primary education

In order to reach the target for primary education, three conditions must be met: all children must enrol in primary school at the mandatory age, no child may drop out of school and no child may repeat a grade.[15] Given the baseline results, meeting these conditions require additional public expenditures on education (see Table 4.9). By construction, solely targeting the goal for primary education does not directly influence progress towards the other goals. However, there may be indirect effects through changes in per capita consumption (as compared to the baseline scenario). For instance, tax financing could affect disposable incomes of households and hence per capita consumption, thereby affecting progress towards MDGs 4 and 7.

As primary education goals are met, wages for skilled workers rise (see Table 4.9) and their unemployment rate declines. The additional public spending in education increases the demand for teachers pushing up the average remuneration for skilled workers. Real wages for other types of workers decline slightly (with respect to the baseline scenario) in the case of the domestic borrowing scenario. This is caused by a crowding out of private investment which slows economic growth and the demand for semi-skilled and unskilled workers as compared with the baseline. For its part, financing through taxation reduces disposable household incomes and private spending on primary education, thus requiring additional public spending on education in order to meet the target.

Achieving the MDG for primary education is more costly than achieving those for health and basic sanitation when measured in terms of the required public spending (as a percentage of GDP), independent of the source of financing used. As Table 4.9 shows, the total additional spending (as compared to the baseline scenario) expressed as the annual average for 2003-2015 is equivalent to 0.7 or 0.6 points of GDP, respectively for the scenarios of domestic resource mobilization (taxes or domestic borrowing) and external borrowing.

Child mortality

The additional public spending in health required (with respect to the baseline scenario) to meet the target for reducing child mortality is estimated at 0.8 per cent or 0.6 per cent of GDP per year on average for the 2003-2015 period, respectively for the scenarios with domestic borrowing or the other two financing options. The required additional spending increases towards the end of the period, as the marginal costs of interventions increases the closer one gets to the target. It is important to recall that, according to the microeconometric analysis, public spending on health has a weak effect on infant mortality. Furthermore, the target for MDG 4 is close to zero.

Financing the increase in health spending through domestic borrowing has an adverse simulated effect on GDP growth, caused by the "crowding-out" effect on private investment (Table 4.9). Since per capita consumption—an important determinant for MDG 4—is also affected as compared with the baseline scenario, the government must increase health spending by more than, for instance, the scenario of foreign borrowing in order to meet the target set for 2015.

As in the case of the MDG 2 scenarios, real wages of skilled workers show a slight increase, as a result of the expansion of health services and as a high share (approximately 45 per cent) of the labour employed in the health sector has completed higher education.

As Table 4.9 shows, reaching the child mortality goal does not have a significant direct impact on the primary education goal. Based on the econometric estimates presented, it is assumed that the behaviour of the students (graduating, repeating grades, dropping out, and others) has a weak relationship with child mortality. To the extent that better education of parents influences child mortality, this likely will take effect beyond the simulation period given the time lags involved.

Water and sanitation

As indicated above, there has been progress in providing the population with drinking water and basic sanitation. Deficits remain large in the area of sanitation, however. Marginal costs of raising coverage in water and sanitation are relatively low, such that with modest additional investments (around 0.2 GDP points per year) the targets for water and sanitation could be met by 2015 (see Table 4.9). Consequently, the macroeconomic repercussion effects of this scenario are negligible and achieving the goals for water and sanitation would be quite affordable, especially if recent trends in economic growth could be sustained.

Reaching the MDGs simultaneously

The macroeconomic costs of achieving MDGs 2, 4 and 7 simultaneously are lower than the corresponding sum for the previous three scenarios, owing to synergies that emerge are the goals are achieved. The synergy effects are relatively small, however, in part because Argentina has already made substantial progress towards the targets. It can be deduced from Table 4.9 that reaching all the goals simultaneously would reduce the required additional public spending by between 0.2 and 0.3 percentage points of GDP per year, as compared with pursuing each goal separately, respectively for the domestic and external financing scenarios.

Tax financing seems the more viable option to fund the additional government spending required to achieve the MDGs, even though it would affect disposable household incomes and private consumption. Domestic borrowing would cause total public debt to increase to likely unsustainable levels of over 100 per cent of GDP by 2015 and it would also slow economic growth as it would crowd out private investment. Resorting to external borrowing would go counter to Argentina's objective of reducing its foreign debt and equally would push up public indebtedness to high levels (87 per cent of GDP by 2015). Furthermore, external financing would lead to an appreciation in the real exchange rate, causing a drop in export volumes by -0.3 per cent compared with the baseline. This, in turn, will affect tax revenue from international trade, thus increasing the need for public resources to finance the MDG strategy.

Microsimulations and extreme poverty

The policy scenarios of MAMS only optimize towards the achievement of MDGs 2, 3, 4 and 7. Poverty is assumed to be a result of the overall performance of the economy, in particular labour market outcomes, rather than of specifically targeted public policies. Poverty and inequality outcomes are estimated through the microsimulation methodology after imposing labour market changes of the scenarios simulated with MAMS on the full income distribution derived from household survey data. The labour market shifts were simulated sequentially for the following components: unemployment rate (U), the sectoral composition of employment (S), relative wages (W1), the average wage (W2) and the composition of employment according to the skill level of those employed (M). Since the microsimulation methodology is non-parametric and involves a randomized process, each estimation procedure was repeated several times in Monte Carlo fashion in order to obtain 95 per cent confidence intervals for the simulated changes in poverty and inequality indicators.

The EPH from the second semester of 2005 was used as the basic set of micro data. The results of MAMS used in the microsimulations cover the period from 2005 to 2015.[16] The final effects on moderate poverty and inequality (measured through the Gini coefficient) correspond to the cumulative effects of the various changes in labour market parameters (that is, U+ S+W1+W2+M). The analysis of the target for MDG 1 is based on the official (moderate) poverty line, since as discussed in the third section, the international poverty line of one dollar a day is not very relevant for Argentina.

Baseline scenario

Poverty declines in the baseline scenario, owing to the drop in the unemployment rate and the increase in the average real wage. The decline in unemployment alone helps to reduce the poverty incidence by 2.6 percentage points between 2005 and 2015.

The simulated changes in the sectoral structure of employment and the composition of employment by skill level do not have a significant impact on poverty. All labour market effects combined contribute to a reduction of poverty of 7.2 percentage points over the simulation period. This is not sufficient, however, to meet the target of reducing poverty to 9.9 per cent by 2015.

The baseline scenario also records a slight fall in inequality, which is mainly on account of the decline in the unemployment rate. As mentioned, inequality in labour incomes across types of workers and sectors does not change much in the baseline scenario, except that wages of skilled workers increase slightly more than those of unskilled workers. Overall, however, the simulated shift in relative wages does not significantly affect the distribution of per capita household income.

MDGs scenario

Most scenarios in which the goals are achieved generate weaker effects on poverty and inequality than the baseline scenario. Hence, as in the baseline scenario, the target of halving poverty by 2015 is not met and this applies to poverty as measured by any of the four poverty lines. The degree of poverty reduction is somewhat less under the scenarios of tax financing and domestic borrowing, while the scenario with foreign borrowing reaches a similar degree of poverty reduction as in the baseline. These outcomes are driven by the fact that the economy would grow more slowly in the scenarios with domestic resource mobilization for the explained reasons. Slower growth implies a smaller reduction in the unemployment rate and a more modest increase in the average real wage. At the same time, the stronger shift in relative wages in favour of skilled workers counteracts poverty reduction in the MDGs scenario as compared to the baseline scenario.

Conclusions and policy recommendations

Between 1990 and 2005, Argentina made visible progress towards the achievement of MDGs 2, 4 and 7. There have been considerable setbacks with respect to reducing poverty (MDG 1), despite the introduction of targeted social welfare programmes. The MDG scenarios analyzed in this chapter indicate that, despite the progress made, business as usual is not good enough to meet the targets set for MDGs 2, 4 and 7. As a consequence, additional public spending efforts are needed. Given the existing pattern of economic growth, however, the increased social spending in order to achieve the goals for education, health, and water and basic sanitation would not provide the employment impetus and redistributive effects needed to also achieve the target of halving poverty by 2015. Furthermore, achieving MDG 1 by 2015 has become more challenging, because of the substantial rise in poverty caused by the economic crisis just prior to the base year used for the scenario analysis. Recently, however, the Argentine government has extended its programme of targeted conditional cash transfers, which could help accelerate achievement of the poverty reduction target. Whether this will work will depend on a multiplicity of factors whose analysis exceeds the scope of the present study, including the effects of the economic and financial crisis that hit the world in 2008.

The way in which the MDG strategy is financed matters for the macroeconomic trade-offs generated by the scaling up of public spending. If the government finances the additional expenditures through increasing its domestic debt, it would tend to crowd out resources available for private investment which would, in turn, adversely affect growth. This slows progress towards the poverty-reduction goal as it diminishes employment and real wage growth. This trade-off is much less of a problem in the tax-financing scenario in which case it is disposable household income that is affected by the higher direct taxes and private consumption fall (including in MDG-related areas). This, in turn, requires that public spending is increased further in order to ensure that the goals are reached. The external financing strategy avoids the previous trade-offs, but instead generates an appreciation of the real exchange rate with negative repercussions on the volume of exports which, in turn, affects government revenues.

While all financing options generate macroeconomic trade-offs, the tax-financing strategy is considered more viable for Argentina, as it would not significantly slow output growth during the simulation period and does not push up public debt to unsustainable levels, as the other two financing options would do. The trade-offs generated in the increased tax-financing scenario are the result of the assumption of the model that only income tax rates adjust endogenously to mobilize the resources for the additional government spending. Tax reform options may be considered to minimize the impact on disposable household income, especially of lower income groups. The scenarios of external or domestic borrowing seem less desirable given Argentina's recent history of defaulting on public debt, which conditions access to future financing.

Alternatively, improving the efficiency of social public spending might also contribute by reducing the need for additional financing, but this option was not analyzed for the present study. In any case, the model-based analysis suggests that reaching MDGs 2, 4 and 7 is affordable in the case of Argentina, though specific measures will also have to be taken to ensure reaching the goal of poverty reduction as well. The analysis has focused on achievement of nation-wide targets. The policies as discussed may not suffice to eliminate all differences in human development and MDG achievement across regions of the country. In fact, as proposed in PNUD (2006), additional targets have been set to eliminate regional differences in MDG achievement by 2015.

Notes

1   As explained below, this high degree of public indebtedness relative to GDP affects the viability of some financing scenarios for the additional public expenditures required to reach the MDGs.

2   The base year of the CGE model is 2003 but, for similar reasons, this year is not used as the starting point for the poverty analysis using the microsimulation methodology because in 2003 the economy just started recovering from the crisis of the early 2000s. Hence, 2005 is used instead as the year of reference for this part of the modelling analysis.

3   The growth rate varies depending on the type of poverty measure used. It would be 4.7 per cent annually using the official estimate for the extreme poverty incidence or 5.6 per cent using that for the moderate poverty incidence.

4   This includes the expenditures of programmes aimed at the poor—primarily monetary transfers.

5   As explained in Chapter 3, MAMS can also be used to simulate reaching the goal of maternal mortality (MDG 5). However, the lack of reliable information on maternal mortality, as well as the expected small impact of an increase in overall public health spending on reaching this goal in the case of Argentina, makes it less viable and interesting to evaluate MDG 5 (see also PNUD, 2006).

6   A detailed presentation of the procedure followed to construct the SAM is found in Cicowiez and others (2006).

7   Notice that the specification of some of the independent variables in the estimated microeconometric models differ somewhat from the determinants identified in the MDG bloc of MAMS. For more details on the latter, see Chapter 3.

8   See, for example, Gertler and Glewwe (1990), Glewwe (1999), Bedi and others (2004) and Vos and Ponce (2004).

9   The Argentine education system is traditionally divided into three levels. The primary level, which is mandatory, generally has a cycle of 7 years, from 6 to 12 years of age. Secondary school includes 5 or 6 years of study and the relevant age cohort is from 13 to 17/18 years of age, while higher education includes short tertiary degrees of 2 or 3 years and university degrees of 4 to 6 years. In the early 1990s, several provinces changed their education system, extending primary education to 9 years, dividing it into three cycles, and renaming it into Basic General Education. The secondary level was shortened to 3 years, and renamed to the "Polymodal." For this analysis, the information pertinent to these provinces was adapted in order to work solely with the traditional structure of the educational system.

10   For more details about the models of determinants of access to health services and health outcomes, see, for example, Gertler and others (1987) and Mwabu and others (1993).

11   According to the Office of Health Information and Statistics of the Ministry of Public Health, the annual rate for infant mortality is the number of deaths among children under one year of age in the population of a particular geographic area during a particular year, divided by the number of live children born and recorded in the population of that geographic area during the same year.

12   Galiani and others (2005) find that the privatization of water services led to a significant increase in access to water and a significant drop in infant mortality. As a result, the MAMS model used here assumes that an increase in the provision of potable water would cause mortality rates to fall for children under five.

13   For the estimation of the capital stock of Argentina, see Coremburg (2003).
14   Graduation rates and students' enrolment increase for all three education levels during the entire period.
15   This way, the indicator associated with MDG 2 only considers the students who belong to a particular age cohort. This is consistent with the goal of reducing the number of over-age students in education as set by the Argentine government for 2015 (PNUD, 2006).
16   The results of MAMS are transmitted to the micro dataset to implement the micro-simulations as deviations from the value simulated for 2005 and not for 2003 which is the base year of the model.

References

Becker, Gary (1964). "Human Capital: A Theoretical and Empirical Analysis with Special Reference to Education". Cambridge (MA): National Bureau of Economic Research.

Bedi, Arjun S., Paul Kimalu, Damiano Kulundu and Nancy Nafula (2004). "The Decline in Primary School Enrolment in Kenya". *Journal of African Economies* 13 (1): 1-43.

Cicowiez, Martín, Luciano Di Gresia and Leonardo Gasparini (2006). "Metodología para el Cálculo de la SAM de Argentina 2003 para el Modelo MAMS." Documento preparado para el Proyecto *"Assesing Development Strategies to Achieve the MDGs in Latin American and the Caribbean"*. CEDLAS. La Plata (mimeo).

Coremberg, Ariel Alberto (2003). "El Crecimiento de la Productividad de la Economía Argentina Durante la Década de los Noventa: "Mito o Realidad"". *XXXVIII AAEP*.

Deaton, Angust (2003). "How to Monitor Poverty for the Millennium Development Goals". Research Program in Development Studies. Princeton University.

Díaz-Bonilla, Carolina, Eugenio Díaz-Bonilla, Valeria Piñeiro and Sherman Robinson (2004). "El Plan de Convertibilidad, Apertura de la Economía y Empleo en Argentina: Una Simulación Macro-Micro de Pobreza y Desigualdad". In Ganuza, Enrique, Sam Morley, Sherman Robinson and Rob Vos (eds.) *¿Quién se beneficia del libre comercio? Promoción de exportaciones y pobreza en América Latina y el Caribe en los 90*, Bogotá, PNUD-AlfaOmega.

Galiani, S., P. Gertler and E. Schargrodsky (2005). "Water for Life: The Impact of the Privatization of Water Services on Child Mortality". *Journal of Political Economy* 113: 83-120.

Gasparini, Leonardo, and Martín Cicowiez (2005). "Meeting the Poverty-Reduction MDG in the Southern Cone. Monitoring the Socio-Economic Conditions in Argentina, Chile, Paraguay and Uruguay". *CEDLAS-The World Bank*.

Gertler, P., L. Locay and W. Sanderson (1987). "Are User Fees Regressive? The Welfare Implications of Health Care Financing Proposals in Peru". *Journal of Econometrics* 36(1/2): 67-80.

__________, and Paul Glewwe (1990). "The Willingness to Pay for Education in Developing Countries: Evidence from Rural Peru". *Journal of Public Economics* 42: 251-275.

Glewwe, Paul (1999). *The Economics of School Quality Investments in Developing Countries: An Empirical Study of Ghana*. London: Macmillan.

Lofgren, Hans, Rebecca Lee Harris and Sherman Robinson (2002). "A standard computable general equilibrium (CGE) model in GAMS". Microcomputers in Policy Research 5, Washington, D.C. International Food Policy Research Institute.

MECON (Ministry of the Economy and Production) (2005). "Evolución Reciente de la Economía Argentina y Perspectivas de Sostenibilidad: Un Enfoque Comparado". *Análisis Económico* 4, Buenos Aires: Ministry of the Economy and Production.

Mwabu, G., M. Ainsworth and A. Nyamete. (1993). "Quality of Medical Care and Choice of Medical Treatment in Kenya: An Empirical Analysis". *Journal of Human Resources* 28 (4): 838-862.

PNUD (2006). *Objetivos de Desarrollo del Milenio. Informe País 2005*. Programa de las Naciones Unidas para el Desarrollo. Proyecto PNUD/ARG/04/046.

Schultz, Theodore W. (1971). *Investment in Human Capital: The Role of Education and Research*. New York: The Free Press.

Vargas de Flood, María Cristina (2006). "El Gasto en Educación". In Vargas de Flood, María Cristina (ed.). *Política del Gasto Social: La Experiencia Argentina*, Buenos Aires: ASAP.

Vos, Rob, and Juan Ponce (2004). "Education". In World Bank and Inter.-American Development Bank (2004), *Ecuador: Creating Fiscal Space for Poverty Reduction: A Fiscal Management and Public Expenditure Review*. Volume II, Report No. 28911-EC, Washington, D.C.: World Bank and IDB.

5
Bolivia

Wilson Jiménez, Mirna Mariscal and Gustavo Canavire

Introduction

The favourable international economic environment during 2002-07 generated an export boom in Bolivia, primarily in hydrocarbons, minerals and agricultural products. At the same time, however, the country went through a period of political instability that has weakened institutions, severely worsened the investment climate and reduced the room to manoeuvre for public policy making.

In 2006, Bolivia began implementing the National Development Plan (PND) called *"Bolivia digna, soberana, y productiva para vivir bien"* (A Dignified, Sovereign and Productive Bolivia for a Better Life) with policies aimed at reducing malnutrition and illiteracy (Ministerio de Planificación del Desarrollo, 2006b). The government also introduced a cash transfer programme as an incentive to keep children in public primary schools.[1] Further, the Policy for Social Protection and Comprehensive Community Development (PPS-DIC) which seeks to strengthen community organizations in municipalities with high poverty levels (Ministerio de Planificación del Desarrollo, 2006a), was also put in place.

The government has enhanced state participation in the production and marketing of strategic natural resources. It has also formulated a strategy for developing production by strengthening small-scale enterprises. In addition, Bolivia has received substantial external debt relief from bilateral and multilateral creditors.

The PND embraces the Millennium Development Goals (MDGs) among its core objectives. This study provides an empirical assessment of the feasibility of achieving the MDGs in Bolivia under alternative financing scenarios. The costs in terms of requirements for scaling up of public spending are estimated through an application for Bolivia of the computable general equilibrium (CGE) model called MAMS, which is described in Chapter 3. This model establishes the functional relationships between a series of determinants, including some macroeconomic aggregates, and a series of indicators associated with the MDGs: the percentage of the population that begins primary education and completes it on time (MDG 2), the child mortality rate (MDG 4), the maternal mortality rate (MDG 5) and the percentage of the population with access to water and basic sanitation services (MDGs 7a and 7b, respectively). The scenarios simulated by using MAMS provide macroeconomic and labour-market outcomes that are subsequently imposed on household survey data, using the microsimulations method described in Appendix A2.1 of Chapter 2. This methodology makes it possible to estimate the simulated impact of enhanced public spending on education, health, and water and sanitation on poverty and income inequality.

Performance of the Bolivian economy

During the 1980s, Bolivia went through a severe crisis that also hit other countries in Latin America. During the crisis, the country witnessed a sharp increase in its public debt and a chronic fiscal deficit. Monetary financing of increasing fiscal deficits led to an episode of hyperinflation of unprecedented proportions, causing a collapse of investment and a contraction of the economy.[2]

In August 1985, a drastic economic stabilization programme was introduced, including fiscal austerity measures, a floating exchange rate, liberalization of the current account, and deregulation of the financial system, among other things. Deeper structural reforms were introduced at a later stage, including public finance reforms, renegotiation of external debt, and targeted interventions aimed at reactivating private sector activity, especially non-traditional agricultural and manufacturing export production.

Between 1985 and 1990, some economic recovery took place, according to the macroeconomic indicators of Table 5.1. GDP grew at an annual average of 2.2 per cent, almost at the same pace as population growth. Tax revenues reached 6.5 per cent of GDP per year, but even so, the fiscal deficit remained high at 5.9 per cent of GDP and had to be financed almost entirely by external borrowing. Consequently, external public debt remained high at more than 80 per cent of GDP. Exports averaged 14 per cent of GDP during the same period.

During the first five years of the 1990s, the Social Investment Fund (FIS) played a central role in the government's enhanced social policy strategy of increased investment in human resources. In that period, GDP grew at an annual average rate of 4.1 per cent, inflation fell to two-digit rates, and the rate of depreciation of the real exchange rate slowed to below 9 per cent (see Table 5.1). Tax revenues increased to 9 per cent of GDP but continued to be insufficient for covering all of the social spending. The fiscal deficit was cut to 4 per cent of GDP, but the dependence on external financing remained practically unchanged and external debt levels remained high at around 72 per cent of GDP.[3]

Table 5.1   Bolivia: main macroeconomic indicators, 1985-2006[a]

	1985-1990	1990-1995	1995-2000	2000-2005	2006
Prices (%)					
Annual inflation rate	1,384.9	12.2	6.4	3.4	4.9
Annual rate of devaluation	3,286.0	8.9	5.3	5.0	-0.6
Real sector					
GDP (millions of Bs)	9,642	23,487	43,054	61,470	89,434
GDP (millions of 1990 Bs)	14,261	17,061	20,856	23,871	27,137
Annual growth of GDP (%)	2.2	4.1	3.4	3.0	4.6
Fiscal sector[b] (% of GDP)					
Total income	27.4	32.2	31.7	30.2	40.9
Tax revenue	6.5	9.0	15.7	18.2	16.6
Total expenditures	32.9	36.2	32.5	31.7	31.8
Capital expenditures	6.5	8.9	7.5	8.6	10.6
Fiscal balance	-5.9	-4.0	-3.1	-5.9	4.6
Domestic financing	2.2	0.4	0.5	2.1	-5.0
External financing	3.7	3.6	2.6	3.8	0.4
External sector (% of GDP)					
Current account balance	-4.1	-3.7	-5.9	-0.4	12.5
Trade balance	-0.6	-3.9	-7.5	6.6	9.9
Exports	14.0	14.6	14.4	20.2	36.4
Imports	-14.6	-18.5	-21.9	-13.6	-26.5
FDI	0.7	2.5	8.8	4.4	2.2
Reserves (months of imports)	4.39	4.89	7.52	7.64	14.03
External debt	82.4	72.2	59.0	55.5	33.1
Total investment (% of GDP)	14.2	15.2	18.6	14.5	15.7
Public	7.6	8.9	6.8	5.5	8.3
Private	6.6	6.3	11.8	9.0	7.4

Source: Unidad de Análisis de Políticas Sociales y Económicas (UDAPE).

[a] Estimates for 1985-2005 are final; data for 2006 are preliminary.

[b] Data correspond to the finances of the non-financial public sector.

In addition, the current account of the balance of payments continued to show a deficit, partly financed through rising foreign direct investment (FDI) which increased by almost two percentage points of GDP.

Deeper, second-generation reforms were introduced in the second half of the 1990s and included measures for recapitalizing some strategic public enterprises and decentralizing public service delivery, including education and health. At the same time, grassroots participation was promoted at the municipal level and the pension system was reformed.

Between 1995 and 2000, economic growth was volatile owing to the indirect impact of the Asian crisis which affected the economies of Bolivia's main trading partners, Argentina and Brazil. In 1999, for example, growth was only 0.43 per cent, which led to an increase in open unemployment and a reduction in labour income (Landa, 2003). Despite these trends, however, the average inflation rate for the five-year period was reduced to one digit and the rate of exchange-rate depreciation moderated (see Table 5.1). Tax revenue increased to 15.7 per cent of GDP and, along with greater fiscal austerity, made it possible to reduce the fiscal deficit to 3.1 per cent of GDP. Higher inflows of FDI helped strengthen the net international reserve position to a level sufficient to cover seven months of imports. The external debt ratio was reduced to 59 per cent of GDP, as a result of the debt relief received in the context of the Heavily Indebted Poor Countries (HIPC) Initiative.[4]

During the first five years of the present decade, a period of economic downturn, Bolivia experienced a severe institutional crisis and high political instability. This led to social conflict and a constitutional change of government in 2003. In response to social and regional demands, a political agenda was put forward that included the convocation of a Constituent Assembly, a referendum on regional autonomy, a referendum on the control of natural gas resources, and earlier than anticipated general elections. Economic recovery began in 2004 helped by favourable world market prices which gave a boost to export earnings of hydrocarbons, minerals and agricultural products. Helped further by the initiation of exports of natural gas to Brazil, exports rose to 20 per cent of GDP on average during 2000-05. At the same time, however, FDI dropped significantly as the programme of capitalization and privatization of public enterprises ended. The reduction in private capital inflows forced a reduction in the level of imports, resulting in a trade surplus and a decrease in the current account deficit. Inflation stayed low, providing proof of macroeconomic stability.

Government revenues grew as a result of improved tax collection and the introduction of a special tax on hydrocarbons. At the same time, however, the government substantially increased spending in response to social demands. In 2003, the non-financial public sector deficit jumped to around 8 per cent of GDP, of which 4 percentage points corresponded to the cost of the reform to the pension system. Between 2002 and 2005, the fiscal deficit remained high, but the degree of external indebtedness fell nonetheless to 55.5 per cent of GDP as a result of debt renegotiation and relief. The resources received through the HIPC Initiative were directed to municipalities to support the fight against poverty.[5] The potential impact of debt relief on public finances was weakened as much of public investment was financed through external borrowing.

In January 2006, the International Monetary Fund (IMF) cancelled the equivalent of $233 million of Bolivia's foreign debt. In July of that same year, the World Bank approved a debt cancellation of $1.5 billion. Additional debt relief of approximately $1.0 billion was also agreed upon with the Inter-American Development Bank (IDB) in the context of the Multilateral Debt Relief Initiative (MDRI). All of this together allowed the external debt ratio to be reduced to 33.1 per cent of GDP in 2006 (see Table 5.1). The debt was reduced even further later in 2007 when the relief from the IDB came into effect.

Trends and prospects for meeting the MDGs

The fourth official MDG Progress Report for Bolivia suggests that it is feasible to achieve several of the goals through the application of the PND. Particularly beneficial would be the social programmes for small farm holder communities targeted at municipalities with a high level of extreme poverty. The reports on the progress towards the MDGs and cost studies presented by the Ministry of Planning of Bolivia are used to describe the trends that are presented below (see Table 5.2).

MDG 1: Incidence of extreme poverty

The target is to reduce by half the percentage of the population with an income of less than one dollar per day at purchasing power parity (PPP) between 1990 and 2015. A similar poverty concept is used for monitoring poverty reduction in Bolivia, but the poverty incidence is measured using a national extreme poverty line that is based on a basket of basic food commodities.

In 1996, extreme poverty measured with the national line was estimated at 39 per cent, but increased to 45 per cent in the year 2000. The target is to lower the extreme poverty rate to 24 per cent by 2015.[6] When using the one-dollar-a-day threshold, 27 per cent of the population lived in extreme poverty in 2000, well short of the target of 14 per cent to be reached by 2015 (see Table 5.2).

Since the late 1980s, poverty fell with episodes of economic growth. Between 1999 and 2003, however, growth was dismal, affecting in particular, construction, manufacturing and services, sectors that are important sources of urban job creation. Agricultural incomes were also affected by a decline in the growth of internal demand. As a consequence, poverty increased (Jiménez and Landa, 2005).

The urban unemployment rate showed an upward trend, increasing from 4.4 per cent in 1997 to 7 per cent in 2000, surpassing 8.5 per cent in 2003, and staying around 8 per cent levels until 2006.[7] The high levels of unemployment that persisted during the last few years were accompanied by a reduction in the time spent looking for work (Canavire and Landa, 2005). Since people were spending less time looking for work, an increase in the share of the inactive

Table 5.2   Bolivia: indicators for monitoring MDGs and goals for 2015

	Starting year		Base year for MAMS		Target for 2015
MDG 1: Eradicate poverty					
Incidence of extreme poverty using national poverty line (%)[a]	41	(1996)	45	(2000)	24
Incidence of extreme poverty using one-dollar-a-day poverty line at PPP (%)	29	(1990)	27	(2000)	14
MDG 2: Universal primary education					
Net primary school enrolment rate (%)	n.a.	--	94	(2003)	100
Gross completion rate for eighth grade of primary (%)	52	(1992)	70	(2001)	99
Percentage of students who begin primary school and complete eighth grade[b]	n.a.	--	71	(2003)	--
MDG 4: Reduce child mortality					
Infant mortality rate (per 1,000 births)[c]	89	(1989)	54	(2003)	30
Coverage of pentavalent vaccine (%)	64	(1994)	80	(2003)	95
MDG 5: Reduce maternal mortality					
Coverage for hospital births (%)	27	(1995)	55	(2003)	70
Maternal mortality rate (per 100,000 births)	416	(1989)	230	(2003)	104
MDG 7: Ensure environmental sustainability					
7a. Potable water coverage (%)	57	(1992)	70	(2001)	78.5
7b. Sewage system coverage (%)	28	(1992)	40	(2001)	64

Source: UDAPE (2005b) and authors' estimates.

[a] The first data for the incidence of extreme poverty measured with the national line is for the year 1996. Extrapolating from this information, a value of 48 per cent was estimated for 1990 and the goal for 2015 was based on this.

[b] Estimated from the reconstruction of a cohort of students who registered in the first year of primary school.

[c] Deaths of children under one year of age.

n.a.: data not available.

population was recorded. The net loss of jobs, especially in manufacturing, caused a displacement of employment towards services and commerce, sectors with high participation in the informal sector (World Bank, 2005). Income inequality rose between 1997 and 2002. The Gini coefficient for per capita family income in urban areas increased from 0.51 in 1996 to 0.54 in 2002, while inequality in rural areas showed pronounced fluctuations.[8]

Economic growth in Bolivia has not been pro-poor. Exports of natural gas have only weak linkages with other production sectors and do not benefit small and medium-sized enterprises (PNUD, 2005). In the PND framework, initiatives have been developed to boost the processing of primary natural resource production and promote rural development, empowering small-farm holders through credit schemes. These measures could help make growth more supportive of poverty reduction.

MDG 2: Completion of primary education

Primary education in Bolivia has a cycle of eight years of education, rather than six years as is more common internationally. Consequently, the gross completion rate for eighth grade has been selected as the indicator for evaluating the goal of achieving universal primary education.[9] According to official estimates, this indicator increased from 55 per cent in 1992 to 70 per cent in 2001 (Table 5.2) and stood at 77.8 per cent in 2005.[10] Based on secondary education records for 2004, a somewhat lower rate is estimated; that is, for each cohort of 100 students who enrolled in primary school, 71 per cent of them had completed eighth grade.[11] In any case, if this trend continues, the primary school completion rate would be expected to near 90 per cent by 2015.

Since the early 1990s, education reforms have promoted actions for increasing school infrastructure through teacher training programmes, bilingual education and other actions aimed at improving the quality of education (Ministry of Education, 2004). In recent years, education policies have sought to increase the internal efficiency of the system, by contributing to raising promotion rates in the first five grades of primary school to over 90 per cent. However, these rates are reduced when students get to sixth grade, due to the insufficient supply of school infrastructure in rural areas, the lack of continuity between the primary school cycles, and students dropping out in the last cycle of primary school.

Both educational infrastructure and the number of teachers have increased with enrolment. In 2002, teachers received an exceptional increase in salary to partially make up for past reductions in pay in real terms. The resources released as a result of the debt relief received under the HIPC II Initiative helped finance the related increase in public spending. Education spending increased to 6.2 per cent of GDP in 2004, up from 5.2 per cent in 1997.

Even though the Bolivian government spends more on education than many other Latin American countries, existing projections suggest that the country will not be able to achieve the target of universal primary education by 2015, as measured here, primarily because of the persistence of high drop-out rates in the last years of the cycle (UDAPE, 2005b).[12]

A cost-effectiveness study in the education sectors identified the obstacles Bolivia faces to meet education targets (De Jong and others, 2005). The study recommends improving access to education in rural areas, primarily through the use of demand subsidies. It also recommends expanding school infrastructure, ensuring greater availability of trained teachers and enhancing school autonomy. The study also estimates that an additional 2 per cent of GDP per annum will need to be spent in order to meet the objective of universal primary education. A study by UDAPE comes to similar findings (Vera, 2006).

MDG 4: Reducing child mortality

The target for MDG 4 is to reduce the under-five child mortality rate by two thirds between 1990 and 2015. In order to monitor this goal, however, the infant mortality rate is used instead, since most child deaths in Bolivia occur among children under one year of age. The high infant mortality rates in Bolivia show that barriers to health access have not yet been overcome (see Table 5.2). Infant mortality rates are closely related to the deficient living conditions in which children are living (UDAPE and UNICEF, 2006a).

The infant mortality rate shows a sustained decline between 1989 and 2003, falling from 89 to 54 per 1,000 live births. Projections of UDAPE (2005a) suggest, however, that with existing trends the target will not be reached by 2015. In order to reach the target of 30 deaths per 1,000 live births, it will be necessary to ensure that all health care measures envisaged in the PND are effectuated.

The observed reduction in infant mortality can be explained primarily by increases in prenatal care coverage, hospital births, coverage of immunizations and by the reduction in the prevalence of diarrheal diseases and respiratory diseases (Ministerio de Salud y Deportes, 2004). An increase in the coverage of water and sanitation services also played a role in the decline of the disease prevalence.

Neonatal deaths happen most often during the first week of life, due to the deficiencies in care at the time of birth, neonatal asphyxia and infections that occur because of the malnutrition and poor health of the mothers. In 2003, only 55.3 per cent of all births took place in hospitals or health care centres, and in rural areas the rate is as low as 30.5 per cent. The lack of adequate prenatal care is one of the primary factors that explain why infant mortality is still high in Bolivia.

MDG 5: Reducing maternal mortality

The target for MDG 5 is to reduce maternal mortality by three quarters between 1990 and 2015. The third official MDG Report for Bolivia estimated the maternal mortality rate on the basis of data from the National Demographic and Health Survey (ENDSA). According to this survey, there were about 416 maternal deaths per 100,000 live births in 1989. The ENDSA for 2003 recorded a rate of 229, suggesting maternal mortality declined by 45 per cent between 1989 and 2003. Yet, the country is still far from the target of 104 deaths per 100,000 live births to be reached by 2015.

The Ministry of Health and Sports (MSD) identified various interventions that could improve health conditions and make it feasible to meet the target of reducing maternal mortality, including increasing coverage of health insurance, immunization programmes, family planning programmes and hospital deliveries (Ministerio de Salud y Deportes, 2004).

In effect, the proportion of births attended in hospitals increased by 37 percentage points between 1994 and 2005 to reach 65 per cent. Healthcare policies of the past 15 years have focused on overcoming economic barriers to the provision of services. In 1996, the National Maternal and Child Insurance (SNMN) programme was launched and two years later that of Basic Health Insurance (SUMI) was introduced, with an extended benefits package. The programme, called EXTENSA, expanded healthcare services in rural areas (UDAPE and UNICEF, 2006a). The Unique Health Insurance (SUS) system was designed in 2006 to expand free healthcare for the population between 5 and 21 years of age, but by mid-2008 it was yet to be implemented. In addition, the Expanded Immunizations Programme (PAI) included the pentavalent vaccine that strengthens the immune system against various diseases that afflict children under five (UDAPE, 2005b). The first two insurance programmes mentioned above and the PAI sought to reduce maternal and infant mortality, while the other plans were aimed at overcoming exclusion from health services.

The risk of maternal mortality increases when haemorrhaging or infections occur during delivery. Miscarriages, eclampsia and anaemia also increase the risk.[13] Even when pregnant women receive care at public health centres, complications in obstetric delivery explain two thirds of the maternal mortality in hospital centres (Ministerio de Salud y Deportes, 2004). In order to reduce infant and maternal mortality and meet the targets for MDGs 4 and 5, UDAPE estimates that it is necessary to increase hospital delivery coverage to at least 70 per cent in 2015. Public spending on health insurance systems has grown on average by 2.5 per cent per year, but in order to expand hospital delivery coverage to the levels required for reaching the mortality goals, it would be necessary to increase health spending by 3.5 per cent per year (Vera, 2006).[14]

MDG 7a and 7b: Increasing the coverage of drinking water and basic sanitation

In order to ensure environmental sustainability, the MDGs also seek to decrease the percentage of the population without access to drinking water and basic sanitation. In the case of Bolivia, the coverage of potable water and basic sanitation was 57 per cent and 28 per cent, respectively, in 1992. In 2001, these levels had risen to 70 per cent and 40 per cent, and it is estimated that they reached 72 per cent and 42 per cent in 2005. The target is to reduce the percentage of the population without access to potable water to 21.5 per cent (MDG 7a) and that without basic sanitation to 36 per cent (MDG 7b) by 2015.

Coverage of drinking water and basic sanitation increased during the 1990s, thanks to the investments made through the social investment funds (SIF), the Popular Participation Law,[15] and private investments in the sector. Beginning in 2001, the National Compensation Policy (PNC) was established in the context of the National Dialogue. This facilitated a greater allocation of resources for social spending by the poorest municipalities. The programmes implemented between 1992 and 2005 were framed within the National "Water for Everyone" Plan and the Ten Year Plan for Basic Sanitation (VSB, 2005). Despite these efforts, investments in the sector have been insufficient. Towards the middle of the current decade, the coverage of services stagnated and the services of providers became less efficient, causing discontent among the population and becoming a source of repeated social conflict.

In 2006, the Ministry of Water was created with a mandate to redefine the regulation of the sector and increasing the role of the government and civil organizations in the provision of basic services. In the context of the PND, further action is to be undertaken to increase services to the population, especially in suburban areas and small cities. According to UDAPE's evaluation for 2006, it is feasible to reach the water and sanitation goals. To that end, programmes are being designed to increase the coverage of these services to the required level.

Model for assessing the MDG strategy: an application for Bolivia

The CGE model that this study uses for evaluating the MDGs is described in detail in Chapter 3. This model, MAMS, permits the construction of a baseline scenario and scenarios in which several of the MDGs are met.

The baseline scenario reproduces trends of key macroeconomic aggregates as observed up to 2006. The business-as-usual scenario assumes that public expenditures grow at the same rate as observed in recent years. The model is calibrated in the baseline such as to achieve a constant real growth of GDP (at market prices) of 3.56 per cent per year during the entire simulation period of 2000-15. This growth rate reflects the performance of the hydrocarbon and mining sectors and takes into account investment projects in the framework of export contracts signed with Argentina and Brazil.[16] Spending on education and health are assumed to increase by 3 per cent and 2 per cent per year, respectively, based on past trends, while spending on water and basic sanitation, as well as infrastructure, is assumed to increase by 2.35 per cent annually. The model assumes that world market prices will increase at trend rates, with the price of imports rising faster than that of exports.[17] The baseline scenario also takes into account the amount of debt relief the country has received in the context of the HIPC Initiative during 2001-05, as well as that received through the MDRI which became effective in 2006. The debt relief received from the IDB in 2007 is not considered, however.[18]

In the MDG scenarios, the assumptions mentioned are maintained, but public spending (recurrent and investment spending) adjusts endogenously to reach the goals as a result of which GDP growth can also be affected. Increased public spending can be financed alternatively through foreign aid (donations), direct taxes, external borrowing or domestic borrowing.

Various macroeconomic closure rules and factor market rules exist for solving for the general equilibrium of the baseline scenario (for more detail, see Chapter 3). Initially, direct tax rates adjust to finance any imbalance in the government current account, keeping the flow of domestic and external borrowing and foreign grants fixed.[19] It is important to mention that this type of macroeconomic adjustment departs from reality in the sense that taxation rates have hardly been modified in Bolivia at all during the last decade, while public investment has been paid for primarily through external financing. On the other hand, consistent with the actual functioning of Bolivia's currency market, the exchange rate is flexible to balance the demand and supply of foreign exchange.

Investment is assumed to be a fixed share of aggregate demand, and the marginal propensity to save of households and firms adjusts to bring savings in line with investment. The model allows changes in the rate of unemployment to achieve equilibrium in the labour market. When wages fall below a 'reservation' (minimum) wage at which workers are not willing to work, the market adjusts through a rise in unemployment. When wages are above the reservation level, the labour market clears through wage adjustment. In contrast, the model assumes full employment of capital.

These closure rules are maintained for all simulations, except for the alternative financing scenarios. According to the latter, emerging fiscal imbalances are no longer financed through direct-tax revenue but rather by flows of, respectively, foreign grants, domestic borrowing or external borrowing.

The model has been estimated using a number of data sources. Many of the model's parameters are directly derived from the Social Accounting Matrix (SAM) for Bolivia. The SAM was built on the basis of national accounts data for the year 2000 provided by the National Statistical Institute (INE).[20] Further, information from the Fiscal Programming Unit (UPF) was used along with balance of payments statistics and financial and monetary statistics from the Central Bank of Bolivia. The SAM specifies key production sectors along with disaggregated accounts for social service delivery, including a breakdown of education and health services by public and non-governmental (private) providers.[21] Overall accounting consistency of the SAM was achieved using the cross-entropy balancing technique proposed in Robinson and others (2001).

Parameters and elasticities not derived from the SAM were directly estimated or derived from other studies. For example, the link between MDG achievement and the provisioning of services of education, health, and water and sanitation is established through logistical functions, according to which, when the level of provision of these services increases and as the indicators approach the targets set for 2015, the contribution of an additional unit of spending decreases. In order to obtain intermediate values for these logistical functions, a series of elasticities needs to be estimated. Owing to limited social sector and household level data, not all of these could be estimated directly and it was necessary to use other studies and estimates derived from the information and assessments of the relevant social sectors.[22]

The elasticities for the determinants of the infant mortality rate and those for water and basic sanitation coverage were obtained from municipal-level data. These indicators were elaborated based on two population censuses (1992 and 2001), administrative records for health and sanitation and budget data from the General Accounting Office.[23] Variation in infant mortality rates across municipalities was tested econometrically in relation to coverage of water and sanitation coverage, municipal per capita consumption, health spending, and public spending on infrastructure for the years 1992 and 2001.[24] Per capita consumption, sector spending, and spending on public infrastructure were tested as determinants of access to drinking water and sanitation.

In the case of primary education, annual series were obtained for enrolment, repetition and graduation rates. These outcomes were related in econometric regressions to per student education expenditures, public spending on infrastructure and per capita household consumption. The regression estimates for the education model were not found to be very robust statistically; hence, they were subject to further scrutiny and sensitivity analysis in the calibration of MAMS, ensuring feasible and plausible outcomes.

In addition to the elasticities associated with the MDG functions, elasticities of substitution between domestic and imported products were estimated through available series provided by INE. Elasticities of substitution for household production and household consumption are based on assumptions, along the lines of other studies of applied CGE analysis for Bolivia (Jemio and Wiebelt, 2003). In addition, the model uses exogenous growth rates for the population and labour force obtained on the basis of household survey data and demographic projections.

Analysis of policy simulations

Baseline scenario

Detailed results on required financing for all scenarios are found in Appendix A5. The baseline presents a plausible trajectory for the economy, even though outcomes for the external sector deviate somewhat from those observed mainly because the SAM could not be constructed for a more recent base year.[25] For example, the baseline of the model underestimates the actual export performance during the 2000s. The model predicts a 4 per cent annual increase in exports, but in reality exports grew by 15 per cent per year between 2003 and 2006. The model also only partially captures the surge in world market prices for minerals in that period.

Exports increase more strongly than imports in the baseline, resulting in an appreciation of the exchange rate by 0.3 per cent per year, which in turn mitigates the initial impact on the current account deficit. Ultimately, foreign savings fall from 8.2 per cent to 7.5 per cent of GDP between 2000 and 2015.[26] Private and government consumption fall as a share of GDP, though government consumption grows according to the aforementioned assumptions. At the same time, the debt relief in the context of the HIPC Initiative and the MDRI allows external borrowing to stay within the limits of debt sustainability.[27]

Under the baseline trends and assumptions, none of the selected MDGs would be achieved by 2015 (see Figure 5.1).[28] In this scenario, by 2015 the percentage of students that begin primary school and complete it would rise to 93 per cent; infant mortality would fall to 40 infants per 1,000 live births (the target being 30); maternal mortality is reduced to 159 per 100,000 live births, which is higher than the target of 104; and the coverage for water and sanitation increases, but stays, respectively, around 2 and 7 percentage points short of the target. A comparison of the scenarios where one or several goals are met with the baseline scenario indicates how much it would cost to close these gaps in order to reach the goals in what follows.

Scenarios for achieving the MDGs separately

According to the model, the additional public expenditure needed (as compared to the base scenario) to meet the target of getting all children to enrol in primary school and to complete it on time, would be the equivalent of 1.3 per cent of GDP per year, if financed with external resources, or 1.8 per cent of GDP per year, if financed through domestic resource mobilization, and if none of the other MDGs are being pursued at the same time (see Table 5.3). Most of this percentage corresponds to government final consumption expenditures (0.9 or 1.1 percentage points, depending on the source of the financing, respectively). Other costs relate to additional investments in infrastructure and specific programmes to promote school retention.

Furthermore, the simulation results suggest that meeting MDG 2 would be least costly in terms of required additional public spending when financed through foreign grants or external borrowing. In the case of foreign aid, for example, Bolivia would need to receive additional amount of donations of 4 per cent of GDP per year between 2005 and 2010 to meet MDG 2, but this amount would gradually fall to 0.2 per cent of GDP in 2015. Each year on average 2.5 per cent of GDP would need to be mobilized in the form of foreign aid to achieve MDG 2 during 2000-15. This source of funding would ensure

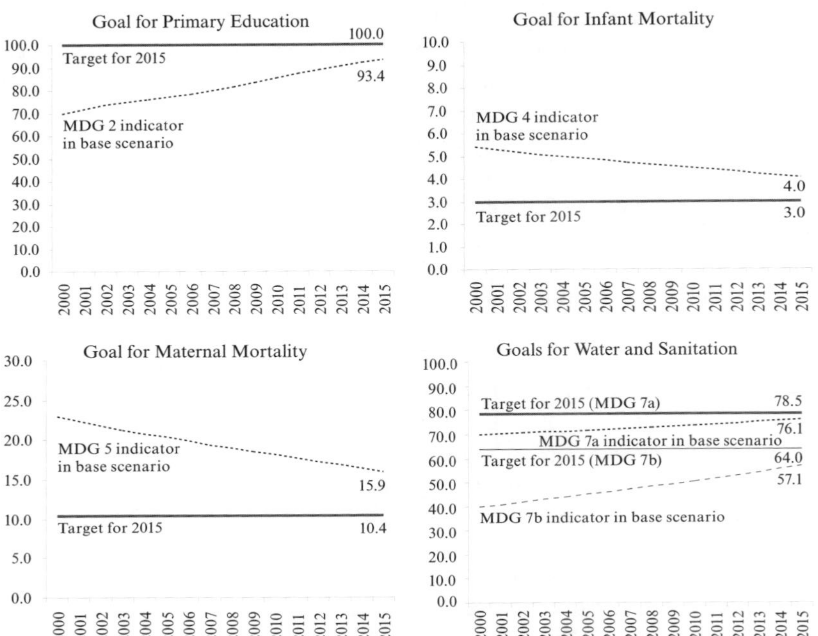

Figure 5.1   Bolivia: Projection of MDG indicators in the baseline and targets for 2015

Source: MAMS model for Bolivia.

fiscal sustainability. Financing through external or domestic borrowing would increase public debt to unsustainable levels (respectively, 66.3 per cent and 70.5 per cent of GDP by 2015). If the additional spending is financed by increasing direct-tax rates, total government revenue should increase by 2.5 per cent of GDP compared with the baseline during the period of 2005-10.

Achieving the goal of primary education through foreign grants would allow an increase in public investment and consumption spending in primary education, without elevating the fiscal deficit. At the same time, in this scenario, the GDP growth rate would reach 3.7 per cent per year, slightly higher than the baseline growth rate. In other words, this financing option would not generate a trade-off with growth effects as it would with the alternatives. As in the case in the external borrowing scenario, increased foreign aid would cause an appreciation of the exchange rate which in turn would discourage exports. Consequently, in this scenario, domestic demand becomes a more important source of economic growth. The resulting Dutch-disease effects are reflected in a reduction in the exports-to-GDP ratio and this also explains why the required aid inflows (2.5 per cent of GDP per annum) exceed the required financing to back the additional public spending of 1.3 per cent of

Table 5.3   Bolivia: Annual additional public spending required to meet the MDGs separately, under different financing scenarios, 2000-2015 (Percentage of GDP)

Millennium Development Goals	Financing scenarios with:			
	foreign grants	direct taxes	external borrowing	domestic borrowing
Universal primary education	1.3	1.8	1.3	1.8
Reducing infant and maternal mortality	1.0	1.1	1.0	1.1
Increased access to drinking water and basic sanitation	0.1	0.1	0.1	0.1

Source: MAMS for Bolivia.

GDP per annum to achieve MDG 2. A similar outcome is also obtained in the scenario in which all MDGs are achieved simultaneously, as discussed further below.

In order to meet only the targets for reducing infant and maternal mortality, annual public spending would need to scale up by 1.0 per cent of GDP, on average, during 2000-15, if financed with external resources. It would need to increase by 1.1 per cent of GDP per year if paid for by additional domestic resource mobilization (see Table 5.3). Most of the additional resources would be needed for investments in health infrastructure and equipment; the larger share of these investments would need to be made between 2005 and 2010 in order to timely achieve the targets for MDGs 4 and 5. The macroeconomic trade-offs are similar as in the case of increased spending to achieve the education target, but weaker as the health targets can be achieved with a smaller rise in public spending.

Finally, to meet the goals in the area of water and basic sanitation separately, public spending in the sector would only have to increase modestly as a share of GDP: around 0.1 points per year. Achieving these goals, however, involves concurrence with private sector investments.[29]

Scenarios for achieving the MDGs simultaneously

According to the predictions of the MAMS scenarios, in order to meet all of MDGs 2, 4, 5 and 7 simultaneously, rather than separately, the government would have to spend an additional amount of between 1.7 per cent and 2.8 per cent of GDP per annum during 2000-2015 (see Table 5.4), but most scaling up of public spending is needed during 2005-2010. This seems affordable, but the viability of the MDG strategy will further depend on the trade-offs caused by financing strategy.

If the attainment of all of the goals is financed through direct taxes, tax revenue would need to increase to 26 per cent of GDP between 2005 and 2010, almost 5 additional points with respect to the baseline scenario. Government savings grow as a result of the increase in direct taxes; however, less available income causes a reduction in private consumption of around 4 percentage

Table 5.4   Bolivia: additional public spending required annually in order to achieve MDGs for education, health, water and sanitation, simultaneously, under different financing scenarios, 2000-2015 (Percentage of GDP)

	Financing scenarios with:			
	foreign grants	direct taxes	external borrowing	domestic borrowing
Final consumption expenditures				
Primary education	0.7	0.8	0.7	0.8
Health	0.4	0.5	0.4	0.5
Water and sanitation	0.0	0.0	0.0	0.0
Investment spending				
Primary education	0.3	0.6	0.3	0.6
Health	0.3	0.7	0.6	0.7
Water and sanitation	0.1	0.2	0.1	0.2
Total public spending	1.7	2.8	2.0	2.8

Source: MAMS for Bolivia.

points of GDP in the same period. When additional public spending is paid for through domestic borrowing, government savings would turn negative (on average -4 per cent of GDP per year in the 2005-10 period). Domestic public debt would already surpass 50 per cent of GDP by 2010—and would level off at 80 per cent of GDP by 2015—which would be considered well above critical debt sustainability levels. Financing the increased spending through taxation or domestic borrowing would only generate a mild appreciation of the exchange rate compared with the baseline, only moderately slowing the rate of export growth.

The external financing scenarios show a different picture. If donations are used, they could increase and surpass 4.4 per cent of GDP per year between 2005 and 2010 when most spending would need to be scaled up—after which they would decline gradually, reaching little less than 2 per cent of GDP by 2015. With external borrowing, on the other hand, the government must borrow an equivalent of 6.7 per cent of GDP per year for the 2005-10 period—though the percentage would gradually go down to 5.0 per cent by 2015, but that strategy would not be viable since the accumulated external debt would reach 75 per cent of GDP by the end of the whole simulation period, surpassing by far the limits of sustainability. Using external resources, as opposed to internal resources, would generate a more marked exchange rate appreciation. Between 2005 and 2010, for example, there would be more than 13 per cent appreciation with respect to the baseline. This would affect the current account and the capacity to export, forcing the country to mobilize additional foreign resources to finance a widening trade deficit, in amounts exceeding those required to source the increase in public spending for the MDGs.

Microsimulation results for extreme poverty

The analysis of the previous goals is based directly on the results of simulations with MAMS. The goal of reducing extreme poverty, however, was analysed after application of the microsimulation methodology. As explained in Chapter 2 (see, specifically, Appendix A2.1), sequential changes in the labour market produced by MAMS' scenarios are linked with household survey data in order to evaluate the variations in income distribution and measure extreme and total poverty using national and international (one- and two-dollar-a-day) poverty lines. The 2000 household survey used was conducted in the context of the project Improving Surveys for the Measurement of Living Conditions (MECOVI).

The population that lives on less than one dollar a day falls from 27.1 per cent in 2000 to 23.9 per cent in 2015 in the baseline scenario; that is to say, the target for MDG 1 of halving extreme poverty is not met. Similarly, the target is also not met when using the national poverty line, since the degree of poverty reduction is of a similar magnitude as in the case of applying the international poverty line (see Tables 5.2 and 5.5). The scenarios for achieving the MDGs for education, health and basic sanitation do not achieve much more poverty reduction. Only the scenarios with external financing reduce extreme poverty slightly more (by 0.7 percentage points during 2000-15).

The insufficient decrease in poverty is caused in part because inequality remains high in the baseline scenario. Both the Gini coefficient of labour income and per capita household income remain virtually unchanged (see Table 5.5). The poverty reduction that would be achieved under any of the scenarios is largely explained by changes in the overall level of employment and changes in average remunerations. Poverty reduction falls short of the target because the increase in remuneration for unskilled workers is negligible and insufficient to take many of them out of extreme poverty (see Table 5.6). In addition, the supply of unskilled and semi-skilled workers increases relatively more than the supply of skilled workers, so at going wages, workers who join the labour market or find new jobs have limited possibilities of getting out of poverty. The growth pattern under both the baseline and MDG scenarios mainly generates employment for unskilled workers at low wages and pushes up the relative remuneration for skilled workers, thus preventing a reduction in income inequality.

In the MDG scenarios, the supply of services of education, health, and water and sanitation increases. This causes a stronger increase in average labour incomes as compared with the baseline, but the real wage increase remains stronger for skilled workers, given the relatively high skill intensity of the delivery social services. However, also when pursuing the MDGs, the average wage increase remains insufficient to meet the target for reducing extreme poverty.

Similarly, the reduction in unemployment is not significant enough to reduce poverty because the open unemployment rate is relatively low (5 per cent), and

Table 5.5   Bolivia: results of the microsimulations in the baseline and all MDGs scenarios, 2000-2015

	2000	2005	2010	2015	2000	2005	2010	2015
	National poverty lines							
	Total poverty (%)				Extreme poverty (%)			
Baseline scenario	66.4	65.1	62.8	60.6	45.2	43.8	41.5	39.4
All MDGs with foreign grants	66.4	64.0	60.9	59.2	45.2	42.9	40.0	38.4
All MDGs with direct taxes	66.4	64.6	62.5	60.5	45.2	43.4	41.5	39.5
All MDGs with external borrowing	66.4	64.0	60.9	59.3	45.2	42.9	40.0	38.4
All MDGs with domestic borrowing	66.4	64.7	62.5	60.5	45.2	43.5	41.6	39.5
	International poverty lines							
	1 dollar a day (PPP) (%)				2 dollars a day (PPP) (%)			
Baseline scenario	27.1	27.0	26.0	24.7	43.3	42.8	41.0	39.0
All MDGs with foreign grants	27.1	26.5	24.8	24.0	43.3	42.0	39.3	37.8
All MDGs with direct taxes	27.1	26.9	25.9	24.7	43.3	42.3	40.9	39.0
All MDGs with external borrowing	27.1	26.6	24.8	24.0	43.3	42.0	39.2	37.8
All MDGs with domestic borrowing	27.1	26.9	26.0	24.7	43.3	42.5	41.0	39.0
	Gini Coefficient							
	Labour income				Per capita household income			
Baseline scenario	0.59	0.60	0.60	0.60	0.62	0.62	0.62	0.62
All MDGs with foreign grants	0.59	0.60	0.60	0.59	0.62	0.62	0.62	0.61
All MDGs with direct taxes	0.59	0.60	0.60	0.60	0.62	0.62	0.62	0.62
All MDGs with external borrowing	0.59	0.60	0.60	0.59	0.62	0.62	0.62	0.61
All MDGs with domestic borrowing	0.59	0.60	0.60	0.60	0.62	0.62	0.62	0.62

Source: MAMS for Bolivia and microsimulations based on 2000 household survey data.

given that unemployment is concentrated among unskilled workers and given their low remunerations and the high degree of informality in the sectors where they work, the increase in the employment rate has little impact on poverty.

The microsimulations demonstrate that reducing extreme poverty requires policy actions that go beyond expanding social programmes. It is necessary to adopt complementary measures in order to improve the overall level of productivity in the economy allowing for higher wages, among others by improving production conditions in low-productivity sectors, enhancing the accumulation of human capital and removing infrastructural bottlenecks. The MDG strategy and the PND pursue such objectives, but these will take time to produce the desired outcomes. In the case of investment in human capital, for instance,

Table 5.6   Bolivia: rate of growth in employment and labour income by type of worker in the baseline scenario and all MDGs scenarios under different forms of financing, 2000-2015

	Baseline scenario	Financing with:			
		foreign grants	direct taxes	external borrowing	domestic borrowing
Employment	2.2	2.2	2.3	2.2	2.3
Unskilled workers	2.1	2.0	2.2	2.0	2.2
Semi-skilled workers	2.4	2.5	2.5	2.5	2.5
Skilled workers	1.9	2.1	2.0	2.1	2.0
Real income per worker	1.4	1.9	1.5	1.9	1.5
Unskilled workers	1.5	1.9	1.4	1.9	1.4
Semi-skilled workers	0.9	1.0	0.8	1.0	0.8
Skilled workers	1.8	2.2	2.1	2.2	2.1

Source: MAMS for Bolivia.

most of the desired impact on productivity likely will take effect beyond 2015, given the time lags involved in enhancing the overall educational level of the labour force.

Conclusions and policy recommendations

Achieving all MDGs in Bolivia by 2015 is a major challenge. In a 'business-as-usual' scenario the goals are not achieved. Scaling up public expenditures to meet the targets for education, health, water and sanitation in itself is not sufficient to produce the employment and income effects needed to also achieve the target of halving extreme poverty by 2015.

The model simulations analysed here suggest that the goals for achieving universal primary education, reduce infant and maternal mortality, and enhanced access of the population to water and basic sanitation would be reachable if public spending is increased by between 1.7 per cent and 2.8 per cent of GDP per year during 2005 and 2015, depending on the financing scenario. Achieving all these goals simultaneously would be less costly than in the hypothetical where they would be pursued in uncoordinated fashion, as there are important synergy effects between the MDGs to take advantage of.

Financing through direct taxes would require increasing tax revenue by between 4 and 5 GDP points per year between 2005 and 2010 when most spending needs to be scaled up. This amounts to nearly 3 percentage points of GDP on average for the whole period up to 2015. Raising taxes would negatively affect private consumption, part of which is also important to achieve the different goals. If financing is through domestic borrowing, the fiscal deficit would increase substantially and domestic public debt would increase to an unsustainable level of over 80 per cent of GDP in 2015.

Financing through external borrowing produces less trade-offs with GDP growth and private demand as in the scenarios with domestic resource mobilization, but would also induce chronic fiscal deficits and intensify the existing external debt dependence. The required additional external borrowing in this scenario would be in the order of 4 per cent of GDP between 2005 and 2010, or around 2 per cent of GDP in the whole period to 2015, and external debt would increase to over 75 per cent by 2015, surpassing the limits of debt sustainability. Alternatively, the annual flow of grants from external donors would need to increase by around 4.4 per cent or 3 per cent of GDP per year during 2005-10 or up until 2015 in order to finance the scaled-up public spending to meet the MDGs. Both forms of external financing would cause a marked appreciation in the exchange rate eroding export competitiveness and which would further increase external financing needs over and above those needed to finance the public spending increase that is required to achieve the MDGs.

Bolivia thus would need additional external support to embark on a more viable strategy towards achieving some of the MDGs. This will require allocation of the additional resources towards universalizing access to social services and improving their efficiency. There is a particular need to provide demand incentives to enhance access to education services in rural areas, to improve teacher performance, and to expand the supply of schools that provide secondary-level education. In the area of health, it is necessary to consolidate immunization programmes and expand primary health care services, provide health centres with the necessary equipment, and enhance preventive health programmes in order to reduce the prevalence of diseases and reduce maternal and infant mortality. In addition, public and private investment in water and sanitation must be stepped up further to enhance coverage, especially in rural areas and small municipalities.

Achievement at the same time of the targeted reduction in extreme poverty would require additional, aggressive policies promoting productive development in Bolivia and boosting factor productivity to facilitate more substantial increases in labour income. In this sense, the PND should give priority to measures that strengthen linkages between the modern economy (gas and mining sectors) and other sectors, not only through transfers (tax on hydrocarbons, departmental royalties, or national dialogue account) but also through projects that support the development of non-traditional activities that can also find a niche in world markets. Removing infrastructural deficits in transportation and communications systems and improving business support services will also be critical in order to achieve significant increases in factor productivity. Greater progress in social and human development may be expected to facilitate increases in productivity in the future. The PND is promoting a Policy for Social Protection and Comprehensive Community Development aimed at supporting communities in rural areas as well as small-scale producers in urban areas. The challenge is to follow through on these promises and cautiously deal with the short-term macroeconomic trade-offs that scaling up of public spending may generate.

Appendix A5

Table A5.1 Bolivia: flows of financing in the baseline and MDG scenarios, 2000-2015 (Percentage of GDP)

Financing and savings variables	Base scenario	MDG Scenarios with:							
		foreign grants	direct taxes	external borrowing	domestic borrowing	foreign grants	direct taxes	external borrowing	domestic borrowing
		MDG 2				*MDGs 4 and 5*			
Direct and indirect taxes	20.9	20.5	23.6	20.5	20.6	20.8	22.1	20.8	20.9
Government savings	2.4	0.2	3.1	-0.2	-0.5	1.7	3.0	1.6	1.6
Foreign savings	7.7	10.4	7.7	10.8	7.7	9.0	7.7	9.1	7.7
Domestic borrowing (flow)	1.6	1.6	1.6	1.6	5.2	1.6	1.6	1.6	3.1
External borrowing (flow)	2.1	2.0	2.1	4.9	2.1	2.1	2.1	3.4	2.1
Foreign grants (flow)	0.0	2.5	0.0	0.0	0.0	1.2	0.0	0.0	0.0
Domestic public debt (stock)	20.4	19.9	20.2	19.9	39.8	20.2	20.3	20.2	26.9
External public debt (stock)	37.3	34.8	36.8	51.4	36.8	36.4	37.2	42.4	37.2
		MDG 7				*MDGs 2, 4-5 and 7*			
Direct and indirect taxes	20.9	20.9	21.0	20.9	20.9	20.5	24.7	20.5	20.7
Government savings	2.4	2.3	2.5	2.3	2.3	0.1	3.9	-0.4	-0.7
Foreign savings	7.7	7.8	7.7	7.9	7.7	11.0	7.7	11.5	7.7
Domestic borrowing (flow)	1.6	1.6	1.6	1.6	1.7	1.6	1.6	1.6	6.3
External borrowing (flow)	2.1	2.1	2.1	2.3	2.1	2.0	2.1	5.5	2.1
Foreign grants (flow)	0.0	0.1	0.0	0.0	0.0	3.1	0.0	0.0	0.0
Domestic public debt (stock)	20.4	20.4	20.4	20.4	21.0	19.8	20.2	19.8	44.1
External public debt (stock)	37.3	37.2	37.3	37.9	37.3	34.4	36.8	53.7	37.0

Source: MAMS for Bolivia.

Notes

1   The programme includes the "Juancito Pinto" cash transfer, of 200 Bs per year (about US$ 25) to all students enrolled in first through eighth grades in the public schools.

2   In 1985, inflation reached a level of 8,170.5 per cent. Between 1981 and 1985, the economy shrank at a pace of nearly 2 per cent per year. Later, in 1986-87, foreign debt came to represent more than 90 per cent of GDP.

3   The fiscal deficit has been affected by the costs of the reform to the pension system which is estimated at about 4 per cent of GDP. If there are no further adjustments to the system, those costs should start going down in 2011.

4   Bolivia entered the HIPC Initiative in 1997. In 2001, with the elaboration of the Bolivian Poverty Reduction Strategy (BPRS), the country's participation in the expanded HIPC-II Initiative was approved.

5   The HIPC Initiative established that the resources freed by the debt relief should be directed to poverty reduction programmes, based on the contents of the BPRS.

6   The Third Progress Report on the MDGs defined the specific target for extreme poverty reduction based on an extrapolation of values between 1996 (initial year) and the goal for 2015, establishing it at 24 per cent. However, according to PND projections, extreme poverty incidence could fall to 20 per cent by 2015.

7   Unemployment data from 2000 come from the capitals of the nine departments and the municipality of "El Alto", largest cities in the country. The longest unemployment series were available only for these geographic areas. According to the 2001 Census, 55 per cent of the Bolivian population live in these cities.

8   Measuring income in the rural areas is more difficult because of the high percentage of production going directly to self consumption among small producers. Inequality in income distribution fluctuates between 0.6 and 0.65 and is at least as high as what is seen at the national level (Landa, 2003).

9   The gross completion rate for primary school is defined as the ratio of the total number of students promoted to the eighth year of primary school in a given year over the total population with the official age for attending this grade (13 year-olds). This rate does not restrict the age of those who finish eighth grade.

10   Information in the Fourth MDG Progress Report.

11   This percentage corresponds to the survival rate in the system at the eighth grade level of primary school and includes the students who repeat the grade and enroll again. When these students are excluded, the rate drops to 58.1 per cent. Similar estimates of the promotion rates per grade have been obtained by Zambrana (2005).

12   In 2003, the Ministry of Education projected the indicators in education and estimated the spending necessary to reach the MDGs for the sector.

13   According to 2003 ENDSA data, blood haemoglobin tests reveal that one third of all women of child-bearing age have anaemia and 7 per cent have moderate to severe anaemia, something that tends to affect a higher percentage of pregnant women and women with lower levels of schooling, especially in the western regions of the country.

14   The cost estimates are based on a procedure designed by UDAPE and presented in Vera (2006) and include, among other actions, interventions related to the strengthening of health insurance programmes, networks, quality control, expansion of coverage, universal health insurance and nutrition (for children and mothers).

15   The Popular Participation Law of 1994 allocated 20 per cent of the fiscal revenue of more than 300 municipal governments—whose competencies in local social service administration had been broadened—primarily to the areas of education, health and provision of water.

16   The growth rate is consistent with the medium- and long-term projections made by UDAPE and the Central Bank. The projections, however, do not consider the nationalization of hydrocarbons and the installation of projects in strategic sectors (mining, hydrocarbons and electricity), measures that are part of the PND of the government of President Evo Morales. The PND foresees reaching an investment rate of nearly 24 per cent of GDP per year through 2010, more than doubling the rate achieved in 2004 (11.2 per cent). The growth projection also does not account for the renegotiation of contracts with foreign companies nor does it take into consideration the effects of the global economic crisis that started in 2008.

17   In the last few years, the prices of minerals and hydrocarbons stayed high in international markets, which translated into a surplus in the Bolivian balance of trade starting in 2004. The assumptions of the model, looking towards the horizon of the year 2015, recognize the possibility of a tendency toward more accelerated growth in the prices for imported goods.

18   The debt relief from the IDB was still in the process of being approved when this study was undertaken.

19   In a strict sense, Bolivia does not have a direct tax on personal income. Rather, it has a regime that complements the value added tax and taxes the labour income of persons. In MAMS for Bolivia, however, the tax is treated as a levy on household income.

20   An input-output matrix, the integrated economic accounts table, and complementary matrices with information of transfers, interest payments and other inter-institutional transactions were used to build the SAM.

21   The disaggregation of this sector was carried out using data from national accounts and from health sector financing, as well as reports from non-governmental organizations linked to the sector and public and private health care funds. The production of private education services was estimated based on the distribution of enrolment and the directories of private establishments, among others.

22   Various national and international agencies drew up projections and costs based on partial equilibrium models. Those developed by Ministerio de Educación (2004), Ministerio de Salud y Deportes (2004), De Jong and others (2005) and UDAPE (2006a) were particularly useful. For the water and sanitation sector, the estimates of costs and coverage presented in Salguiero and Castrillo (2002) and VSB (2005) were used.

23   The municipal data on sectoral spending show incomplete coverage, which is why they are only taken as a reference and in several cases yielded estimated elasticities that were not statistically robust.

24   For maternal mortality, elasticities were defined based on infant mortality results. The elasticities are lower than those estimated for infant mortality, which leads to the assumption that decreasing the number of maternal deaths could become more difficult in the future.

25   The SAM was built for the year 2000 and its estimates are influenced by the impact of the economic crisis starting in 1999.

26   Because of export revenues, modifications in the tax on the hydrocarbons sector, and to some degree low budgetary spending, Bolivia's government has recorded a fiscal surplus in the last few years.

27   The HIPC initiative defines the debt sustainability threshold as a value of the debt that is no more than 150 per cent of exports. Since the model does not reproduce this indicator, the Andean Community indicator is used, which defines debt as unsustainable when it surpasses 50 per cent of GDP.

28   With some differences due to differing methodologies, the results of this study resemble the projections drawn in the Third Report on the MDGs (UDAPE, 2005b).

29   The National Plan for Basic Sanitation 2001-10 estimated that to achieve the MDGs
     in the sector, a total investment of $2,408 million would be required through the year
     2025. Because of natural population growth, an additional $65 million to $85 million
     per year would be required (less than 1 per cent of GDP), including public and private
     financing, in order to cover water and sanitation needs.

References

Canavire, G., and F. Landa (2005). "Duración del desempleo en el área urbana de Bolivia un análisis de los efectos de los niveles de instrucción y características socioeconómicas". *Revista de Análisis Económico* 22, Unidad de Análisis de Políticas Económicas y Sociales (UDAPE), La Paz.

De Jong, Nick, Arjun Bedi, Juan Ponce and Rob Vos (2005). "Presupuestación para la educación: Bolivia, Honduras y Nicaragua", Evaluating Poverty Reduction Strategies in Latin America – 2005, Stockholm and The Hague: Swedish International Development Cooperation Agency (Sida) and Institute of Social Studies.

Jemio, L., and M. Wiebelt (2003). "¿Existe Espacio para Políticas Anti-Shocks en Bolivia? Lecciones de un Análisis basado en un Modelo de Equilibrio General Computable", *Revista Latinoamericana de Desarollo Económico* 1(1): 37–68.

Jiménez, W, and Bolivia Landa (2005). "¿Tuvo crecimiento pro-pobre entre los años 1993-2002?" *Revista Análisis Económico* 20, UDAPE, La Paz.

Landa, Fernando (2003). *Pobreza y distribución del ingreso en Bolivia: Entre 1999 y 2002.* UDAPE Working Paper, La Paz.

Ministerio de Educación (2004). *Plan de trabajo del sector educación en el contexto de las metas del milenio (2004-2006)*, La Paz.

Ministerio de Planificación del Desarrollo (2006a). *Marco Conceptual, Políticas y Estrategias de Protección Social y Desarrollo Integral Comunitario*, La Paz.

__________ (2006b). *Plan Nacional de Desarrollo. "Bolivia digna, soberana y productiva para vivir bien*, La Paz.

Ministerio de Salud y Deportes (2004). *El sector salud en el contexto de las metas del milenio. Plan de trabajo 2004-2006*, La Paz.

PNUD (2005). *Informe Temático del Desarrollo Humano. Economía más allá del gas*, Programa de Naciones Unidas para el Desarrollo, La Paz.

Robinson, S., A. Cattaneo and M. El Said (2001). "Updating and Estimating a Social Accounting Matrix Using Cross Entropy Methods", *Economic System Research* 13(1): 47-64.

Salgueiro, René, and Castrillo, Luis (2002). *Plan de acción para el logro de las metas del milenio en agua potable y saneamiento en Bolivia. Metodología de estimación de inversiones. Viceministerio de servicios básicos*, La Paz.

UDAPE (Social and Economic Policy Analysis Unit) (2005a). *Informes Económico y Social 2003 – 2004*, Social and Economic Policy Analysis Unit, La Paz.

__________ (2005b). *Tercer informe 2003-2004. Progreso de los Objetivos de Desarrollo del Milenio Asociados al Desarrollo Humano*, Comité Interinstitucional de las Metas de Desarrollo del Milenio, La Paz.

__________ (2006). *Objetivos de desarrollo del milenio*, Cuarto informe de progreso, UDAPE – Comité Interinstitucional para las Metas del Milenio: La Paz.

UDAPE (Social and Economic Policy Analysis Unit) and UNICEF (2006a). *Evaluación de impacto de los seguros de maternidad y niñez*, UDAPE-UNICEF: La Paz.

__________ (2006b). *Gasto social funcional y el gasto social para la niñez*, UDAPE–UNICEF: La Paz.

UNDP (United Nations Development Programme) (2005). *Informe Temático del Desarrollo Humano. Economía más allá del gas*, UNDP, La Paz.

Vandermoortele, J., and Roy, R. (2004). "Making sense of MGD costing", Bureau for Development Policy, New York.

Vera, Miguel (2006). "Costeo de las metas sociales prioritarias del plan nacional de desarrollo (PND)", Consulting Report, Ministry of Planning for Development, Vice-Minister of Planning and Coordination, Social and Economic Policy Analysis Unit, La Paz.

VSB (Vice-Ministry of Basic Services) (2005). *Plan Bolivia – Sector Agua y Saneamiento Básico*, La Paz.

World Bank (2005). *Bolivia Poverty Assessment: Establishing the Basis for Pro-Poor Growth*, Washington.

Zambrana, Gilmar (2005). *Cumplimiento de los Objetivos del Milenio en Educación*. Universidad Católica Boliviana (UCB), La Paz.

6
Chile

Raul O'Ryan, Carlos J. de Miguel and Camilo Lagos

Introduction

Chile has committed to meeting its Millennium Development Goals (MDGs) by the year 2015. Over the last two decades, the country made great progress towards these goals, possibly more than any other country in Latin America.

This chapter looks at whether it is likely that Chile will be able to achieve the MDGs within the specified time period and —to the extent the country appears to be off track towards some of the goals—recommend specific policies to make their achievement possible. The analysis has been carried out by simulating alternative scenarios of economic growth and public spending through the year 2015. The simulations are conducted using the computable general equilibrium (CGE) model called MAMS, described in Chapter 3. The distributive repercussions of the various scenarios simulated with MAMS—working through the labour market—are also analysed using a microsimulation method described in Chapter 2 (See Appendix A2.1).

The next section describes Chile's economic performance and its progress thus far towards meeting the MDGs during the 1990-2005 period. The subsequent section analyses the main determinants of progress towards specific MDGs and the estimation of some key MDG-related elasticities of MAMS for Chile. The fourth section looks at the results obtained from comparing the achievement of the goals in a baseline scenario, where public spending increases at the same pace as that of recent years, with a series of scenarios where public spending is adjusted endogenously in order to achieve each of the goals separately, as well as to achieve all of them simultaneously. The minimum rates of economic growth required to achieve the goals or speed up the achievement of some of them are also determined. The fifth section analyses the distributive repercussions of the main policy scenarios analysed and the final section presents the main conclusions and policy recommendations.

Economic and social context for achieving the MDGs in Chile

Over the past 15 years, macroeconomic stability, improved social policies and targeted public spending have allowed Chile to make significant progress not only in terms of economic growth, but also in terms of many of the indicators used to monitor MDG progress towards pre-established targets. According to government officials, the country is in a position to be able to achieve many of the targets ahead of schedule (MIDEPLAN, 2005a). The following section looks at the social and economic context of public policies developed and the achievement of the MDGs.

Social and economic performance

Historically, growth in Chile has been based on renewable and non-renewable natural resources. Copper is the main export product, accounting for about 45 per cent of total exports in 2005 (DIRECON, 2006). A continuous process of export diversification has taken place in the last quarter century, however.

The last decade of the twentieth century was characterized by a high degree of economic and political stability. Prosperous growth was achieved in an environment of reliable institutions, continuity in economic policies, and strengthened market functioning, along with trade liberalization. These factors also attracted new foreign investment to Chile in spite of the economy's relatively small domestic market (ICEX, 2003).

The process of privatization of public services, initiated in the mid-1990s, has continued in the last 15 years. Policies have also promoted private investment in infrastructure, telecommunications, electricity and air transportation, and most domestic markets have been liberalized. Important trade agreements have been signed. Reforms have been made in the education system. At the same time, regulation of some key markets such as the electricity market and the capital market has been enhanced. As a result, domestic market functioning has become more efficient and import tariffs are close to zero for countries with whom Chile has trade agreements. Since the early 1990s—once development policies designed in the period of authoritarian government could be left behind—the State has also re-established its role as protector of the common good and has taken the lead on resolving pressing social and environmental problems.

All these factors have contributed to Chile's strong economic performance. Between 1995 and 2003, GDP grew at an annual average rate of 4.9 per cent (Central Bank, 2006), a much higher rate than in other countries of the region where economic growth barely hovered around 2 per cent during the same period (CEPAL, 2005a).[1] As a result, per capita GDP reached $7,000 at current prices in 2005, more than double that of 15 years earlier. Growth rates of 6.2 per cent in 2004 and 6.3 per cent in 2005 generated expectations that high growth rates could be sustained, leading to average growth projections in some studies of around 5.5 per cent per year up to 2010 (Eyzaguirre, 2005).

These expectations have turned out to be too optimistic, however. GDP growth in 2006, which was at first expected to be around 5 per cent, ended up reaching only 4.4 per cent, and projections have become more conservative as a reflection of greater economic uncertainty. Current discussions suggest that, prior to the global crisis of 2008-09, the slowdown in growth was due to structural causes and that only fundamental macroeconomic and microeconomic reforms could reverse this trend.

A competitive exchange rate was an important variable driving strong growth of the Chilean export sector during the latter half of the 1980s. The real exchange rate depreciated by nearly 100 per cent between 1980 and 1990, contributing to the 98 per cent increase in Chilean exports in real terms during that period. Furthermore, in spite of the fact that the real exchange rate appreciated again by approximately 75 per cent in the late 1990s as compared to its 1990 value, exports still continued to grow by 9.3 per cent annually. Total exports increased by 165 per cent over the decade. In 1999, Chile adopted a floating exchange-rate regime, eliminating the exchange-rate band with respect to the dollar. In addition, in order to improve the competitiveness of the Chilean financial sector, restrictions on the foreign-exchange market were relaxed. Limits to capital outflows were eased and reserve requirements on capital inflows were eliminated.

The terms of trade improved during the mid-2000s, due to an unexpected sharp increase in the international price for copper, which rose 64 per cent between 2005 and 2006. Fiscal revenues have increased markedly as a result, leading to a fiscal surplus equivalent to 4.2 per cent of GDP in the first semester of 2006. Fiscal expenditures have remained stable. Starting in the year 2000, Chile's fiscal policy began to be guided by the structural balance rule, with the target of reaching a surplus of 1 per cent of GDP. The adoption of this policy has helped to strengthen public finances and modernize the country's macroeconomic framework, contributing to a stable financing for social policies (MIDEPLAN, 2005a). In fact, growth of central government debt represents a low fiscal risk in the medium term, due primarily to the low existing level of debt in relationship to GDP (around 6 per cent) and the prudent macroeconomic policy rules (OECD, 2005).

Other macroeconomic variables are also under control and are remaining within acceptable limits. Since the early 1990s, the Central Bank has made it a priority to meet annual inflation targets. As a result, inflation fell from 27 per cent in 1990 to 1.1 per cent in 2003 and was around 3 per cent in the mid-2000s.

Gross domestic investment has increased considerably, reaching an average of 26.2 per cent of GDP for the 1990-2003 period, 10 percentage points of GDP more than in the 1980s. However, domestic savings have not grown very much and most of the increase in investment has been financed through external savings.

Good macroeconomic performance has also translated into real wage growth of 3.2 per cent per annum in the 1990s. Wage growth has been less than productivity growth, however. The unemployment rate on average fell markedly from 18 per cent in the 1980s to 6 per cent in the subsequent decade when approximately 1.4 million new jobs were created. Unemployment surged again to near 10 per cent between 1999 and 2004, despite government efforts to reduce it and despite sustained economic growth. In 2005, the rate of unemployment did fall somewhat to about 8 per cent.[2]

Social policies have undergone profound changes since the early 1990s as social policy action has been significantly strengthened (Schkolnik and Bonnefoy, 1994; Baytelman and others, 1999). During the 1980s, the prevailing idea was that of a "subsidiary social welfare state", when the delivery of public sector services was decentralized and the private sector was encouraged to take a greater role in the provisioning of social services. Universal social programmes were cut back and spending was targeted to specific objectives like the eradication of extreme poverty, protection for newborns and maintenance of basic services.

While social spending fell considerably in that period, better targeted spending contributed to greater progress in human development indicators, especially in terms of reductions in infant mortality and illiteracy and increased school enrolment. However, lower public spending did increasingly lead to a general deterioration in the access to and quality of social services and goods. Poverty levels also rose significantly. In 1987, nearly 45 per cent of the population lived in conditions of poverty—almost twice the incidence of 15 years earlier (Martin, 1998).

To redress these problems, the government shifted to an "integrated policy approach" in the 1990s.The new focus privileged social investment more than social welfare spending with the aim of establishing a greater balance between growth and macroeconomic stability, on one hand, and equity and poverty reduction, on the other. Changes in budgetary priorities and a reorientation towards social programmes, along with economic growth and a sustainable and counter-cyclical fiscal policy, have allowed Chile to maintain, if not increase, resources available for social spending even during periods of economic slowdown (MIDEPLAN, 2005a). Social expenditures increased from 61 per cent of total public spending to a share of 68 per cent in 2003, representing nearly 15 per cent of GDP (see Table 6.1). The social policy shift allowed the government to concentrate its efforts on the most disadvantaged sectors of the population and achieve greater efficiency in the use of fiscal resources.

Several flagship social programmes were developed, as discussed in Raczynski and Serrano (2005). About 400 such programmes were put in place

Table 6.1   Chile: change in public social spending (Percentage of GDP)

	1990-1991	1996-1997	2002-2003
Education	2.4	3.0	4.0
Health	1.9	2.4	3.0
Social security[a]	8.2	7.2	7.6
Housing	0.2	0.2	0.2
Total	12.7	12.8	14.8

Source: CEPAL (2006b).

[a] Includes spending on labour-related programmes.

with the participation of nearly 80 institutions. The most important programmes among these are: *Chile Solidario,* for the elimination of extreme poverty; *Chile Barrios,* with a goal of eradicating informal urban settlements in the country; *Orígenes,* aimed at the rural indigenous population; *Chile Joven,* for vocational training; and *Plan AUGE,* aimed at reforming the Chilean health sector.

These programmes have contributed to the continuous trend of poverty reduction observed since 1990. In fact, the percentage of people living in poverty fell from 45 per cent to 18.8 per cent between 1987 and 2003.[3] However, income inequality has remained high in Chile. At the beginning of this millennium, the wealthiest 20 per cent of households received 15 times the income of the poorest 20 per cent, and the Gini coefficient was around 0.57. This degree of inequality is little different from that of the 1970s.

MDG progress

Chile's progress towards the MDGs has been recorded in two official reports: the government report (MIDEPLAN, 2005a) and the report of the Economic Commission for Latin America and the Caribbean (CEPAL, 2005b). The key findings of these reports are presented in Table 6.2 and examined in the below.

MDG 1: Eradicating extreme poverty and hunger

The percentage of the population whose income is less than the international poverty line of one dollar a day at purchasing power parity (PPP) dropped from 3.5 per cent in 1990 to 2.3 per cent in 2000. According to MIDEPLAN (2005a), if the target to be reached by 2015 is set at 1.7 per cent of the population, "extreme poverty would only need to be reduced by 0.04 percentage points per year to meet this target. Considering the speed at which the percentage of the population with an income of less than one dollar a day (PPP) was reduced between 1990 and 2000, it can be inferred that it is feasible to reach this target."

According to CEPAL (2005b), an extreme poverty line based on the cost of satisfying the basic food consumption needs of the population is "more relevant for measuring the magnitude of poverty and for identifying the most

Table 6.2   Chile: change in indicators associated with the MDGs and targets to be reached by 2015

MDG	Goal	Indicator	1990	2003	2015 (target)
MDG 1	Reduce by half, between 1990 and 2015, the percentage of the population whose income is less than one dollar a day (at PPP)	Percentage of the population living with one or less than one dollar a day	3.5	2.3	1.7
MDG 2	Ensure that all girls and boys complete the entire cycle of primary school.	Primary school completion rates (%)	84.5	81.6	100.0
MDG 4	Reduce by two-thirds the child mortality rate	Under-five mortality rates (per 1,000 live births)	19.3	9.6	6.4
MDG 5	Reduce the maternal mortality rates by three quarters between 1990 and 2015	Maternal mortality rate (per 100,000 live births)	40	19	10
MDG 7a	Reduce by half the percentage of people who lack sustainable access to drinking water by 2015	Percentage of households with access to drinking water in urban areas.	97.4	99.8[a]	99.9[a]
MDG 7b	Reduce by half the percentage of people who lack sustainable access to basic sanitation services by 2015.	Percentage of households with access to sewage systems in urban areas.	82.6	94.4	97.2[a]

Source: MIDEPLAN (2005b) for MDG 1; MINEDUC (2005) for MDG 2; CEPAL (2005b) for MDG 4; and MIDEPLAN (2005b) for MDGs 5, 7a and 7b.
[a] Since the goal was already achieved in 2003, for the purposes of simulation exercises using MAMS, the target was re-estimated using 2003 as the base year.

affected population groups." Extreme poverty as measured with these alternative thresholds also decreased significantly in Chile. According to the CASEN household survey, moderate poverty and extreme poverty, as measured by the official national lines, affected 38.6 per cent and 12.9 per cent of the population, respectively, in 1990. By 2003, these indicators had fallen markedly to 18.8 per cent and 4.3 per cent. On the basis of these trends, it can be asserted that by 2003 Chile had already met the internationally established target to halve extreme poverty.

MDG 2: *Achieving universal primary education*

As explained in MIDEPLAN (2005a), the net enrolment rate in basic education increased to 91 per cent in 2000 from 88 per cent in 1990, and the target is to reach 95.5 per cent by 2015.[4] At the same time, the percentage of students who begin first grade and complete fifth grade was 91.6 per cent in 2000, 8.4 percentage points less than the target.

CEPAL (2005b) estimates that net primary school enrolment decreased from 87.7 per cent in 1990 to 86.5 per cent in 2002.[5] The primary school completion rate rose, however, from 95.5 per cent in 1992 to 97 per cent in 2002. According to CEPAL, Chile is among the countries where, based on current trends, at least 95 per cent of the children that are under five today will finish primary school by 2015. At the same time, however, it indicates that efforts should be made to identify the households where children are least likely to finish primary school.

While enormous progress has been made in terms of coverage, results are not as auspicious with respect to retention rates. According to the Ministry of Education (MINEDUC, 2005), 84.5 per cent of those who entered first grade finished the primary school cycle (completing 8th grade) in 1990. By 2003, this rate had dropped to 81.6 per cent. Thus, the objective of the education policy should be to concentrate efforts not only on education coverage, but also on attaining 100 per cent retention.

Furthermore, the Chilean government has also proposed that by 2015, all girls and boys should be able to complete the entire education cycle through high school. This was formalized through a Constitutional Reform in 2003, when the government was entrusted with the responsibility of guaranteeing at least 12 years of schooling for all.

Most of the population of 15 to 24 years of age is already literate and by 2015 it is estimated that 99.8 per cent of this age group will be able to read and write (MIDEPLAN, 2005a).

Notwithstanding the improvements in access to education for lower income groups and the progress made in promoting gender equality,[6] the big challenges in the area of education continue to be the quality of education and the low coverage for preschool education. This situation is reflected in the results of international tests, according to which the acquired cognitive skills of Chilean children are under par. Inequalities also persist between socio-economic classes, regions and type of schools (private, subsidized or public) in terms of the quality of education received, as evidenced through school tests administered by the System for Measuring Educational Quality (SIMCE), and more recently through the University Selection Test (PSU).[7]

MDG 4: Reduce under-five child mortality

Over the last decade, Chile has made significant improvements in reducing child mortality. The under-five child mortality rate per 1,000 live births was reduced from 19.3 in 1990 to 9.6 in 2003, a decline of 75 per cent. At ongoing trends, it is expected that the rate will decline further to 6.4 in 2015.

MDG 5: Reduce maternal mortality

Maternal mortality rates have also fallen significantly since the 1990s, going from 40 to 17 deaths per 100,000 live births between 1990 and 2002. This 2002 number is quite a bit lower than the average of 87 deaths per 100,000 live births recorded for the Latin American and Caribbean region as a whole in 2000. Chile has made 70 per cent progress towards the target of reducing maternal mortality rates by three fourths between 1990 and 2015.

The progress report on the MDGs for Chile (MIDEPLAN, 2005a) indicates that the observed decrease in maternal mortality is associated with the impact of several programmes of the Ministry of Health. The Maternal Health Programme, which includes a series of prenatal check-ups that allow early detection of pregnancy-related pathologies, has been particularly effective. Other programmes, like family planning programmes, have helped reduce unwanted pregnancies.

MDG 7: Increase access to drinking water and basic sanitation services

In 2003, 99.8 per cent of all residential houses located in urban areas of the country were connected to public drinking water systems; reflecting an increase by 2.4 percentage points compared with coverage in 1990. In rural areas, coverage increased from 76.5 per cent in 1990 to 98.5 per cent in 2004.[8] The percentage of the urban population with access to the sewage system increased from 82.6 per cent in 1990 to 94.4 per cent in 2003, while coverage in rural areas expanded from 19.1 per cent to 40 per cent in the same period.

There has also been a spectacular increase in wastewater treatment. In the early 1990s, Chile had wastewater treatment levels of less than 5 per cent, comparable only to countries with much lower levels of development. However, water treatment has expanded dramatically since, reaching 35 per cent in 2001 and close to 80 per cent in 2005. It is expected that more than 95 per cent of all wastewater will be treated by 2010.

Determinants of MDG-related achievements in MAMS

MAMS was used to simulate the impact of alternative policies aiming at the achievement of the MDGs (see Chapter 3). A special module of this model links a set of socio-economic variables or determinants with the indicators used to monitor progress towards these goals. To quantify this link, a series of elasticities needs to be estimated. For the case of Chile, the estimations have been documented in detail in O'Ryan and others (2007).[9] Below we provide a summary and justify the chosen values for these elasticities as these were used to calibrate the MDG module of MAMS.

Education

In MAMS, a series of macroeconomic and social variables are assumed to determine progress towards improving completion rates of primary education. Elasticities quantify the impact of these determinants of educational behaviour of individuals by educational category on achievement towards MDG 2. In the case of Chile, these were estimated using data from the Ministry of Education (children who passed, failed, graduated and enrolled in first year); information from the Ministry of the Interior (infant mortality at the district level, average public spending and investment per district); and the 2003 CASEN household survey.

From these data sets, it was possible to estimate the influence of the variables with the greatest effect on student enrolment and retention (that is, the decision to begin primary school at the correct age, passing a grade, and completing one cycle and going on to the next). Results show that public infrastructure provision and the reduction of infant mortality have only a minor impact on decisions to enter the school system or on later education-related behaviour. The main reason for this is that Chile has already achieved high rates of primary school enrolment and very low infant mortality rates. The wage premium and household consumption also have a relatively weak effect, but greater than that of the previously mentioned determinants.[10] Finally, the level of public spending in education per student comes out as a positive and significant determinant of decisions to enter the school system and for continuing in the system.

Data limitations, both in quantity and quality, did not permit full model specification and may explain the lack of sufficiently robust econometric results on the determinants of primary school performance. However, it was possible to make plausible inferences regarding the sign of the parameters and the range in which the values should move, which in most cases were consistent with the opinion of experts in the field of education. The final elasticities for the key relationships, plugged into MAMS, were based on a combination of the empirical results indicated above, the expert opinion on the relative importance of each factor in education-related decisions and a sensitivity analysis conducted with the CGE model.

MAMS also requires the estimation of a series of basic educational indicators, including average rates for students that pass a grade, drop out, repeat, continue their studies and graduate in each education cycle, as well as the number enrolled in each grade and cycle per year, children who enter first grade at age seven, and new students entering each educational cycle, among others. These indicators were computed with official information from the Ministry of Education (MINEDUC, 2005) and from CEPAL-UNESCO (2005).

Mortality

The determinants of mortality for children under five were estimated using district-level data for 2003 from the Ministry of Health and the 2003 CASEN survey. The results suggest there is a negative—yet not in all cases statistically significant—relationship between infant mortality and the following determinants: access to basic sanitation and drinking water, per capita household income (as a proxy for per capita consumption), average district levels of investment in health and some infrastructure variables like the number of primary health care units per capita. However, only the level of investment in health per district—used as a proxy for household spending on health for which no data were available—was found to be statistically significant.[11] For lack of better information, and considering that the sign and absolute and relative magnitudes of the estimated coefficients appeared plausible, the decision was made to use the estimated values as reported in O'Ryan and others (2007), but allowing for some adjustment following sensitivity analysis and consistent calibration of the full CGE model.[12]

The very low maternal mortality rate did not allow us to estimate the determinants that influence the reduction of that indicator with the required statistical rigour, so the decision was made to assume determinants and related elasticities are similar to those of child mortality, on the basis of a general understanding from international studies that there tends to be a high correlation between the determinants of trends in both mortality rates.[13]

In summary, in order to calibrate the MDG module of the MAMS model, it is assumed that all of the variables considered previously are weakly correlated with mortality among children under five and with maternal mortality. This assumption is reasonable for the Chilean case, since the mortality rate is very low (see Table 6.2), and corresponds to isolated cases generally associated with high risk situations and not to specific socio-economic variables.

Drinking water and basic sanitation

In order to quantify the influence of the determinants of drinking water coverage and those of access to sewage systems, data from the 2003 CASEN survey and statistics from the Ministry of the Interior (Infopais) were used. The elasticities obtained indicated that access to drinking water and sewage systems is positive and strongly correlated with total consumption of both services (1.13); and positive, but weakly correlated with public investment in sanitation services (0.025) and with per capita household consumption (0.096). In addition, the probabilities of having access to drinking water and sewage systems are very similarly correlated to the aforementioned determinants, which is not surprising given the high coverage of the two services in urban areas (see Table 6.2). The urban areas without coverage of these services tend to border on rural areas, so coverage in these areas may be expected to improve along with the expansion of drinking water and sewage networks in rural areas.

General equilibrium analysis

Progress towards the MDGs in Chile was examined by analyzing the general equilibrium results obtained through MAMS. In addition to the elasticities associated with the econometrically-estimated MDG models and another series of related parameters mentioned previously, MAMS for Chile was solved by using also the following sources of additional data: a Social Accounting Matrix (SAM); elasticities that characterize the behavioural relationships associated with decisions around trade, production, spending and savings; and the growth levels and rates of some exogenous variables. Having made due reference to these additional inputs for the calibration of the model, the rest of this section focuses on the analysis of the simulated scenarios.

SAM and additional data for model calibration

The SAM for Chile that was used to provide MAMS with an accounting framework was constructed for 2003 by updating an earlier SAM built around the 1996 input-output matrix (Central Bank, 2003).[14] The 2003 SAM provides a realistic picture of the structure of the Chilean economy in that year and its accounts follow the structure of the prototype matrix of MAMS (see Chapter 3). The matrix has a separate entry for the copper sector, however, given its importance in the Chilean economy and because copper is produced almost entirely for export. In MAMS, natural resources are specified where appropriate as an additional production factor and this feature was used in the specification of the production function for the copper sector in the model for Chile. Another peculiar characteristic of the Chilean SAM is that "water and sanitation" are provisioned through the private sector rather than the public sector, owing to the fact that this type of infrastructure has been either given in concession or has been privatized. Consequently, the public policy impact on water and sanitation goals has not been modelled. This does not affect the analysis of assessing the resources needed to achieve the MDGs, however, since the targets for water and sanitation were already met in 2003, well ahead of time. These and other details about the construction of the SAM, as well as the matrix itself, are presented in O'Ryan and others (2007).

The behavioural elasticities for trade, production, consumption and savings were derived from existing sources, including the elasticities used in the calibration of the ECOGEM-Chile model (O'Ryan and others, 2001, 2003, 2006), as well as those found in international literature. Some adjustments were made to the parameters derived this way during the calibration process of MAMS but ensuring that values were kept within possible and plausible ranges.[15] The model also uses a series of parameters and annual exogenous growth rates that are essential to its functioning. For example, for the definition of a baseline scenario under moderate economic growth assumptions introduced in the following section, government expenditures grow 4.5 per cent annually, consistent with the performance of the six years preceding 2005 and existing projections (Central Bank, 2005). The labour force was calculated by economic activity and skill level based on information from the 2003 CASEN survey and assuming an average annual population growth of 1 per cent, consistent with demographic statistics provided by CELADE-CEPAL.

Baseline scenario

After calibrating and solving the model, two baseline scenarios were defined for MAMS for Chile, for the 2003-15 period. The great uncertainties in growth prospects and related uncertainties regarding the feasible growth of public spending are the main reasons to have two baselines. In the first, "moderate" baseline scenario, GDP and public spending are assumed to grow by 4.5 per cent per year, while in the second, "optimistic" baseline, both variables grow at the same rate by 5.5 per cent per year. MAMS's initial macroeconomic closure rules—used in all country studies of this volume—come into play in the generation of both baseline scenarios, and they only vary in the scenarios for reaching the goal of primary education which is analysed further below (see Chapter 3).

Table 6.3 shows the annual growth rates of key macroeconomic aggregates under both baseline scenarios. In the moderate baseline, the annual growth rate for domestic absorption is greater than that of GDP (4.8 per cent versus 4.5 per cent), consistent with stronger growth of imports than of exports and with an appreciation in the real exchange rate (by 3.5 per cent between 2003 and 2015). Foreign savings and substitution of domestic with external public

Table 6.3   Chile: initial value and annual growth rate of key macroeconomic aggregates in two baseline scenarios, 2003-2015

	Initial value in 2003 (billions of pesos)	Annual growth rate (per cent)	
		Moderate scenario	Optimistic scenario
GDP	50,731	4.5	5.5
Household consumption	31,230	4.9	5.8
Government consumption	6,314	4.5	5.5
Investment	10,769	5.1	6.3
Private	9,132	5.4	6.5
Public	1,638	3.3	5.1
Exports of goods and services	18,553	4.3	5.2
Imports of goods and services	16,529	5.0	6.1

Source: MAMS for Chile.

debt make it possible to maintain a robust growth in private consumption and investment in spite of the fiscal pressure which is also greater.

Production in the natural resources sector grows by more than average economic growth (5.2 per cent and 6.0 per cent, respectively, in the moderate and optimistic baseline scenarios) because of the higher relative profitability of this sector. The water and sanitation sectors would expand at a lower rate than the economy as a whole (2.6 per cent and 3.4 per cent, respectively), reflecting that most of the population in Chile has already been covered by these services. Output in most other activities (agriculture, industry and services) grows at more or less the same rate as the economy as a whole in both baseline runs. The provision of private health and education services expands at slightly higher than annual average growth rates (4.8 per cent and 5.3 per cent, respectively, for the two scenarios), owing to the above-par profitability of these private services.

As mentioned in the sixth section, the rate of unemployment did not fall in the 1999-2004 period. Depending on their skill level, workers were affected differently by unemployment. In 2003, for example, the unemployment rate of workers with only primary education was 6 per cent while that of workers with secondary and tertiary education was 9 per cent and 12 per cent, respectively, much higher than the "natural" rate of unemployment which has been estimated at around 5 per cent for the 1990s (MIDEPLAN 2005b). For this reason, and considering the strong influence of adjustments in employment and wages on poverty and income distribution, the labour market was modelled in detail, following the MAMS specifications, including the possibility of unemployment.

The composition of the labour supply depends on the level of schooling of the workers, who may be unskilled, semi-skilled or skilled, and is therefore determined by the graduation rates of each education cycle. If graduation from a particular educational cycle increases, the supply of the associated labour category increases and, *ceteris paribus,* the market rate for wages falls. The model assumes that there is a "reservation" (minimum) wage that is sensitive to changes in the employment rates by skill level. The higher the employment rate (or the lower the unemployment rate), the stronger the upward adjustment of the reservation wage for each labour category. Wages respond relatively slowly to changes in prices, according to the relationship established by other elasticities in the model (O'Ryan and others, 2007). In addition, the demand for labour (by occupational category) depends on output in each economic sector. After matching this demand with supply of labour, the model determines the degree of unemployment for each occupational category.

Figure 6.1 shows the change in unemployment for the two baseline scenarios. Unemployment rates for unskilled and semi-skilled workers drop abruptly in the first three years in both scenarios. This is broadly consistent with observed data for late 2006, which recorded an unemployment rate of 5.8 per cent for unskilled workers. The unemployment rate of 9 per cent recorded for semi-skilled

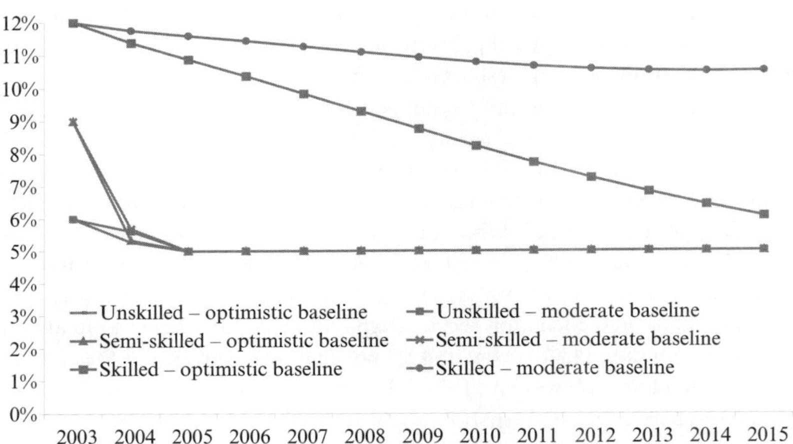

Figure 6.1 Chile: Changes in employment by type of worker in the two baseline scenarios, 2003-2015

Source: MAMS for Chile.

workers turned out to be a little greater than that predicted by the model's baseline. Unemployment among workers with the highest skill levels shows a somewhat different simulated trend: it falls gradually, though more substantially in the optimistic scenario. With an annual economic growth of 4.5 per cent in the moderate scenario, unemployment for skilled workers remains worrisome at above double digits in 2015.

Real wages increase throughout the simulation period in both baseline scenarios. Unskilled and semi-skilled workers gain in this sense. In the moderate baseline scenario, for example, their average remunerations grow by 6.7 per cent and 5.9 per cent per year, respectively, in contrast to the remuneration of skilled workers, which only grows by 0.2 per cent per year. At this pace, in 2015 the wage gap between unskilled and skilled workers decreases 9.7 times and that between semi-skilled and skilled workers falls 8.1 times as compared with the gap that existed in the base year.

These variations in labour incomes are explained by both supply and demand factors. As the average level of schooling rises, the growth in the supply of unskilled labour decelerates and starts falling short of demand for this type of workers. Their wages increase as a consequence. Increased demand for skilled workers keeps the wages for these workers from falling even as their supply increases with improved education outcomes. In the moderate scenario, the total number of employed people would rise from 5.9 million in 2003 to 6.8 million in 2015. The number of unskilled workers would remain constant at around 1.6 million, that of semi-skilled workers rises slightly (from 3.4 million to 3.6 million), while that of skilled workers would almost double (from 900,000 to 1.6 million).

Will the MDGs be reached with the assumed rate of growth in public spending in the baseline scenarios? As Table 6.4 shows, Chile's goals will be reached even before 2015 in both baselines, except for the target for primary education, which would be almost reached in the optimistic scenario, but fall somewhat short in the moderate baseline. This makes it possible to come to a first and important conclusion: considering the expected growth rates for the country and the public policies that have been applied for more than 15 years now, almost all of the internationally set MDG targets have already been achieved or are within close reach in Chile.

Table 6.4   Chile: achieving the MDGs in the two baseline scenarios[a]

Goal	Moderate scenario	Optimistic scenario
Primary education	98.1%	99.2%
Under-five child mortality	Reached in 2006	Reached in 2006
Maternal mortality	Reached in 2005	Reached in 2005
Water	Reached in 2008	Reached in 2007
Sanitation	Reached in 2008	Reached in 2007

Source: MAMS for Chile.

[a] MDG 1 for extreme poverty is examined in detail in the following section.

Policy scenarios for achieving the MDGs

This section looks at scenarios that are alternatives to the baseline scenarios, in which increased public spending and its financing will assure that all MDGs will be reached. In Chile's case, the exercise is relevant only for the target for primary education, which, as mentioned, is not met in the baseline scenarios. The results of these scenarios are only examined with respect to the moderate baseline scenario, since the results of the MDG scenario differ very little from those obtained by the more optimistic baseline. While the model allows consideration of four alternative mechanisms for financing the new public spending required to reach the goals, only increases in direct taxes or internal borrowing are considered relevant options in the case of Chile.[16]

The results of these new scenarios are detailed in Appendix A6 (Table A6.1). In terms of the main components of the output on the demand side, it can be seen there is very little variation with respect to the baseline scenario. Results also show that the greater public effort required to achieve the goal here set for MDG 2 has only minor repercussions on the rest of the economy given that Chile is so close to meeting this goal. The simulation results also suggest there would be a small reduction in the average GDP growth rate for the period with respect to the baseline scenario, which is explained by the "crowding-out effect" of increased public spending on private consumption in the case of the tax-financing scenario, or of private investment in the case of domestic borrowing. As Figure 6.2 shows, the final consumption spending of the government must be frontloaded—to immediately enrol those children at the relevant age for primary school—at a rate

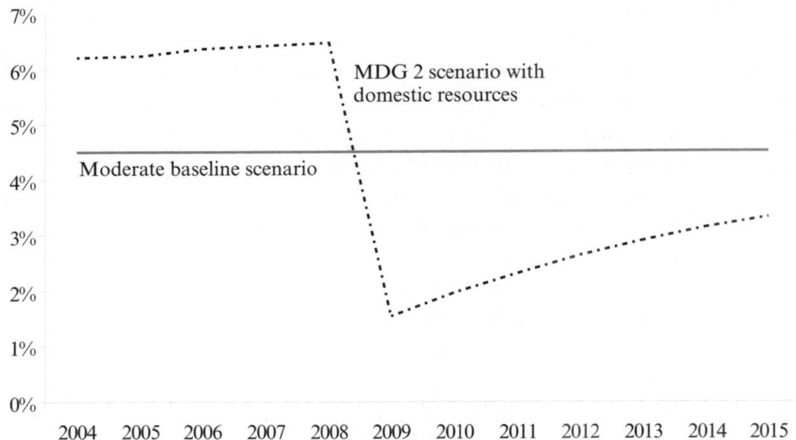

Figure 6.2 Chile: Growth of final government consumption spending in the "moderate" baseline and MDG 2 scenarios
Source: MAMS for Chile.

that is two percentage points per year higher than in the baseline during the first five years of the simulation period (2004-08), after which it can grow at lower rates. If the official social discount rate is applied,[17] the additional final consumption spending of the government aimed at meeting the primary education goal for 2015 comes out 2.3 per cent higher than that of the baseline scenario. Public investment would also need to increase—in tandem with frontloaded final consumption spending—at a rate slightly above that of the moderate baseline scenario through the year 2008 in order to converge to the baseline path thereafter. During that 2004-08 period of spending frontloading, public investment increases on average by almost 1 per cent per year. Relative to GDP, the additional required public spending (with respect to the baseline scenario) to achieve the education goal is minimal, amounting to just 0.003 per cent per year.

Nonetheless, under the tax-financing scenario there would be a visible impact on direct tax rates. In order to reach the goal for primary education, direct tax revenue must increase in the first five years of the simulation period (through 2008), after which this source of government income could be allowed to gradually fall again. Direct tax revenue should be 22 per cent higher on average during the 2005-10 period as compared with the baseline. In the subsequent period of five years till 2015, they could be allowed to drop on average by 6 per cent with respect to the baseline. As a result, direct tax income would need to be 8.5 per cent higher than in the baseline on average for the whole period. Should this apparently strong impact on direct taxes be considered politically less desirable, the alternative would be to try and finance the strategy towards achievement of MDG 2 through domestic borrowing. This option would not increase outstanding public debt substantially and would not affect economic growth or consumption any differently than in the tax-financing scenario.

Turning to the dynamics of the labour and capital markets, the moderate baseline suggests that by 2015 a slight substitution of capital for labour would have taken place, mainly benefiting unskilled and semi-skilled workers, as compared with the base year 2003 (see Table 6.5). As this leads to a rise in wages for these categories of workers, the policies and growth patterns currently in place would tend to close existing wage gaps. In the scenarios in which the primary education goal is achieved, there is a slight, but further increase in the income share of unskilled labour and there is also a slight increase in the share of capital with respect to the baseline. These shifts would be to the detriment of the income share of skilled workers. The shifts are mainly on account of a reduction in the supply of unskilled labour following further progress towards the education target. This puts upward pressure on the wages of unskilled workers and this effect dominates the employment effect.

Table 6.5   Chile: structure of factor incomes in the base year and in 2015 in the moderate baseline and MDG 2 scenarios (percentage)

	Unskilled workers	**Semi-skilled workers**	**Skilled workers**	**Capital**
Base year (2003)	5.8	14.4	24.3	55.5
Baseline scenario (in 2015)	7.2	17.7	24.3	50.8
MDG 2 scenario with direct taxes or domestic borrowing (in 2015)	7.3	17.7	23.8	51.2

Source: MAMS for Chile.

Minimum growth requirements for achieving the MDGs

The previous evaluations assume that the annual growth rate of the economy is 4.5 per cent. MAMS for Chile was also used to explore alternative, more pessimistic, baseline scenarios. It is found that there are two economic growth rates that mark the difference as to whether the MDGs will be met or not (see Table 6.6). Should the economy grow at 3.5 per cent per year, all of the goals can still be met except that associated with MDG 2 (as well as that of eradicating extreme poverty, as explained ahead). As shown above, achieving MDG 2 requires an economic growth rate higher than that of the most optimistic scenario in the absence of additional public policy action. If average annual growth is between 1.5 per cent and 3.5 per cent, the goals for water and sanitation would no longer be met. If the economy grew at less than 1.5 per cent per year, the under-five mortality rate would also not be met. These results show the importance of assuring high and sustained growth rates, which should also allow an increase in social spending in order to facilitate achievement of the agreed upon development goals.

Table 6.6   Chile: progress towards the MDGs by 2015 under different baseline assumptions for economic growth[a]

	Base year (2003)	Target for 2015	Annual GDP growth rate (%) in the baseline scenario							
			1.0	1.5	2.0	2.5	3.0	3.5	4.5	5.5
Percentage of children who begin primary school and complete it on time	81.6	100.0	90.0	92.0	93.0	95.0	96.0	97.0	98.0	99.0
Under-five mortality rate (per 1,000 live births)	10.0	6.0	7.0	6.0 (2015)	5.0 (2011)	5.0 (2009)	5.0 (2008)	5.0 (2008)	5.0 (2007)	5.0 (2007)
Maternal mortality rate (per 100,000 live births)	19.0	10.0	10.0 (2005)	10.0 (2005)	10.0 (2005)	10.0 (2004)	10.0 (2004)	10.0 (2004)	10.0 (2004)	10.0 (2004)
Percentage of households with access to drinking water.	98.0[b]	99.0[b]	97.2	97.5	98.0	98.5	98.9	99.2 (2011)	99.4 (2008)	99.5 (2007)
Percentage of households with access to basic sanitation	94.4	97.2	92.2	93.2	94.4	95.6	96.8	97.8 (2011)	98.9 (2008)	99.4 (2007)

Source: MAMS for Chile.

[a] The year in which the target is achieved is in parentheses.

[b] Since the goal was reached in 2003, and given the most pessimistic indicator for that year (99.1%), the maximum gap for achieving the 100% goal was established as one percentage point. Because of this, and with the goal of facilitating a convergence in the scenarios simulated through MAMS, 98% coverage was established as a starting point with a goal of increasing it by one percentage point by 2015.

MDG achievement as a legacy of the bicentennial

In the year 2010, Chile will celebrate the bicentennial of the constitution of the first Governing Board *(Junta de Gobierno)*. This is serving as a milestone for achievements of public policies. In this context, the spending requirements for reaching all of the MDGs by the end of 2010, and the economic impact of doing so, has also been examined. The moderate baseline scenario, in which the economy grows by 4.5 per cent annually, is used as a reference for this exercise. The analysis is focused on reaching the primary education goal since the other goals are expected to have been reached before 2010.

In order to reach the primary education goal in 2011, public spending in education must be frontloaded in even greater amounts starting from the first year of the simulation period (2004), considering the primary education cycle lasts eight years. With this spending frontloading, the share of government consumption in GDP increases almost two percentage points in the 2003-05 period and should remain higher than that of the baseline scenario through 2011. The fiscal adjustments required in 2004 are significant: government consumption spending must increase by 33 per cent and public investment by 40 per cent with respect to 2003.

When the spending is financed with domestic resources (direct taxes or borrowing), a "crowding-out" effect is observed with greater public spending, reducing private consumption especially during the first years. Private consumption would fall as a share of GDP by almost two and a half points in the 2003-05 period and by a little more than one point between 2005 and 2010. Both GDP and domestic absorption show an average growth similar to that of the baseline scenario.

Finally, results show that speeding up the achievement of MDG 2 to 2011, in addition to requiring a greater public effort, would generate a slight delay in the achievement of the other goals if financed through domestic resource mobilization. For example, MDG 4 could have been reached in 2007 instead of in 2006 if the primary education target would have been reached earlier. A similar delay would apply in the case of the target associated with MDG 5, but not in the case of water and sanitation.

Impact on poverty and income distribution

In order to examine the distributive impacts of the various scenarios, the microsimulation methodology described in Appendix A2.1 from Chapter 2 was applied. The 2003 CASEN survey (MIDEPLAN, 2005b) provided the micro dataset for implementing this methodology. Several poverty lines were used to estimate alternative poverty measures once the full distributive impacts had been accounted for: one dollar a day at PPP (308 Chilean pesos a day at the 2003 exchange rate); two dollars a day at PPP (615 Chilean pesos a day at the 2003 exchange rate); the national extreme poverty line (20,000 Chilean pesos a month); and the national moderate poverty line (38,000 Chilean pesos a month).[18]

Baseline scenarios

The target for MDG 1 is to reduce by 50 per cent extreme poverty measured through the international poverty line of one dollar per day at PPP between 1990 and 2015. For Chile, this means reducing the extreme poverty incidence from 3.2 per cent to 1.7 per cent of the population. By 2003, extreme poverty by that measure had decreased to 2.5 per cent. As Table 6.7 shows, the target is met quite easily under the two baseline scenarios as the extreme poverty incidence would fall to 0.9 per cent in 2015. There would be an equally strong reduction in the other poverty indicators. For example, when measured with the 2-dollar-a-day poverty line, the poverty incidence would drop by 7.4 and 7.5 percentage points, respectively, in the moderate and optimistic baseline scenarios. This means that maintaining the already existing social policy efforts in Chile, as well as the projected growth rates, would be sufficient to achieve the MDG goal for extreme poverty.

The reduction of poverty in the moderate scenario is explained by increases in both per worker labour income and per capita household income of around 5 per cent per year. It is notable that the annual growth in labour income for women (5.3 per cent) is higher than average, surpassing the rate of labour income growth for male workers by 0.5 percentage points.

As shown in the previous section, total employment grows at an annual average rate of 1.2 per cent and job growth for skilled workers is faster than that for semi-skilled and unskilled workers (4.4 per cent, 0.5 per cent and 0.0 per cent,

Table 6.7   Chile: poverty and income distribution in the base year and in 2015 in the baseline scenarios

		2015	
Indicators for poverty and inequality	**Base year (2003)**	**Moderate scenario**	**Optimistic scenario**
Incidence of poverty (% of the population)			
1-dollar-a-day poverty line at PPP	2.50	0.90	0.90
2-dollar-a-day poverty line at PPP	9.33	1.93	1.80
Gini coefficient			
Labour income	0.54	0.49	0.48
Per capita household income	0.56	0.47	0.46
Average monthly labour income (Chilean pesos)	285,820	512,865	588,327
Women	218,993	409,224	467,724
Men	325,975	575,142	660,797
Average monthly per capita household income (Chilean pesos)	113,660	202,920	234,146

Source: MAMS for Chile and microsimulations using the 2003 CASEN survey.

respectively). As a result, wage growth for unskilled and semi-skilled workers is stronger than that for skilled workers.

These simulation results may seem optimistic, but are consistent with the results of the more recent 2006 CASEN survey, which reveals a notable decline in poverty indicators as well as improvements in the income distribution. In fact, between 2003 and 2006, poverty measured through the national poverty line fell from 18.7 per cent to 13.7 per cent, and the Gini coefficient for per capita household income (before transfers) fell from 0.57 to 0.54.

Poverty and income distribution effects of achieving MDG 2

No matter which financing mechanism is used, achieving the target for primary education would only slightly change the results of the (moderate) baseline scenario for poverty and income distribution. Inequality as measured through the Gini coefficient of per capita household income would fall slightly, reaching 0.46 in 2015 compared with 0.47 in the baseline. The incidence of poverty measured using the one-dollar-a-day poverty line would fall to 0.80 per cent by 2015 compared with 0.85 per cent in the baseline and to 1.9 per cent (compared with 1.93 per cent in the baseline) when measured by the two-dollar-a-day poverty line. These outcomes are mainly driven by further improvements in the real wages of unskilled and semi-skilled workers. Thus, the increase in public spending associated with achieving the primary education target strengthens the positive effects of the baseline scenario to some extent.

Conclusions and policy recommendations

Chile has made visible progress towards the MDGs since 1990, specifically in the areas of poverty eradication, access to primary education, reduction of child and maternal mortality and access to drinking water and sewage systems. The fact that Chile has enjoyed both macroeconomic and political stability since the 1990s has contributed significantly to this progress. Increased public spending, especially through targeted social spending, during this period of democratic governments has also been fundamental. The better targeting of social spending is especially essential for understanding the progress made thus far in Chile and for the results it hopes to achieve by the year 2015.

Given that it is not easy to maintain high economic growth rates for a prolonged period of time, this study looked at the evolution of MDG indicators under alternative growth scenarios. A scenario of a moderate GDP and public expenditure growth of 4.5 per cent is seen as consistent with Chile's policy of fiscal austerity and structural budget rule, which closely links the evolution of both variables in order to maintain macroeconomic stability.

The conclusion that emerges from the results of the moderate growth scenario is that the MDG targets, except for one, will almost definitely be achieved if the current public policy is maintained. The primary school completion rate would reach 98.1 per cent by 2015 in this scenario, just short of the target. The targets set for the other goals would be met during the first few years of the simulation period. In other words, if they have not been met yet, the goals are well within reach in the case of Chile.

The situation at the starting point for the model, the year 2003, goes a long way towards explaining these results. Increased social spending and reforms in education have opened up great opportunities, in particular for the poorest sectors of the country. In terms of access to primary and secondary education, Chile's indicators are quite satisfactory. There are a few pending issues to deal with, however. One is the fall in retention and graduation rates observed in recent years. Another is that the quality of education services must be improved, especially in the case of public schools. Indicators are also showing a lack of access to preschool education.

Significant progress has also been made in reducing child and maternal mortality in the last decade. According to the modelling exercise carried out, the MDG targets for reducing maternal and child mortality will be met within three years from the base year, if current policies are continued. Chile's increase in health system coverage and the high level of births attended to by professionals, among other things, lead us to believe that current mortality rates are explained in large part by situations of specific vulnerability (for example, extremely premature births in the case of child mortality and complications in pregnancy or miscarriage in the case of maternal mortality). In order to improve the mortality rates beyond the MDG targets, additional policies targeted at high-risk groups would be required. The costs of enacting these more focused and specialized interventions would be exponentially higher. Unfortunately, the aggregate modelling used in this study cannot be used to determine whether Chile should spend its resources towards this objective or if it should use its resources for other social priorities.

Soon there will be 100 per cent coverage and access to potable water in both urban and rural areas. In fact, the baseline scenario of moderate growth suggests that Chile should have reached the targets for drinking water and sewage systems by 2008. In addition, one of the main achievements since the 1990s has been the spectacular increase in wastewater treatment. This service reached around 80 per cent of the population in 2005, even though coverage was close to zero just a decade earlier. Current policies aimed at reaching a coverage of 95 per cent of the population by 2010.

The percentage of poor people living on less than one dollar a day in 1990 decreased significantly to around 2.3 per cent of the population by 2003. This is not only quite low by Latin American standards, but it is also very close to the target for 2015 (1.7 per cent). In spite of economic growth and targeted policies, however, income distribution has remained highly skewed in Chile and ranks among the least equal in Latin America. Between 2003 and 2006, there was only a small reduction in inequality.

The baseline scenario of moderate growth shows that the percentage of the population with income of less than one dollar a day has been substantially reduced. In fact, findings show that it will drop to 0.9 per cent by 2015, so it appears that the target for extreme poverty can be easily met if economic growth can be sustained, at least at a moderate pace. Importantly, income inequality at the household level falls under the simulated scenarios, suggesting a possible break with historic trends of unchanged, high inequality. Both of these results can be explained by two important effects in the labour market. One is an expected increase in the demand for labour in the most dynamic sectors of the economy, generating a decline in the rate of unemployment. On the supply side, the simulation results project a relative stagnation in the supply of unskilled labour and a rapid increase in the supply of skilled labour. As a result, the wages of unskilled and semi-skilled workers rise at an annual average rate that is higher than that of workers with higher skill levels. This also allows for an increase in the average wage level and for a reduction in the wage gap between skilled and less skilled workers.

These results depend a great deal on the assumed rates of growth of GDP and public spending. If public spending were to drop below 3 per cent per year, the targets for coverage of drinking water and sanitation would not be met with existing patterns of resource allocation. If economic growth were to fall to, say, 1 per cent per year, the target for reducing the child mortality goal would no longer be met either.

Reaching the target for primary education would require a small increase in public spending compared with the moderate baseline scenario, and the related increase in government expenditures would only have modest macroeconomic repercussions. The required increase in taxation to finance the new spending would be quite significant, though, suggesting the government may prefer to resort to domestic borrowing instead in order to mobilize the required additional resources. The MDG 2 scenario does not alter to any significant degree the outcomes for income distribution of the moderate baseline scenario, though it does help to reduce poverty a slight bit further.

Given this auspicious panorama, it is worth asking whether Chile might be able to achieve its primary education goal ahead of time, for example by the time of its bicentennial (end of 2010). The modelling shows that, if this were to happen, the other targets would still be met before the bicentennial, though some of them might be achieved one year later. However, the immediate fiscal cost would be quite significant due to significant frontloading of additional spending and could, with time, destabilize public finances.

In summary, Chile does not require much additional public spending to meet the MDGs. Public spending and GDP would by and large suffice if it continues to grow at current rates until 2015. To also achieve the primary education goal, some additional efforts are needed in that area over the next few years. At the same time, future analysis and policy discussions should expand beyond the modelling of this study to include such aspects as: the insertion of women in the labour market; improvements in access to public health services and in the quality of (public) education; and the promotion of sustainable development.

Appendix A6

Table A6.1   Chile: detailed results of the moderate baseline and MDG 2 scenarios under different forms of financing, 2003-2015

		MDG 2 scenario with:		
	Baseline scenario	**direct taxes**	**external borrowing**	**domestic borrowing**
Key macroeconomic aggregates (annual average growth rate for 2003-2015)				
GDP at factor cost	4.53	4.51	4.53	4.51
Total absorption	4.8	4.8	4.7	4.8
Household consumption	4.9	4.9	4.9	4.9
Government consumption	4.500	4.105	4.117	4.105
Investment	5.1	5.0	5.0	5.0
Private	5.4	5.3	5.3	5.3
Public	3.3	3.1	3.1	3.1
Exports of goods and services	4.3	4.3	4.4	4.3
Imports of goods and services	5.0	5.1	5.0	5.1
MDG-related public spending (percentage of GDP in 2015)				
Final consumption				
Primary education	2.1	1.5	1.5	1.5
Health	2.5	2.5	2.5	2.5
Water and sanitation	0.0	0.0	0.0	0.0
Investment				
Primary education	0.01	0.01	0.01	0.01
Health	0.01	0.10	0.10	0.10
Water and sanitation	0.00	0.00	0.00	0.00
Savings and financing (percentage of GDP in 2015)				
Revenues from direct taxes	5.7	5.0	5.7	5.7
Government savings	2.3	2.2	2.8	2.7
External savings	1.5	1.5	0.9	1.5
Government domestic borrowing (flow)	0.1	0.1	0.1	-0.4
Government foreign borrowing (flow)	0.3	0.3	-0.2	0.3

Table A6.1 (cont'd)

	Baseline scenario	MDG 2 scenario with:		
		direct taxes	external borrowing	domestic borrowing
Public domestic debt (stock)	6.2	6.2	6.2	11.3
Public foreign debt (stock)	7.7	7.7	12.1	7.7
Labour market (Annual average growth rate for 2003-2015)				
Employment	1.2	1.1	1.1	1.1
Unskilled workers	0.0	-0.1	-0.2	-0.1
Semi-skilled workers	0.5	0.6	0.6	0.6
Skilled workers	4.6	4.4	4.4	4.4
Wage per worker	4.4	4.3	4.3	4.3
Unskilled workers	6.7	6.9	7.0	6.9
Semi-skilled workers	5.9	5.8	5.9	5.8
Skilled workers	0.2	0.1	0.1	0.1

Source: MAMS for Chile.

Acknowledgements

The authors are grateful for the technical assistance of Mauricio Pereira, research assistant from the Department of Industrial Engineering, and for the support of FONDECYT Project No. 1040701.

Notes

1   Economic growth was spectacular between 1989 and 1998 when the country grew at a remarkable rate of 8 per cent per year.
2   Unemployment among workers with tertiary education is considerably higher than the national average and reached 12.5 per cent in 2003. Unemployment among unskilled and semi-skilled workers, on the other hand, was 6 per cent and 10 per cent respectively (MIDEPLAN, 2005b). The unemployment rate for youth (workers between 15 and 24 years of age) is double the average, reaching 17.5 per cent in 2005. Furthermore, a breakdown shows a high level of inequality according to income levels and gender; the poorest quintile has an unemployment rate of 39 per cent and women have 30 per cent higher probability of becoming unemployed than men (ECLAC, 2006a).
3   Even though the methodologies used to measure poverty are not strictly comparable for those two years, there is no doubt that there has been a significant reduction in poverty as measured through the nationally defined poverty line.
4   Basic education includes basic primary education (1st to 6th grade, according to the CINE-97 classification) and the first two years of secondary education (7th and 8th grades). It is worth highlighting that the net enrolment rates for Chile at the primary school level tend to be systematically lower than those of most countries. This is because the annual school cycle begins in early March but children turning six after March 31st would not be allowed by Chilean law to enroll in 1st grade until the following year. Therefore, the low net enrolment rates recorded do not necessarily mean that children are not incorporated into the education system (MIDEPLAN, 2005a).

5   CEPAL (2005b) also warns that the number for Chile underestimates the net primary school enrolment rate by around ten percentage points because the cohort it uses in its calculation includes all 6 year old children but according to current laws, most children turn seven while they are in first grade.

6   One result of greater access to education for the poorest sectors is that in the first decile, youth between the ages of 15 and 24 have 2.5 times more years of study than their grandparents and 1.5 times more than their parents. In terms of gender equity, the enrolment of girls in high school is 1.02 times greater than that of boys. At the level of higher education, the ratio of women to men grew from 0.81 to 0.87 between 1990 and 2000.

7   A report of the OECD (2004) provides a complete and independent evaluation of educational policies in Chile since 1990, identifying the primary problems and making a series of short-, medium- and long-term recommendations.

8   CEPAL (2005b) estimates a much lower coverage, with 59 per cent of the rural population having access to drinking water in 2002.

9   Microeconometric estimations were carried out to select the values of the key elasticities of the MDG module of MAMS. The data utilized came from the 2003 CASEN socioeconomic determination survey and from the data bases of the Ministry of Health (MINSAL), Ministry of Education (MINEDUC) and Ministry of Development and Planning (MIDEPLAN). The best information available was used to confirm the ranges in which these parameters likely move.

10   A study by Sapelli and Torche (2004) concludes that the income variable is a significant determinant but with little influence on drop-out rates.

11   The use of aggregate data at the district level and the already low infant mortality rates in Chile explain, in large part, the results obtained.

12   Castañeda (1985) evaluates the determinants of the decrease in infant mortality rates in Chile between 1975 and 1982, showing results that are consistent with those used.

13   For more detail, see MIDEPLAN (2005b).

14   A new input-output matrix for 2003 was published in 2006, but it was not yet available when this study was being conducted. The 1996 SAM, on the other hand, was carried out in the framework of the ECOGEM-Chile project (for more details, see O'Ryan and others, 2001, 2003, 2006).

15   The values of all elasticities and other key parameters used in MAMS for Chile are documented in O'Ryan and others (2007).

16   The scenario of financing through foreign aid is not realistic given the relatively high level of Chile's development. At the same time, it is also believed that it would not make much sense to finance the new public spending required through external debt, since there is already a high level of achievement of the goals in the baseline scenario.

17   MIDEPLAN applies a discount rate for the evaluation of the social impact of projects of 8 per cent.

18   The two national lines were calculated as the population weighted average of the urban and rural poverty lines established by MIDEPLAN.

References

Baytelman, Y., Cowan, K., De Gregorio, J. and González, P. (1999). "Política Económica-Social y Bienestar: El Caso de Chile". *UNICEF Document.*

Castañeda, T. (1985). "Determinantes del Descenso de la Mortalidad Infantil en Chile: 1975-1982", *Cuadernos de Economía*, año 22., No. 66 (August), Santiago, Chile.

Central Bank (2003). *Matriz de Insumo Producto para la Economía Chilena 1996*, Santiago,Chile.

__________ (2005). *Anuario de Cuentas Nacionales 1996-2004*, Santiago, Chile.

__________ (2006). *Anuario de Cuentas Nacionales 2005*, Santiago, Chile.

CEPAL (Comisión Económica para América Latina y el Caribe) (2005a). *Anuario Estadístico de América Latina y el Caribe 2004*, Santiago de Chile.

__________ (2005b). *Objetivos de Desarrollo del Milenio: Una Mirada desde América Latina y el Caribe*, Santiago de Chile.

__________ (2006a). *Juventud y Mercado Laboral: Brechas y Barreras*, Santiago de Chile.

__________ (2006b). *Panorama Social de América Latina 2005*, Santiago de Chile.

CEPAL-UNESCO (Comisión Económica para América Latina y el Caribe - United Nations Educational, Scientific and Cultural Organization) (2005). "Invertir mejor para invertir más. Financiamiento y gestión de la educación en América Latina y el Caribe", *Serie Seminarios y Conferencias*, No. 43, Santiago de Chile.

DIRECON (2006). "Informe de Comercio Exterior. Cuarto Trimestre 2005," Santiago, Chile.

Eyzaguirre, Nicolás (2005). "Exposición sobre el Estado de la Hacienda Pública." Presentation of the Ministry of Treasury, October (mimeograph).

ICEX (2003). *Claves de la Economía Mundial*, Spanish Institute for Foreign Trade and the Complutense Institute for International Studies, Madrid.

Martin, M. (1998). "Integración al desarrollo: una visión de la política social", in Toloza, C. y E. Lahera (eds.), *Chile en los noventa*, Dolmen ediciones: Santiago, Chile.

MIDEPLAN (Ministry of Development and Planning) (2005a). *Los Objetivos de Desarrollo del Milenio: Primer Informe del Gobierno de Chile*, Santiago, Chile.

__________ (2005b). *Resultados de la Encuesta de Caracterización Socio-Económica 2003 (CASEN)*, Santiago, Chile.

MINEDUC (Ministry of Education) (2005). *Indicadores de la Educación en Chile 2003-2004*, Ministry of Education, Santiago, Chile.

OECD (2004). "Reviews of National Policies for Education - Chile", Paris.

__________ (2005). "Estudios Económicos de la OCDE: Chile", Volume 19/2005, November. Supplement No. 1, Paris.

O`Ryan R., De Miguel, C. and Lagos, C. (2007). "Estrategias para alcanzar los objetivos del milenio en Chile," *Documentos de Trabajo,* Centre for Applied Economics, Department of Industrial Engineering, University of Chile (publication forthcoming).

O`Ryan R., De Miguel, C. and Miller, S., (2001). "Environmental Taxes, Inefficient Subsidies and Income Distribution in Chile: A CGE Framework," *Working Papers, CEA*, No. 98, Santiago, Chile.

__________ (2003). "The Ecogem-Chile Model: A CGE Model for Environmental and Trade Policy Analysis", *Working Papers*, Central Bank, Santiago, Chile.

__________ (2006). "The Environmental Effects of Free Trade Agreements: A Dynamic CGE Analysis for Chile", Santiago, Chile (mimeograph).

Raczynski, D., and Serrano, C. (2005). "Las políticas y estrategias de desarrollo social. Aportes de los años 90 y desafíos futuros", in Patricio Meller (ed.), *La paradoja aparente. Equidad y Eficiencia: resolviendo el dilema*, Taurus Ediciones: Santiago, Chile.

Sapelli, C., and Torche, A. (2004). "Deserción Escolar y Trabajo Juvenil: ¿Dos Caras de una Misma Decisión?" *Cuadernos de Economía*, Vol. 41 (August), Santiago, Chile.

Schkolnik, M., and Bonnefoy J. (1994). "Una Propuesta de Tipología de las Políticas Sociales en Chile". *UNICEF document.*

7
Costa Rica

Marco V. Sánchez

Introduction

The degree of progress made towards the Millennium Development Goals (MDGs) has been uneven in Latin America and the Caribbean (See Chapter 2 and ECLAC, 2005). Costa Rica has shown notable progress towards most of the goals, and this has been possible in large part because the country's social policies historically have gone hand in hand with economic policy making. This policy approach contributed to the country's good economic performance. Real GDP per capita grew by 1.8 per cent per year in the 1960s and by 3.4 per cent per year in the 1970s. Improvements in prosperity were temporarily interrupted by the foreign debt crisis in the period between 1980 and 1983, when real GDP per capita fell by 4.3 per cent per year. Stabilization policies were introduced in response to the crisis, followed by a series of structural adjustment reforms that allowed the country to resume growth of per capita output at a pace of 1.7 per cent per year between 1983 and 1989. During the 1990s, this pace was stepped up to slightly above 3 per cent per year, less than the growth achieved in the 1970s and below the outcome expected from the structural reforms. During 2000-05, growth of per capita output decelerated to 1.9 per cent per year, close to the rate of income improvement of the 1960s, but under circumstances of a more unequal income distribution.

These historic trends raise the question of whether Costa Rica's economy has the capacity to sustain a rate of growth that is sufficient to support increased social investments needed to achieve the MDGs. Nonetheless, per capita income stood at \$4,580 in 2005, a high development level by Latin American standards. Furthermore, the country's social policies have proven to be highly effective, also during periods of economic turbulence. Broadly, main social indicators have kept improving since the foreign debt crisis. The country has progressed satisfactorily towards the achievement of most of the MDGs and several of the internationally agreed targets linked to the MDGs have already been reached ahead of schedule. Paradoxically, though, given the degree of progress made, meeting all targets has become a greater challenge.

This chapter attempts to do three things: quantify the public spending required to achieve the MDGs in primary education, under-five child mortality, maternal mortality and coverage for drinking water and basic sanitation systems; determine the most viable financing mechanism for covering that expenditure; and identify macroeconomic trade-offs as well as any repercussions there might be in terms of poverty and inequality if public spending increases and is financed for this purpose. The methodological framework used is provided by a computable general equilibrium model called MAMS, which has the unique characteristic of including a module of determinants for the MDGs that are the subject of this study (see Chapter 3 of this volume). The goal for reducing extreme poverty is an exception in that MAMS does not identify any public spending that can be directly associated with that goal and the model further lacks sufficient detailed specification of the income distribution in order to analyse poverty changes in a rigorous manner. The analysis with MAMS is therefore combined with the application of a microsimulation methodology (see Chapter 2, Appendix A2) in order to determine how changes in the labour market affect poverty and inequality, with and without increases in public spending aimed at meeting the other MDGs.

The chapter is structured as follows. The next section reviews the main reforms that have been part of Costa Rica's economic development in the last few years, in order to place the economic changes of the 1985-2005 period in context. It also identifies the key vulnerabilities of the economy. The third section deals with social policy aspects and the progress made towards the MDGs and the prospects of achieving the pre-established targets in the future. The steps for implementing the modelling techniques with Costa Rican data are explained in the fourth section. The subsequent section analyses the various scenarios simulated through MAMS and the microsimulations. The final section presents the main conclusions as well as some policy recommendations.

Economic reforms, performance and vulnerabilities

Once the foreign debt crisis had been overcome and the economy was stabilized, Costa Rica chose to reorient its pattern of economic development towards deeper integration with the rest of the world. Trade reforms were introduced, including measures of export promotion that were effective until the late 1990s and various rounds of unilateral, bilateral and multilateral trade liberalization.[1] Taxes on exports were by and large eliminated and the average tariff on imports had fallen to 2 per cent by 2000-03 as a result of these reforms (Sánchez, 2005). The impact on trade can be seen from Table 7.1. For example, total trade in goods and services expanded markedly, reaching 93 per cent of

GDP on average between 2000 and 2005. Imports of intermediate and capital goods increased significantly, dominating the structure of imported goods. Imports of fuel and lubricants, in particular, increased in importance, representing almost 7 per cent of imports on average during 2000-05, after expanding at 31.4 per cent per annum in that same period. The rising dependence on imported oil products made the production sectors more vulnerable to external shocks, especially in the light of rising world market prices for oil from 2002.

Exports grew strongly in the 1990s, especially during the second half of the decade when they increased at a rate of almost 15 per cent per year (see Table 7.1). After a precipitous decline of 14.2 per cent per year in 2000-01—the result of a contraction in INTEL microprocessor exports and lower export prices for coffee and bananas—exports recovered in the next biennium at a pace of 8.9 per cent per year.[2] Future export growth is highly dependent on the performance of the microprocessor sector. Traditional vulnerability to falling primary commodity prices is much less, as export production has become much more diversified. Non-traditional exports represented on average almost 87 per cent per year of total merchandise exports during 2000-05. Because of the good export performance, the trade deficit averaged around 2.6 per cent of GDP in 2000-05; much less than that recorded at the beginning of the 1990s. As Sánchez and Sauma (2006) show, economic growth has been export-led over the past two decades.

Exchange-rate policies have been crucial to the export performance. A regime of mini-devaluations of the *colon*, using the multilateral real effective exchange rate as a reference for the adjustments, kept the real exchange rate relatively stable and competitive during the period between 1985 and 2005, with the exception of the short period between 1990-95 when the exchange rate appreciated following the elimination of capital controls and the resulting strong influx of capital (see Table 7.1). As the exchange rate had become predictable with the system of mini-devaluations and the economy had become increasingly dollarized, a mechanism of managed floating of the currency was adopted in October 2006 with bands determined by the Central Bank of Costa Rica (BCCR).

As mentioned, the elimination of capital controls in 1991 boosted capital inflows (see Table 7.1). Much of the capital inflows are invested in productive activities, stimulated by the economic reforms, the political and economic stability of the country, as well as by special guarantees to foreign investors created for this end. Annual inflows of net foreign direct investment (FDI) increased to an average of 3.2 per cent of GDP in 2000-04.

Domestic price controls and state monopolies on trade in basic consumption goods have been eliminated. Fiscal reforms have been slower, though tax collection has been improved, public employment has been reduced, and spending policies have become more restrictive. Tax revenues have increased, but less than spending (see Table 7.1). The fiscal deficit of the central government

Table 7.1   Costa Rica: indicators of production, employment, external sector and public finances, 1985-2005 (annual period averages)

	1985-1989	1990-1994	1995-1999	2000-2005
Production and employment				
Real GDP (annual percentage change)	4.7	5.6	5.4	3.7
Employment (annual percentage change)	4.5	2.9	2.8	5.7
Real wages per employed person (annual percentage change)[a]	n.a.	3.3	1.0	-1.5
External sector				
Trade balance of goods and services (% of GDP)	-2.2	-5.4	-1.5	-2.6
Total trade in goods and services (% of GDP)	67.8	75.3	88.1	93.9
Exports of goods and services (annual percentage change)	8.8	9.2	14.8	4.3
Non-traditional exports (% of exports of goods)[c]	46.0	64.1	76.9	86.8
Imports of goods and services (annual percentage change)	11.7	9.9	9.2	9.1
Imports of intermediate and capital goods (% of imports of goods)	78.3	78.0	79.4	89.2
Gross private capital inflows (% of GDP)[b]	6.4	5.3	8.7	9.8
Net foreign direct investment (% of GDP)[b]	2.0	2.7	3.6	3.2
Nominal exchange rate (index, 1995 = 100)	36.3	72.1	129.4	214.3
Real exchange rate (index, 1995 = 100)	106.0	106.9	102.6	108.2
Public finances				
Tax revenues (% of GDP)	13.8	9.1	12.2	13.0
Total expenditures (% of GDP)	17.7	14.7	15.2	15.8
Fiscal deficit (% of GDP)	2.7	2.9	3.1	2.8
Domestic financing (% of fiscal deficit)	56.3	99.4	91.3	69.7
Domestic financing (% of GDP)[b]	1.8	2.7	3.0	1.9
External financing (% of fiscal deficit)	43.7	0.5	8.7	30.7
External financing (% of GDP)[d]	0.1	0.0	0.0	0.9
Domestic debt of non-financial public sector (% of GDP)[b]	11.3	13.6	24.3	27.7
External public debt (% of GDP)[b]	64.1	38.1	22.4	20.2

Source: Based on data from the Central Bank of Costa Rica, except for gross private capital inflows and foreign direct investment for which data come from the World Bank's World Development Indicators, and for real average wage growth which was estimated based on data from the National Institute of Statistics and Census (INEC).

[a] Real average monthly wage in July. Starting in 2001, it refers to the real average monthly wage of the main occupation of workers. The change in measure is due to methodological adjustments to the household surveys.

[b] Data for the last sub-period are for 2000-2004.

[c] Includes export processing zones known as 'perfeccionamiento activo' and 'zona franca'.

[d] Data for the first sub-period refer to 1988-1999.

n.a.: Data not available.

widened continuously as a percentage of GDP between 1995 and 1999. Despite some improvement in the 2000-05 period, the large deficit formed a constraint to pursuing the MDGs.[3] Domestic public sector debt has ballooned in order to finance the widening fiscal deficit. Government debt expanded at onerous terms, since the government has had to issue bonds at very high interest rates to attract private savings, affecting private investment negatively. The servicing of domestic debt has become increasingly costly and has become itself a main source of the deficit increases and this has crowded out resources available for public investment. These problems led the government to seek more external financing. In addition, given the low tax burden—an average of 13 per cent of GDP in the 2000-05 period—various tax reform measures came under consideration to enhance tax revenue. Measures to improve tax collection were implemented with visible positive outcomes from 2005.[4]

The economic reforms did contribute to changes in the structure of the economy during 1985-2005. The share of agriculture in total output fell, while that of industry kept its significance. Service sectors linked to international trade, finance and tourism have become the main source of value added generation in the economy since the beginning of the 1990s. This structural change was accompanied by significant growth in overall output, employment and real wages (see Table 7.1). The economy grew by 5.5 per cent per year in the 1990s, slowing thereafter on the back of weaker export performance, the finalization of the construction of INTEL's installations and the rise in oil prices. During the first five years of the new millennium, the economy grew by 3.7 per cent per year on average, even though growth accelerated to 6 per cent per annum between 2003 and 2005.[5] Employment increased by almost 3 per cent per year during the 1990s, much less than output as a result of productivity growth. The increase in labour productivity can be associated with the impact of the economic reforms and the use of more skill-intensive technologies in production and increased use of imported capital goods (Sanchez, 2004). Rising productivity allowed for real wage increases, especially in the early 1990s. The decline in production during the 2000-02 downturn was accompanied by a substantial rise in the level of employment that actually reflected a cyclical increase in informal services jobs. Average real wages fell by 1.5 per cent per year between 2000 and 2005 as a result of the years of downturn and did not recover at the same pace as production thereafter.

Social policy and progress towards the MDGs

Social progress has gone hand in hand with economic development in Costa Rica. Since the beginning of the previous century, institutions of governance and the legal framework of the country have given high importance to social policy development.[6] Irrespective of changes in the pattern of economic growth, there has been no noticeable change in the orientation of social policies that have kept focus on the universal coverage and the promotion of social programmes.

The country's institutional framework for conducting social policy has been supported by adequate levels of government spending. From 1987 to 1999, the country dedicated an average of 15 per cent of GDP per year to public social spending and this share increased to 18.3 per cent in the 2000-04 period (see Table 7.2). Spending on education has increased since the mid 1980s, though it has not reached the level of 6 per cent of GDP required by the Constitution, since its reform of 1997.[7] A similar pattern can be seen in the areas of healthcare and social welfare since the early 1990s. Public social spending has been relatively efficient considering that, in per-capita terms, it has been associated with a relatively low incidence of poverty, something only seen elsewhere in Latin America in countries like Chile and Uruguay (Sanchez, 2007a). The results of social policies have also been reflected in visible progress towards the achievement of the MDGs.[8]

As mentioned in the introduction, the MDGs considered in this study are those related to extreme poverty reduction, primary education, child mortality, maternal mortality and coverage of drinking water and basic sanitation. Table 7.3 presents the indicators that are internationally used to evaluate progress towards the achievement of these goals. These are complemented by some national indicators.

In the Millennium Declaration, countries made a commitment to reduce by half the percentage of the population who are living on an income of less than one dollar a day, as well as halving the percentage of the population experiencing hunger and resolved to do so between 1990 and 2015 (MDG 1, targets 1 and 2). The percentage of Costa Ricans who live on less than one dollar a day was 3.4 per cent in 1990 and this share should thus be reduced to 1.7 per cent in 2015 to meet the target. The poverty incidence has indeed fallen since 1991 to as low as 1.6 per cent in 1998, thus achieving the MDG target ahead of time. The progress in poverty reduction has experienced setbacks thereafter, however, for reasons explained below.

Table 7.2   Costa Rica: public social spending by sector as a percentage of GDP, 1987-2004

	1987-1989	**1990-1994**	**1995-1999**	**2000-2004**
Education	3.7	4.0	4.2	5.3
Health	4.9	4.7	4.7	5.4
Social assistance	5.5	4.9	5.6	5.8
Housing	2.1	1.8	1.6	1.7
Other	0.2	0.2	0.2	0.1
Total	16.4	15.6	16.4	18.3

Source: Databases of the Technical Secretariat of the Budget Authority, Ministry of the Treasury of Costa Rica (for social spending data) and the BCCR (for GDP data).

Table 7.3   Costa Rica: progress towards the MDGs, 1990-2005 and targets for 2015

Indicator	1990	1995	2000	2002[a]	2004[b]	2015 Target
Poverty						
Percentage of the population living on less than one dollar a day at purchasing power parity (MDG 1, target 1)	3.4	2.8	1.8	2.8	n.a.	1.7
Percentage of the population below the national extreme poverty line[c]	9.1	6.2	6.1	5.7	5.6**	
Percentage of the population below the national moderate poverty line[c]	27.4	20.4	20.6	20.6	21.2**	
Primary education						
Percentage of students that begin first grade and get to fifth grade	80.3	84.8	88.9	89.4	n.a.	
Percentage of students who begin primary school and complete it (MDG 2, target 3)	76.7	80.3	83.7	84.1	n.a.	100.0
Repetition rate in primary education (%)	11.3	9.3	8.2	7.6	7.4	
Net enrolment rate in primary education (%)	98.5	99.8	99.4	99.2	98.5	
Mortality						
Under-five child mortality rate per 1,000 live births (MDG 4, target 5)	18.0	16.0	12.0	9.6	13.0	6.0
Infant mortality rate per 1,000 live births	16.0	14.0	10.0	n.a.	11.0	
Maternal mortality rates per 100,000 live births (MDG 5, target 6)	15.0	20.0	36.0	41.0	30.0**	8.3[d]
Water and sanitation						
Percentage of the population with access to potable water (MDG 9, target 10)	50.0[e]	69.0	76.0	78.4	79.5*	75.0
Percentage of the population with access to toilet connected to sewage system or septic tank (MDG 10, target 11)	75.8[e]	83.5[f]	90.6	93.4	93.5*	91.2

Source: Data on the percentage of the population with income of less than one dollar a day are from Consejo Social del Gobierno de la República de Costa Rica and Sistema de las Naciones Unidas en Costa Rica (2005), and national poverty data are from INEC. Information on education is from the Ministry of Public Education. Mortality data are from UNICEF, except for maternal mortality data which come from the Ministry of Health. Information about water is from the Costa Rican Institute of Water and Sewage (AyA) and information on sanitation comes from INEC.

[a] Base year of the modelling methodology used in the study.

[b] Data with one asterisk are for 2003 and those with two asterisks are for 2005.

[c] Calculated using the INEC national poverty or extreme poverty line as applicable.

[d] Target defined using the 1991 maternal mortality rate (33 per 100,000 live births).

[e] Data for the two indicators related to water and sanitation are for 1991 and 1989, respectively.

[f] Data for 1994.

n.a.: Data not available.

Costa Rica aspires to meet the same target of halving poverty as measured on the basis of national poverty lines defined by INEC.[9] In 1990, 9.1 per cent of households were living in extreme poverty by the nationally set threshold. In order to be on track towards the 2015 target, the poverty incidence would need to decline at a rate of 2.7 per cent per year, implying that by 2005 the extreme poverty incidence according to the national measure would need to have reached 6.1 per cent or less. Despite the fluctuations in the economy, the measure had fallen in fact to 5.6 per cent in 2005, suggesting Costa Rica is on track to meet the target. The total poverty incidence as measured through the moderate national poverty line, which next to food also covers non-food basic needs, affected about 27.4 per cent of the population in 1990. This poverty rate fell in the early 1990s, but the reduction could not been sustained from the mid-1990s and there was a temporary increase in poverty after 2003, which was reversed no sooner than in 2006.

Effective social policies have contributed to poverty reduction, especially during the period prior to the end of the 1990s. Improvements in the quality of new jobs also contributed, as reflected in particular in an increase in formal sector jobs (Sánchez and Sauma, 2006). Trade reforms and keeping the exchange rate competitive also exercised a positive influence in the early 1990s, as shown by Sánchez (2004, 2005). Sánchez further indicates that foreign direct investment and enhanced foreign-exchange earnings facilitated technological change which stimulated productivity and real wage growth during the 1990s by employing the country's relatively large pool of skilled labour.

. The decline in total poverty could not be sustained after the mid 1990s because of the volatility in output growth, the related decline in real wages and the rise in income inequality. The share of the poorest quintile in national income has fallen steadily since 1996 and has stayed below 5 per cent since. The Gini coefficient of the per capita household income distribution increased from 0.37 in 1990 to 0.43 in 2002. This increase in inequality is consistent with the observed trend showing that the poorest of the poor have become poorer. As indicated, the share of the population living on less than one dollar a day increased after 1998. Therefore, reaching the goal of reducing this incidence to only 1.7 per cent by 2015 will thus not only depend on the level and stability of economic growth, but also on trends in the income distribution.

Recent data from INEC show that there was a significant reduction in total poverty between 2006 and 2007, as it fell from 20.2 per cent to 16.7 per cent, to reach the lowest level recorded in three decades. This reduction is due to the acceleration of economic growth referred to earlier and to lower inflation and government subsidy programmes, rather than to any visible reduction in income inequality. It remains to be seen whether this recent trend towards poverty reduction can be sustained. In considerable degree, this will also depend on whether or not adverse external factors will affect economic growth.

MDG 2 (target 3) aims to ensure that all children in the appropriate age group will be able to finish the complete cycle of primary education by the year 2015. The net enrolment rate for primary school in Costa Rica is one of the highest in Latin America and the Caribbean, averaging nearly 99 per cent between 1999 and 2004. The number of children that started school but failed to finish the entire cycle of primary education has been systematically reduced since 1990. Only about 15.9 per cent of the children fell in this category in 2002. Higher numbers of students starting first grade and getting to fifth grade, and lower repetition rates reflect this progress. In order to raise completion rates further, however, drop-out rates must be reduced and classroom performance must be improved. Regional gaps in school performance should be closed by prioritizing the areas that are lagging the farthest behind. Equally important for lowering the school drop-out rates will be the continuation of government support programmes like the voucher system, scholarships and transportation subsidies for those who truly need it.[10] Increasing public social spending on education to 6 per cent of GDP, as required by the Constitution, would likely contribute to putting the country on track towards meeting the primary education target by 2015.

Another goal is to eliminate gender inequalities in primary and secondary education, preferably by the year 2005, and for all levels of education before the end of the year 2015 (MDG 3, target 4). At present, gender inequality is no longer a serious problem in Costa Rica's education. If anything, the net enrolment rates for female students have surpassed—though only slightly—those of males between 1990 and 2004, especially at the highest levels of education.

In health, the targets are to reduce by two thirds the under-five child mortality rate between 1990 and 2015 (MDG 4, target 5) and to reduce maternal mortality by three quarters during the same period (MDG 5, target 6). The under-five mortality rate was 18 per 1,000 live births in 1990 to fall steadily to one of the lowest rates in Latin America and the Caribbean by 2003.[11] Using a linear projection, however, the child mortality rate should have fallen to 9.7 by 2004 in order to be on track for achieving the 2015 target of 6 deaths per 1,000 live births, but in practice 13 deaths per 1,000 live births were recorded in that year. In order to achieve the target, the under-five mortality rate would have to be reduced further by little more than 50 per cent between 2004 and 2015, which at the relatively low rate achieved could pose a challenge.

Death in infancy is the most common cause of child mortality (see Table 7.3). The problem has been reduced primarily because of advances in the medical field, but also because of the expansion of preventative healthcare treating infectious diseases and parasites, including improved coverage of vaccination programmes. The National Immunizations Programme and food assistance programmes have also been vital. Social welfare programmes have also had an effect, especially those related to housing and poverty reduction. Even so, resource constraints could limit the scope for further reductions in infant mortality, as neonatal mortality (death within the first 28 days after birth) has become the principal cause of death (more than two thirds of the cases in 2000-03). The neonatal death rate has decreased more slowly than that of post-neonatal mortality since 1993; and it has to do primarily with premature births, low birth weight and congenital deformations. Dealing with problems like congenital deformations, for example, requires technological resources and facilities that hardly exist in developing countries and are not available in Costa Rica. Furthermore, even if serious problems could be detected in the foetal stage, current laws do not permit therapeutic abortions. Minimally, public spending must be increased further to strengthen the National System for the Analysis of Infant Mortality (SINAMI) and the National Plan for the Prevention of Infant Mortality, and to ensure full coverage of vaccination programmes. Resources must be targeted at the primary care level, especially in the areas with the least access to child health services.

Maternal mortality is also relatively low with 15 recorded deaths per 100,000 live births in 1990. Data limitations hamper the analysis of trends in maternal mortality. In 1991, for instance, the rate jumped to 33 deaths per 100,000 live births after improvements in the data collection. Available statistics show fluctuating trends over time. Over the period from 1991 to 2005, the rate fell only modestly (from 33 to 30), according to these data. The main causes of maternal death suggest that making further progress towards the MDG target will be costly, as these include complications before and during birth, post-partum haemorrhaging, pregnancy-induced hypertension, miscarriages and post-partum complications. Non-compliance with maternal and perinatal healthcare standards and the lack of risk classifications for pregnant women should also be added to the list (Ministerio de Salud, 2001). In addition, currently, pregnant women who are not insured by the Costa Rican Social Security Fund (CCSS) can obtain only one free professional medical consultation during pregnancy.

Because maternal death records have improved, the most sensible base year for measuring progress towards the target for MDG 5 is 1991. Even so, the target remains overly ambitious. To go from 33 to 8.3 maternal deaths per 100,000 live births between 1991 and 2015 would require lowering the maternal mortality rate by 5.6 per cent per year. The government set a more realistic national target of 20 maternal deaths per 100,000 live births (Consejo Social del Gobierno de la República de Costa Rica and Sistema de las Naciones Unidas en Costa Rica, 2005). The prospects of achieving this adjusted target are still challenging but not too poor either, considering that a high percentage of maternal deaths could have been prevented by providing better care to pregnant women. Therefore, greater prevention should be a social policy priority.[12] This will require better training for general practitioners and nurses so that they can classify and appropriately care for women with high-risk pregnancies and it will mean that more gynaecologists and obstetricians must be hired in the CCSS system.

Progress made in recording and assessing maternal mortality should also have an influence on the improved design of policies and strategies for alleviating the problem. Public health services should also be required to provide care to all pregnant women in labour, whether they are insured or not.

Finally, the MDG targets of reducing the percentage of the population without access to drinking water in half (MDG 7, target 10) and improving access to basic sanitation (MDG 7, target 11) have been achieved ahead of time (Table 7.3).[13] In the case of sanitation, in particular, the level of progress is explained primarily by achievements made in enhancing coverage in rural areas.[14] Costa Rica must continue increasing public spending on water and sanitation at a rate high enough to provide the service to the growing population and at least maintain the existing rate of coverage. At the same time, new resources must be allocated to address negative environmental externalities associated with sanitation systems. The collection and evacuation of wastewater through a sanitary sewage system does not mean that the water is being treated adequately as it is disposed. In the case of septic tanks, businesses empty their waste directly into the rivers without any prior treatment and they are not required to have their own treatment plant. This means that contamination produced in dwellings is transmitted to water sources, implying that the country could actually be moving backwards in terms of sustainable development. Furthermore, the use of septic tanks should be reduced in densely populated areas.

Modelling approach

As indicated, MAMS—explained in Chapter 3—was used to simulate various scenarios. The base-year accounting framework for the model is provided by a Social Accounting Matrix (SAM) built for 2002. A salient feature of MAMS is the specification of functional relationships for the MDG indicators and their main determinants. Through MAMS, a baseline scenario and alternative scenarios for achieving the MDGs are simulated for the 2002-15 period. Ideally, the baseline scenario should fully replicate observed economic trends between 2002 and 2007, the most recent year for which observed data were available when conducting this study. Unfortunately, this is not exactly the case due to limitations of the model, including its inability to account for some key policy changes, the fact that certain parameters are assumed to be fixed, and the existence of a number of restrictive assumptions about the closure rules for factor markets and macroeconomic balances. In the baseline scenario, final consumption of the government is assumed to grow at a fixed rate, but based on observed trends between 2000 and 2005. The baseline scenario serves as the reference for assessing alternative scenarios under which public spending is adjusted to the levels needed to achieve one or more MDGs. The alternative scenarios assess the implications of scaling up public spending under different financing options: through foreign aid, increased income taxes, domestic borrowing or external borrowing.

The model distinguishes three types of workers: those who have not completed secondary education (unskilled), those with at least completed secondary education (semi-skilled) and those who have completed some degree in tertiary education (skilled). In all of the scenarios, if the unemployment rate by type of worker exceeds a minimum unemployment rate, the real wage (with respect to the consumer price index) is equivalent to a "reservation wage" such that the market reaches equilibrium through adjustments in the unemployment rate (or, by the same token, through changes in the level of employment). Alternatively, if the unemployment is at the minimum rate, the labour market reaches equilibrium through adjustments in the real wage. Meanwhile, the capital market reaches equilibrium through adjustments in the price of capital under the assumption of full capital utilization.

The macroeconomic closure rules in the base scenario are as follows. Government investment spending, which depends on the demand for capital in the public services sector, is covered through current savings and fixed levels of borrowing (domestic and external) and foreign aid. The government is assumed to cover any remaining imbalances by adjusting income tax rates. This may be a good representation of the government's actual behaviour between 1990 and 2005, when tax revenue increased as a percentage of government spending (see Table 7.1). Capital flows from abroad are assumed fixed, such that the real exchange rate adjusts to clear the current account of the balance of payments. This external closure rule does not adequately capture the regime of mini-devaluations, and this has some implications for the interpretation of the baseline results as discussed further below. The third macroeconomic closure rule assumes that, once the level of government investment has been determined, private investment adjusts such that total investment equals total savings. The closure rule for the fiscal balance changes for the MDG scenarios that allow increased spending to be financed through either domestic borrowing, foreign aid or external borrowing. In these cases, the relevant financing mechanism is made flexible, while the income tax rates become fixed.

As is usually the case in most general equilibrium models, MAMS only defines the distribution of mean incomes across representative groups of workers and households, but not that within those groups. Thus, it is not possible to obtain results for shifts in the full income distribution, as needed to assess the implications of the scenario analysis on poverty. This limitation is overcome by using the microsimulations methodology described in Appendix A2 of Chapter 2. With this methodology, the changes in the labour market structure in each scenario simulated in MAMS are imposed on a database representative for all households.[15] A randomized process of movements of workers between labour-market segments and occupational condition (for example, being employed or unemployed) is assumed—including the imputation of labour incomes for new labour market entrants, but by repeating the random reallocation of workers sufficient times, confidence intervals of 95 per cent are constructed for the indices of poverty and inequality.

In order to calibrate MAMS, the 2002 SAM for Costa Rica documented in Sánchez (2006b) was adapted, as described in Annex 1 of Sánchez (2006a). Insufficient data were available to estimate all key elasticities for the MDG determinants. Parametric and non-parametric estimates could only be produced for MDG 4 (target 5) and MDG 7 (targets 10 and 11).[16] These estimations were combined with a sensitivity analysis that allowed the identification of feasibility ranges (upper and lower bounds) within which the values of the elasticities of MDG determinants would need to fall in order to enable a feasible solution of MAMS for Costa Rica.

The parametric estimates were calculated using the Quasi-Maximum Likelihood Estimation suggested by Papke and Wooldridge (1996) and they are all presented in Sanchez (2008, Appendix A9, Table A9.1). These estimation results suggest that child mortality is inversely correlated with per capita household consumption, public infrastructure (other than that in education, health, and water and sanitation; hereafter, "other public infrastructure") and the coverage of the population with access to basic sanitation services. All related coefficients were found to be statistically significant and hence these were used to define the corresponding elasticities of MAMS. Other determinants, including public spending on health services and access of the population to drinking water, were not found to be statistically significant and, moreover, the related parameters had the wrong sign, possibly owing to deficiencies in the data. Econometric estimates also indicated that, as expected, access to adequate water and basic sanitation services (MDG 7, targets 10 and 11) is positively correlated with public spending on water and sanitation, per capita household consumption and "other public infrastructure". The level of statistical confidence was found to be below 95 per cent for a few regression coefficients only. The derived elasticities for the determinants of MDG 7 turned out to be rather high, though, probably because of omitted variables in the functional relationship and the way in which the data were transformed for the estimation procedure.[17] The value of these elasticities consequently exceeded the upper limit of the range that would enable solving MAMS, and were not used in the model for that reason.

The econometric analysis was complemented by the estimation of point elasticities of the MDG determinants which are also presented in Sanchez (2008, Appendix A7, Table A7.1). These elasticities had the expected sign and were found to be low for most determinants. In the case of the determinants of progress towards MDG 7, the computed point elasticities are much lower than those estimated through the parametric model. The non-parametric estimates produced elasticities that fell within the feasibility ranges of MAMS.

Some additional assumptions were made to complete the set of MDG elasticities. The elasticity of the degree of achievement on MDG 7 (for targets 10 and 11) with respect to the level of public spending on water and sanitation was assumed to be less than 1. Determinants of maternal mortality were assumed to be closely associated with those of infant mortality the occurrence of which, as indicated earlier, essentially explains under-five child mortality. Consequently, elasticities for MDG-5 determinants are assumed to be identical to those for MDG 4. Further, the effect of improvements in access to drinking water on the outcome for the health indicators related to MDGs 4 and 5 is assumed to be the same as that of progress towards the target for access to basic sanitation. Generally, the elasticities of the analysed determinants of child and maternal mortality are low, because some of the main causes of death are not captured in MAMS. Given the high degree of progress already made towards the education target, elasticities for the determinants of MDG 2 were assigned a value near the lower limit of the feasibility ranges for MAMS. The assumed elasticity values were validated after checking whether the MDG indicators showed plausible trends in the baseline scenario of MAMS. All elasticity values used for MAMS are presented in Table A7.1 of Annex A7.

Another important set of elasticities of MAMS relate to the degree of substitution in production and consumption with respect to changes in relative prices and changes in income. For these, the values estimated for Costa Rica by Sánchez (2004) were adopted. Because of the high level of sectoral disaggregation of the elasticities available in this study, and in order to adapt them to the relatively more aggregated structure of MAMS, the values were reweighed using information from the SAM presented in the same study (as reported in Sánchez, 2006a). In general terms, those elasticities suggest that relatively low degrees of substitution in production and consumption prevail in Costa Rica. As for the income-expenditure elasticity, these are relatively low for education and health, as evidence households consider these services to be part of their basic consumption basket.

Analysis of simulation results

A summary of main simulation results is presented in Annex A7 (Tables A7.2-A7.3) and complementary to these are the more detailed results —of scenarios in which only the primary education goals or the mortality goals are achieved by 2015—that can be found in Sánchez (2008, Annex A9, Tables A9.3-A9.4). The discussion in this section focuses on the main findings. The results of the scenarios of financing MDG-related expenditures through foreign aid are not analysed here, as Costa Rica, being a middle-income country, has little access to this source of financing. The results of simulations aiming at achieving more ambitious targets for increasing access to water and sanitation are also not presented either, as, in line with the discussion above, it would seem that greater priority should be given to reversing the negative environmental externalities of existing sanitation systems. Finally, since the target of reducing the maternal mortality rate to 8.3 per 100,000 live births by 2015 is considered unrealistically ambitious, the resource requirements of reaching the national target of 20 are analysed instead.[18]

Baseline scenario

The baseline or 'business-as-usual' scenario broadly reproduces observed trends in key macroeconomic indicators during 2002-05, though with a few notable discrepancies. As the external closure of the model does not consider the mechanism of mini-devaluations, the real exchange rate appreciates gradually in the baseline. Consequently, the model underestimates the observed real export growth and overestimates the need for foreign savings as a larger-than-observed trade deficit is projected. As a result, real GDP (at market prices) increases by 5 per cent per year in the baseline—0.5 percentage points below the trend rate of the early 2000s. The real exchange-rate appreciation induces higher imports and an expansion of non-tradable goods production, as well as an increase of private consumption as a share of GDP. Final government consumption decreases with respect to GDP in the baseline but, on average, it increases by 1.1 per cent per year between 2002 and 2015 after correcting for inflation—following the observed trend of 2002-05. Investment increases slightly as a percentage of GDP.

Government savings is -4 per cent of GDP in the base year, but the government's current account deficit narrows gradually until turning into a surplus at the end of the simulation period on account of a strong rise in revenue from direct and consumption taxes. In addition, data from the BCCR indicate that government domestic borrowing was 2.9 per cent of GDP while the level of external borrowing was 1 per cent of GDP in 2002. The model overestimates domestic borrowing needs and underestimates demand for foreign financing in the base year, as a consequence of adjustments in the model calibration needed to reach initial equilibrium. In subsequent years, though, observed trends are reproduced by MAMS for Costa Rica reaching on average 3 per cent and 1.4 per cent of GDP per year for domestic and external borrowing, respectively, for the 2002-05 period. As the government deficit falls, domestic borrowing requirements are also less, but these are added the outstanding domestic public debt which ultimately increases over time. The level of external debt in local currency falls as a result of the real exchange rate appreciation.

Employment growth in the baseline is stronger for skilled workers (4.8 per cent on average per year) than for semi-skilled (3.3 per cent) and unskilled workers (0.6 per cent). Total employment increases by 1.8 per cent per year, given the smaller share of skilled workers in the total. According to INEC data, observed employment growth was 2.9 per cent per year in 2002-05, compared with 2.4 per cent in the baseline during those years. The difference is explained by the increase in school enrolment in the model, which reduces the participation rate for less skilled workers.

In the baseline scenario, the average real wage rate increases by 2.8 per cent per year. In contrast to employment growth, labour income growth favours unskilled workers more than semi-skilled and skilled workers: these groups would see their wages increase by 4.6 per cent, 1.2 per cent, and -1.2 per cent per year, respectively.

These changes in the labour market translate into a drop in the percentage of the population with income of less than one dollar a day, but the target for MDG 1 would not be reached under the assumptions of the baseline scenario (see Figure 7.1). The higher real wages for unskilled workers do not have a strong enough effect to lift the poorest out of extreme poverty. The shifts in employment and real wages have more or less offsetting effects on income distribution and, consequently, the Gini coefficient only shows a very marginal decline in inequality around 2010 (see Table A7.3). However, the national targets of reducing moderate and extreme poverty (using national poverty lines) to, respectively, 13.7 per cent and 4.6 per cent by 2015, would be easily met.

Public social spending grows at the same pace as that observed in 2002-05 throughout the baseline. Even at this relatively low rate of increase, substantial progress is made towards the MDGs (see Figure 7.2). Other factors also contribute to this outcome, though, including the rise in household consumption spending on MDG-related services, the expansion of "other public infrastructure",

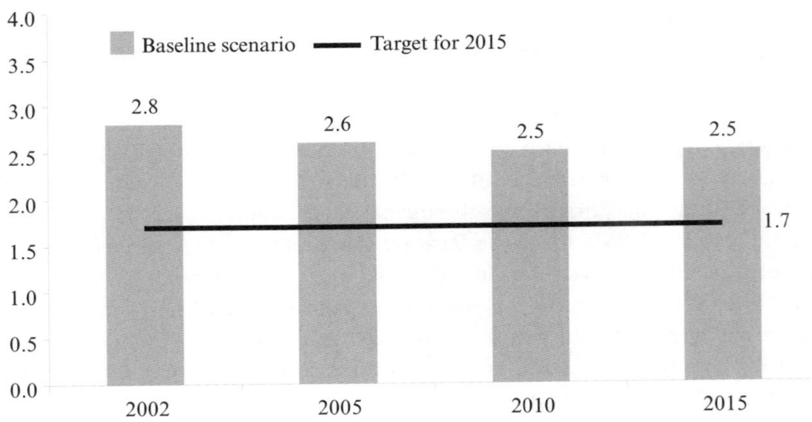

Figure 7.1 Costa Rica: Percentage of the population that live on less than one dollar a day, 2002-2015

Source: MAMS for Costa Rica and microsimulations based on the 2002 household survey (EHPM) of INEC.

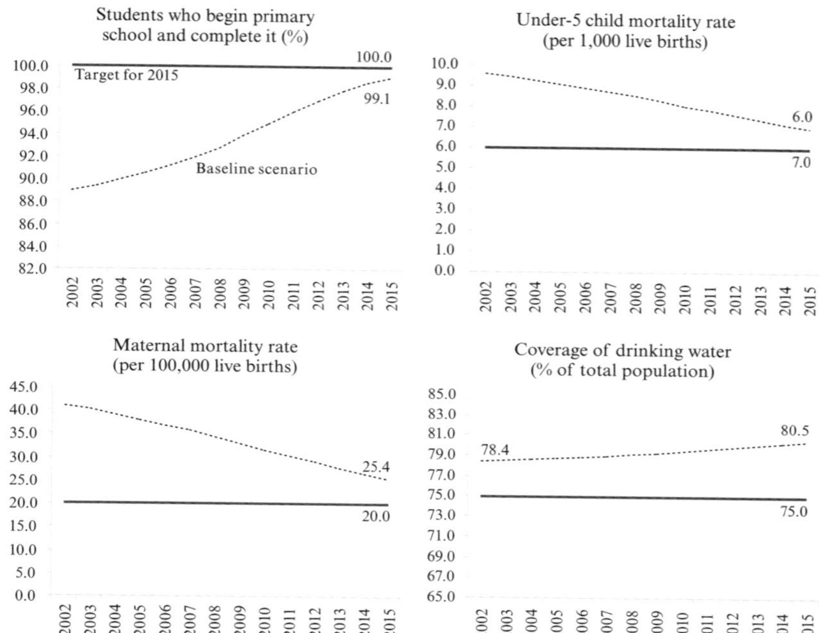

Figure 7.2   Costa Rica: Evolution of MDG indicators in the baseline scenario of MAMS, 2002-2015

Source: MAMS model for Costa Rica.

the positive influence of the "wage premium" to education in school enrolment, and the expansion of water and sanitation coverage, which helps to decrease child mortality.

MDG scenarios

The additional public spending (with respect to the baseline scenario) required to achieve only the goal of primary education is around one half of a percentage point of GDP per year (see Table 7.4). This spending would need to be frontloaded in the beginning of the simulation period, in order to ensure all students of the relevant cohort are enrolled and can graduate timely so as to meet the MDG 2 target by 2015. The frontloading of spending creates macroeconomic trade-offs, which may explain why the cost estimate may be higher than those obtain by partial-equilibrium analyses or sector studies. Towards the end of the simulation period additional education spending may taper off. The study by ECLAC and UNESCO (2005), for example, estimates that to make primary education universal in Costa Rica, public spending on primary education would gradually drop from 2.05 per cent of GDP in 2000 to 1.9 per cent in 2005, 1.8 per cent in 2010, and 1.7 per cent in 2015, under the

Table 7.4   Costa Rica: public spending on MDG-related services in the baseline and MDG scenarios, 2002-2015 (Percentage of GDP)

	2002 Base year	BS	TF	EB	DB	TF	EB	DB
			Additional public spending with respect to the baseline scenario (2002-2015)					
			Scenario for MDG 2			*Scenario for MDGs 4 and 5*		
Primary education	2.6	2.0	0.4	0.4	0.4	0.0	0.0	0.0
Current	2.5	2.0	0.3	0.3	0.3	0.0	0.0	0.0
Investment	0.1	0.0	0.1	0.1	0.1	0.0	0.0	0.0
Health	5.4	4.1	0.0	0.0	0.0	0.8	0.8	0.9
Current	4.9	3.9	0.0	0.0	0.0	0.6	0.6	0.7
Investment	0.5	0.2	0.0	0.0	0.0	0.2	0.2	0.2
Water and sanitation	1.6	1.1	0.0	0.0	0.0	0.0	0.0	0.0
Current	1.4	1.1	0.0	0.0	0.0	0.0	0.0	0.0
Investment	0.3	0.0	0.0	0.0	0.0	0.0	0.0	0.0
Total	9.6	7.3	0.4	0.4	0.5	0.8	0.8	0.9
			Scenario for MDG 7			*Scenario for MDGs 2, 4-5 and 7*		
Primary education	2.6	2.0	0.0	0.0	0.0	0.3	0.3	0.3
Current	2.5	2.0	0.0	0.0	0.0	0.2	0.2	0.2
Investment	0.1	0.0	0.0	0.0	0.0	0.1	0.1	0.1
Health	5.4	4.1	0.0	0.0	0.0	0.9	0.8	0.9
Current	4.9	3.9	0.0	0.0	0.0	0.7	0.6	0.7
Investment	0.5	0.2	0.0	0.0	0.0	0.2	0.2	0.2
Water and sanitation	1.6	1.1	0.1	0.1	0.1	0.1	0.1	0.1
Current	1.4	1.1	0.0	0.0	0.0	0.1	0.0	0.1
Investment	0.3	0.0	0.1	0.1	0.1	0.1	0.1	0.1
Total	9.6	7.3	0.1	0.1	0.1	1.4	1.1	1.4

Source: MAMS for Costa Rica.

Abbreviations: BS: Baseline scenario; TF: tax financing; EB: External borrowing; DB: Domestic borrowing;

assumption of an average annual GDP growth rate of 2.6 per cent, the same as that observed during 1990-2002. According to MAMS for Costa Rica in a scenario of an annual rate of 5 per cent economic growth, in contrast, total public spending on primary education needed to achieve MDG 2 would need to be slightly over 3 per cent of GDP in 2005, 2.5 per cent in 2010 and 1 per cent in 2015.

The spending needed to achieve the MDG 2 target should be financed, preferably, through higher income taxes. The additional tax burden would be no more than 0.6 percentage points of GDP per year with respect to the baseline scenario and it tends to decrease when nearing 2015 (see Sanchez, 2008, Table A9.3). In this financing scenario, government savings increase slightly and the public debt burden remains unchanged. In contrast, in the other two financing scenarios, either the external or internal debt ratio rises to, respectively, 24.5 per cent or 48.6 per cent of GDP in 2015, up from 19.5 per cent or 28.7 per cent of GDP in 2002. Domestic borrowing also "crowds out" private investment, which would be negligible in the case of the tax-financing scenario. Borrowing from the private sector in order to finance the additional public spending on primary education, generates a larger budget deficit and real GDP grows 0.2 percentage points less than in the baseline. Raising income taxes causes a decline in disposable private income, affecting final consumption and savings, but these adjustments do not affect overall growth because of the rise in public spending.

Achieving the goal for primary education has little to no impact on the other goals during the simulation period. In fact, the general equilibrium effects would cause a slight increase in extreme poverty compared with the baseline scenario, as inequality rises somewhat around 2010 as a consequence of a small decline in employment of semi-skilled and skilled workers in the export sectors (see Sánchez, 2008, Tables A9.3 and A9.4).

Owing to a slight appreciation of the real exchange rate with respect to the baseline, the profitability of some export sectors falls, affecting employment for some workers. This effect is also present, and stronger, in the other scenarios analysed below. In those cases, required public spending in social services is higher leading to a stronger increase in the supply of these services. As the government needs new inputs and workers (doctors, teachers and others) the supply of which is limited, the prices for inputs and wages of workers tend to increase, pushing up government production costs. As a result, the price of MDG-related services, which are considered "non-tradables", increases with respect to that of "tradable goods", which is reflected in the appreciation of the real exchange rate. This effect becomes much more pronounced if the government decides to finance the MDG strategy through external borrowing.

The additional public spending required to achieve the two targets for reducing child and maternal mortality is practically double that needed for achieving the primary education goal (see Table 7.3). The main part of that new spending would be needed to cover the increased wage bill in the public health sector. More than 70 per cent of the new public spending in health would be allocated to primary care and to medical consultations, which is consistent with findings from health sector studies that point at the need to correct the deficiencies in preventative care in order to reduce infant and maternal mortality rates.

The composition of GDP spending in this scenario changes in the same way as in the MDG 2 scenario, but the adjustments are stronger (see Sánchez, 2008, Table A9.3). With domestic borrowing—leading to a stronger "crowding out" effect on private investment—GDP growth would drop by 0.2 percentage from the baseline to 4.8 per cent per year—whereas external borrowing would not affect growth.

According to the model, reaching the targets for reducing child and maternal mortality seems affordable (see Sánchez, 2008, Table A9.3). Tax financing, again, would appear to be the most convenient option since government savings grow 0.2 percentage points of GDP with respect to the baseline scenario. Annual income tax revenues would increase by around 1.6 percentage point of GDP per year, growing from 2.8 per cent of GDP in 2002 to 4.4 per cent of GDP in 2015. Increased public borrowing would be less desirable because of its repercussions on the public debt burden. Financing achievement of MDGs 4 and 5 through domestic borrowing would lead to a reduction in government savings by 1.6 percentage points of GDP on average during the simulation period compared with the baseline. The domestic public debt ratio would increase to 51.2 per cent of GDP in 2015, up from 28.7 per cent in 2002. Debt sustainability is less endangered in the external borrowing scenario. In this case, government savings as a share of GDP fall on average by 0.7 percentage points with respect to the baseline during 2002-15, while the external debt ratio would increase 7.8 percentage points of GDP on average to reach 27.3 per cent of GDP in 2015, up from 19.5 per cent in 2002.

Reaching the health goals generates positive synergy effects easing the achievement of the goal for primary education. In addition, more skilled workers are hired, with small positive effects on productivity and average real wages. As a result, poverty decreases, but the impact is only very small. The scenario with domestic borrowing does not yield this outcome, however, as employment levels for unskilled and semi-skilled workers in industrial sectors fall due to the "crowding-out" effect on private investment. This leads to a slight decrease in the average real wage per worker, causing poverty to increase, also when measured using the national poverty lines. In general, no matter the chosen financing option, inequality in the distribution of per capita income rises as a result of these labour-market shifts, which—next to the adverse effect of the currency appreciation on employment in export sectors—prevents any significant reduction in poverty from taking place.

The results of scenarios that simulate the joint achievement of the primary education and health goals by and large magnify the outcomes described above. The cost of achieving the primary education goal are somewhat less, however, as achieving the under-five mortality goal generates positive synergy effects, as mentioned. Current government spending on education needs to be on average 0.1 percentage points of GDP less as compared with the scenario that only targets MDG 2 (see Table 7.4). The total additional public spending required for achieving both the goals for education and health would be, respectively, 1.4 per cent, 1.1 per cent, and 1.4 per cent of GDP per year on average during 2002-15, depending on whether it is financed through higher income taxes, external borrowing, or domestic borrowing.

The mobilization of domestic resources tends to make the strategy more costly in terms of the required extra public spending. As a result of the decline in investment and private consumption in sectors linked to the MDGs, the government must spend relatively more on MDG-oriented interventions in order to meet the given targets. In the scenario with domestic borrowing, the economy grows 0.5 percentage points less than in the base scenario. In the scenario with higher direct taxes, on the other hand, the injection of public spending makes it possible to maintain an annual growth rate similar to that of the baseline scenario. Achieving the goals by using the external borrowing option allows the economy to grow at an average of 5.1 per cent per year—only 0.1 percentage points more than in the baseline.

Even though the additional public spending required in order to achieve the three MDGs simultaneously is relatively less when financed with external resources, it would be more feasible from a macroeconomic point of view to use income taxes in the case of Costa Rica, for the same reasons outlined above. When spending is financed by raising income taxes, tax revenue needs to increase by 1.6 percentage points of GDP more than in the baseline scenario, which on balance improves public finances (see Table A7.2). When recurring to more public indebtedness, government savings would fall markedly with respect to the baseline scenario. External borrowing would raise the external debt ratio on average by 7.8 percentage points of GDP compared with the baseline scenario and would reach 33 per cent of GDP in 2015. This level of borrowing could be manageable for a country like Costa Rica where, in 1993, for example, external debt was 32.8 per cent of GDP, having declined gradually from 71.1 per cent of GDP in 1984. According to the model-based analysis, the option of domestic borrowing would seem least advisable as the level of domestic public debt would increase by 13.6 percentage points of GDP on average with respect to the baseline and reach 66.9 per cent of GDP in 2015. This level of indebtedness is well above historical levels, as over the past quarter century the domestic debt burden never was higher than 40 per cent of GDP.

The degree of real exchange-rate appreciation is more pronounced in the scenario when all three MDGs are targeted simultaneously as the required increase in public spending is larger (see Table A7.2). The resource allocation to non-traded goods production drives economic growth in the MDG scenarios. In this case, around 2010 the drop in employment (primarily of skilled workers) and real wages (primarily of semi-skilled and skilled workers) in export sectors is such that aggregate labour-market outcomes deteriorate with respect to those of the baseline scenario. As a consequence, there is a slight increase in moderate and extreme poverty compared with the baseline in 2010 (see Table A7.3). This also happens in 2015 when the additional public spending is financed through internal borrowing because of the "crowding-out" effect on private investment, which has a marked adverse effect on exports and real wages paid in export sectors. While national poverty targets continue to be met no matter the source of financing, the share of the population that lives on less than one dollar a day does not fall sufficiently to meet the established target of 1.7 per cent by 2015, primarily because the MDG strategy does not induce the required income redistribution and employment is affected by the reduction in competitiveness of export sectors. In the case of the domestic borrowing scenario, private investment, and with it economic growth, is affected in addition to the just mentioned adverse effects.

Conclusions and policy recommendations

Since 1990, robust economic performance and effective social policies have supported notable progress in most social areas critical to the achievement of the MDGs in Costa Rica. The targets for improving coverage of water and sanitation were reached ahead of schedule, and the target for reducing extreme poverty was achieved temporarily in 1998. Paradoxically, because of the amount of progress already made, the country faces a major challenge of further reducing child and maternal mortality rates that are already at low levels.

According to the model-based analysis, continuing the economic trajectory that Costa Rica has followed since 2002—with growth of around 5 per cent per year and public social spending increasing by 1.1 per cent per year in real terms—would generate a reduction in poverty and significant progress towards the targets for improving primary education completion rates and reducing child and maternal mortality. Poverty reduction would be insufficient to meet the MDG target for halving extreme poverty, though nationally defined poverty targets would be reached by 2015. The scenarios in which the targets for education and health are met, suggest that the cost of doing so would be quite modest in terms of additional public spending. Specifically, the cost would be 1.4 per cent, 1.1 per cent, or 1.4 per cent of GDP per year, respectively, depending on whether the extra public spending is financed through increased income taxes, external borrowing, or domestic borrowing. Most of the additional expenditures would be needed for the health sector. The spending requirements could be less if efficiency in the delivery of services can be improved.

In the case of education, spending should be targeted at addressing the known problems of high drop-out and repetition rates, as well as towards expanding coverage of school infrastructure in rural areas. Sufficient allocation of resources could be ensured without delay if public spending in education were to increase to at least 6 per cent of GDP as stipulated by law. The targets for reducing child and maternal mortality in turn could be achieved by enhancing preventative health care inter alia by increasing the coverage of vaccination programmes and providing adequate care for pregnant women in order to prevent complications before and during childbirth, among other measures. The largest share of additional public spending in health should be aimed at training for maternity and obstetric personnel. To the extent progress is made towards reducing mortality rates, positive synergy effects are triggered that support advancement towards the primary education goal.

According to the simulated scenarios, financing the required public spending through direct taxes or external borrowing will be viable. Raising income taxes for this purpose would be recommended as the more desirable option because of the country's urgent need to put its public finances on sound footing, even though it implies that the direct tax burden would practically need to be doubled as a percentage of GDP with some "frontloading" required before 2010. In the alternative of financing through public borrowing, the simulations suggest that the fiscal deficit would increase beyond the impact induced by the immediate additional public spending requirements in education and health. External borrowing remains a possible option, though, as it does not lead to an explosive rise in public indebtedness as was found for the domestic borrowing scenario. The latter scenario would generate an additional trade-off by substantially crowding out funds available for private investment.

Possibly, the most convenient option would be to combine financing sources in such a way that the scaling up of public spending for the MDGs would sustain an economic growth rate of around 5 per cent per year on average. It will be important that the fiscal reform needed to mobilize the additional public resources be implemented in such a way that it will also help to contribute to a more equal income distribution. At the same time, continued efforts should be made to enhance the efficiency of the existing tax collection system and allocating public spending more effectively on the basis of social development priorities. Resolving these fiscal problems should help reduce dependence on borrowing and enhance government's creditworthiness internationally.

Finally, the model simulations indicate that real wages could increase and inequality could fall with the progress made towards the education and health goals. This would translate into a reduction in poverty, but insufficiently to also achieve the MDG for reducing extreme poverty. The achievement of this goal will depend, not only on how strong and stable economic growth is, but also on how well it is distributed. Further, poverty reduction would also help accelerate progress towards the other development goals.

Appendix A7

Table A7.1   Costa Rica: Elasticities of determinants of progress towards the MDGs as specified in MAMS

a) MDG Goals	Determinants					
	PSW	**OPI**	**IMT10**	**IMT11**	**PHC**	**PHS**
MDG 4 (Target 5)		-0.96[a]	-0.09[a]	-0.09[a]	-0.49[a]	-0.94[b]
MDG 5 (Target 6)		-0.96[a]	-0.09[a]	-0.09[a]	-0.49[a]	-0.94[b]
MDG 7 (Target 10)	0.65[d]	0.21[b]			0.46[b]	
MDG 7 (Target 11)	0.65[d]	0.24[b]			0.11[b]	

b) Educational Behaviour/ by cycle	**IM5**	**OPI**	**WPS**	**WPT**	**PHC**	**QE**
Percentage of students at the age for entering primary school who enrol in the cycle	0.05[c]	-0.06[c]	0.12[c]	0.06[c]		0.08[c]
Percentage of students who passed their grade in primary school.	0.05[c]	-0.02[c]	0.09[c]	0.04[c]		0.08[c]
Percentage of students who passed their grade in secondary school	0.05[c]	-0.02[c]	0.21[c]	0.04[c]		0.10[c]
Percentage of students who passed their grade in tertiary education.	0.05[c]	-0.01[c]	0.47[c]		0.08[c]	0.10[c]
Percentage of primary school graduates who go on to secondary education.	0.05[c]	-0.01[c]	0.21[c]	0.04[c]		0.09[c]
Percentage of secondary school graduates who go on to tertiary education.	0.05[c]	0.00[c]	0.47[c]		0.09[c]	0.10[c]

Source: Author's estimates and imputations.

Abbreviations: PSW: Public spending on water and sanitation; OPI: "Other public infrastructure"; IMT10: Indicator for MDG 7 (Target 10); IMT11: Indicator for MDG 7 (Target 11); PHC: Per capita household consumption; PHS: Per capita health spending; IM5: Indicator for MDG 5; WPS: Wage premium: Secondary vs no education; WPT: Wage premium: Tertiary vs Secondary; QE: Quality of education.

[a] Parametric estimates.

[b] Non-parametric estimates.

[c] Value near the lower limit of the feasibility range of MAMS for the elasticity in question.

[d] Value imputed by author on the basis that it falls within the feasibility range of MAMS as determined through sensitivity analysis of the baseline scenario.

Table A7.2   Costa Rica: Key macroeconomic results in selected scenarios simulated with MAMS, 2002-2015

		Scenario for primary education and mortality goals with:						
	Baseline scenario		direct taxes		domestic borrowing		external borrowing	
	Base year	**2002-**		**2002-**		**2002-**		**2002-**
	2002	**2015**	**2015**	**2015**	**2015**	**2015**	**2015**	**2015**	**2015**
Macroeconomic indicators								
Exchange rate (2002 index = 100)	100.0	96.5	98.2	96.4	98.1	96.0	97.9	96.4	97.8
Growth rate of real GDP (%)		5.6	5.0	5.5	5.0	4.8	4.5	5.6	5.1
Private final consumption spending (% GDP)	67.7	78.9	73.7	78.7	72.7	82.7	75.2	78.9	73.7
Govt. final consumption spending (% GDP)	14.9	9.8	12.4	10.2	13.4	10.8	13.6	10.0	13.2
Gross formation of fixed private capital (% GDP)	19.5	20.9	20.1	20.8	19.8	16.9	17.3	20.9	20.1
Gross formation of fixed public capital (% GDP)	3.1	3.3	3.3	3.4	3.7	3.4	3.6	3.4	3.7
Exports of goods and services (% GDP)	42.3	38.8	40.2	38.7	39.8	37.4	39.2	38.7	39.2
Imports of goods and services (% GDP)	47.5	51.7	49.7	51.8	49.4	51.2	49.0	51.9	50.0
Foreign savings (% GDP)	5.3	10.9	8.4	10.9	8.4	11.5	8.6	11.8	10.0
Government savings (% GDP)	-4.0	0.6	0.3	0.8	0.7	-4.3	-2.6	-0.1	-0.9
Income taxes (% GDP)	2.8	3.1	5.0	3.7	6.6	3.2	5.1	3.1	5.0
Domestic government borrowing (% GDP)	6.9	1.7	2.1	1.7	2.1	6.7	5.3	1.7	2.1
External government borrowing (% GDP)	0.4	0.9	0.9	0.9	0.9	1.0	0.9	1.8	2.5
Domestic government debt (% GDP)	28.7	33.7	34.1	33.9	34.1	66.9	47.7	33.5	33.9
External government debt (% GDP)	19.5	18.1	18.9	18.2	18.9	19.1	19.3	33.0	26.7
Labour market								
Employment[a]	1,586,491	1.9	1.8	1.9	1.7	1.9	1.8	1.9	1.8
Unskilled workers	1,025,519	0.5	0.6	0.5	0.6	0.5	0.6	0.5	0.6
Semi-skilled workers	420,096	3.5	3.3	3.5	3.3	3.5	3.3	3.5	3.3
Skilled workers	140,877	5.1	4.8	4.7	4.8	4.4	4.6	4.8	4.8

Table A7.2   (cont'd)

| | Base year 2002 | Baseline scenario | | Scenario for primary education and mortality goals with: | | | | | |
| | | | | direct taxes | | domestic borrowing | | external borrowing | |
		2015	2002-2015	2015	2002-2015	2015	2002-2015	2015	2002-2015
Real wage per worker[b]	115,254	3.4	2.8	3.1	2.8	2.4	2.3	3.2	2.8
Unskilled workers	78,782	5.4	4.6	5.5	4.6	4.5	4.1	5.5	4.7
Semi-skilled workers	145,530	1.7	1.2	1.2	1.1	0.5	0.6	1.3	1.1
Skilled workers	290,465	-0.7	-1.2	-1.1	-1.2	-1.3	-1.4	-1.1	-1.3

Source: MAMS for Costa Rica.

[a] Number employed in base year and growth rate in scenarios.

[b] *Colones* in base year and rate of growth in scenarios.

Table A7.3   Costa Rica: Poverty and inequality results of microsimulations for selected scenarios simulated with MAMS, 2002-2015[a]

	Moderate poverty (% of population)				Extreme poverty (% of population)			
	2002	2005	2010	2015	2002	2005	2010	2015
Baseline scenario								
U	20.6	19.7	19.7	19.6	5.7	5.3	5.4	5.6
U+S	20.6	19.9	19.4	20.0	5.7	5.5	5.2	5.6
U+S+W1	20.6	19.9	18.6	18.7	5.7	5.5	5.0	5.3
U+S+W1+W2	20.6	19.9	14.6	12.2	5.7	5.5	4.0	3.7
U+S+W1+W2+ M	20.6	19.9	14.6	12.8	5.7	5.5	4.2	4.3
Scenario for MDGs 2, 4 and 5 with tax financing								
U	20.6	20.5	20.5	19.6	5.7	5.6	5.6	5.6
U+S	20.6	20.3	20.6	20.0	5.7	5.6	5.8	5.6
U+S+W1	20.6	20.3	20.1	18.7	5.7	5.6	5.6	5.3
U+S+W1+W2	20.6	20.3	16.2	12.2	5.7	5.6	4.5	3.7
U+S+W1+W2+ M	20.6	20.4	16.0	12.8	5.7	5.7	4.6	4.3
Scenario for MDGs 2, 4 and 5 with domestic borrowing								
U	20.6	19.6	19.7	20.0	5.7	5.3	5.2	5.6
U+S	20.6	19.7	19.8	20.2	5.7	5.3	5.3	5.8
U+S+W1	20.6	19.7	20.0	19.4	5.7	5.3	5.4	5.6
U+S+W1+W2	20.6	19.7	15.8	13.8	5.7	5.3	4.3	4.2
U+S+W1+W2+ M	20.6	19.7	16.0	14.1	5.7	5.3	4.7	4.7
Scenario for MDGs 2, 4 and 5 with external borrowing								
U	20.6	19.4	19.6	19.6	5.7	5.3	5.4	5.3
U+S	20.6	19.5	19.8	19.9	5.7	5.4	5.5	5.5
U+S+W1	20.6	19.3	19.3	18.6	5.7	5.4	5.4	5.3
U+S+W1+W2	20.6	19.3	15.4	12.1	5.7	5.4	4.3	3.7
U+S+W1+W2+ M	20.6	19.5	15.4	12.5	5.7	5.5	4.7	4.1

Table A7.3   (cont'd)

	Population living on less than 1 dollar a day (%)				Gini coefficient of per capita household income			
	2002	2005	2010	2015	2002	2005	2010	2015
	Baseline scenario							
U	2.8	2.5	2.7	2.8	0.43	0.43	0.42	0.42
U+S	2.8	2.5	2.7	2.8	0.43	0.43	0.42	0.42
U+S+W1	2.8	2.5	2.5	2.8	0.43	0.43	0.41	0.41
U+S+W1+W2	2.8	2.5	2.1	2.0	0.43	0.43	0.41	0.41
U+S+W1+W2+ M	2.8	2.6	2.5	2.5	0.43	0.43	0.41	0.41
	Scenario for MDGs 2, 4 and 5 with tax financing							
U	2.8	2.7	2.7	2.8	0.43	0.43	0.43	0.42
U+S	2.8	2.8	2.9	2.8	0.43	0.43	0.43	0.42
U+S+W1	2.8	2.8	2.9	2.8	0.43	0.43	0.42	0.41
U+S+W1+W2	2.8	2.8	2.4	2.0	0.43	0.43	0.42	0.41
U+S+W1+W2+ M	2.8	2.8	2.6	2.5	0.43	0.43	0.43	0.41
	Scenario for MDGs 2, 4 and 5 with domestic borrowing							
U	2.8	2.5	2.6	2.9	0.43	0.43	0.42	0.42
U+S	2.8	2.5	2.6	3.1	0.43	0.43	0.42	0.42
U+S+W1	2.8	2.5	2.6	3.0	0.43	0.43	0.42	0.41
U+S+W1+W2	2.8	2.5	2.1	2.3	0.43	0.43	0.42	0.41
U+S+W1+W2+ M	2.8	2.6	2.6	2.9	0.43	0.43	0.42	0.42
	Scenario for MDGs 2, 4 and 5 with external borrowing							
U	2.8	2.4	2.7	2.6	0.43	0.42	0.42	0.42
U+S	2.8	2.5	2.9	2.8	0.43	0.42	0.42	0.42
U+S+W1	2.8	2.5	2.9	2.8	0.43	0.42	0.41	0.40
U+S+W1+W2	2.8	2.5	2.4	1.9	0.43	0.42	0.41	0.40
U+S+W1+W2+ M	2.8	2.6	2.8	2.5	0.43	0.42	0.42	0.41

Source: MAMS for Costa Rica and microsimulations based on the 2002 EHPM of INEC.

[a] Sequential and cumulative effects are presented for changes in: U, unemployment rate by skill level; S, employment structure by sector of activity; W1, structure of labour income per sector of activity; W2, average labour income; and, M, employment structure by skill level. For more detail on methodology, see Chapter 2 (Appendix A2.1).

Acknowledgements

The author is grateful to Matthew Hammill from the Subregional office of ECLAC in Mexico for processing household survey information and for conducting econometric estimations and also to Lourdes Colinas from the same office for her review of literature. Conversations with Martín Cicowiez, Hans Lofgren and Carolina Díaz-Bonilla were essential for the proper application of the model framework used for this study. Thanks are also due to the other coordinators of the project for their invaluable contributions, especially to Enrique Ganuza and Rob Vos, and further to the Social Council of the Government of Costa Rica and the agencies of the United Nations system represented in the country, who served as the national counterpart for conducting this study. Finally, special thanks are owed to José Manuel Hermida and Adriana Murillo.

Notes

1   For more detail on the main trade reforms of the last few years, see Sánchez and Sauma (2006) and Sánchez (2004, 2005, 2007b).
2   Furthermore, as Sánchez (2004) shows, eliminating subsidies for non-traditional exports in 1990 provided a disincentive to foreign sales, especially of agricultural products.
3   Part of the fiscal problem is the cost of implementing the trade reforms. Electoral cycles have also put pressure on spending. In addition, there have been repercussions from the growth of public pensions charged to the government budget as a result of generous adjustments to pension regimes made previously.
4   Since 2002, public debt declined to 45 per cent of GDP in 2007, down from an average of 47.9 per cent of GDP in the 2000-05 period, as shown in Table 7.1. The reduction is explained by economic growth during this period, which allowed tax revenues to increase, as well as by lower interest rates, which reduced the cost of government debts and by higher government savings generated as a result of higher revenues and a control on spending. In fact, the government registered a primary surplus, which was 2.17 per cent, 2.74 per cent and 3.73 per cent of GDP in 2005, 2006 and 2007, respectively. These trends would suggest the government has now more fiscal space to increase social investment. Over the medium term, however, the economy would need to grow steadily at the same pace as that of 2004-07, in order to sustain higher levels of social spending without jeopardizing fiscal sustainability.
5   According to data from the BCCR, GDP grew by 8.8 per cent and 6.9 per cent in 2006 and 2007, respectively.
6   The development of social policy has been characterized by three stages that began early in the last century and are described in detail in Sauma and Garnier (1998).
7   In 1997, production was estimated based on the productive structure of 1966, the base year of the prevailing national accounts system. In 1998, the BCCR changed the base year for calculating GDP and began using the 1991 productive structure as a base instead. The new GDP in 1998, then, was 33 per cent higher than the previous GDP. Since public funds for education were not adjusted to reflect the adjustment of GDP, it has not been possible to allocate 6 per cent of GDP to education expenditures. To correct the problem, a decree was signed on 22 June 2000 establishing a mechanism that

would allow spending to move gradually from 6 per cent of the old GDP to 6 per cent of the current GDP.

8   The rest of this section is broadly based on the First National Report on the MDGs (Social Council of the Government of Costa Rica and the United Nations System in Costa Rica, 2005).

9   The extreme poverty incidence is the measure of the percentage of individuals with an income insufficient to cover the cost of a basic food basket that would allow them to satisfy minimum nutritional needs. By this definition, the measure may also be seen as an indirect measure of the share of the population experiencing conditions of hunger or malnourishment.

10 One explicit target of the "Education for All" Action Plan of the Ministry of Public Education is to lower the percentage of students who repeat a grade in primary school to 2 per cent by 2015 (MEP, 2004).

11 According to UNICEF data, only Cuba (8) and Chile (9) had lower under-five mortality rates than Costa Rica (10) among Latin American countries in 2003.

12 According to the National System for Evaluating Maternal Mortality, about 80 per cent of maternal deaths could have been prevented in the year 2000. This represents 19 lives that could have been saved according to technical criteria (Ministerio de Salud, 2001).

13 According to AyA and OPS (2002), the country could aspire to reaching 96 per cent coverage for potable water in 2020.

14 Progress in rural areas is explained in part by including latrines as a sanitary option.

15 INEC's 2002 Household and Multipurpose Survey (EHPM) was used for this purpose.

16 The reduction in the maternal mortality rate is inversely related to its determinants in the MAMS model. This causality could not have been reproduced empirically since, as explained, the maternal mortality rate has experienced some increases. Therefore the estimates are omitted in this case.

17 Data on public spending for water and sanitation and health were disaggregated by *cantón* (geographical division similar to district) using population weights by *cantón* in each of the 7 regions as defined for the national planning process. The estimated coefficients could be biased in the sense that they might measure the distribution of the population rather than the extension of the provision of the respective services in case this is weakly correlated with population by *cantón*.

18 This national target is proposed in the First National Report of the MDGs. For more detail, see, Consejo Social del Gobierno de la República de Costa Rica and Sistema de las Naciones Unidas en Costa Rica (2005).

References

AyA, and PAHO (2004). "Situación de la tecnología de tratamiento de las aguas residuales de tipo ordinario en Costa Rica," San José: Costa Rican Institute of Water and Sewage (AyA) and Pan-American Health Organization (PAHO).

CEPAL (2005). *Objetivos de Desarrollo del Milenio. Una mirada desde América Latina y el Caribe*, Economic Commission for Latin America and the Caribbean, Santiago de Chile: United Nations (June 2005).

CEPAL, and UNESCO (2005). "Invertir mejor para invertir más. Financiamiento y gestión de la educación en América Latina y el Caribe", Economic Commission for Latin America and the Caribbean and United Nations Educational, Scientific and Cultural Organization, *Serie Seminarios y Conferencias*, No. 43, CEPAL, Santiago de Chile.

Consejo Social del Gobierno de la República de Costa Rica y Sistema de las Naciones Unidas en Costa Rica (2005). *Objetivos de Desarrollo del Milenio: Informe sobre el avance del país en su cumplimiento*, San José.

MEP (2004). *Plan de Acción de la educación para todos 2003-2015*, San José: Ministry of Public Education (MEP).

Ministerio de Salud (2001). "Memoria Anual 2000", San José: Ministry of Health of Costa Rica.

Papke, L. E., and J. M. Wooldridge (1996). "Econometric methods for fractional response variables with an application to 401(k) plan participation rates," *Journal of Applied Econometrics* 11(6): 619-32.

Sánchez, Marco V. (2004). *Rising inequality and falling poverty in Costa Rica's agriculture during trade reform. A macro-micro general equilibrium analysis,* Maastricht: Shaker.

__________ (2005). "Reformas económicas, régimen cambiario y choques externos: efectos en el desarrollo económico, la desigualdad y la pobreza en Costa Rica, El Salvador y Honduras," *Serie de Estudios y Perspectivas*, No. 36, Subregional Office of ECLAC in Mexico City, Mexico.

__________ (2006a). "Gasto público para el logro de las metas del milenio en Costa Rica: viabilidad de financiarlo y sus efectos en la asignación de los recursos, la pobreza y la desigualdad", Final report for the project *Public Policies for MDGs in Latin America and the Caribbean*, UNDP/UN-DESA/World Bank, November (mimeograph).

__________ (2006b). "Matriz de contabilidad social (MCS) 2002 de Costa Rica, y los fundamentos metodológicos de su construcción," *Serie de Estudios y Perspectivas*, No. 47, Subregional office of ECLAC in Mexico City, Mexico.

__________ (2007a). "Crecimiento exportador en Centro América: alcances y limitaciones para el bienestar social", in Ana Sojo and Andras Uthoff (editors), *Desempeño Económico y Política Social en América Latina y el Caribe: Los Retos de la Equidad, el Desarrollo y la Ciudadanía*, Mexico City: ECLAC, FLACSO, GTZ and INDESOL, pp. 257-307.

__________ (2007b). "Liberalización comercial en el marco del DR-CAFTA: efectos en el crecimiento, la pobreza y la desigualdad en Costa Rica," *Serie de Estudios y Perspectivas*, No. 80, Subregional office of ECLAC in Mexico City, Mexico.

__________ (2008). "Capítulo 9: Costa Rica," in Rob Vos, Enrique Ganuza, Hans Lofgren, Marco V. Sánchez, and Carolina Díaz-Bonilla (eds), *Políticas Públicas para el Desarrollo Humano ¿Cómo lograr los Objetivos de Desarrollo del Milenio en América Latina y el Caribe?* Santiago de Chile: Uqbar Editores y Programa de las Naciones Unidas para el Desarrollo (PNUD), pp. 313-47.

__________, and Pablo Sauma (2006). "Costa Rica - export-orientation and its effect on growth, inequality and poverty," in Rob Vos, Enrique Ganuza, Samuel Morley and Sherman Robinson (eds.), *Who Gains from Free Trade? Export-led growth, inequality and poverty in Latin America*, London, New York: Routledge, pp. 204-30.

Sauma, Pablo and Leonardo Garnier (1998). "Política Social, Política Económica, y Pobreza en Costa Rica", in Enrique Ganuza, Lance Taylor and Samual Morley (eds.), *Políticas macroeconómicas y pobreza en América Latina y el Caribe*, pp. 311-353, Madrid: Mundi-Prensa Libros S.A.

8
Ecuador

Mauricio León, José Rosero and Rob Vos

Introduction

The social and economic development of Ecuador has been uneven in recent decades. Progress has been made on some dimensions of human development, but stagnation or deterioration has occurred in other areas. This chapter seeks to assess the feasibility of achieving the United Nations' Millennium Development Goals (MDGs) by 2015, using a dynamic general equilibrium framework. The general equilibrium focus is especially relevant considering that the achievement of these goals has dynamic effects on the economy as a whole. It creates changes in the skill composition of the labour force, for example, and produces endogenous growth effects, which may make it easier to achieve these goals. At the same time, however, the upfront public spending efforts needed to meet the goals could generate macroeconomic trade offs and hence obstacles to sustained growth and poverty reduction. The objective of the analysis is to generate results regarding the level of public spending that would be required to achieve the goals, to assess the viability of alternative forms of financing the required increase in public spending, and to identify possible tradeoffs.

This chapter has five additional sections. The next section briefly reviews the social and economic context of Ecuador since the 1980s. It examines the main social and economic policy reforms undertaken along with recent trends in the indicators that evaluate progress towards the achievement of the MDGs. It will also summarize the results of partial equilibrium analyses of the determinants of MDG-related outcomes in education, health, and access to drinking water and sanitation. The subsequent section presents the results of the dynamic computable generable equilibrium analysis based on MAMS, as well as the main characteristics and assumptions made for applying the model to the Ecuadorian economy. The fourth section presents the results of the microsimulations that were conducted to estimate the impact of the policy simulations on extreme poverty. The last section summarizes the main conclusions and provides some policy recommendations.

Ecuador's challenge for achieving the MDGs: a problem of resource abundance?

Stabilization, growth, inequality and poverty

It may be argued that Ecuador has lost nearly two and a half decades in terms of its economic development. During about one-third of the years between 1980 and 2005, the country experienced economic crises characterized by declines in GDP per capita (see Figure 8.1), lowering the standard of living for its population. Since the debt crisis in the early 1980s, poor macroeconomic management, a series of exogenous shocks, and political instability have all contributed to the high degree of economic volatility.

During the 2000s, rapid economic recovery has been driven by the construction of a new oil pipeline for the transport of heavy crude and by the significant increase in the price of oil. Economic growth until the global crisis of 2008 was also supported by increasing remittances from Ecuadorian migrants living abroad. Remittances accounted for nearly 5 per cent of GDP by the middle of the first decade of the 21st century. The strong expansion of the oil sector has not been accompanied by a similar economic dynamism in the rest of the economy, however, which has increased the economy's dependence on oil (see Table 8.1).

Though Ecuador has not experienced periods of hyperinflation, the annual average inflation rate for the period analysed has been over 20 per cent. The economy experienced a financial and banking crisis in 1999, and in the midst of a very unstable political and economic situation, in January 2000, the decision was made to adopt the US dollar as the official currency in an attempt to stabilize the

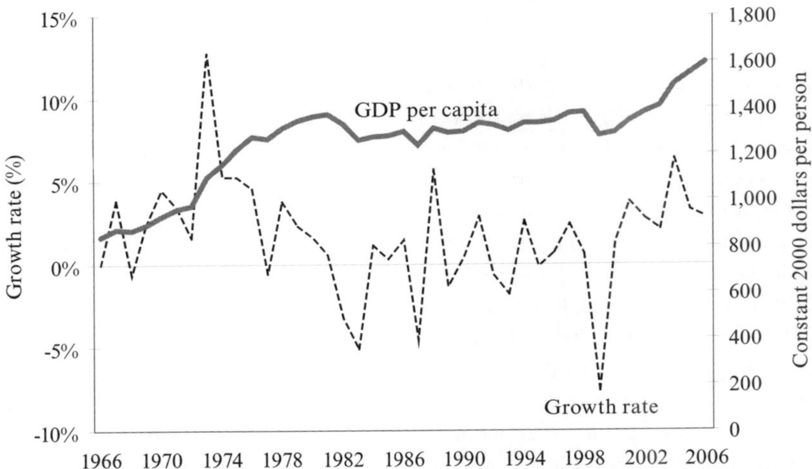

Figure 8.1 Ecuador: GDP per capita (constant 2000 dollars) and growth rate, 1966-2006
Source: Central Bank of Ecuador (BCE), Monthly statistical information.

Table 8.1   Ecuador: Economic growth by sector, 1994-2004 (Percentage)

	1994-1998	1998	1999	2000-2004	2005-2006
Total GDP	2.6	2.1	-6.3	4.8	4.5
Agriculture and Livestock	3.6	-5.0	13.0	4.2	3.2
Fishing	8.4	6.1	-6.7	-1.9	9.7
Mining and quarrying	-0.2	-1.6	1.4	7.2	2.0
Manufacturing	4.7	5.5	-5.2	1.6	6.3
Oil refinery	7.9	0.9	26.8	7.5	4.3
Electricity, gas, and water	1.3	8.5	23.0	1.7	0.0
Construction	1.0	-0.2	-24.9	11.9	5.0
Wholesale and retail trade	2.6	0.7	-11.2	3.4	4.9
Transportation and storage	3.8	4.2	0.0	2.2	3.9
Financial intermediation services	1.5	-16.9	-47.3	0.9	12.0
Other services	5.8	7.2	-3.2	4.4	5.2
Imputed banking services	1.0	-15.3	-33.0	1.6	7.6
Public administration and defence	-0.1	6.0	-5.6	3.7	2.6
Domestic services to households	3.1	3.0	3.4	3.1	-1.5
Other components of GDP	3.2	2.7	-4.5	7.9	7.2

Source: Central Bank of Ecuador, Monthly statistical information.

economy (Vos, 2000). The monetary "shock" initially generated a greater adjustment of prices, and inflation soared to 100 per cent in 2000. It took three years after the official dollarization of the economy to bring the rate of inflation down to one digit (see León and others, 2008). The slow convergence of the inflation rate with respect to international rates caused a significant appreciation in the real exchange rate; a trend which showed a mild reversal from 2003 (see Figure 8.2). Real wages recovered along with the appreciation of the exchange rate, as they did during the early 1990s when a macroeconomic stabilization programme was applied using the exchange rate as a nominal anchor, in the framework of a system with exchange rate bands. Also at that time, no major restrictions existed on the availability of foreign exchange, and the increase in real wages was a significant factor in the reduction of urban poverty, similar to the trends observed after 2000 (see Figure 8.2).

Growth in the oil sector, accompanied by the appreciation in the exchange rate, the recovery of real wages, and the very weak growth in labour productivity in non-oil tradable sectors are symptoms of the so-called "Dutch disease." This syndrome has negatively affected the economic development of Ecuador since the early 1970s when oil exploitation began (see Vos, 1989, among others). Though oil resources have helped to promote public spending on infrastructure and social development, they have not been enough to reduce inequality and to promote sufficient competitiveness and productivity in the productive sector, thus limiting a process of greater diversification of the economy. Instead, because of the dependence on oil, the volatility of

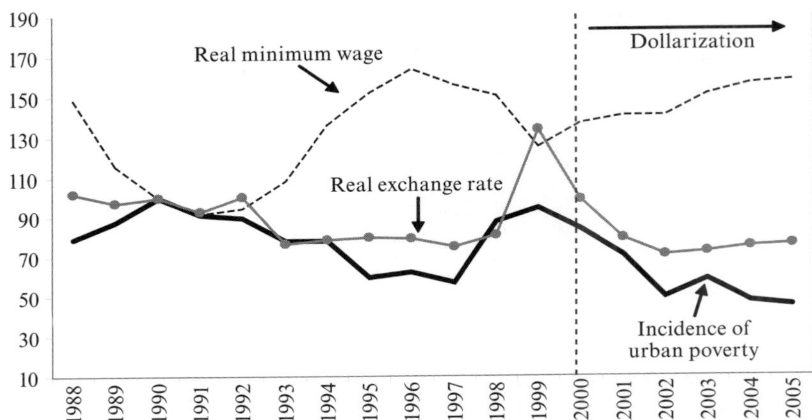

Figure 8.2 Ecuador: Incidence of urban poverty, minimum wage, and real exchange rate, 1988-2005 (Index 1990=100)

Source: INEC, Urban employment, underemployment, and unemployment surveys; Central Bank of Ecuador (BCE), Monthly statistical information.

international markets has been transferred to the national economy, while "pro-cyclical" macroeconomic policies have further intensified the cyclical ups and downs of the economy, increasing investment uncertainty. As seen in other cases, the inability to implement "counter-cyclical" macroeconomic policies has contributed to a lower pace of economic growth in the long term (Ocampo and Vos, 2008; United Nations, 2006).

Income inequality has increased over the last 15 years (see Figure 8.3). According to Vos and León (2003), the factors associated with the structural reforms introduced in the 1990s, such as trade liberalization and financial liberalization, have tended to widen the income gap between skilled and unskilled workers. In addition, information on income poverty collected from employment surveys suggest that absolute poverty in urban areas increased during the years of high inflation and decreased in periods when inflation was reduced, when the economy recovered after the strong contraction of 1999, and when real wages increased. As mentioned previously, wage increases coincided with episodes of exchange rate appreciation (see Figure 8.2). Since dollarization in the year 2000, currency appreciation has been caused by the inflationary trends of the first years of dollarization, the rising price of oil, and a substantial increase in remittances received from Ecuadorans living abroad. In this sense, poverty reduction has not been the result of a more dynamic non-oil economy and broad-based employment growth, but rather that of a temporary favourable external environment, especially rising oil prices.

Information from living standards surveys suggest that rural poverty also declined after dollarization. According to this information, the rural poverty

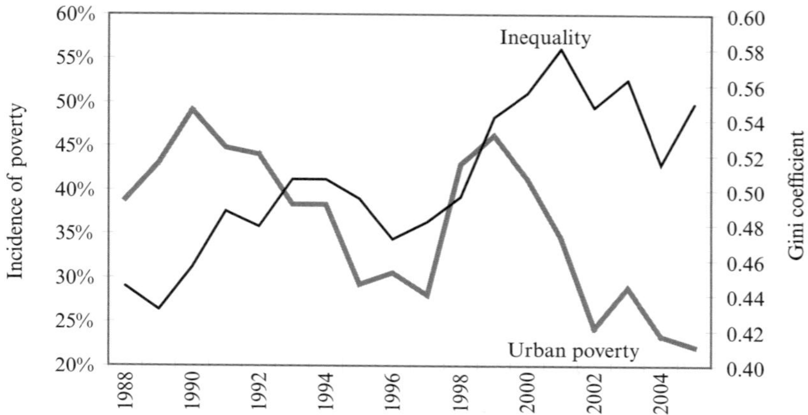

Figure 8.3 Ecuador: Incidence of poverty and inequality in urban areas, 1988-2005[a]
Source: INEC, Urban employment, underemployment, and unemployment surveys.
[a] The incidence of poverty is measured using per capita income data and a poverty line of 2 dollars a day per person. Inequality is measured by the Gini coefficient for income per capita.

rate measured by consumption fell from 75 per cent to 62 per cent between 1999 and 2006. The same source also confirms that there has been a decline in urban consumption poverty, though this is less pronounced than when measured in terms of income: specifically, from 36 per cent to 25 per cent in the same period. National consumption poverty fell from 52 per cent in 1999 to 38 per cent in 2006.[1]

Progress towards the Millennium Development Goals[2]

MDG 1: Eradicate extreme poverty and hunger

The chapter on poverty in the *First Report on the Millennium Development Goals (MDG) of the Republic of Ecuador* (SODEM, 2005) uses a methodology based on the elasticity of poverty with respect to economic growth, for a given distribution of income. This methodology, originally developed by UNDP-ECLAC-IPEA (2003), aims to estimate the efforts that must be made in economic growth and re-distribution in order to achieve the first target for MDG 1. This analysis considers the target of reducing the national level of extreme poverty from 15.5 per cent in 1999 to 7.7 per cent in 2015, using the poverty line of one dollar a day per person at purchasing power parity (PPP). The report, which looks at three different scenarios regarding assumptions of per capita annual GDP growth (1 per cent, 2 per cent, and 3 per cent), concludes that not even 3 per cent per year growth would be enough to reach the target and that, therefore, significant complementary redistributive efforts will be required. The Gini coefficient would have to be reduced from 0.539 in 1999 to 0.513, 0.522, and 0.533 in 2015, respectively, for each one of the three scenarios of economic growth in order to meet the target.

As indicated, economic volatility has an adverse impact on long-term growth in the sense that, as observed in other countries, there is increased uncertainty and risk for investment, which tends to affect both private and public investment in long term social and economic development projects (United Nations, 2006). Therefore, in order to achieve the target for reducing extreme poverty, the country would need to preserve economic stability, sustain rapid growth of per capita income at rates above 3 per cent per year, as well as achieve a redistribution of income towards the poor. These conditions pose quite a challenge since the country would have to look for ways to increase the pace of economic growth above long-term historic levels and be able to reverse the trend towards greater inequality of the last few decades.

In summary, with the existing trends and policies, the target of halving extreme poverty by 2015 would not be met. The greater economic stability achieved by macroeconomic policy since around 2002 has not been accompanied by a notable improvement in productivity. Also, trade liberalization has done little to dynamise the economy, while it did produce greater inequality. The country has improved is social protection system, and that helps attenuate, to a certain degree, the situation of extreme poverty, but efforts must be redoubled to increase productivity and find redistributive mechanisms that can effectively bring about more opportunities for the economic inclusion of poor groups.

MDG 2: Achieving universal primary education

According to information from the 1990 and 2001 population census, the net rate of enrolment in primary education was practically stagnant during 90 per cent of this period, which is worrisome. The average level of schooling of the population age 24 and older grew just slightly, from 6.7 years to 7.3 years; in other words, it grew by only 0.6 years in the entire last decade, when previously, the same progress had been made in 1.5 years. These indicators are aggravated by high drop-out and repetition rates, where the highest levels occur during first grade. On average, 14 per cent of the children enrolled drop out of first grade. In recent years there has been a significant improvement in access to education, however. In fact, according to the living standard surveys, the net primary school enrolment rate increased from 90.3 per cent to 94.3 per cent between 1999 and 2006. It should be noted, however, that only 67.4 per cent of the students finished primary education in 1990 and that the level of repetition and desertion remains high.

The econometric analysis of Vos and Ponce (2004) indicates that it is possible to achieve access to primary education for all girls and boys who live in the urban areas at a very reduced additional cost (between 0.1 per cent and 0.2 per cent of GDP per year), but only if resources are allocated to more "cost-effective" interventions. Possible interventions would include, increasing the number of trained teachers, increasing access to cash transfer programmes in the poor urban sectors (Human Development Bonus),[3] reducing the number of children per classroom, and promoting greater participation of schools and local authorities in decision-making related to education. In rural areas, adult literacy programmes and the universalization of the first year of basic education would also have a significant impact.

Unlike the Vos and Ponce (2004) study that focused on primary and secondary school *enrolment*, this study looks at the education target for primary school *completion*. To this effect, three different behaviours were modelled, which together determine the probability that a person might complete the educational cycle: that is, enter first grade, successfully complete the school year, and continue on to the next grade. The determinants of these three behaviours were analysed using logit probabilistic models, and the conclusion was that the primary school completion rate is a function of per capita household consumption, school infrastructure, and the quality of education (see León and others, 2008). While the dependent variable of these models differs from the one used in the Vos and Ponce study, the conclusions are similar. Increasing the number of trained teachers and having fewer students per classroom are considered measures that improve both quality of education and school completion. Finally, an increase in per capita household consumption can be induced through cash transfer programmes, like that of the Human Development Bonus (*Bono de Desarrollo Humano*), which have been shown to have a positive effect on school attendance among the poor in Ecuador (see Vos, León and Brborich, 2002; Schady and Araujo, 2005; Ponce, 2008). In addition to the kind of variables also considered in the Vos and Ponce study, the primary education completion model also includes as explanatory variables, the health status of children (approximated through the reduction in the child mortality rates) and the wage premium provided by education.

In addition to being consistent with the theories of human capital and modern empirical models of access to education (see, for example, Glewwe, 2002), the estimated functional relationship makes it possible to analyse the interaction between the progress made towards reaching the education and child mortality targets (MDG 2 and MDG 4, respectively),[4] as well as the consequences of the changes in supply of education on the wage differential between workers with higher and lower skill levels. Table 8.2 summarizes the quantitative dimensions of the determinants for access to and completion of education, which served as a base for calibrating MAMS.

MDG 4: Reducing under-five child mortality

The infant mortality rate (for children under one year of age) has fallen continuously from 30.3 per 1,000 live births in 1990 to 17.3 in 2001. Likewise, the under-five child mortality rate was reduced from 42.3 to 24.8 deaths per each 1,000 live births during the same period. If these trends are maintained, the

Table 8.2　Ecuador: Elasticities of the MDG module of MAMS

	IF	MDG 4[a]	QE[b]	WP1[c]	WP2[d]	PCC	MDG 7a[e]	MDG 7b[f]	PCH	PCS
glentry – primary[g]	0.162	-0.035	0.111	0.059		0.126				
grd – primary[h]		-0.013	0.050	0.041		0.030				
grd – secondary[h]	0.080	-0.025	0.253	0.046						
grd – tertiary[h]	0.080	-0.025	0.253	0.046						
grdcont – secondary[i]	0.086	-0.019		0.034		0.087				
grdcont – tertiary[i]	0.821				0.203	0.097				
MDG 4[j]	-0.194					-0.325	-0.400	-0.400	-0.989	
MDG 5[j]	-0.194					-0.325	-0.400	-0.400	-0.989	
MDG 7a[j]	0.100					0.200				1.000
MDG 7b[j]	0.200					0.100				1.000

Source: León and others (2008).

Abbreviations: IF: Infrastructure; QE: Quality of education; WP: Wage premium; PCC: Per capita consumption; PCH: Per capita supply of health services; PCS: Per capita supply of water and sanitation services

[a] Under-five child mortality.

[b] Number of teachers with training

[c] Wage gap: secondary vs. no education

[d] Wage gap: tertiary vs. secondary

[e] Percentage of the population with sustainable access to drinking water.

[f] Percentage of the population with access to basic sanitation services.

[g] "glentry" represents the probability that a child (6 years old) will enter the first grade of primary school.

[h] "grd" represents the probability of graduating from (passing) some grade of the respective educational cycle.

[i] "grdcont" represents the probability of graduating from the last grade of the respective cycle and continue on to the next.

[j] "MDG" refers to the models estimated for the child mortality goal (4), the maternal mortality goal (5), the goal for water (7a) and that for basic sanitation (7b).

child mortality rate will reach 11.8 deaths for each 1,000 live births in 2015, or even earlier, a number that would surpass the target of reducing the 1990-value of that rate by two-thirds.

Despite this progress, large inequalities in health conditions remain. The probability that an infant of poor parents will not survive his or her first year of life is 1.6 times higher than the probability for an infant born to non-poor parents, while the probability that an indigenous infant will die is twice as high as that of non-indigenous infants. The Vos and others study (2005) on the determinants of child mortality in Ecuador shows that these disparities are caused by a lower level of education among mothers, less knowledge about reproductive health (such as the importance of breast feeding), limited access to professional prenatal care and care during the birth process, and the difficulty of accessing basic sanitation services.[5] This study shows, furthermore, that the millennium goal for child mortality could be reached by making access to immunization universal and by improving the access to health services for poor and indigenous people through an expansion of the Free Maternal Care Programme. Such a "cost-effective" allocation of resources would demand an additional cost for the health sector of $7.2 million per year between 2004 and 2015, which would be the equivalent of an additional annual effort of no more than 0.02 per cent of GDP.

For the purposes of this study, a more limited econometric analysis of the determinants of child mortality was conducted, which focuses on health policy interventions that would come into play in MAMS. A child mortality model is estimated under the assumption that the highest probability of dying during the first five years is concentrated in the first year of life (see León and others, 2008). As in the education model, a logit model was estimated. According to this analysis, public investment in health (used as a proxy for the coverage and quality of maternal and infant healthcare services), per capita household consumption (which approximates the access to these services), and the provision of water and basic sanitation services are key determinants (see Table 8.2).[6]

MDG5: Improving maternal health

While some doubts exists about the quality of the information sources on maternal mortality, available data suggest that the number of deaths has declined. According to INEC's vital statistics, the maternal mortality rate fell from 203 per 100,000 live births in 1971 to 117 in 1990, and further to 52 in 2002. A linear continuation of this decreasing trend would be enough to achieve the MDG target for this indicator (which is to reduce the rate by 75 per cent between 1990 and 2015). However, according to other sources of information, the maternal mortality rate is still at around 87 deaths per 100,000 live births.

Due to the lack of sufficient observations on maternal deaths in the survey on demographics and maternal and infant health, it is difficult to conduct an econometric analysis of the determinants of maternal mortality. Public health experts generally consider improvement in access to professional care before, during, and after delivery, as well as the general level of sanitation conditions, as key factors for lowering maternal mortality in developing countries. As mentioned previously, these factors have also been decisive for reducing child mortality rates in the country. Therefore, this study used the assumption that the interventions aimed at reducing child mortality have a similar impact in lessening maternal mortality.

MDG 7: Improving the provision of basic drinking water services and waste treatment services

According to the Population and Housing Census, the percentage of the population with access to piped-in drinking water increased from 60.8 per cent to 77 per cent between 1990 and 2001. The percentage of the population with access to sewage elimination services also increased from 37.1 per cent in 1990 to 44.9 per cent in 2001. Rural, indigenous, and Afro-Ecuadorian residents have less access to these basic services. The MDG target for drinking water supply would be achievable long before the year 2015 if coverage keeps increasing at the pace of the last decade. Meeting the target for access to basic sanitation services, in contrast, would require a greater public policy effort. Ecuador's self-established targets are more ambitious than the international ones. According to these, access to drinking water and sanitation services should have reached at least 89 per cent and 73 per cent, respectively, by the year 2015. Reaching these targets would require additional efforts over and above existing policies.

No econometric studies of the determinants of access to sanitary services are available for Ecuador, nor are there studies on the cost-effectiveness of public investment towards achieving the targets for water and sanitation. For the purposes of this study, a simple probabilistic model was estimated that relates access to drinking water and sanitation to public investment and per capita consumption (see Table 8.2 for results and León and others, 2008 for methodological aspects).

Brief overview of social and economic policy reforms[7]

Public policy related to the achievement of the MDGs has relied primarily on social programmes. In practice, however, the millennium goals have not featured as key priorities in the policies conducted by the various ministries that deal with social issues.[8] Furthermore, the level of public social spending (excluding the social security system)[9] is one of the lowest in Latin America, fluctuating between 4 per cent and 5 per cent of GDP during the 1980s and 1990s. Per capita spending on education fell sharply from the early 1980s to recover only from the year 2000 onwards, although most of the recovery is explained by increased teacher salaries. During the 1980s and 1990s, public spending in health was only 1 per cent of GDP (and 2 per cent when health spending by the social security system is included). However, the ongoing expansion of the low-cost immunizations programme and some other relatively cost-effective programmes—along with the process of urbanization and the reduction of fertility rates—have helped to improve health indicators.

Economic policy, for its part, has never been managed with a clear and explicit vision of fighting poverty. Rather, as mentioned earlier, macroeconomic policy has responded strongly "pro-cyclical" to external shocks, influenced in particular by the volatility in oil prices. More structural economic reforms, such as the liberalization of finance and trade, were introduced primarily with the expectation of improving efficiency in production and, therefore, accelerating economic growth. Poverty would be reduced, in the best-case scenario, as a result of the expansion of the economy as a whole.

Certain changes in social and economic policy were introduced in the mid-2000s, however, that could mark a turning point towards more accelerated progress in the attainment of the MDGs. For example, the Fund for Stabilization, Social and Productive Investment, and Reduction of Public Debt (FEIR-EP) was reformed in 2005. This fund was financed out of the surplus of oil revenues, that is all revenues obtained when oil prices rose above the reference price defined in the pro forma government budget. Twenty percent of the fund went to the oil stabilization fund, 10 per cent to investment projects in health and education, and 70 per cent towards public debt repayment. With the reform, FEIREP was transformed into the Special Account for Social and Productive Reactivation of Development in Science and Technology and for Fiscal Stabilization (CEREPS) and with a different distribution of the resources: 35 per cent going towards the production stimulus projects and the servicing of public debt (which includes up to 10 per cent for productive infrastructure), 15 per cent for education and culture, 15 per cent for health and sanitation, 5 per cent for road maintenance, 5 per cent for environmental clean-up, 5 per cent for science and technology projects, and 20 per cent towards the oil stabilization fund. In addition, in 2006 the government increased its share in private oil company profits earned at oil prices over 15 dollars a barrel. These resources would also contribute to the funding of CEREPS, and it is estimated that they would amount to about 3 per cent of GDP. In summary, these reforms aim at mobilizing substantial resources for the financing of public investments in MDG-related services. With sustained high oil prices, the necessary investments will be affordable. Furthermore, CEREPS should also provide the mechanism to put an end to the "pro-cyclical" macroeconomic policies, by imposing a "counter-cyclical" automatic stabilizer and a tool for smoothing social spending over time.

In 2008, however, the Constituent Assembly established during the administration of President Rafael Correa decided to eliminate the oil funds and incorporate these resources into the central government budget. At the same time, the government has maintained the cap on growth in current spending. With these decisions, oil resources are now largely used for investment in road and energy infrastructure, which in the medium term are expected to contribute to increased productivity of the economy as a whole. In addition, public spending on health and education has practically doubled under this arrangement. One reason for eliminating the oil funds, including CEREPS, was that, while rising oil prices had allowed large quantities of resources to accumulate in the funds in the world markets, the resources were restricted in terms of their ability to be aimed at investment projects. The reforms lifted these restrictions.

In the social policy arena, a series of measures were implemented in the 1990s with the explicit goal of contributing to the achievement of the millennium goals. For example, the unconditional cash transfer programme (*Bono Solidario*) created in 1998 sought to compensate the poor for the rising price of energy. In 2003, the programme was converted into a programme of conditional cash transfers (the *Bono de Desarrollo Humano*, mentioned earlier) aimed at increasing access to schools and the retention of students in the school system, on one hand, and at improving health conditions for children, on the other. A recent evaluation of the impact of the monetary transfers, conducted by the Technical Secretariat of the Social Cabinet and the World Bank indicates that the programme has generated a significant increase in enrolment rates. In fact, the probability that a child who lives in a household that receives the cash transfer is enrolled in a school is 10 percentage points higher than the probability for a comparable child whose family does not receive the Bond (Schady and Araujo, 2005).[10] In this sense, the transfer programme has reinforced the school meals programme, which dates back to 1990s and provides schools with breakfasts and lunches not only to provide nutrition to children, but also with the aim of improving enrolment and retention rates. Several local governments have also implemented free textbook programmes and adult literacy programmes. Finally, the Ministry of Education and Culture has begun a programme aimed at universalizing the first year of the ten-year cycle of basic education, as well as a nation-wide programme to provide free textbooks.

One important step towards universalizing access to reproductive health services was the passage of the Free Maternal and Child Care Law in 1998. The law includes a wide range of benefits such as: prenatal controls, deliveries, caesarean sections, obstetric emergencies, family planning, care for healthy newborns and newborns with pathologies, and care for children under five in the prevailing childhood diseases (UNFPA-CONAMU, 2004). By providing these free services to the low-income population, steps have been taken on both the supply side and the demand side that have a significant influence on infant mortality, as pointed out previously. However, the application of the Free Maternal and Child Care Law has been affected by the increasing de facto "privatization" of health care in Ecuador (Vos and others, 2005),[11] as visible from the reduction of physician's work shifts in the public sector to only four hours and an expansion of hours in private sector medical centres. The shift to private practices as well as a reduction in the use of health services in general resulted from the cost-recovery policy implemented in the health sector at the same time the law was enacted. All of this has affected both the supply and the demand of public health services and, therefore, its current coverage and functioning are exiguous for reaching the millennium goals in health.

Another effort aimed at improving the health of the population is the Universal Health Insurance Programme enacted by the administration of President Alfredo Palacios in 2006. This programme was initially directed at the poorest 40 per cent of the population, and it has been implemented in the municipalities of Ecuador's three largest cities: Quito, Guayaquil, and Cuenca. The expectation is that these programmes will increase the demand for health services, especially among the poorest groups, while reducing their out-of-pocket expenses and improving their health status. This is also expected to reduce maternal and infant mortality. However, a better system of health insurance does not, in and of itself, guarantee a better supply of services, so the effectiveness of the programme will also depend on whether maternal and infant care is improved at the same time.

Finally, the Ministry of Urban Development and Housing has begun the PRAGUAS project with the goal of providing drinking water and sewage systems to poor areas. In addition, since the mid 1990s, the Central Government has been transferring 15 per cent of the current income to the municipalities for investment, including investment in water and basic sanitation. Local governments also have access to the resources of Ecuador's Solidarity Fund and to loans from the Ecuadoran Development Bank for the same purposes.

In spite of these favourable changes, social policy has been negatively affected by the instability of resources available for investment in human development, due to economic volatility and ongoing changes in the management of social reforms. There is still much to do, therefore, to improve efficiency in public spending and ensure more equitable access to social services (see World Bank and Inter-American Development Bank, 2004; Vos and others, 2003). The achievement of these millennium goals requires a better integration of social and economic policies with a long term vision and mechanisms that prevent volatility in social investment. The high prices of oil and CEREPS were providing an opportunity to confront this challenge. The flexibilization of the use of oil resources is now allowing more resources to be allocated to public investment in basic infrastructure. It also keeps excessive quantities from accumulating in oil funds. However, there is a risk of not being able to activate a "counter-cyclical" mechanism with sufficient resources when the world market conditions are less favourable. An unfavourable situation of this type would undoubtedly mean that the achievement of the MDGs would be delayed.

General equilibrium analysis of the achievement of the millennium goals

While a partial equilibrium analysis provides useful information about the budgetary efforts needed to achieve the millennium goals, such an analysis does not take into consideration interactions between the goals or the relationship between these goals and the performance of the economy (and vice versa). To avoid this restriction, this study has used a dynamic general equilibrium model called MAMS, which is detailed in Chapter 3. This model allows the quantification of macroeconomic effects and the fiscal costs required by various scenarios aimed at reaching the millennium goals. It provides a general economic framework that relates the achievement of the goals—through financing mechanisms and policies—to the effects that these mechanisms have on the various sectors of the economy and, therefore, on the adjustment of the labour market, relative prices, public resources, and household income, which in turn have an effect on the achievement of these goals. The next section will present the most important aspects of the calibration of the model for the case of Ecuador, the assumptions of the baseline scenario, and the main results in this scenario and 16 other scenarios where the millennium goals are met through simulation.

Aspects related to the calibration of MAMS for Ecuador

The MAMS was calibrated with a Social Accounting Matrix (SAM) for Ecuador. The base year for the SAM is 2001, the year when the Ecuadorian economy stabilized significantly in the context of dollarization. Thus, the SAM takes into account the new structure of transaction flow between sectors and agents that emerged after the 1999 crisis. The SAM was constructed especially for the purposes of this study, following the accounting structure required in MAMS, as presented in Chapter 3.[12] The novelty of the matrix lies in the detailed disaggregation of social services: education (public and private, and by cycle), heath (public and private, and with separate levels of care in the case of public health), the public provision of water and sanitation, other public infrastructure services, and other government services. At the same time, 17 other production sectors are distinguished (covering various sectors in agriculture, mining, industrial and services), next to three types of labour: unskilled workers, with incomplete primary and secondary education; semi-skilled workers, with complete secondary education and incomplete tertiary education; and skilled workers, with some level of completed tertiary education.

The SAM provides the accounting structure and point of departure for the calibration of the model. The initial values of the endogenous variables and many of the parameters are determined on the basis of the SAM, as are the exogenous variables, including employment and population data, which are specified in satellite tables to the SAM for Ecuador. To complete the solution of the base year (2001) of the model, however, it was necessary to estimate a number of elasticities through partial equilibrium methods. The functions referring to the millennium goals, using the elasticities reported in Table 8.2, were calibrated in such a way that they replicated the levels observed in the social indicators associated with them for the year 2001. In the same way, the calibration of the logistical function of MDG achievement requires the estimation of certain elasticities that define the magnitude of the change of the determinants of those goals (for example, per capita consumption, the quality of education, and others) in a way that is consistent with reaching the related targets in 2015. A methodological note about the estimation of these elasticities is presented in León and others (2008, Annex 5). Finally, the elasticities that define substitution for production and consumption and the income-expenditures relationship of households were taken from prior studies (Kouwenaar, 1988; De Janvry and others, 1991; Jaramillo, 1992; Vos and León, 2003).[13]

Assumptions and results of the baseline scenario

Once the model was calibrated in the base year, a baseline scenario was simulated defining the trajectory of the economy from 2001-2015, under the assumption that no additional public policy effort is made to achieve the millennium goals. The scenario assumes that public social spending changes at the same pace of the trends observed in past and recent years, and that other exogenous variables stay constant or change according to prior trends. In the particular case of Ecuador, the scenario assumes that the export price for crude oil and the import price for refined petroleum products increase between 2001 and 2005, following the trends observed, and that they do not fluctuate in subsequent years.

The macroeconomic closure rules in the baseline scenario are the following. In the case of the *government,* an endogenous adjustment of the current account balance (or government savings) is assumed. The difference between government investment spending and its financing (through income, in the case of a current account surplus, and through a fixed level of internal and external borrowing) is covered by adjusting income tax rates. For the *external sector,* a flexible adjustment of the real exchange rate is assumed, while the capital account variables of the balance of payments are fixed. This rule is quite realistic for Ecuador's dollarized economy, in which all adjustment falls on domestic prices, and external prices are fixed, leaving the real exchange rate to either appreciate or depreciate. Finally, *private investment* adjusts to balance total savings, once the government investment spending has been determined.

The baseline scenario shows that if external conditions and policies do not change, there will be more progress in human development, but it will be insufficient for achieving the millennium goals (see Table 8.3). The percentage of children who complete primary school on time is almost five points less than what is required to reach the established target for MDG-2 by 2015. The indicator does show a significant increase, however, which is explained by an increase in the quality of education (measured by the per student supply of education services) and per capita household consumption, to such an extent that this increase compensates for, and even outweighs, the effect of the decrease in the wage premium on education and scant public investment in infrastructure (see Figure 8.4). These results in education are consistent with the trend observed in the last five year period and the effects of recent programmes aimed at stimulating demand for education—in particular, the Human Development Bonus.

Table 8.3   Ecuador: MDG achievement in the baseline scenario, 2001-2015

MDG and associated indicator	2001	2005	2010	2015	Target for 2015
MDG 1: Percentage of the population living on less than 1 dollar a day.	15.5	14.77	10.59	9.4	7.7
MDG 2: Completion rate for primary education	71.9	82.7	91.4	95.4	100.0
MDG 4: Child mortality rate (per 1,000 live births)	24.8	20.7	17.6	15.7	14.3
MDG 5: Maternal mortality rate (per 100,000 live births)	96.9	67.2	46.6	36.0	29.3
MDG 7a: Access to drinking water (% of population)	77.0	79.1	81.6	83.6	89.0
MDG 7b: Access to sanitation services (% of population)	44.9	50.0	56.0	60.9	73.0

Source: MAMS for Ecuador and microsimulations for MDG 1.

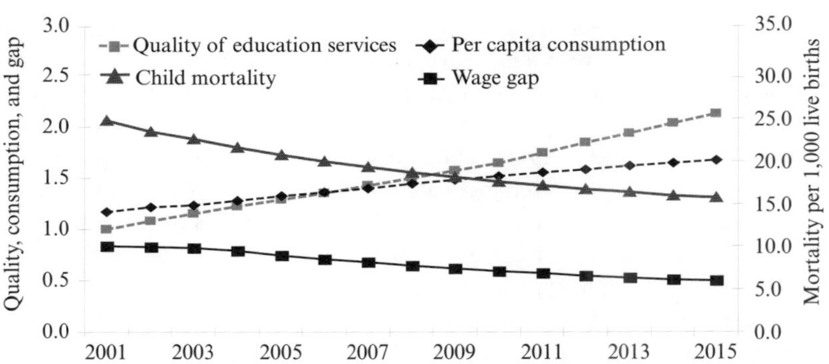

Figure 8.4 Ecuador: Trends in the determinants of the primary education goals in the base scenario, 2001-2015[a]

Source: MAMS model for Ecuador.

[a] Quality of education services is measured using an index of the supply of education services per student enrolled in primary schools. Per capita consumption is expressed in thousands of dollars, child mortality in deaths per 1,000 live births and the wage gap refers to the gap in earnings between semi-skilled and skilled workers.

The mortality rate among children decreases from 24.8 deaths per 1,000 live births to 15.7 between 2001 and 2015, closely approaching the target (MDG 4), and contributing also to improvement in the MDG 2 target (see Table 8.3 and Figure 8.4). The maternal mortality rate would decline from 96.9 to 36.0 per 100,000 live births; but in spite of this, there remains a gap of almost seven points above the stipulated target (see Table 8.3). The trends in both mortality indicators are explained primarily by an increase in per capita household consumption, an increase in the per capita consumption of total health services, and by a slight improvement in access to water and sanitation (see Figure 8.5). Thus, the baseline scenario does not reproduce the child and maternal mortality outcomes that would result from projecting past trends linearly forward, according to which the health targets would be achieved by 2015. The results of the baseline scenario can be considered more realistic since, in practice, neither type of mortality behaves in a linear fashion, much less when they are relatively low.

The model simulates a slight improvement in access to drinking water (MDG 7a), from 77 per cent in 2001 to 83.6 per cent in 2015, though it misses the target by slightly less than 6 percentage points (see Table 8.3). Likewise, access to sanitation services (MDG 7b) increases from 44.9 per cent in 2001 to 60.9 per cent in 2015, leaving a gap of 12 percentage points that would have to be overcome in order to meet the MDG target. The insufficient expansion of the per-capita supply of water and sanitation services, in the order of 2.6 per cent per year, is the main reason why both goals are not met.

Finally, the goal for reducing extreme poverty (MDG 1) is not met, according to the methodology of microsimulations which is introduced in the next

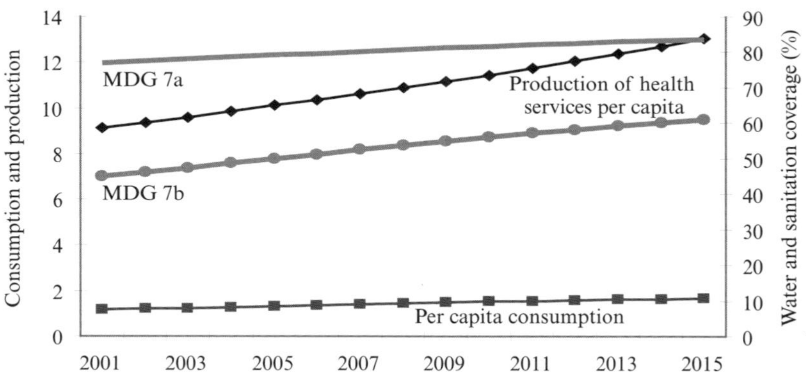

Figure 8.5 Ecuador: Trends in the determinants of the health goals in the baseline scenario, 2001-2015[a]

Source: MAMS model for Ecuador.

[a] Per capita consumption is expressed in thousands of dollars, MDG 7a and MDG 7b are the percentage of the population with access to drinking water and sanitation, respectively, and per capita production is expressed in dollars per person and refers to the supply of health services.

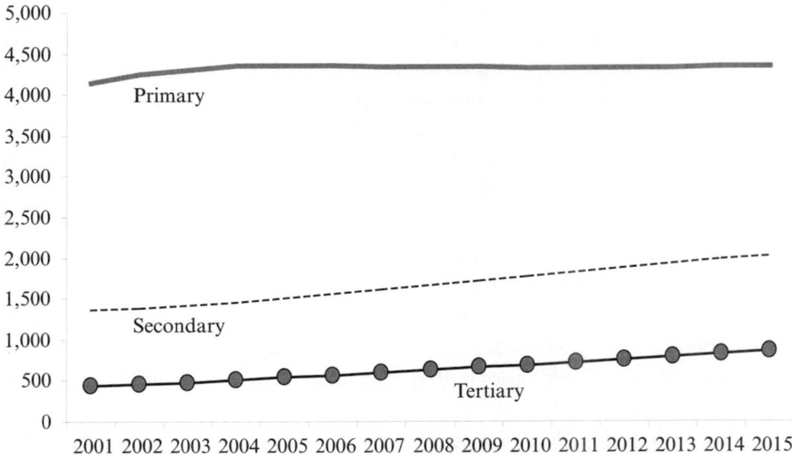

Figure 8.6 Ecuador: Labour supply in the base scenario, 2001-2015 (Thousands of people)
Source: MAMS model for Ecuador.

section. While the percentage of people living on less than one dollar a day is reduced from 17 per cent in 2001 to 9.4 per cent in 2015, it does not reach the target of 7.7 per cent. The significant—but insufficient—reduction in extreme poverty is explained primarily by an increase in per capita household consumption and a redistribution of income generated for the reduction in the previously mentioned wage gaps between skilled and unskilled workers. It is worth mentioning that improvements in education in the baseline scenario cause significant changes in the structure of the labour market.

The total labour supply increases to an annual average rate of 1.4 per cent, while the supply of semi-skilled and skilled workers grows at higher rates (2.9 per cent and 2.9 per cent respectively). In contrast, the supply of unskilled workers grows at a pace of 0.3 per cent per year (see Figure 8.7). The labour market is adjusted through wages or unemployment depending on the gap between unemployment in 2001 and the parameter for the minimum (or natural) rate of unemployment for each labour factor. Based on this process and the changes observed in the labour supply and demand, the following occurs: on one hand real labour income per employed person grows at an annual average rate of 2.2 per cent less than the economy as a whole. On the other hand, due to the adjustments in the supply and demand by type of worker, the real labour income of unskilled and semi-skilled workers grows by 4.1 per cent and 0.3 per cent per year, respectively, while that of skilled workers actually falls by 1.9 per cent per year (see Figure 8.7).

The real wage of unskilled workers increases because of the relative decline of their labour supply, which occurs because: 1) a growing number of people

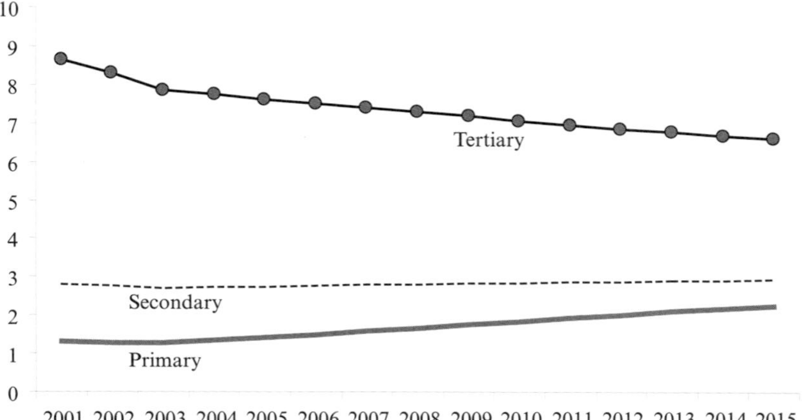

Figure 8.7 Ecuador: Average real wage by type of worker in the baseline scenario, 2001-2015 (Thousands of dollars)
Source: MAMS model for Ecuador.

are remaining in the educational system; and 2) they are acquiring higher skill levels. For these reasons, the unemployment rate of these workers decreases until it arrives at its natural rate. In the same way, the greater demand of semi-skilled workers (with secondary education) initially exerts pressure on the real wages of these workers, which, therefore, tend to rise. Once the supply of these workers grows—in other words, once an entire cohort complete secondary education successfully and enters the labour market—the upward pressure on their wages is mitigated and unemployment of this factor is reduced until it reaches its natural rate in 2015. Finally, the greater supply of skilled workers with tertiary education exceeds demand, causing a decline in real wages for this type of worker. However, since these wages cannot be reduced below the minimum wage, the unemployment rate of skilled workers increases until it reaches the level of 25.7 per cent in 2015. In this way, the wage gaps between skilled and unskilled labour tends to be reduced (see Figure 8.7).

Results discussed thus far are derived from a baseline scenario in which real GDP grows at an annual average rate of 4 per cent—one percentage point higher than the average rate of the last 12 years—but, one percentage point lower than the average recorded between 2000 and 2007. It is assumed that government consumption (total and by sector) grows at the same pace as real GDP and that private borrowing (external and internal) and government borrowing increase by an average of 2.5 per cent per year.

Assumptions about the growth of the public sector and the macroeconomic closure of the government do not adhere strictly to the fiscal rules established by the Organic Law for Fiscal Responsibility, Stabilization, and Transparency enacted in June 2002 and reformed in July 2005. According to this law, government current spending cannot grow by more than 3.5 per cent annually in real terms[14] and the fiscal deficit (without including income from oil exports) must be reduced by 0.2 per cent of GDP each year until it is eliminated. In addition, the law establishes that the total public debt must be reduced until it represents 40 per cent of GDP, a percentage that then would become the ceiling. In spite of all of this, the baseline scenario sufficiently approximates what is established in the fiscal rule during the period in question (see León and others, 2008). Government tax revenue decreases from 3 per cent of GDP in 2001 to 1.5 per cent in 2015 (see Table 8.5 below). Government savings decreases from 2.4 per cent to 1.3 per cent of GDP and external savings goes from 2.9 per cent to 2.5 per cent of GDP. Internal public debt is reduced from 13.2 per cent to 8.8 per cent of GDP, and the external public-debt ratio from 53.7 per cent to 45.7 per cent. The horizon of the fiscal rule comes in sight, however, since the total public debt-to-GDP ratio must be reduced until it reaches 40 per cent in 2010. The time horizon of this study is 2015 and, therefore, it can be said that, while its trends are moving in the directions established by the fiscal rule, the baseline scenario implies a more expansionary fiscal stance for a longer period of time.

The results of the baseline scenario further show that private investment grows by 4.3 per cent per year between 2001 and 2015, while government investment actually declines by 0.5 per cent per year. Private consumption, exports, and imports grow at an annual average rate of 4 per cent, 3 per cent, and 3.2 per cent respectively. The external deficit (and, hence, foreign savings) is slightly reduced, consistent with trade performance and the reduction in public debt, which in turn reduces debt service payments. In line with observed trends, the baseline scenario projects a tendency towards an appreciation of the real exchange rate.

In summary, under the assumptions of the baseline scenario, without changes in public policy, the country would get closer to the MDG targets but none of them would be fully met. Public spending will thus need to be scaled up in order to meet the targets.

Assumptions and results of the scenarios for achieving the millennium goals

Using the baseline scenario as a reference point, 16 policy scenarios were simulated wherein public spending (current and investment spending) associated with the previously mentioned millennium goals—except for the goal of reducing extreme poverty—increases in order to achieve one or two of the goals separately, or all of them simultaneously.[15] The results of these scenarios are contrasted with those of the baseline scenario in order to reach conclusions about: (i) the macroeconomic viability of achieving the goals; (ii) the cost and the most effective options of financing; and (iii) the macroeconomic tradeoffs that may emerge with possibly undesirable effects on economic growth. For the MDG scenarios, public expenditures are scaled up to the level required to meet the MDGs in 2015, using the behavioural functions of the MDG determinants. The closure rules are the same as those of the baseline scenario, except that the government rule is adjusted in the case of the alternative financing scenarios of domestic borrowing, external borrowing or financing through foreign aid. In those cases, the direct tax rates are fixed and the alternative financing sources are made endogenous.

The costs of achieving the millennium goals

As shown in Table 8.4, the simulation results show that the additional cost for achieving the targets for education, mortality, and water and sanitation would be around 1.5 per cent of GDP per year, on average, for the period of 2005-2015. It also shows that the cost tends to increase towards the end of the period, when it comes to represent 2.7 per cent of GDP. This incremental cost is due to the assumption that there is a decreasing effectiveness of the interventions and decreasing marginal returns to other determinants the closer one gets to the targets. The cost analysis shows that it is more difficult to get the "last" group of children to enter and complete primary school. Likewise, the lower the child mortality rate, the higher the cost for reducing it further. Therefore, it is highly relevant to consider the requirements at the end of the period since they reflect the probable cost of maintaining the level reached in education and health after 2015.

Table 8.4 also shows that synergies exist when the attempt is made to reach all of the goals at once; in fact, the additional cost at the end of the period (2.7 per cent of GDP) is less than the sum of the cost of reaching the goals separately (3.4 per cent of GDP). The "savings" are obtained in particular in the form of lowering the required additional costs in health (0.6 per cent) and, to a lesser extent, in education (0.1 per cent of GDP). The reduction of child mortality has a positive impact on the achievement of the education goal, and better access to drinking water and sanitation services accelerates the achievement of the mortality goals. The effects of the simultaneous achievement of all of the goals also have an influence on the economy as a whole (among others, the contraction of the wage differential among workers with higher education reduces the cost for the production of education and health services).

It is worth noting that these results occur without taking into consideration improvements in efficiency such as efficiency in the delivery of social services or efficiencies that could come from reallocating the budget towards more "cost-effective" interventions than those that exist. Since there is ample scope for improving the efficiency of public spending, the estimates given can be considered the upper limit of the additional costs required.[16]

Financing alternatives

The MDG strategy is more costly when using more domestic resources (taxes or domestic borrowing) as compared to the external borrowing scenario. The

Table 8.4   Ecuador: Simulated additional costs for achieving the MDGs separately and simultaneously, at the end of the period simulated and average for period as a whole (Percentage of GDP)[a]

	Public spending in the base year	Only the primary education goal	Only the mortality goals	Only the water and sanitation goals	All MDGs
		Additional public spending needed to achieve the following MDGs:			
		The end of the period (2015)			
Primary education	1.1	1.2	0.0	0.0	1.1
Current spending	1.0	1.2	0.0	0.0	1.1
Public investment	0.1	0.0	0.0	0.0	0.0
Health	2.0	0.0	1.6	0.0	1.0
Current spending	1.6	0.0	0.9	0.0	0.6
Public investment	0.4	0.0	0.7	0.0	0.4
Water and sanitation	0.3	0.0	0.1	0.5	0.5
Current spending	0.0	0.0	0.0	0.0	0.0
Public investment	0.3	0.0	0.0	0.5	0.5
		Annual average for the period (2005-2015)			
Total	3.4	1.2	1.7	0.5	2.7
Primary education	1.1	0.8	0.0	0.0	0.8
Current spending	1.0	0.7	0.0	0.0	0.7
Public investment	0.1	0.1	0.0	0.0	0.1
Health	2.0	0.0	0.6	0.0	0.4
Current spending	1.6	0.0	0.3	0.0	0.2
Public investment	0.4	0.0	0.3	0.0	0.2
Water and sanitation	0.3	0.0	0.1	0.3	0.3
Current spending	0.0	0.0	0.0	0.1	0.1
Public investment	0.3	0.0	0.0	0.3	0.3
Total	3.4	0.8	0.7	0.3	1.5

Source: MAMS for Ecuador.

[a] Additional costs are estimated as the difference between estimated public spending in each scenario for reaching the MDGs and the public spending recorded in the baseline scenario. The results presented correspond to scenarios where the public spending is financed through domestic resources (direct taxes or borrowing). The additional costs tend to be around 0.2 percentage points of GDP less in the scenarios where the spending is financed through external resources (aid or borrowing).

difference is 0.2 percentage points of GDP. Domestic resource mobilization also tends to slow economic growth somewhat as compared with the foreign financing scenario (see Table 8.5). Using higher direct taxes produces a situation with lower household consumption, which means less private spending on education and health. In order to compensate for that effect and still make sure the goals are reached by 2015, there must be an additional increase in public spending on education and health. In the case of financing the MDG scenario through domestic borrowing, the amount of domestic credit available for financing private investment is reduced and hence private investment is less than in the other scenarios (see Table 8.5). This scenario also would generate the lowest GDP growth with respect to the baseline scenario, though the difference is not very large.

The real exchange rate appreciates in all scenarios, even in the baseline scenario, given the increase in spending on non-tradable activities associated with the MDGs. Nevertheless, the level of currency appreciation is greater when external borrowing is used to finance the additional public spending required to reach the goals (see Table 8.5). This erodes the competitiveness of exports, particularly of non-traditional exports, a situation that further increases the dependence of the economy on oil and agricultural export production. Because of the limited time horizon of the simulation period (through 2015) and given time lags in education, productivity gains from higher levels of human development are insufficient for stimulating the production of exports with a higher technological content.

It should be said that the baseline scenario incorporates the increases in the world market price of oil that took place during the 2000s and which lifted some of the country's financial constraints. The model assumes that this price would stay high during the period of the simulation, which could be considered very optimistic since these prices have fluctuated a great deal historically. At the same time, however, results show that the current situation could favour the achievement of the millennium goals. It would require policies that allow public consumption to remain stable at adequate levels over a prolonged period of time. The fiscal responsibility law and the oil stabilization fund, as well as the subsequent reforms, could provide an adequate framework to do this, if decision-makers implement policies in a consistent way. Furthermore, while trying to protect social spending, this fiscal framework also aims at reducing the burden of public debt. The sustainable level of external debt in the current fiscal policy framework is 40 per cent of GDP (World Bank and Inter-American Development Bank, 2004). The scenarios simulated here suggest that this critical level could be exceeded by a substantial margin in either of the two cases where the new public spending required for reaching all the goals—except that of extreme poverty—is financed through external or internal debt, as shown in Table 8.5.

In the domestic borrowing scenario, internal public debt would increase to almost 30 per cent in the year 2015 from an initial level of 13 per cent in the base year (see Table 8.5). Public domestic debt in Ecuador has been low historically because of the lack of a developed bonds market. However, the model assumes that this market exists; therefore it allows domestic borrowing to increase at a given interest rate. It is quite likely that the real cost of the financing strategy is

Table 8.5   Ecuador: Selected macroeconomic results of some scenarios simulated with MAMS, 2001-2015

Variable and scenario	2001	2005	2010	2015
Real exchange rate (2001=100)				
Base	100.0	95.8	94.1	92.7
Achieving the goals with direct tax financing	100.0	95.7	93.8	92.3
Achieving the goals with external borrowing	100.0	95.3	92.8	90.6
Achieving the goals with domestic borrowing	100.0	95.7	94.0	92.7
GDP (annual growth rate)[a]				
Base		4.1	3.6	2.9
Achieving the goals with direct tax financing		4.2	3.6	2.7
Achieving the goals with external borrowing		4.1	3.6	2.7
Achieving the goals with domestic borrowing		4.1	3.4	2.5
Private consumption (annual growth rate)[a]				
Base		4.6	3.9	3.1
Achieving the goals with direct tax financing		4.3	3.3	2.8
Achieving the goals with external borrowing		4.6	3.8	3.0
Achieving the goals with domestic borrowing		4.5	3.7	2.9
Private investment (annual growth rate)[a]				
Base		3.6	3.4	3.0
Achieving the goals with direct tax financing		3.2	2.8	2.6
Achieving the goals with external borrowing		3.6	3.5	2.8
Achieving the goals with domestic borrowing		1.7	0.4	1.4
Exports (annual growth rate)[a]				
Base		4.3	3.4	2.3
Achieving the goals with direct tax financing		4.2	3.1	2.1
Achieving the goals with external borrowing		3.5	2.1	1.7
Achieving the goals with domestic borrowing		4.1	2.7	1.8
Domestic public debt (% GDP)				
Base	13.2	11.7	9.9	8.8
Achieving the goals with direct tax financing	13.2	11.7	9.9	8.8
Achieving the goals with external borrowing	13.2	11.7	9.9	8.8
Achieving the goals with domestic borrowing	13.2	12.3	16.3	29.2
External public debt (% GDP)				
Base	53.7	48.8	44.4	42.4
Achieving the goals with direct tax financing	53.7	48.8	44.3	42.3
Achieving the goals with external borrowing	53.7	49.2	49.7	61.7
Achieving the goals with domestic borrowing	53.7	48.8	44.7	43.3
Income taxes (% GDP)				
Base	3.0	0.2	0.5	1.5
Achieving the goals with direct tax financing	3.0	0.9	3.1	4.7
Achieving the goals with external borrowing	3.0	0.2	0.5	1.5
Achieving the goals with domestic borrowing	3.0	0.2	0.5	1.5

Source: MAMS for Ecuador.

[a] Variable expressed in real terms after deflating for the consumer price index.

being underestimated since, given the poor development of the domestic capital market, the government could only issue bonds at high interest rates. Even so, higher debt levels are a problem in both financing scenarios since public debt rises to slightly over 70 per cent of GDP in 2015, a situation that would be very difficult to manage even with the current price of oil. Furthermore, given that Ecuador has declared several moratoriums with its international lenders in the past, there would be serious restrictions on the possibility of financing new public spending through external borrowing in the context of the international financial markets.

In a scenario where spending would be financed through higher taxes, these restrictions could be avoided, but at the cost of lower growth in investment and private consumption. MAMS suggests that to reach the goals, income tax revenues would have to increase around three percentage points of GDP in 2015 as compared to the tax level recorded in the baseline scenario (see Table 8.5). On the other hand, the advantage of this type of scenario is that there would be a significant reduction of public indebtedness. Ecuador has a great deal of room to manoeuvre for implementing further tax reforms, particularly a reform aimed at improving the collection of direct taxes. According to the data used in MAMS, direct tax revenue is only 1.5 per cent of GDP in the base year, which is low by any international standard. However, tax reforms are politically difficult to implement in Ecuador, especially if they affect high-income groups. Thus, the challenge of the government would be to convince elites to contribute part of their wealth to human development and the long-term benefit of the country. At the same time, the high price of oil offers certain additional fiscal flexibility to mobilize the resources that would be necessary to undertake such a distributive effort in order to achieve the MDGs.

Analysis of the poverty reduction goal

Using the results of the MAMS scenarios for the simulated changes in the level and composition of employment and the average level and distribution of labour earnings, the microsimulations technique described in Chapter 2 (see Appendix A2.1) was applied to analyse the distributive impact and the impact on poverty in these scenarios. The technique was applied using data from the 2001 INEC Employment, Underemployment, and Unemployment Survey.

As indicated in the previous section, extreme poverty falls in the baseline scenario, but the reduction is not sufficient for achieving the goal outlined for MDG 1 (see Table 8.3). The results of the microsimulations also show that achieving the goals for education, mortality, and water and sanitation do not lead to any greater reduction in poverty by the year 2015.

The supply of skilled workers exceeds demand in all of the scenarios, producing a reduction in the wage gap for that type of worker. On the other hand, unskilled workers are the ones who gain the most from the strategy of achieving the goals, as their average labour income increases almost 4 per cent per year. The sum of these effects translates into a substantial reduction in income inequality of more than 10 per cent between 2001 and 2015 (measured by the Gini coefficient for per capita household income). This, combined with moderate growth in per capita income of around 2 per cent per year, results in a considerable reduction of extreme poverty, though not enough for reach the goal by 2015.

These trends are already present in the baseline scenario. The scenarios for reaching the millennium goals do not change the aggregate labour market outcomes very much, in part because the effect of better educational performance on the labour supply is just beginning to be felt at the end of the period of analysis. Also, the results in the labour market are very similar in the various financing scenarios for reaching the goals, though it must be said that the increase in the real average wage is relatively higher when external borrowing is used, because of the effect of the currency appreciation. This situation does not translate into a greater reduction in poverty because employment does not expand quite as much in this case.[17] In summary, the extreme poverty target is not met in any of the financing scenarios and the remaining shortfall from the target is similar in all of them, though it is very slightly larger in the case of domestic borrowing where, as explained, GDP and real wages grow less than in the other scenarios (see Figure 8.8).

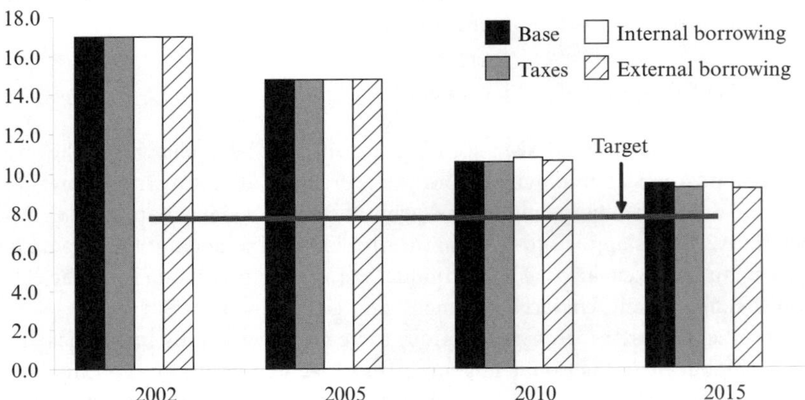

Figure 8.8 Ecuador: Incidence of extreme poverty in the baseline and MDG scenarios under alternative financing options[a]

Source: MAMS for Ecuador and microsimulation methodology.

a The incidence of poverty is measured using per capita income data and a poverty line of 1 dollars a day per person.

MDG achievement, macroeconomic tradeoffs and policy recommendations

In order to achieve the MDGs, Ecuador must give higher priority to the goals and ensure these are fully integrated in economic and social policies of all ministries and other government institutions. This must occur in the framework of a government policy that is based on public management by results and a real strategy for human development and poverty reduction that integrates social and economic policy in a coordinated fashion, eliminating the historic volatility in social spending.

Efforts must be redoubled in order to achieve the MDGs

The dynamic general equilibrium analysis presented indicates that without better-targeted public policies, none of the millennium goals will be reachable. The scenarios simulated for achieving the goals of education, mortality, and water and sanitation show that their achievement would require a significant increase in public spending and that the government would face significant macroeconomic tradeoffs in managing the financing of the additional expenditures. Apparent conflicts between different objectives of fiscal management must be resolved. If the current fiscal rules are not strictly adhered to as directed by the Organic Law for Responsibility, Stabilization, and Fiscal Transparency, public debt would reach unsustainable levels, requiring the government to generate undesirable levels of primary surplus in the future. At the same time, fiscal rules prevent the accumulation of domestic and external public debt and the kind of increased government current spending required to finance the achievement of the goals. Financing the spending through foreign donations is not a viable scenario either, since Ecuador does not qualify as a Highly Indebted Poor Country or as an otherwise aid-eligible low-income country. In order to make progress towards reaching the millennium goals, the limits imposed by fiscal rules would have to be applied with some flexibility, but preserving economic stability within the limited policy space of a dollarized economy.

Tax reform is required

According to the analysis of this chapter, the most feasible scenario for achieving the MDGs simultaneously would be to finance the public spending required through increases in direct income taxes. Direct tax revenue would have to be raised by three percentage points of GDP from current levels, up to 4.6 per cent of GDP in the year 2015. This strategy would also demand the elimination of the current restriction on increasing current spending. Obviously, the tax reform that must be sought in order to create the additional fiscal space necessary could face political opposition. However, the current income tax burden is very low and the additional cost for reaching the goals does not appear to be prohibitive.

These are important arguments for justifying such a tax reform. Since income inequality is very high in Ecuador, it is most reasonable to suggest that the burden of such a reform should fall on the high-income groups.

"Counter-cyclical" stabilization mechanisms and the financing of the strategy

Oil resources could contribute significantly to the achievement of the millennium goals, especially if they complement the financing sources considered here—primarily tax reform. The use of these resources will also allow a "counter-cyclical" mechanism to be established that will counteract economic volatility and protect social spending in times of crisis. The high price of oil today presents an opportunity to create the fiscal space necessary for implementing this kind of macroeconomic management. The resources accumulated in the stabilization fund must be used prudently with a view towards stabilizing social spending in the medium term and keeping it at an adequate level. Fiscal policy is extremely important, since monetary and exchange policy are not as relevant in a dollarized economy. CEREPS and other oil funds were eliminated in 2008 in order to increase flexibility in the use of oil funds. This has allowed more resources to be directed at public investment in basic infrastructure and has prevented an excessive accumulation of resources in these funds. There is a risk, however, of not being able to activate a "counter-cyclical" mechanism, with sufficient funding, that is aimed at confronting more adverse conditions in the world markets. Therefore, establishing this mechanism, while maintaining flexibility in the allocation of the resources for financing public investment in a way that is consistent with existing "counter-cyclical" fiscal rules, should be considered a priority in order to keep adverse external shocks from working against the achievement of the MDGs.

More fiscal space through efficiency in public social spending

The general equilibrium perspective applied in this study looked at the interactions and synergies between the achievement of the various goals, and it is clear that fewer resources are needed if public action is directed at achieving all of the goals simultaneously. Achieving the under-five child mortality goal has a significant influence on the achievement of the goal for primary school completion. In the same way, achieving the goals for water and sanitation increases the likelihood of achieving the previously mentioned mortality goal. Likewise, interventions aiming at achieving the goal of reducing extreme poverty will contribute to the attainment of all of the other goals. According to the estimates of this study, the synergies can generate a savings in costs of approximately one percentage point of GDP per year with respect to a hypothetical situation in which the objective is only to reach one or two goals at a time.

According to the analysis, in order to achieve the goals examined here—with the exception of the target for extreme poverty—public spending must increase gradually to a point of 2.7 per cent of GDP at the end of the projected period (2015). On average, this additional cost is estimated at 1.5 per cent of GDP per year during the period from 2005-2015. This estimate of additional costs takes into account the general equilibrium effects of the adjustments in the economy as a whole generated by increased government investment and an improvement in human development. However, it does not include the possibility of improving efficiency in the delivery of social services, in order to be more effective in allocating resources at a lower cost, in spite of the fact that this is feasible for Ecuador. In education, this would mean strengthening the cash transfer programme (Human Development Bonus), as well as looking for ways to improve teacher skill levels and education infrastructure and to facilitate greater autonomy in the delivery of teaching services. While these changes are in progress, it would be possible to reduce costs by minimizing absenteeism among teachers and avoiding the current situation where each teacher is assigned a large number of students. In health, on the other hand, cost-effective interventions include working towards universal coverage of the immunization programme and the expansion of the Free Maternal and Infant Care Programme. Meanwhile, according to Vos and others (2005), more structural changes in financing (for example, through a system of universal medical insurance) and the reorganization of public medical services could lead to cost savings in the sector. This study assumes that increased public social spending will result in a direct improvement in the access to education and health services, facilitating the achievement of the MDGs, but it has not included the possible cost savings that would result from greater efficiency in the delivery of social services. In this sense, it is possible that the MDGs could be achieved at a lower cost than the one estimated here, as long as successful efforts are made to achieve greater efficiency along the lines suggested.

Increasing social spending is not enough

This study has found that, while a sufficient increase in social spending could result in the achievement of the goals for primary education, child and maternal mortality, and water and sanitation, and that this would generate a certain redistribution of income, the goal for reducing extreme poverty measured by income would not be achieved. This is true when the assumption is of an economy that grows between 3 per cent and 4 per cent per year, which means that the growth of per capita income is less than 2 per cent per year. With this growth rate, which is higher than the levels Ecuador has actually experienced in the last few decades, income inequality would need to be reduced further. This could be achieved if the economy increases its capacity to absorb the growing supply of labour, primarily that of workers with higher educational levels. The greater availability of skilled workers could have favourable repercussions on productivity, but it is not a sufficient condition for reducing poverty. In the case of Ecuador, greater diversification of the economy must be sought and, in order to attack extreme poverty, productivity must be improved and more economic activities that provide employment for the poorest citizens must be promoted. In this sense, programmes that favour this kind of redistribution and also provide incentives for equity in access to credit and to productive assets (an agrarian reform or the implementation of a microfinance programme, for example) should be created and strengthened. At the same time, it will be important to overcome deficiencies in existing physical infrastructure in order to facilitate greater economic integration of the various regions of the country. To the extent that these interventions help improve productivity and the productive capacity, they could also limit (and possibly prevent) the adverse impact the real exchange rate appreciation could have on the competitiveness of exports, something that would be expected in a context of the application of a strategy focused only on increased social spending.

Acknowledgements

The authors would like to thank Hans Lofgren, Carolina Díaz-Bonilla, Martín Cicowiez and Marco V. Sánchez for their technical support and suggestions in the process of the specification and calibration of MAMS. Special thanks to Marco V. Sánchez for his valuable comments on a previous draft of this chapter. Many thanks are also due to Wilson Pérez for his observations, and to those who attended the presentations of the results of this study in FLACSO-Ecuador and in the workshop in Santiago, Chile. Finally, the authors are also grateful to SIISE analyst Rosario Maldonado for her assistance in conducting the microsimulations and to the UNDP office in Ecuador for their logistical support. Any error or omission in this report is the exclusive responsibility of the authors.

Notes

1   There is a significant methodological difference in how urban and rural areas are identified in the 1999 and 2006 surveys, which affects the ability to compare this information with precision.
2   Data in this section come from the First MDG Report of the Republic of Ecuador (SODEM, 2005).
3   The Human Development Bonus programme is a conditional cash transfers programme which, in principle, only pays out if the boys and girls that belong to beneficiary households attend school. However, no mechanism has been put in place to verify school attendance, making the transfer unconditional in practice. However, see also further below in the sub-section of social policy reforms.
4   Also the interaction between the goals for education and extreme poverty (MDG 2 and MDG 1, respectively) is considered, if per capita consumption is taken as a proxy of changes in the incidence of poverty.

5   This study applies a combination of two models for Ecuador: one, a multinomial model of the determinants of access to health services for maternal and infant care and the other, a survival model applied to children under one year of age. In both cases, the problems of endogeneity and multicollinearity are corrected.

6   The study by Vos and others (2005) did not find a statistically significant relationship between access to drinking water and sanitation and the infant mortality rate, however. The authors point out that this result could be explained by the influence of other variables such as the area of residence (urban/rural) and the education level of the head of household, which, in turn, are determinants of the access to drinking water and sanitation. They also conclude that while access to potable water and sanitation does not appear to be a direct determinant of infant mortality, it is at least a conditioning factor for the statistical significance of other determinants.

7   This section analyses the main social and economic policy reforms through 2006. Therefore, it does not cover the changes introduced in 2007 by the government of President Rafael Correa.

8   The National Secretariat for the Millennium Goals (SODEM) was created in 2005 as a ministry-level body with the objective of promoting a policy agenda aimed at achieving the millennium goals. This body was eliminated two years later, however, and its functions were transferred to the National Secretariat for Planning (SENPLADES).

9   Spending on social security benefits is also low in Ecuador, since less than 20 per cent of the population is covered by the social security system.

10   A more recent study by Ponce (2008, Chapter 2) confirms these results, though with certain qualifications. It indicates, furthermore, that the positive impact occurs in spite of the fact that in practice there is no system to verify that all of the beneficiaries of the Human Development Bond are complying with the conditions (in other words, that they actually attend school). Therefore, the impact of the cash transfer is greater among beneficiaries who believe that the conditionality could be applied at some point to the cash transfer. The third chapter of the same study does not find a significant impact on the quality of education as measured by test scores. In other words, the programme helps to improve access to education, but not necessarily the quality of the education.

11   De facto "privatization" refers to the growing relative participation of private medical personnel and services in the last decade (Vos and others, 2005).

12   The construction of the SAM was part of an institutional effort through which integrated social and economic accounts are continuously generated based on the methodology of the national accounts systems of the United Nations (INEC-ISS-SIISE, 2003). The methodology of the construction of the matrix is described in León and others (2008, Annex 2) and can also be found on the web page of the Ministry of Social Development Coordination (*Ministerio de Coordinación del Desarollo Social*) (http://www.meds.gov.ec/content/view/121/72/).

13   According to these studies, the substitution elasticities between domestic production and imports (Armington), as well as those that define the transformation of products for the domestic and international markets, are relatively low, in the rage of 0.4-1.5 in both cases. The substitution between the factors, and between the factors and intermediate goods is even lower, defined by elasticities in the range of 0.2 – 0.95. The range of income-consumption elasticities is the smallest (0.8-1.3).

14   The July 2005 reform restricted the fiscal rule only to current spending. Initially, the rule was applied to the primary government budget deficit.

15   The achievement of each of the goals in education, mortality, and water and sanitation is simulated separately, and then the simultaneous achievement of all of these goals is

simulated. These four scenarios, in turn, are simulated using four alternative financing strategies (foreign donations, internal borrowing, external borrowing, and increased taxes), so that a total of 16 scenarios are simulated. The scenarios where financing occurs through foreign donations are not analysed here since Ecuador is not eligible to receive substantial quantities of foreign aid.

16   Vos and Ponce (2004) and Vos and others (2005) offer recommendations aimed at achieving greater effectiveness in public spending on primary education and maternal and infant health at a smaller cost.

17   A more detailed analysis of the results of the microsimulations is presented in León and others (2008, Annex 6).

References

De Janvry, Alain, Elizabeth Sadoulet and André Fargeix (1991). "Politically feasible and equitable adjustment: Some alternatives for Ecuador", *World Development*, 19 (11): 1577-1594.

Glewwe, Paul (2002). "Schools and skills in developing countries: education policies and socioeconomic outcomes", *Journal of Economic Literature*. Vol. XL (June 2002), pp. 436-482.

INEC-ISS-SIISE (2002). *La Matriz de Contabilidad Social para Ecuador, 1993*, Quito: Ediciones Abya Yala (for INEC, the Institute of Social Studies, and the Technical Secretariat of the Social Cabinet).

Jaramillo, Fidel (1992). "Apertura, integración y competencia imperfecta en un modelo de equilibrio general computable", Quito: UNDP, CONADE (mimeo).

Kouwenaar, Arend (1988). *A Basic Needs Policy Model: A General Equilibrium Analysis with Special Reference to Ecuador*, Amsterdam: North-Holland.

León, Mauricio, José Rosero and Rob Vos (2008). *El Reto de Alcanzar los Objetivos de Desarrollo del Milenio en Ecuador. Un análisis de equilibrio general de los requerimientos de financiamiento*, Estudios del SIISE, Quito: Technical Secretariat of the Social Front.

Ocampo, José Antonio, and Rob Vos (2008). "Policy space and the changing paradigm in conducting macroeconomic policies in developing countries", in: Bank for International Settlements, *New Financing Trends in Latin America: A Bumpy Road towards Stability*, BIS Papers No. 36, Basel: Bank for International Settlements and Federal Reserve Bank of Atlanta, pp. 28-45.

Ponce, Juan (2008). *Educational Policy and Performance: Evaluating the Impact of Targeted Education Programs in Ecuador*, PhD Thesis, Institute of Social Studies, The Hague (published with Shaker Publishers, Maastricht).

Schady, Norbert, and María Caridad Araujo (2005). "Cash transfers, conditions, school enrollment, and child work: Evidence from a randomized experiment in Ecuador", World Bank Policy Research Working Paper 3930, Impact Evaluation Series No. 3, The World Bank.

SODEM (2005). *Primer Informe de los Objetivos de Desarrollo del Milenio (ODM) de la República del Ecuador*, Quito: National Secretariat of the Millennium Goals.

UNFPA-CONAMU (2004). *Ecuador: 10 años después. Ecuador 1994-2004. Evaluación del cumplimiento de los compromisos del Ecuador en la Conferencia Internacional sobre Población y Desarrollo, El Cairo 1994*, Quito, Ecuador: UNFPA-CONAMU.

United Nations (2006). *World Economic and Social Survey 2006: Diverging Growth and Development*, New York: United Nations (www.un.org/esa/policy).

UNDP-ECLAC-IPEA (2003). *Hacia el objetivo del milenio de reducir la pobreza en América Latina y el Caribe*, Santiago, Chile: United Nations Development Programme, the Economic Commission for Latin America and the Caribbean, and the Institute of Applied Economic Research.

Vos, Rob (1989). "Ecuador: windfall gains, unbalanced growth and stabilization", in: E.V.K. FitzGerald and Rob Vos, *Financing Economic Development. A Structural Approach to Monetary Policy*, Aldershot: Gower.

__________, (2000). *Development and the Colour of Money. Should Developing Countries have their own Currency?* The Hague: Institute of Social Studies.

__________, José Cuesta, Mauricio León, Ruth Lucio and José Rosero (2005). "Reaching the Millennium Development Goal for Child Mortality: Improving Equity and Efficiency in Ecuador's Health Budget", ISS Working Papers No. 410, The Hague: Institute of Social Studies (www.iss.nl).

__________, and Mauricio León (2003). *Dolarización, dinámica de exportaciones y equidad: ¿cómo compatibilizarlas en el caso de Ecuador?* SIISE Studies and Reports, No. 5, SIISE-ISS, Quito-The Hague.

__________, Mauricio León and Wladymir Brborich (2002). "Are cash transfer programmes effective to reduce poverty?" Quito and The Hague: Technical Secretariat of the Social Front and the Institute of Social Studies (mimeo).

__________, and Juan Ponce (2004). "Meeting the Millennium Development Goals in Ecuador: a cost-effectiveness analysis for Ecuador", ISS Working Papers No. 402, The Hague: Institute of Social Studies (www.iss.nl).

__________, Juan Ponce, Mauricio León and José Cuesta (2003). *¿Quién se beneficia del gasto social en Ecuador?* Studies and Reports of SIISE No. 4, SIISE-ISS, Quito-The Hague.

World Bank and Inter-American Development Bank (2004). *Ecuador: Creating fiscal space for poverty reduction. A fiscal management and public expenditure review*, Report No. 28911-EC, Washington D.C.: The World Bank and IDB.

9
Honduras

Maurizio Bussolo and Denis Medvedev

Introduction

Over the past ten years, Honduras has achieved important progress in terms of education attainment and provision of basic social infrastructure. This augurs well for the possibility of accomplishing the Millennium Development Goals (MDGs). Yet, compared with other countries in the Latin America and Caribbean (LAC) region, Honduras lags behind in growth and remains off track in terms of achieving the goal of halving poverty by 2015 (MDG 1). Without a significant acceleration in per-capita growth rates over the next decade, attaining the MDGs is likely to be very difficult because growth and MDG achievements reinforce each other. Improved health and educational outcomes can increase productivity, with positive synergies when service access improves simultaneously in different areas (health, education, water and sanitation). At the same time, growth and higher incomes can generate increased funding for services and raise service demand, creating a virtuous circle of growth and MDG achievement.

Improving service delivery is only one part of the challenge—it is also necessary to consider demand-side incentives and capabilities. In a stagnant economy with virtually no growth in per capita income, as Honduras has been in the last decade, large programmes aimed at expanding social services may not work as effectively as in a faster-growing economy. In fact, the need to finance investments in MDG-related services may crowd out investment and growth in other parts of the economy. Progress on the MDG front may also be slowed by the increasing marginal resource requirements as governments reach out to populations that are more difficult to reach physically due to geography (for example, populations residing in remote areas with underdeveloped infrastructure) and/or that are less capable of making use of services due to low incomes and a low level of initial MDG attainment. Inefficiencies in service delivery due to rapid scaling up may add to incremental resource requirements.

In this chapter, we explicitly consider the above mechanisms and, by using the MAMS framework that all country studies in this volume have used, provide estimates of the resources required to reach the MDGs and evaluate different strategies for their achievement. The chapter is structured as follows. The next section describes the current macroeconomic and MDGs performance in Honduras. A brief assessment of the forthcoming challenges for the expansion of social services and their (partial equilibrium) costs estimation are also provided. The third section describes the methodology and data. The subsequent section discusses alternative model-simulated scenarios. In particular, it contrasts a baseline simulation where Honduras continues on current trends and does not achieve the MDGs against a scenario where increased public social spending helps reach the full set of MDGs. The final section offers concluding remarks and policy recommendations.

Macroeconomic performance and existing progress towards the MDGs

Recent macroeconomic trends

Between 1990 and 2004, Honduras' real GDP grew at an average rate of 3.3 per cent per year, slightly faster than during the 1980s but barely above population growth. As shown in Table 9.1, this has resulted in virtually no improvement in real per-capita household consumption expenditure between 1990 and 2000. Growth in government expenditures, both recurrent and capital, has been constrained by the slow growth of the economy, current account financing needs and the public debt overhang. From the 1980s to 2004, total debt has hovered above 80 per cent of gross national income and servicing this debt cost about one third of total exports of goods and services. Thanks to the Highly Indebted Poor Countries (HIPC) initiative, the debt burden has lessened significantly after the country reached HIPC completion point in 2004. The debt situation is likely to continue improving, which should free up resources for the large infrastructure and social spending needs in order to meet the objectives of the Poverty Reduction Strategy (PRS) and the MDGs.

On top of this already limited room to manoeuvre, the government of Honduras also has had to respond to large adverse shocks such as the 1994 internal energy crisis[1], hurricane Mitch in 1998 and several cyclical declines in coffee prices. On the positive side, remittances sent by Hondurans working abroad have been a steadily increasing and important source of financing for the economy. In 2004, remittances represented about 10 per cent of GNI, up from the 4 per cent yearly average of the 1990s. The country has also joined the DR-CAFTA (Dominican Republic-Central American Free Trade Area) agreement with the US and the resulting increased integration with this important commercial partner is likely to provide increased export opportunities and potentially larger inflows of FDI.[2]

Table 9.1   Honduras: Macroeconomic performance, 1980-2004

	1980	1990	2000	2004
GDP at market prices (millions 2000 US$)	3,393	4,313	5,963	6,798
Household consumption per capita (units, 2000 US$)	680	633	652	714
Population (millions)	3.57	4.87	6.46	7.13
General government consumption (millions 2000 US$)	617	727	944	877
Gross investment, public sector (millions 2000 US$)	313	242	350	293
Period averages		1980-1990	1990-2000	2000-2004
GDP (growth rate)		2.4	3.3	3.3
Household consumption expenditure per capita (growth rate)		-0.7	0.3	0.6
Population (growth rate)		3.2	2.9	2.5
General government consumption (growth rate)		1.7	2.6	-1.8
Gross investment, public sector (growth rate)		-2.5	3.8	-4.4
General government Consumption (% of GDP)		13.5	11.3	13.5
Gross Investment, public sector (% of GDP)		7.7	8.3	5.8
Trade (% of GDP)		60.3	86.6	92.5
Agriculture, value added (% of GDP)		21.6	20.7	13.3
Total debt (EDT)/GNI		81.9	118.6	86.0
Debt service (TDS)/Exports of goods and services		26.9	26.8	12.0
Remittances received/GNI		0.6	3.9	10.0

Source: World Bank, World Development Indicators.

Table 9.1 further shows that Honduras openness has increased considerably, up to 90 per cent on average in 2000-04 from the already high average level of 60 per cent in 1980-90, and that at the same time, agriculture is becoming a smaller (but still relevant) share of the nation's GDP.

Progress towards the MDGs

Honduras is the third poorest country in LAC after Haiti and Nicaragua. In 2004, its per capita GDP reached a mere $952 (at constant 2000 prices), compared with $3,935 on average for the region as a whole. More than 64 per cent of the country's population lives below the national poverty line, while almost 45 per cent are in extreme poverty (Table 9.2). Measured on the basis of the international poverty line of $1 PPP per person, per day, the poverty headcount rate is 26 per cent in 2004. Although these poverty rates are high by both international and regional standards, it should be acknowledged that Honduras has made important strides towards poverty reduction since 1990, particularly when considering the rather anaemic pace of growth in per-capita income and consumption. This suggests that growth in Honduras, albeit slow, has been quite pro-poor over the last decade and half. The performance on other MDGs has been similarly encouraging (Table 9.2), although nearly all indicators remain substantially below the averages for LAC.[3]

Table 9.2   Honduras: Progress towards the MDGs

	Honduras		
MDG and related indicator	**1990**	**2004**	**2015 Target**[a]
MDG 1: People living on less than $1 (PPP) a day (% of population)	38	26	19
MDG 1: People living below the national poverty line (% of population)	84	65	42
MDG 2: Primary completion rate (% of relevant age group)[b]	65	76	100
MDG 4: Under-five mortality rate (per 1,000 live births)	59	31	24
MDG 5: Maternal mortality rate (per 100,000 live births)	280	108[c]	70
MDG 7a: Access to an improved water source (% of population)	73	82	87
MDG 7b: Access to improved sanitation facilities (% of population)	66	77	83

Source: Sistema de Información de la Estrategia para la Reducción de la Pobreza (SIERP); available at www.sierp.hn.
[a] These are the targets as defined in the UN Millennium declaration. The Government of Honduras, on the other hand, has set more or less ambitious targets for several indicators. For example, the water and sanitation coverage is to be expanded to 95 per cent of the population, significantly exceeding the MDG of improving access by one-half. Also, the child mortality rate target is set slightly above the MDG definition at 24 instances per 1000 live births.
[b] Corresponds to the net completion rate.
[c] 2000 value.

Several positive signs have been recorded for the education goal: the literacy rate among the young has increased from 79.7 per cent to 85.5 per cent between 1990 and 2001 and net enrolment rate for primary education reached 89.3 per cent in 2004. Additionally, no apparent gender gap is recorded in the data for primary education with boys and girls having almost identical access and completion rates. These positive trends are, however, not sufficient for the achievement of universal primary education completion.

Despite this progress, a number of studies question the quality of education received by many Honduran pupils and the efficiency public education spending. For example, World Bank (2001) cites a study assessing language and math skills in the third and fourth grades of education, where, out of twelve Latin American countries participating in that study, Honduras ranked last in language and next-to-last in mathematics. World Bank (2004) claims that recent expansion in public spending on primary education was accompanied by declining efficiency: even though spending on primary education per student increased from $89 in 1998 to $151 in 2002, two key education achievement indicators—the sixth grade completion rate and test scores—have been stagnant or decreasing over the same period. Finally, De Jong and others (2006) report that only 10 per cent of third-graders in Honduras attain proficiency in language and mathematics.

In health, the under-five mortality rate decreased from 59 to 31 per thousand live births and the infant mortality rate was reduced from 47 to 23 per thousand between 1990 and 2005-06. While data inadequacies do not permit a precise assessment of the evolution of maternal mortality, the available survey results suggest that considerable progress has been achieved: the maternal mortality rate was reduced from about 280 (per 100 thousand) in 1990 to around 108 in 2000.[4] The percentage of childbirths assisted by specialized personnel in health institutions follows a fluctuating but upward trend, rising from 45.6 per cent in 1990-91 to 61.7 per cent in the 2001. Although not large, there still exists a gap between the shares of urban (85.5 per cent) and rural (80.7 per cent) mothers receiving prenatal control. This gap is much larger for medically assisted child-births: in 2001, 82.4 per cent of the childbirths in the urban areas took place in institutions with specialized sanitary personnel, as opposed to only 37.5 per cent in the rural areas.

The observed improvements in health indicators can be attributed to various measures adopted to promote the delivery and efficiency of health services— such as programmes aimed at expanding ambulatory and hospital care and at strengthening the country's epidemiologic capacity to respond to emerging and other infectious diseases. Honduras has also initiated a programme to improve maternal-infantile health, which includes preparing medical protocols to regulate the sector delivering specialized maternal-infantile health services, the expansion of the services of the Integral Care to Childhood (*Atención Integral a la Niñez*) network, and the implementation of a programme for the monitoring and analysis of maternal and child deaths. However, additional progress is likely to require an increase in the coverage of currently under-served rural areas and the provision of more advanced (and more expensive) medical services administered by highly skilled health professionals. The rapid pace of reductions in infant and child mortality rates between 2001 and 2005-06 bodes well for the achievement of MDG 4, but continued progress is conditional on maintaining the recent growth of public health expenditures, which expanded at an annual average rate of 11.7 per cent between 1999 and 2005 (measured in constant lempiras). If this growth is not sustained, additional inroads in improving health outcomes are likely to be minor.

National coverage of the population with access to potable water increased from 73 per cent to 82 per cent between 1990 and 2004, while sanitation coverage increased from 66 per cent to 77 per cent. However, large disparities in coverage are observed across rural and urban areas, and even across large and smaller cities. In addition, Honduras faces serious challenges in reaching its ambitious targets for enhancing coverage given of the high population growth and the low efficiency of delivery mechanisms. According to official forecasts, reaching a 95 per cent coverage rate for water and sanitation in 2015 (a target which is above that set by the Millennium Declaration) means providing access to drinking water for an additional population of 2.6 million in total—1.2 million in rural and 1.4 million in urban areas—and supplying sanitation services to 3.5 million in total (of which 1.3 million would live in rural areas and the rest in urban ones). Although the size of the investments required is large, the government realizes the importance of starting these as soon as possible to start filling out existing gaps and taking advantage of the health and other benefits generated by universal access to these services.

How much will it cost to achieve the goals?

Concerned with the limited progress on many MDG indicators, the government of Honduras, in collaboration with civil society organizations and the international donor community, has commissioned a study to quantify the required additional resources and identify opportunities for increased efficiency in the allocation of public resources and external aid. In June 2004, a Consultative Group started planning and evaluating costs of programmes in six sectors: Education, Health, Agro-Forests, Water and Sanitation, Infrastructure, and Security and Justice. This Group also realized that no sector programme, no matter how comprehensive and well thought through, could succeed in a deteriorating economic environment and decided to include in the planning strategy some key cross-cutting issues, such as economic growth, macroeconomic management, trade and competitiveness, and decentralization and environmental management. The results of the various sector studies were merged in a single government document and its main costing estimates are summarized in Table 9.3.[5]

The first column of Table 9.3 shows the total recurrent and capital expenditures by the central government of Honduras in 2004 on the key MDG and infrastructure sectors. For the same year, their aggregate value represents almost 40 per cent of total government expenditure, and primary education and health are the sectors absorbing the largest shares of government resources. The third column represents the amounts the government should spend in 2015 if the sector plans designed to reach the targets of the MDGs and infrastructure plans were strictly followed; the rows labelled "Baseline" represent instead the amounts spent in a scenario where public MDG-related expenditure (in real terms) grows at the same rate as real GDP.[6] The fourth column shows the total amount of spending for the whole period. This total amount was estimated by sector experts and it is represented in 'real' values; that is, the costs were evaluated at constant prices in 2004 lempiras. These costs can thus be interpreted as the costs required for the expansion of the volume of services delivered by the public sector: this expansion is shown by the growth rates of the last column. The methods used to cost the required interventions and investments vary slightly for each sector, but mainly consist of an estimation of the additional

Table 9.3 Honduras: Estimates of required infrastructure and MDG-related expenditures (millions of 2004 lempiras, unless indicated otherwise)

	2004	2004 GE	2015	2004-2015	Gap	AYG
Infrastructure						
PRSP/MDG government						
Plan	2,219	9.2	6,693	69,528		16.3
Baseline	2,219	9.2	3,795	33,061	36,467	3.9
Primary education						
PRSP/MDG government						
Plan	4,978	20.7	14,528	149,396		15.6
Baseline	4,978	20.7	8,515	74,177	75,219	3.9
Health						
PRSP/MDG government						
Plan	3,733	15.5	11,101	102,282		13.1
Baseline	3,733	15.5	6,385	55,629	46,653	3.9
Water and Sanitation						
PRSP/MDG government						
Plan	690	2.9	1,658	18,927		13.1
Baseline	690	2.9	1,181	10,288	8,639	3.9

Source: Government of Honduras (2005) for the PRSP/MDG government plan, authors' estimates for the baseline as explained in the text.
Abbreviations: 2004 GE: 2004 as % of total government expenditure; AYG: Average yearly growth rate of expenditures.

demand due to the increased coverage rates and a growing population. The 'technology' of delivering services is assumed to be constant throughout the 10 years of the planning period and, further, possible economies (or dis-economies) of scale or externalities among investments are not considered.[7] Table 9.3 shows that the yearly growth rates required to reach the MDGs are considerable and tend to be similar across sectors. According to these estimates, a baseline growth rate of service delivery of 3.9 per cent per year would be well below what is required.

The figures in Table 9.3 only refer to required public spending. However, in the case of the key MDG-related service sectors, the contribution of private services is not very large. For example, World Bank (2004) shows that providers of private education account for 5 per cent to 10 per cent of total enrolment at the primary level, and less than 20 per cent of enrolment at the tertiary level.[8] Moreover, private schools are located almost exclusively in urban areas, implying that service delivery to the rural population is entirely public. Furthermore, most of private delivery of education serves the wealthier parts of the population.

Table 9.4 disaggregates the social spending figures of Table 9.3 by different types of inputs. The provisioning of general public infrastructure and drinking water and sanitation have a much higher investment component—more than 60

Table 9.4   Honduras: The structure of social spending on MDG-related services, 2004

		Expenditure		Employment	
		Millions of lempiras	**% of total**	**Thousands of workers**	**% of total**
Public infrastructure	Intermediates	685	31		
	Labour	114	5		
	Unskilled[a]	30	1	3.2	36
	Semi-skilled[b]	21	1	2.2	25
	Skilled[c]	63	3	3.5	39
	Investment	1,419	64		
	Total	2,219	100	8.9	100
Water and sanitation	Intermediates	96	14		
	Labour	168	24		
	Unskilled[a]	168	24	2.5	100
	Semi-skilled[b]				
	Skilled				
	Investment	427	62		
	Total	690	100	2.5	100
Health	Intermediates	965	26		
	Labour	2,625	70		
	Unskilled[a]	872	23	10.6	55
	Semi-skilled[b]	381	10	3.6	19
	Skilled[c]	1,372	37	5.0	26
	Investment	143	4		
	Total	3,733	100	19.3	100
Primary education	Intermediates	280	6		
	Labour	4,544	91		
	Unskilled[a]	1,216	24	16.4	27
	Semi-skilled[b]	1,514	30	21.8	36
	Skilled[c]	1,815	36	22.8	37
	Investment	154	3		
	Total	4,978	100	60.9	100

Source: SAM and MAMS for Honduras.

[a] Workers with incomplete secondary education.

[b] Workers with incomplete tertiary education.

[c] Workers with complete tertiary education.

per cent of total costs—than other social sectors. In contrast, recurrent spending, especially on labour inputs, is the major cost component in the delivery of education and health services.

The data in the "employment" column of Table 9.4 shows that unskilled workers (those who have not completed secondary education) form a large part of total employment in MDG-related sectors, even those usually considered to be relatively skill-intensive, such as education and health services. This could be part of the explanation of the low quality of service delivery and a reflection of the low performance on test scores of students, as observed earlier. Consequently, without substantial changes in the current input structure, it may be difficult for these sectors to produce the targeted outcomes. In particular, the existing low share of adequately trained teachers and health workers could signal likely shortages in the supply of such workers when scaling up MDG-related spending and could result in faster-than-average wage growth for skilled workers.

The costing approach summarized in Table 9.3, while providing detailed information on each sector, does not account, however, for important feedbacks and indirect effects captured in a general-equilibrium setting. In particular, the partial- equilibrium setting does not account for possible synergies across MDGs. Additionally, unit costs are most likely not constant. More likely, marginal costs may increase the closer one gets to achieving the MDG targets. Reaching two thirds or even three quarters of the relevant population may be relatively easy; however, getting further improvements in school completion rates or reduction of child mortality rates may become more costly as one gets closer to 100 per cent completion or when mortality is already low. The last uncovered fraction of the population usually are poorer, are harder to reach, live in remote communities, and much more may be required than a mere expansion of service supply to satisfy their needs. The MAMS model, as explained in Chapter 3, accounts for the likelihood of increasing marginal costs.

Model and data

Similar to the other studies in this volume, this chapter uses the *Maquette* for MDG Simulations (MAMS) model to provide a quantitative assessment of the economy-wide effects of alternative policies to achieve selected MDGs (see Chapter 3). MAMS does not explicitly track the progress of MDG 1 and we adopt the macro-micro approach explained in Chapter 2 (Appendix A2.1), according to which the labour market results from MAMS simulated scenarios are applied to the full distribution of household survey data using the micro-simulation methodology. The data for the micro-simulations come from the 2004 *Encuesta Permanente de Hogares de Propósitos Múltiples* (EPHPM) survey, which allows us to identify employment and wages by skill and sector. The microsimulation approach in this chapter allows for four main avenues of escaping poverty: moving from agricultural employment to non-farm activities where the wages tend to be higher, upgrading individual skills (through schooling), changes in relative wage changes, and an economy-wide income growth component that equally benefits all households.

The data requirements of MAMS are substantial. The previous section already mentioned the sources of information for the current degree of MDG achievement and the required expansion in public service delivery to reach the targets by 2015. However, many other data are needed to estimate and calibrate MAMS. These include a social accounting matrix (SAM) that provides a breakdown of public activities by the relevant MDG sectors (primary education, health, and so on) and the accounting framework of the model, detailed data on education including graduation, drop-out, and repetition rates by cycle, the volumes of workers and students at each education level, and various elasticity parameters. The following discussion briefly touches upon each of these data components.

The starting point to construct the SAM, along the lines of the accounting requirements of MAMS (see Chapter 3), was a macroeconomic SAM for Honduras at 2004 values, constructed by the authors from national accounts data. In order to disaggregate the SAM, we rely on various sources including detailed information on public expenditure by activity provided by the Ministry of Finance, wage data from the household survey (2004 EPHPM), trade and protection statistics from UN COMTRADE and UN TRAINS, and to a lesser extent an earlier 1997 SAM described in Cuesta (2004). The data on labour volumes comes from the household survey, while the data on stocks of students was obtained from the World Bank's database, EDSTATS. The repetition, graduation, and drop-out rates were obtained from background information for the education indicators published by the Honduran information system for the poverty reduction strategy, SIERP.

Since no econometric estimates are available for the key elasticities (MDG or otherwise) of MAMS for Honduras and their estimation is problematic due to data constraints, the MDG elasticities used in this chapter have been chosen from a range of values identified in other studies in this volume based on the authors' judgement. For example, the elasticity of MDG 4 (child mortality) with respect to a 1 per cent increase in household per capita consumption is approximately -0.4, while the elasticity of MDG 7a (access to clean water) with respect to a 1 per cent increase in household per capita consumption is 0.1. The non-MDG elasticities have been selected from a comprehensive review of econometric and CGE literature in Annabi and others (2006).

Although the lack of precise econometric estimates of these key elasticities likely introduces a degree of imprecision in the model results with respect to Honduras' reality, we believe this approach is justified for three main reasons. First, our elasticity values are within a plausible range (established in the existing CGE literature) and are close to the elasticities used in the other Central American country cases in this volume. Second, the conclusions of this study are not meant to be taken as definitive statements about the precise resource scale-up requirements to reach the MDGs in Honduras. Instead, the purpose is to highlight the relative importance of various determinants of MDG outcomes and, within a consistent economy-wide framework, discuss the relative merits of various sources of financing and the implications of a targeted pursuit of MDGs on the rest of the economy, as well as the several macroeconomic trade-offs involved. Third, moderate changes to the elasticities used in this chapter do not change any of the qualitative conclusions and do not have excessive impacts on the numerical results. Thus, while the exact quantitative findings of this study may be subject to revision if better elasticity estimates become available, the qualitative conclusions should remain applicable.

MDG simulations and results

Baseline scenario

Our baseline scenario defines a benchmark against which other scenarios will be compared. Under the assumptions, of this scenario real GDP per capita grows at 1.8 per cent per year—consistent with the World Bank, IMF, and Government of Honduras growth projections, but much faster than the 0.5 per cent average annual growth recorded over the 1990-2004 period (see Table 9.5).[9] No targeted MDG policies are implemented in the baseline scenario; instead, the level of government service provision in public infrastructure, water and sanitation, health, and education sectors is assumed to grow exogenously at 3.9 per cent per annum (the same rate as real GDP). Spending in the general government sector is also set to grow exogenously at the same rate, so that both public consumption and investment remain fixed as a share of real GDP throughout the model's time horizon (that is, 2004-15).

Additional government financing needs are determined by the required increases in current and capital expenditures on MDGs and the rest of the public

Table 9.5   Honduras: Macro variables in the baseline scenario, 2004-2015

Variable	Units	2004	2010	2015	Annual growth rate
Real GDP at market prices	(billions of LCU)	136	173.9	206.1	3.9
Private consumption	(% of GDP)	85	86	86	4.2
Government consumption	(% of GDP)	12	12	12	3.9
Investment	(% of GDP)	26	26	26	4.2
Private	(% of GDP)	21	21	21	4.2
Public	(% of GDP)	5	5	5	3.9
Exports	(% of GDP)	42	41	39	3.4
Imports	(% of GDP)	66	66	66	4.1
Real GDP per capita	(thousands of LCU)	18,972	21,420	23,186	1.8
Exchange rate	LCU per USD	1.00	0.99	0.97	-0.3
Foreign debt-to-GDP	(%)	68.2	23.6	21.0	
Debt service-to-exports	(%)	2.3	0.8	0.8	

Source: MAMS for Honduras.

sector. The balance between government income and current public spending is cleared by a flexible direct tax rate on household income. Because the skill intensity of the "commodities" produced by the public sector is higher than the economy-wide average (see Table 9.4) and demand for skilled labour grows faster than supply (the evolution of factor prices will be discussed in more detail below), the share of public expenditure in nominal GDP rises from 17 per cent in 2004 to 18.4 per cent in 2015. This requires an increase in direct tax revenue from 4.6 per cent to 5.9 per cent of GDP, accomplished via an increase in the direct tax rate from 4.1 per cent to 5.1 per cent. The fact that direct tax rates must rise in the baseline in order to maintain a constant share of public expenditure to real GDP thus limits the fiscal space available to the government for scaling up spending to meet the MDGs.

The evolution of foreign debt follows the forecast in the joint Debt Sustainability exercise by the World Bank and the IMF. The debt path takes into account the significant easing of Honduras' debt burden under the HIPC initiative, reducing the debt-to-GDP ratio by a factor of more than three. This also more than halves the foreign debt service obligations (as a share of exports), creating important fiscal space for the government's pursuit of MDG objectives. For simplicity, foreign grants are fixed at zero in the baseline.

A flexible foreign exchange rate assures equality between inflows and outflows of foreign currency. It should be noted that the assumption of a flexible exchange rate is not a good representation of the actual exchange-rate regime of Honduras, which has a managed (crawling) peg system controlled through a series of mini-devaluations. However, the distinction of fixed versus flexible exchange rates in the MAMS model is just a matter of convenience, since there is no money in the system and all prices are determined relative to a fixed *numéraire* (i.e., the consumer price index, CPI). Furthermore, the real exchange rate movements implied by the model are quite mild and are certainly within the historical range under the current peg system. In the baseline, the real exchange rate appreciates by approximately 3 per cent between 2004 and 2015, which is caused by shifts in consumer demand towards more manufactured and service goods which also have higher import intensities.[10]

Beyond the major macro indicators, the main variables of interest in the baseline are the levels of MDG attainment and the behaviour of the labour market. Largely due to the fact that the growth of social spending on MDGs falls short of the requirements identified by the sector studies commissioned by the Government of Honduras (2005), the education, health, and water/sanitation MDGs are not attained in the baseline (see Table 9.6). Comparing the MDG levels in 2015 with the targets listed in the fifth column of the table reveals that MDG performance under baseline assumptions varies across different goals: among the non-poverty MDGs, the biggest improvements (more than 60 per cent distance to target) are observed for the education goal. Progress towards

Table 9.6   Honduras: MDG achievement in the baseline scenario, 2004-2015

MDG indicator	Units	2004	2015	2015 target	Distance to target in 2015 (%)
Poverty headcount (npl)	(%)	65	58	42	28
Poverty headcount (ipl)	(%)	26	21	19	76
Primary completion rate	(%)	76	91	100	63
Under-5 mortality rate	(per 1,000 live births)	31	29	24	16
Maternal mortality rate	(per 100,000 live births)	108	102	70	17
Access to safe water	(%)	82	84	95	14
Access to sanitation	(%)	77	79	95	15

Source: MAMS for Honduras and authors' calculations for distance to target.
Abbreviations: npl: national poverty line; ipl: international poverty line of $1 (PPP) a day.

other goals is much more modest, with improvements in MDGs 4 and 5 covering only 16 per cent and 17 per cent of total distance to the MDG goals, respectively, while water and sanitation fare slightly worse at 14 per cent and 15 per cent of total distance to target.

Despite the acceleration in growth from the historical averages, the poverty targets—at both the national and the international poverty lines—remain elusive (the top two rows of Table 9.6).[11] The main reason growth in Honduras' baseline scenario is not more pro-poor is the widening inequality: the Gini coefficient rises by 0.7 base points to 0.599, while the Theil index increases by 2.3 base points to 0.716. This increase in inequality is at odds with the historical trend of declining inequality in Honduras and is driven by rising skill premiums, which causes the incomes of unskilled workers to rise less than the economy-wide average.[12] In order to explain these labour market dynamics, we need to consider impact of the progress in education on the labour markets.

The demographic distribution of Honduras is heavily skewed towards younger age groups—almost 45 per cent of the total population is 16 years old or younger. Any education policy aimed at keeping children in school and encouraging them to continue their education at the next level is bound to have large distributional and temporal effect on the labour force in Honduras—first, as enrolment, completion and continuation to the next education cycle rates rise, the relative share of unskilled labour will decline in favour of more skilled categories, and second, increasingly larger parts of the labour force will leave the labour market (to go to school) and return after having completed their education (see Table 9.7).

Due to the success of previous education policies, secondary school enrolment in Honduras is large relative to the stock of labour with completed secondary education (almost 70 per cent of semi-skilled employment in 2004). Furthermore, the improvements in primary education in the baseline scenario encourage more young adults to continue their education at the secondary level. The

Table 9.7   Honduras: Labour market dynamics in the baseline scenario, 2004-2015

	2004	**2015**	**Annual growth rate (%)**
Employment (thousands)			
Unskilled workers	1,787	2,372	2.6
Semi-skilled workers	492	666	2.8
Skilled workers	172	222	2.4
Labour incomes (thousands of LCU)			
Unskilled workers	23.5	26.8	1.2
Semi-skilled workers	54.5	64.6	1.6
Skilled workers	125.1	167.7	2.7

Source: MAMS for Honduras.

combination of these two factors causes semi-skilled labour to grow slightly faster than unskilled labour (Table 9.7). At the tertiary level, the base year rates of continuation from secondary school are low (around 15 per cent) and cannot rise very rapidly without additional financial infusions into the tertiary school system. This causes the stock of skilled workers (that is, those with some tertiary education) to grow at the slowest rate among the three educational groups, while demand for the services these workers provide rises much more quickly. As a result, wages of skilled workers grow faster than those of other workers. The upward pressure on wages of semi-skilled workers is mitigated by the fact that, over time, stronger increases of wages for jobs for semi-skilled and skilled workers creates additional incentives for students to continue their studies. This factor stimulates some additional growth in the supply of (semi-)skilled labour at the margin, but not sufficiently enough as to meet the growing demand for skills in the baseline scenario for Honduras.

MDG scenarios (with aid financing)[13]

Our second set of scenarios explicitly targets the attainment of MDGs 2, 4, 5, 7a and 7b through the expansion of service delivery in the primary education, health, water and sanitation, and public infrastructure. In order to target the MDGs, we use the growth rates in various categories of government expenditure provided by the sector studies as a starting point. These rates are subsequently adjusted by the model to account for cross-MDG synergies and other general-equilibrium effects. We assume a constant rate of improvement in the water and sanitation, health, and education targets, and use the information above to calculate the required volume of public expenditure necessary to attain these goals over the model horizon (2005-15). In the education sector, the growth rate of primary school expenditure is such that graduation rates reach 100 per cent by 2010,[14] while expenditure on secondary and tertiary schooling is roughly remains at baseline levels. Since the sector studies referenced in the earlier sections explicitly considered improvements in infrastructure as a key part of the government's MDG strategy, our MDG simulation also incorporates faster growth in public infrastructure spending. As a best-case benchmark scenario, we consider the possibility that all of the additional MDG expenditures are financed by foreign donors—that is, domestic taxes are fixed at the baseline levels and any budgetary shortfall is made up by flexible foreign grants. The MDG results and the government expenditure required to reach all but MDG 1 are shown in Table 9.8.

The results of the MDG scenario show that a large, sustained increase in government spending relative to the amount spent in the baseline is required in order to reach the targets by 2015. In all instances, the required growth in current spending is more than twice the baseline growth, and investment in various sectors needs to grow by more than three times the baseline rates.[15] At the same time, comparing the growth rates in government expenditure with the results of sector studies (see Table 9.3) reveals the importance of cross-MDG complementarities

Table 9.8 Honduras: Trajectory towards the MDGs and government spending in the MDG scenario, 2004-2015

MDG and spending indicators	Units	2004	2010	2015	Annual growth rate (%)
Poverty headcount (npl)	(%)	65		55	-1.4
Poverty headcount (ipl)	(%)	26		19	-3.0
Primary completion rate	(%)	76	93	100	2.5
Under-5 mortality rate	(per 1,000 live births)	31	28	24	-2.2
Maternal mortality rate	(per 100,000 live births)	108	92	70	-3.9
Access to safe water	(%)	82	88	95	1.3
Access to sanitation	(%)	77	86	95	2.0
Government consumption					
Primary education	(% of GDP)	3.6	6.0	4.4	7.7
Secondary education	(% of GDP)	1.4	1.2	1.2	3.9
Tertiary education	(% of GDP)	1.1	1.0	0.9	3.9
Health	(% of GDP)	2.6	3.4	4.3	10.3
Water and sanitation	(% of GDP)	0.2	0.3	0.4	12.9
Public infrastructure	(% of GDP)	0.6	0.9	1.5	15.1
Government investment					
Primary education	(% of GDP)	0.1	0.5	0.0	37.6
Secondary education	(% of GDP)	0.0	0.0	0.0	3.9
Tertiary education	(% of GDP)	0.0	0.0	0.0	3.9
Health	(% of GDP)	0.1	0.3	0.3	17.7
Water and sanitation	(% of GDP)	0.3	1.2	1.6	22.7
Public infrastructure	(% of GDP)	1.0	5.0	8.4	27.7

Source: MAMS for Honduras.

Abbreviations: npl: national poverty line; ipl: international poverty line of $1 (PPP) a day.

in assessing the costs of reaching multiple MDGs. In our modelling approach, spending on public infrastructure facilitates access to MDG-related services (and hence higher MDG achievement); therefore, lower sector-specific expenditures are needed with higher levels of infrastructure spending. Additionally, progress in the coverage of drinking water and sanitation exerts a positive influence on health and thus allows for savings in the production of health services; in turn, a healthier student population more easily achieves completion of educational cycles. For example, the growth rate of current spending on water and sanitation is lower than the required growth identified by the partial-equilibrium studies (compare the 12.9 per cent in Table 9.8 with the 13.1 per cent of Table 9.3). The required growth in spending on health, and to a larger extent that on primary education, is also significantly lower than the estimates of the sector studies— reflecting the positive "multiplier" effect of several cross-MDG synergies.

The education sector results deserve more detailed examination owing to the critical importance of the education system as a source of new labour market entrants. Because of the increased rates of enrolment, graduation, and continuation to the next education cycle, the 2015 labour force in the MDG scenario is 2 per cent below the 2015 level for the baseline scenario. Furthermore, the structure of the labour force also changes across the two scenarios: in the MDG simulation, the volume of unskilled labour reaches a level in 2015 which is 3 per cent below that of the baseline, while the stocks of semi-skilled and skilled labour are, respectively, 1.9 per cent and 1.8 per cent higher. The decrease in the number of unskilled workers is driven by the dynamics discussed in the earlier sub-section: as more children enter (and graduate) the secondary school system, fewer individuals enter the unskilled labour market either as out-of-system entrants (those who have never been to school) or secondary dropouts. As the supply of unskilled workers falls, returns to their labour rise (see Table 9.9).

At the same time, the pursuit of MDGs creates additional demand for the services of semi-skilled and skilled workers. This occurs through two channels. First, as mentioned earlier, MDG-related services are more skill-intensive than most other sectors of the economy, which raises the relative demand for skills when these sectors grow faster than the economy-wide average. Second, large inflows of foreign grants lead to faster growth in private income and consumption (as discussed in more detail below), which raises demand for more skill-intensive products which tend to have higher income elasticities. As a result, wage growth for semi-skilled and particularly for skilled workers accelerates significantly relative to the baseline (Table 9.9). In fact, the effects of the increased demand for skills turns out to be stronger than the supply-side effects, and the skilled-unskilled wage gap widens slightly between the baseline and the MDG achievement scenario (compare Table 9.9 with Table 9.7). At the same time, higher wages for semi-skilled and skilled workers also imply higher production costs for the economy as a whole, affecting macroeconomic performance.

The behaviour of the macro variables is summarized in Table 9.10. We have already mentioned that per capita GDP grows substantially faster than in the baseline scenario due to increased public spending financed by foreign grants. Higher private incomes (due to faster growth in real wages) translate into faster growth in private consumption and investment. As a consequence of large foreign grant inflows, the real exchange rate appreciates much more rapidly than in the baseline. While the real appreciation erodes the competitiveness of Honduran producers and reduces export growth by 1.1 percentage points per year, it also benefits consumers by making imports cheaper. Import growth is also bolstered by the fact that part of the intermediate inputs for the supply of MDG-related services tend to be more import-intensive than the economy-wide average (for example, infrastructure and water and sanitation are intensive in

Table 9.9   Honduras: Labour market dynamics in the MDG scenario, 2004-2015

	2004	**2015**	**Annual growth rate (%)**
Employment (thousands)			
Unskilled workers	1,787	2,301	2.3
Semi-skilled workers	492	679	3.0
Skilled workers	172	226	2.5
Labour incomes (thousands of LCU)			
Unskilled workers	23.5	30.2	2.3
Semi-skilled workers	54.5	73.9	2.8
Skilled workers	125.1	220.9	5.3

Source: MAMS for Honduras.

Table 9.10   Honduras: Macroeconomic performance under the MDG scenario, 2004-2015

Variable	Units	2004	2010	2015	Annual growth rate
Real GDP at market prices	(billions of LCU)	136	181.2	224.9	4.7
Private consumption	(% of GDP)	85	83	81	5.1
Government consumption	(% of GDP)	12	15	15	7.5
Investment	(% of GDP)	26	31	34	8.2
Private	(% of GDP)	21	21	21	5.5
Public	(% of GDP)	5	10	14	14.9
Exports	(% of GDP)	42	32	30	2.3
Imports	(% of GDP)	66	68	69	6.1
Real GDP per capita	(thousands of LCU)	18,972	22,321	25,296	2.7
Exchange rate	LCU per USD	1.00	0.89	0.86	-1.4
Foreign debt-to-GDP	(%)	68.2	19.3	15.9	
Debt service-to-exports	(%)	2.3	1.0	0.9	

Source: MAMS for Honduras.

the use of capital goods, which have higher import content than food products). Due to faster growth in public service provision, the share of government consumption in total absorption rises by one third relative to baseline scenario, while the share of public investment in total absorption doubles. At the same time, it should be noted that growth in public consumption and investment is significantly below the average growth in MDG services, reflecting the fact that government services not directly related to MDG production continue to grow at baseline rates.

A major general-equilibrium effect of improved primary education performance is the growth penalty of a smaller total labour force, at least during the transition phase when unskilled workers who would otherwise have entered the labour market stay in school.[16] Although per capita GDP grows faster than in the baseline scenario, it is significantly below what would be expected had the labour supply been growing at the baseline rates. Therefore, additional government education expenditure growth is necessary to offset the lower growth in consumption per capita. Obviously, a better educated labour force would contribute to stronger growth rates in the future. However, in the initial transition phase, Honduras is faced with an important trade-off similar to that faced by poor households who have to decide whether to send their young members to school and forgo their incomes or get them to work but deprive them of potentially higher earnings in the future.

Changes in private consumption, together with the labour market dynamics discussed in the preceding paragraphs, determine the effects of the foreign-grant-financed strategy of scaling up MDG-related spending on poverty and inequality. As shown in Table 9.8, the poverty headcount at the national poverty line falls by 3 percentage points, while the incidence for the one-dollar-a-day poverty declines by 2 percentage points. The poverty reduction is sufficient to meet MDG 1 as defined through the international poverty line, but not in the case of the national poverty line when the reduction falls 42 per cent short of the target covered in this scenario. The degree of poverty reduction is mitigated by the increase in income inequality caused by the wage dynamics described earlier: the Gini coefficient rises by 0.5 percentage points relative to the baseline scenario (in 2015), while the Theil index increases by nearly 2 percentage points. Figure 9.1 sheds more light on this issue by plotting a growth incidence curve for Honduras under the baseline and the MDG achievement (foreign-grant financed) Scenarios. While most of the increase in inequality takes place in the richest part of the distribution (as expected from the results of Table 9.9), all but the poorest parts of the population experience less than the average income gains. Thus, although the growth is beneficial to the extreme poor, it is hardly pro-poor overall.

The financing requirements to reach the MDGs are very large. Foreign grants—the only means of financing the pursuit of MDGs in the current scenario—rise

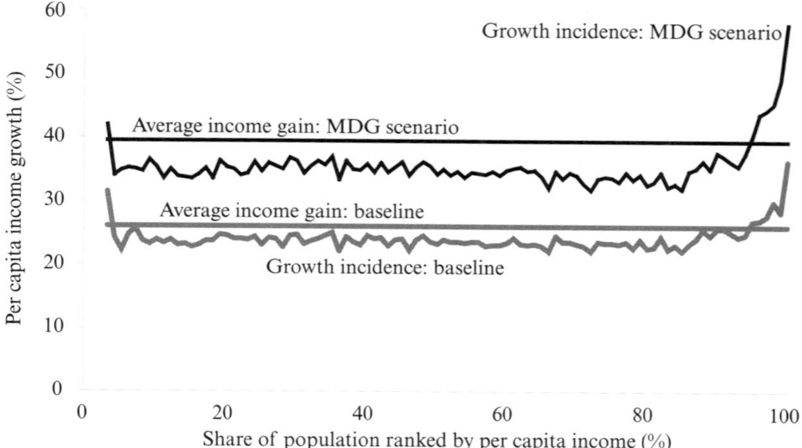

Figure 9.1 Honduras: Growth incidence curve for the baseline and MDG scenarios
Source: MAMS for Honduras and microsimulations based on the 2004 EPHPM.

to 14.2 per cent of GDP by 2015. In per capita terms, this increase translates to $215 for each resident of Honduras. Over the entire model horizon (2004-15), Honduras is likely to require $13.7 billion in order to finance its pursuit of MDGs through foreign grants.

Pursuit of individual MDGs and the role of cross-complementarities

The results and discussion in the previous sections have emphasized the fact that cross-MDG complementarities are a key feature of MAMS. This aspect follows the existing empirical evidence that access to clean water and sanitation improves health indicators and that improved health is beneficial for completing primary school. It also implies that simply costing each intervention and adding up the individual components could lead to serious double-counting. We have seen evidence of this in the previous section, where the required growth rates in MDG service provisions were lower than those suggested by partial equilibrium sector studies. In order to assess the effects of ignoring these complementarities, this section discusses three sensitivity-type simulated scenarios—each of them targeting one set of MDGs (water and sanitation, health, and education) without deliberatively targeting the achievement of others. In each scenario, public infrastructure growth is maintained at the level required for MDG achievement (that is, infrastructure spending grows at the same rate as the full MDG scenario).

Table 9.11 shows the results of implementing a scenario where only MDGs 7a and 7b are targeted. Despite the fact that growth in government expenditure categories other than infrastructure and water-sanitation is kept at baseline

Table 9.11   Honduras: MDG performance and government spending when targeting MDG 7a-b only, 2004-2015

MDG and spending indicators	Units	2004	2010	2015	Annual growth rate (%)
Poverty headcount (npl)	(%)	65		56	-1.4
Poverty headcount (ipl)	(%)	26		19	-2.9
Primary completion rate	(%)	76	81	94	1.9
Under-5 mortality rate	(per 1,000 live births)	31	30	29	-0.5
Maternal mortality rate	(per 100,000 live births)	108	103	97	-0.9
Access to safe water	(%)	82	88	95	1.3
Access to sanitation	(%)	77	86	95	2.0
Government consumption					
Primary education	(% of GDP)	3.6	3.3	3.1	3.9
Secondary education	(% of GDP)	1.4	1.3	1.2	3.9
Tertiary education	(% of GDP)	1.1	1.0	1.0	3.9
Health	(% of GDP)	2.6	2.4	2.3	3.9
Water and sanitation	(% of GDP)	0.2	0.3	0.4	13.0
Public infrastructure	(% of GDP)	0.6	1.0	1.6	15.1
Government investment					
Primary education	(% of GDP)	0.1	0.1	0.1	3.9
Secondary education	(% of GDP)	0.0	0.0	0.0	3.9
Tertiary education	(% of GDP)	0.0	0.0	0.0	3.9
Health	(% of GDP)	0.1	0.1	0.1	3.9
Water and sanitation	(% of GDP)	0.3	1.2	1.7	22.7
Public infrastructure	(% of GDP)	1.0	5.3	8.9	27.7

Source: MAMS for Honduras.
Abbreviations: npl: national poverty line; ipl: international poverty line of $1 (PPP) a day.

levels, significant improvements are seen across all MDGs. In education, 74 per cent of total distance to target is covered, compared with 63 per cent in the baseline scenario. For MDGs 4 and 5, the comparable achievements are 27 per cent and 28 per cent versus 16 per cent and 17 per cent in the baseline scenario. Finally, the poverty headcount rates based on, respectively, the national and international poverty lines, are respectively 2.8 per cent and 1.6 per cent lower than in the baseline scenario. The achievements in terms of the provision of water and sanitation services remain the same as in the full MDG scenario due to the fact that no other MDG enters the production function for water and sanitation. However, public spending in water and sanitation must grow at a slightly faster rate than in the full MDG achievement scenario because the spill-over effects from increased household consumption per capita are smaller due to slower overall economic growth.

Table 9.12 presents a second set of results, for the scenario where we target only the health MDGs. Because the expenditures required to achieve the health targets exceed those needed for improved water and sanitation coverage (and consequently more foreign financing is obtained), the poverty results improve slightly from the MDG 7a-b simulation. Education performance is also improved over the previous simulation, due to the more direct impact of health on primary completion rates. However, both current and capital expenditure in the health sector have to rise more rapidly in this scenario than in the full MDG achievement, since the positive spill-over effects of reaching the water and sanitation goals are now forgone. In fact, total expenditure on health over the 2004-15 period in this scenario is 2 per cent above what would be required under the full MDG achievement scenario (equivalent to a 2.5 billion lempiras increase in costs).

Table 9.12   Honduras: MDG achievement and government spending when targeting MDGs 4-5 only, 2004-2015

MDG and spending indicators	Units	2004	2010	2015	Annual growth rate (%)
Poverty headcount (npl)	(%)	65		55	-1.4
Poverty headcount (ipl)	(%)	26		19	-2.9
Primary completion rate	(%)	76	81	94	1.9
Under-5 mortality rate	(per 1,000 live births)	31	28	24	-2.2
Maternal mortality rate	(per 100,000 live births)	108	92	70	-3.9
Access to safe water	(%)	82	83	85	0.3
Access to sanitation	(%)	77	79	81	0.5
Government consumption					
Primary education	(% of GDP)	3.6	3.2	3.0	3.9
Secondary education	(% of GDP)	1.4	1.3	1.2	3.9
Tertiary education	(% of GDP)	1.1	1.0	1.0	3.9
Health	(% of GDP)	2.6	3.6	4.5	10.6
Water and sanitation	(% of GDP)	0.2	0.2	0.2	3.9
Public infrastructure	(% of GDP)	0.6	0.9	1.6	15.1
Government investment					
Primary education	(% of GDP)	0.1	0.1	0.1	3.9
Secondary education	(% of GDP)	0.0	0.0	0.0	3.9
Tertiary education	(% of GDP)	0.0	0.0	0.0	3.9
Health	(% of GDP)	0.1	0.3	0.4	18.1
Water and sanitation	(% of GDP)	0.3	0.3	0.3	3.9
Public infrastructure	(% of GDP)	1.0	5.2	8.7	27.7

Source: MAMS for Honduras.

Abbreviations: npl: national poverty line; ipl: international poverty line of $1 (PPP) a day.

In our final scenario only the education MDG is targeted (see Table 9.13). Even though the education goal does not have any explicit links to any of the other MDGs, the other indicators show improvements over the seen in the baseline scenario due to the positive influence of expansion in infrastructure. Poverty reduction is slightly less pronounced in comparison with the health-only scenario because the total amount of foreign-grant inflows is lower, which in turn limits the growth boost of additional MDG spending. Unlike earlier simulations, in the scenario that targets only the achievement of MDG 2, the growth of public spending on education is actually *less* than what is observed in the full MDG scenario. This occurs despite the loss of positive externalities from health and despite the "growth penalty" of slower growth in the labour force due to improvements in the education system. The main reason is that the education system itself produces most of the factors required for improved

Table 9.13   Honduras: MDG performance and government spending when targeting MDG 2 only, 2004-2015

MDG and spending indicators	Units	2004	2010	2015	Annual growth rate (%)
Poverty headcount (npl)	(%)	65		56	-1.3
Poverty headcount (ipl)	(%)	26		19	-2.8
Primary completion rate	(%)	76	93	100	2.5
Under-5 mortality rate	(per 1,000 live births)	31	30	29	-0.5
Maternal mortality rate	(per 100,000 live births)	108	103	98	-0.9
Access to safe water	(%)	82	84	85	0.3
Access to sanitation	(%)	77	79	81	0.5
Government consumption					
Primary education	(% of GDP)	3.6	6.1	4.5	7.6
Secondary education	(% of GDP)	1.4	1.3	1.2	3.9
Tertiary education	(% of GDP)	1.1	1.0	1.0	3.9
Health	(% of GDP)	2.6	2.4	2.3	3.9
Water and sanitation	(% of GDP)	0.2	0.2	0.2	3.9
Public infrastructure	(% of GDP)	0.6	0.9	1.6	15.1
Government investment					
Primary education	(% of GDP)	0.1	0.5	0.0	37.3
Secondary education	(% of GDP)	0.0	0.0	0.0	3.9
Tertiary education	(% of GDP)	0.0	0.0	0.0	3.9
Health	(% of GDP)	0.1	0.1	0.1	3.9
Water and sanitation	(% of GDP)	0.3	0.3	0.3	3.9
Public infrastructure	(% of GDP)	1.0	5.2	8.8	27.7

Source: MAMS for Honduras.

Abbreviations: npl: national poverty line; ipl: international poverty line of $1 (PPP) a day.

educational attainments (semi-skilled and skilled workers), while the demand for skills is lower than in the full MDG scenario due to less spending on other skill-intensive MDG-related sectors. As a result, the education system is able to re-orient its "production structure" more towards more productive tertiary-educated employees—enough so that the total costs are lower even though the unit costs of hiring workers with tertiary education is higher.

Alternative financing scenarios

A crucial feature of the MDG scenario presented in the previous section is the assumption that foreign grants will provide all of the financing required to scale up public spending for the MDGs. Given the very large expenditure increases needed to meet the goals, one might ask whether Honduras is likely to secure the necessary amounts of foreign aid and, if not, what effects this might have on the MDGs and the rest of the economy. To test the sensitivity of our results to alternative financing closures, we explore two alternative financing scenarios: one where the required financing is raised through domestic taxation and one where the financing needs are met through domestic borrowing. We do not consider a foreign borrowing scenario—as most other country studies of this volume do -as it will drive up the external debt-to-GDP ratio to likely unsustainable levels.[17] In both of the alternative financing scenarios below, we continue to scale up government spending such that MDGs 2, 4, 5, 7a-b are simultaneously met by 2015.

We begin by allowing the government to vary household direct tax rates in order to obtain the necessary financing.[18] Since the required increase in public spending in this scenario is financed by increasing the tax rate on household income, slower growth in private consumption translates into less progress in poverty reduction. The 2015 poverty headcount at the national poverty line is at 61.9 per cent (3.5 percentage points higher than the projected headcount rate in the baseline scenario), while the proportion of population living on less than $1 PPP per day is 23.2 per cent (2.4 percentage points above the baseline scenario and 4.3 percentage points above the simulated estimate in the foreign grant-financed MDG scenario). At the same time, the indices of inequality (Gini and Theil) remain largely unchanged in this scenario compared with the simulation where financing is obtained through foreign grants. Thus, slower aggregate income growth is the main reason for less poverty reduction.

The behaviour of the main macro variables is summarized in Table 9.14. Although the annual growth rate of real GDP is 0.2 percentage points lower than in the foreign grants scenario, it is still 0.6 percentage points above the baseline scenario. However, private consumption and investment are penalized much more severely. In order to raise the necessary financing, the direct tax rate must rise to 19 per cent in 2015, up from 5 per cent in the baseline. This increases the share of direct taxes in GDP to 22 per cent and results in significant crowding out of private spending by the public sector: household consumption grows almost a full percentage point slower than in the baseline scenario, and the same is true of private investment. Less growth of private consumption also dampens the demand for imports, which results in much less appreciation of the real exchange rate (both compared to the foreign grants and baseline scenarios).

Table 9.15 shows the behaviour of macroeconomic variables under the flexible domestic borrowing closure. In this scenario, the crowding out occurs first and

Table 9.14   Honduras: Macroeconomic performance when scaled-up MDG spending is financed by domestic taxes, 2004-2015

Variable	Units	2004	2010	2015	Annual growth rate
Real GDP at market prices	(billions of LCU)	136	179.4	220.2	4.5
Private consumption	(% of GDP)	85	76	73	3.3
Government consumption	(% of GDP)	12	16	17	7.7
Investment	(% of GDP)	26	29	32	6.8
Private	(% of GDP)	21	18	17	3.2
Public	(% of GDP)	5	11	15	14.9
Exports	(% of GDP)	42	39	38	3.9
Imports	(% of GDP)	66	63	63	4.4
Real GDP per capita	(thousands of LCU)	18,972	22,093	24,773	2.5
Exchange rate	LCU per USD	1.00	0.99	0.99	-0.1
Foreign debt-to-GDP	(%)	68.2	22.7	19.9	
Debt service-to-exports	(%)	2.3	0.8	0.7	

Source: MAMS for Honduras.

Table 9.15   Honduras: Macroeconomic performance when scaled-up MDG spending is financed by domestic borrowing, 2004-2015

Variable	Units	2004	2010	2015	Annual growth rate
Real GDP at market prices	(billions of LCU)	136	172.0	196.0	3.4
Private consumption	(% of GDP)	85	87	89	4.0
Government consumption	(% of GDP)	12	17	19	7.6
Investment	(% of GDP)	26	19	18	0.2
Private	(% of GDP)	21	8	1	-19.7
Public	(% of GDP)	5	11	17	14.9
Exports	(% of GDP)	42	38	36	2.1
Imports	(% of GDP)	66	63	64	3.3
Real GDP per capita	(thousands of LCU)	18,972	21,179	22,050	1.4
Exchange rate	LCU per USD	1.00	0.97	0.94	-0.6
Foreign debt-to-GDP	(%)	68.2	23.2	21.5	
Debt service-to-exports	(%)	2.3	0.9	0.9	

Source: MAMS for Honduras.

foremost on the investment side, as evidenced by the negative growth rate of private investment through the model horizon. As a result, real GDP growth is a full 0.5 percentage points per year lower than in the baseline scenario and, due to overall slower growth in the economy, private consumption growth is also below baseline rates. Domestic debt stocks rise substantially, from 25 per cent of GDP in the baseline scenario (in 2015) to 130 per cent of GDP. Such an increase in domestic debt is unlikely to be feasible in Honduras; in addition, this simulation assumes that the Honduran government will be able to continue paying the relatively low 3.1 per cent interest rates on its bonds regardless of the size of domestic debt. In reality, this condition is unlikely to hold, which means that either additional borrowing or higher taxes would be required in order to finance the higher borrowing costs.

Conclusions and policy recommendations

Despite significant progress on many MDG indicators, Honduras is unlikely to reach the MDG targets for poverty reduction, primary education, and water and sanitation by 2015. Furthermore, unless the recently observed rapid increase in the funding of health services is sustained, the health MDGs are also likely to remain elusive. In order to attain the full set of MDG targets, Honduras needs to expand its social spending significantly, and complement greater public investment in human development with policies aimed at accelerating economic growth.

The general equilibrium approach of this chapter explicitly considers the mechanisms through which service delivery and other determinants of MDG achievements interact, capturing the roles of the demand and supply sides of MDG services. Using the MAMS model, the potential advantages and disadvantages of various strategies for pursuing MDG attainment have been assessed. Our simulation results show that significant cost savings can be realized from pursuing the MDGs together, rather than one or two at a time, due to the presence of important cross-complementarities across targets. In addition, investment in infrastructure is required to support growth and create a positive environment for MDG achievement.

An additional advantage of using the MAMS framework is the ability to analyze competition over scarce resources between MDG services and other sectors as well as the interactions between MDG service provision and the rest of the economy via the labour market. Our simulations show that the focused pursuit of the MDGs considerably raises the demand for semi-skilled and skilled workers, and success is critically dependent upon the ability of the education system to deliver the needed graduates. Although the wages for all categories of workers are likely to rise with the expansion in MDG service delivery, skilled and semi-skilled workers are likely to gain much more than the unskilled.

The application of the MAMS model for Honduras has also enabled assessing the role of alternative MDG financing scenarios on the macro aggregates and the government budget balance. Under the assumption that MDG financing is entirely covered by flexible foreign aid, the per-capita level of foreign grants would need to increase to $215 by 2015 and the total cumulative amount of required aid would total $13.7 billion over 2004-15. As a consequence of these large inflows, the real exchange rate would appreciate much more strongly than under a baseline scenario, eroding the international competitiveness of Honduran exports. Although this might be unproblematic if foreign aid could continue to flow infinitely into the future, it may not be realistic to make the economy vulnerable to a possible sudden cessation of aid which could set off a difficult adjustment period as entry and exit of firms into export markets tends to be asymmetric.

Despite the risks of such Dutch-disease effects, our simulation results show that foreign-grant financing of MDG achievement is likely to be the best strategy for Honduras. We cannot assess how likely Honduras is to obtain all of the needed resources from foreign donors. However, given that it just recently reached HIPC completion point, it is unlikely to be able to borrow the required funding (and even if it could, the stock of foreign debt would skyrocket to 92 per cent of GDP). Raising the resources needed to fund the MDG strategy domestically could generate an important trade off: while the non-poverty targets are still likely to be reached, poverty reduction is much smaller—in 2015, the headcount rate (at the national poverty line) would be 1 percentage point higher compared with the baseline scenario if financing is obtained through domestic borrowing and 3.5 percentage points higher if the funds are raised through increases in direct taxes. Furthermore, raising the funds through domestic borrowing implies taking on a tremendous domestic debt burden (130 per cent of GDP), which is unlikely to be sustainable or even feasible to raise in domestic capital markets. Our results imply that Honduras should attempt to raise the resources domestically only if it is unable to attract foreign donors, and then be aware this could go at cost of lesser growth and poverty reduction.

Acknowledgements

The chapter is the result of team work and benefits from extensive discussions and inputs by Carolina Diaz-Bonilla, Pablo Flores, Hans Lofgren, Shuo Tan, Hans Timmer and Dominique van der Mensbrugghe. It also draws in some parts on previous work by the above team members. The authors are grateful to Marco V. Sánchez and Rob Vos for their helpful comments on earlier drafts of this chapter.

Notes

1   The country is highly oil dependent and the recent sustained increases in oil prices have strained government finances and do not bode well for the future.
2   There are plenty of reasons to be cautious about DR-CAFTA's potential to provide increased export opportunities for Honduran producers. One reason is that the overall level of US protection faced by Honduran exporters is very low, and the agreement primarily locks in the existing CBA (Caribbean Basin Initiative) and GSP (Generalized System of Preferences) preferences rather than open new US sectors for competition. In addition, one of the sectors likely to experience the most marked increase in import competition is non-export crops, which is the largest employer of farm labour in Honduras. This is likely to depress growth of farm wages and reduce the pace of poverty reduction in rural areas. On the other hand, increased investment inflows could result in new opportunities and facilitate transition to higher value-added activities. For a more detailed discussion of the economy-wide consequences of DR-CAFTA accession for Honduras, see Medvedev (2008).
3   For a comparison between Honduras' MDG indicators and the region's, see Table A2.1 in Chapter 2 of this volume.
4   Surveys aimed at measuring maternal mortality rates were administered in 1990 and 1997, and the national statistical institute (INE) estimated the rate for the year 2000.
5   Government of Honduras - Grupo Consultativo, "Avanzando en la planificacion sectorial de mediano plazo. Plan Pluriennal de Ejecución de la ERP", Tegucigalpa, Honduras, May 2005.
6   The macro assumptions of the model, including baseline growth, will be discussed in more detail below.
7   For details on the sectoral estimates see Government of Honduras (2005).
8   However, private schools account for approximately half of enrolment at the secondary level.
9   The GDP growth projections are obtained from the Joint IDA/IMF Debt Sustainability Analysis completed in 2006.
10   Demand for manufacturing and services grows faster than demand for agriculture mainly because the income elasticities of the former are above those of the latter.
11   All poverty estimates are the result of microsimulation analysis, as discussed in the previous section. In order to evaluate poverty at the international poverty line of $1 at PPP, we took the monthly poverty line ($32.74 in 1993 prices at PPP exchange rates) and converted it into a local currency equivalent by multiplying it by the consumption PPP exchange rate and the ratio of the consumer price index (CPI) in 2004 to the CPI in 1993.
12   Labour markets are assumed to be strictly segmented by skill. Within the same skill level, labour markets are characterized by full factor mobility across activities (sectors) such that a single economy-wide, skill-specific wage clears the market. The labour market closure used in this chapter assumes no change in the degree of resource utilization, or a fixed rate of unemployment. On the one hand, this assumption may be reasonable given that the official unemployment rate in Honduras has been fluctuating around 4 per cent over the last five years. On the other hand, however, unofficial estimates place the unemployment rate as high as 28 per cent, in which case the assumption of an unchanged unemployment rate would be much less realistic. Real wages in Honduras have been stable over the same period (Gindling and Terrell, 2006), which provides indirect evidence of significant labour market rigidities. In this case, unless we expect significant institutional improvements that make the Honduran labour market more competitive

(not very likely given the historical performance of the economy, particularly in the baseline scenario), the fixed unemployment rate assumption seems appropriate.

13   Other financial options will be discussed further below.

14   This requirement is due to the length of the primary education cycle and the definition of MDG 2. If the target is defined as reaching (close to) 100 per cent primary school completion in 2015 and the length of the primary education cycle is 6 years, achievement of MDG 2 implies that 100 per cent of children of primary school age must enter the first grade in 2010 and complete grades 1 through 6 at 100 per cent rates by 2015.

15   Note that investment growth in education is reported for the 2004-10 period, since the primary education system is assumed to reach its full potential by then and investment spending in the 2011-15 period is directed only towards maintaining the 2010 ratio of capital stock per student (rather than increasing the capital stock per student, as is the case during the 2004-10 period)..

16   The model version used here does not allow for changes in labour force participation rates between 2004 and 2015. As wages for unskilled workers rise (because unskilled labour becomes scarcer—see Table 9.9 and the accompanying discussion) more unskilled workers may choose to enter the labour force. However, this effect could be mitigated by difficulties in finding employment, which could include formal barriers to labour mobility (such as prohibitive hiring costs), specificity of human capital required for certain tasks, and location challenges (e.g. moving from remote rural areas to cities).

17   Financing the pursuit of MDGs through foreign borrowing would require the foreign debt-to-GDP ratio to rise to 92 per cent in 2015. This is roughly equivalent to Honduras' debt burden in 2000, shortly after its entry into the HIPC initiative.

18   Also the growth rates of public consumption and investment (in real terms) do not change with the choice of financing as long as full MDG achievement is imposed.

References

Annabi, Nabil, John Cockburn, and Bernard Decaluwé (2006). "Functional forms and parametrization of CGE models." MPIA working paper 2006-04, Poverty and Economic Policy (PEP) network.

Cuesta, José (2004). "The 1997 Social Accounting Matrix (SAM) for Honduras", Institute of Social Studies, The Hague. February (mimeo).

De Jong, Niek, Arjun Bedi, Juan Ponce and Rob Vos (2006). "Result-oriented Budgeting for Education: The Cases of Bolivia, Honduras and Nicaragua", Evaluation of Poverty Reduction Strategies in Latin America, Thematic Report 2005, The Hague and Stockholm: Institute of Social Studies and Swedish International Development Agency (SIDA) (http://www.iss.nl/Cross-cutting-themes/PRSP/Informes-temáticos)

Gindling, T. H. and Katherine Terrell (2006). "Minimum wages, globalization and poverty in Honduras", Discussion Paper 2497, Institute for the Study of Labour, Bonn.

Government of Honduras (2005). "Avanzando en la planificación sectorial de mediano plazo. Plan Pluriennal de Ejecución de la ERP", Grupo Consultativo, Tegucigalpa, Honduras, May.

Medvedev, Denis (2008). "Preferential Liberalization and Its Economy-Wide Effects in Honduras", World Bank Policy Research Working Paper 4537, Washington, DC: World Bank.

World Bank (2001). "Honduras Public Expenditure Management for Poverty Reduction and Fiscal Sustainability", Washington, D.C.: World Bank.

__________ (2004). "Honduras Development Policy Review: Accelerating Broad-Based Growth", Washington, D.C.: World Bank.

10
Mexico

Araceli Ortega and Miguel Székely

Introduction

The commitment to reach the Millennium Development Goals (MDGs) is one of the few issues on which a broad consensus has emerged in Mexican society in recent years. An initial report on the MDGs was presented in early 2004 as part of a joint effort on the part of the Government of Mexico and the United Nations Development Programme (UNDP). This report was discussed extensively by many stakeholders, including both chambers of Congress, the state governments, the municipal governments, and the executive branch of the federal government. This appears to have yielded three key results. For the first time in many years, a shared vision has emerged regarding the medium-term objectives the country should aim for. In addition, broad agreement was reached on the need to pursue the MDGs, independent of the political moment and the six-year electoral cycles marked by each change of government. Finally, the need to take action on several fronts was acknowledged, with the participation of all three levels of government and all three branches of government, to ensure the goals will be achieved.

This chapter seeks to contribute to the consolidation of the MDGs in Mexico as an instrument for planning and evaluating public policies, identifying some of the actions that can help ensure they are achieved by 2015. To that end, the quantitative impact of public policies aimed at achieving the MDGs is estimated using a computable general equilibrium model known as MAMS (see Chapter 3). To adequately estimate the impact on poverty, this model is supplemented with a microsimulation technique (see Chapter 2, Appendix A2.1). This methodological approach permits to evaluate the feasibility and effectiveness of alternative policy scenarios to achieve the MDGs, in order to derive recommendations for further public action.

Although Mexico has achieved some of the MDGs ahead of the 2015 deadline and has as yet to attain others, the analysis is important for two reasons.

First, the pace of progress is not yet satisfactory in some areas, specifically in reducing infant and maternal mortality. Therefore, identifying specific scenarios in which the health goals could be achieved is valuable for future planning and allocation of public budgets. Second, while Mexico has made substantial progress towards at least six of the eight MDGs, this does not guarantee that all will be achieved in a timely manner. Any drawback from the degree of economic stability and growth observed in recent years will slow progress towards the MDGs or could even roll back the gains made to date.

To be consistent with the other country studies in this publication, the effort in this chapter will be focused on the goals of poverty reduction, total coverage and completion of primary education, reductions in maternal mortality and under-five child mortality, and expanded coverage of drinking water supply and basic sanitation services. Four more sections are included for that purpose. The next section compares the macroeconomic situation and poverty and inequality in Mexico from 1990 to the most recent year for which information was available at the time of elaborating the study, and briefly describes progress made towards the MDGs. The following section describes some aspects of the application of the modelling methodology using Mexican data. Subsequently, in the fourth section, a series of scenarios are analysed that were simulated to identify the extent to which public spending needs to be scaled up to accelerate progress towards attaining the MDGs, and how the new spending could be financed and the effect that each financing strategy would likely have on the Mexican economy. Finally, the last section presents the conclusions and policy recommendations.[1]

The Mexican economy until the mid-2000s

Comparing economic and social progress between the years 1990 and 2004 provides an encouraging picture as far as progress towards the MDGs is concerned.[2] The macroeconomic context seemed favourable, a series of reforms were introduced that have not necessarily resulted in a further increase in income inequality, and notable gains were observed in the accumulation of human capital and in reducing inequality in access to social services. Nonetheless, as will be observed further on, far from being a period of continuous improvement, the Mexican economy experienced a series of abrupt fluctuations, causing the degree of poverty reduction to be much less than otherwise might have been expected.

The macroeconomic environment

As illustrated in Table 10.1, real per capita GDP grew 23.0 per cent from 1989 to 2004. Inflation fell from 19.7 per cent to 5.6 per cent, the real exchange rate appreciated by 19 per cent, the interest rate fell from 45.0 per cent to 7.1 per cent, and social spending as a share of GDP rose from 6.1 per cent to 11.0 per cent.

At first glance, this macroeconomic context appears to be favourable for reducing both income inequality and poverty. First, it is well-known that inflation tends to hurt the poor more, as they are less able to protect their monetary income and assets from the erosion entailed in a sustained increase in prices. In contrast, high-income groups have access to financial services that enable them to maintain the real value of their assets. A reduction of inflation on the scale observed would thus create a less adverse environment for the poor. Second, since low-income groups tend to depend more on wage labour than the wealthier sectors, an appreciation of the exchange rate (as observed in Table 10.1) would increase their income situation as it is associated with a higher average real wage. Third, a reduction in the interest rate generally benefits net debtors, and it is well known that the greater one's income, the less one will depend on credit, and the greater the likelihood of becoming a net creditor. Therefore, it may be expected that such a substantial decline in interest rates will benefit low-income groups relatively more. Fourth, if social spending is adequately targeted, even if partially, an increase as seen during the first half of the 2000s should be associated with lower levels of poverty.[3] One would also expect that the higher levels of economic growth observed would have allowed for reductions in poverty, even if the relationship between economic growth and inequality is not obvious.[4]

Table 10.1 includes information for 1984, since the differences with respect to this year clearly reflect that since the early 1980s, Mexico has been characterized by enormous macroeconomic volatility and instability. Indeed, as observed in Figure 10.1, the 1984-89 period presents a totally different picture. In this period there was economic contraction, a major devaluation, stagnant social spending, and a high and rising debt-to-GDP ratio. Even though there was lower inflation and, in 1989, a slight appreciation of the real exchange rate, the context was less favourable than that of most of the period from 1989 to 2004 (with the exception of the currency crisis of 1994-95, of course). Figure 10.1 also shows that the volatility and economic recession of the 1984-89 period coincided with contractions in social spending, whereas from 1989 to 2004, with the exception of the brief period of instability around 1994, economic stability predominated and there was a sustained increase in social spending.

A breakdown of public spending by sector makes it possible to verify that spending on public education, health, and poverty reduction programmes has closely followed the trend of total social spending (see Table 10.2). Taxes are a main source of government finance, though total tax revenues remained rather stable as a share of GDP. Income tax revenue, which accounts for the largest share of total taxes, has remained at levels below 5.5 per cent of GDP since 1993, while total tax revenue, not including exports, has remained below 12 per cent (see Figure 10.2).

Table 10.1   Mexico: Overview of socio-economic indicators for the 1984-2004 period

Variables	1984	1989	2004	Percentage change 1989/2004	Effect on inequality[a]
Macroeconomic indicators					
Per capita GDP (baseline 2002)	$52,730	$50,216	$61,574	23%	?
Inflation (annual change in CPI) (%)	59.2	19.7	5.6	-72%	-
Index of real exchange rate	80.2	101	82.0	-19%	-
Real interest rate (Cetes at 28 days)	61.6	45	7.1	-84%	-
Social spending / GDP (%)	6.5	6.1	11.0	80%	-
External debt / GDP (%)	37.8	35.4	12.0	-66%	?
Structural reform indicators					
Index of reforms in Latin America	0.34	0.40	0.57	43%	?
Index of reforms in Mexico	0.29	0.41	0.55	38%	?
Labour reform in Mexico	0.36	0.33	0.30	-10%	-
Financial liberalization in Mexico	0.19	0.43	0.77	78%	?
Trade liberalization in Mexico	0.62	0.87	0.84	-3%	-
Privatization in Mexico	0.00	0.40	0.27	-33%	-
Tax reform in Mexico	0.28	0.34	0.38	12%	?
Indicator of inequality: years of schooling by income deciles					
I	2.32	2.82	4.08	45%	1.26
II	3.10	3.65	4.71	29%	1.06
III	3.49	4.43	5.40	22%	0.97
IV	3.61	4.79	5.95	24%	1.16
V	4.24	5.71	6.72	18%	1.01
VI	4.94	6.18	7.06	14%	0.88
VII	5.96	6.73	7.86	17%	1.13
VIII	7.16	7.94	8.63	9%	0.69
IX	8.06	9.05	10.15	12%	1.10
X	9.52	11.19	12.78	14%	1.59

Source: Based on data from: the National Household Income and Expenditure Survey (ENIGH) of 1984, 1989, 2004; the National Institute of Statistics, Geography, and Informatics (INEGI); the Ministry of Finance and Public Credit (SHCP); Banco de México; and Lora and Barrera (1997) and Lora (2001).

[a] In the case of years of schooling by income deciles, this column shows the absolute difference between 1989 and 2004.

Structural reform policies undertaken since the early 1980s and deepened from around 1990 have transformed the Mexican economy and have had an impact on income distribution. The second panel of Table 10.1 shows the value of a series of indices of reform developed by Lora and Barrera (1997) and Lora (2001). According to these indices, the reforms in Mexico increased 90 per cent towards greater market orientation from 1984 to 2004. Much of this shift was pushed following the intensification of the reform process from 1989. This degree of market liberalization is noteworthy if one considers that the average increase in the degree of market reforms in Latin America was 69 per cent during the same period. The repercussions for income distribution and poverty are not obvious, and, in fact, these depend on the specific type and area of reform.

The general index of reform is an average of five indices in the areas of labour, finance, commerce, privatization and taxation. The impact of the reforms in

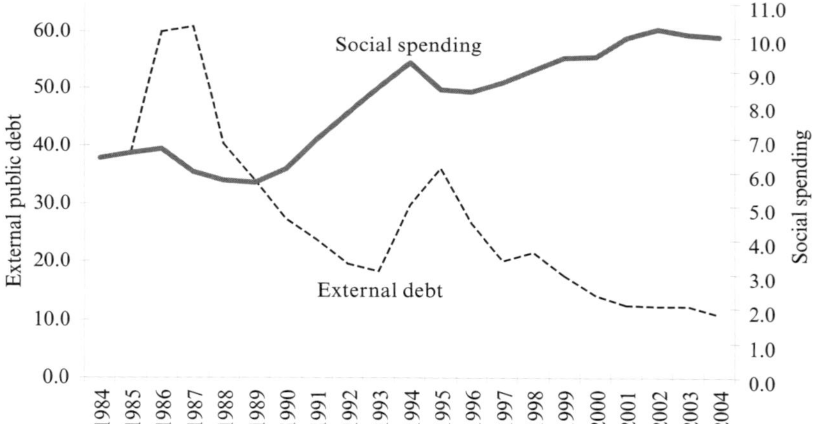

Figure 10.1 Mexico: External public debt and social spending, 1984-2004 (Percentage of GDP)
Source: SHCP, Centre for Studies of Public Finances.

Table 10.2   Mexico: Executed public sector budget by programmes, 2004-2006 (Percentage of GDP)

Item	2004	2005	2006[a]
Total	17.2	17.7	15.4
Social development	10.1	10.4	9.6
Education	3.8	3.8	3.6
Health	2.4	2.7	2.5
Social security	2.2	2.1	2.0
Urban development, housing and regional development	1.4	1.3	1.1
Drinking water and sewerage	0.1	0.1	0.1
Social assistance	0.3	0.3	0.3
Other	7.1	7.3	5.8

Source: Federal public budget for 2004 and 2005, and Budget of outlays of the Federal Government for 2006.

[a] Approved budget as authorized by Congress (Honourable House of Representatives).

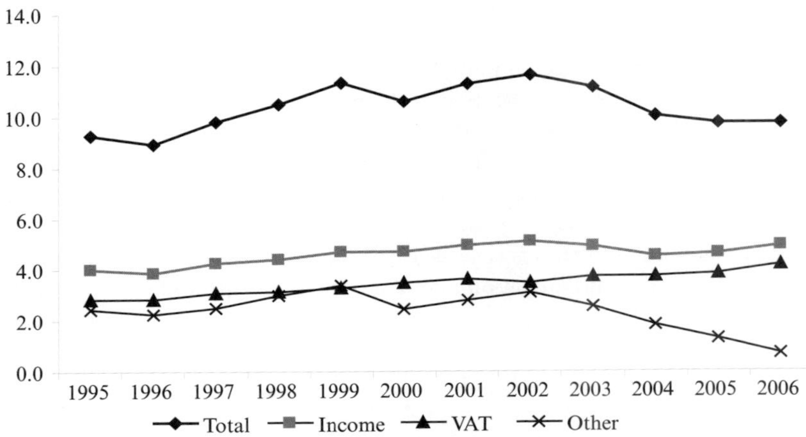

Figure 10.2 Mexico: Total tax burden and main sources of tax revenue, 1995-2006 (Percentage of GDP)

Source: Based on the data base of the SHCP, the statistical office of the Ministry of Finance.

these areas on inequality and poverty is not obvious a priori, since they set in motion a series of favourable and adverse effects, whose net impact depends on the specific conditions and the context of their implementation. In the case of Mexico, the three most important reforms in terms of intensity and repercussions for the well-being of the population are financial liberalization, trade liberalization and privatization.[5]

Given the impact of these reforms on the wage differentials between workers with different education levels, one may expect that differences in years of schooling across income strata are indicative of how the welfare effects are distributed. The third panel of Table 10.1 shows the average number of years of schooling of income earners in each decile of the income distribution. It can be seen that the absolute number of years of schooling of those in the top 10 per cent increased more than for any other decile between 1989 and 2004. The second largest increase was for those in the poorest decile. In relative terms, however, gains in schooling have been greater for the lower income deciles between 1989 and 2004. Indeed, the bottom five deciles have proportional increases greater than the rest, with a 45 per cent increase in the poorest decile. In other words, the distribution of education improved in relative terms, and this might suggest that forces were at play that tended to favour a reduction of inequality and poverty in general.

Inequality and poverty

As shown in Table 10.3, between 1989 and 2004, the income share of the richest decile of the population fell, while that of the rest, but especially that of the

Table 10.3 Mexico: Inequality and poverty indicators, 1984-2004

Indicator	1984	1989	2004	Change 1989/2004[a]
Income share of the poorest 10%	1.4	1.3	1.4	7.7
Income share of deciles 2 to 5	15.7	14.7	15.6	6.1
Income share of deciles 6 to 9	43.4	40.3	42.5	5.5
Income share of the richest 10%	39.5	43.7	40.5	-7.3
Per-capita monthly income of the 10% poorest[b]	266	260	358	37.7
Per-capita monthly income of the richest 10%[b]	7,253	8,828	10,311	16.8
Proportion of per-capita income of the richest 10% with respect to the poorest 10%	27.3	34.0	28.8	-15.3
Number of years for the income of the poorest 10% to converge to the observed income level of the richest 10%[c]	68	73	70	
Gini coefficient	0.43	0.47	0.46	0.0
Percentage of persons in food poverty (extreme)	22.5	22.7	17.3	-5.4
Percentage of persons in income poverty (moderate)	53.0	53.5	47.0	-6.5
Millions of persons in food poverty	16.9	19.0	18.3	-0.7
Millions of persons in income poverty	39.8	44.7	49.6	4.9

Source: Székely (2005b).

[a] Represents the percentage change except for the last five indicators (Gini coefficient and poverty incidence) for which the absolute change is shown.

[b] Constant 2002 pesos.

[c] In a scenario in which the economy grows by 5% annually.

poorest 10 per cent, increased. This led to a 15 per cent reduction in the income gap between these two extremes. Nonetheless, the Gini coefficient remained practically constant in the same period due to shifts in other parts of the income distribution.

As for poverty, the percentage of people in extreme poverty fell by 5.4 percentage points to 17.3 per cent between 1989 and 2004 (see Table 10.3). Moderate poverty fell by 6.5 percentage points in the same period. Nonetheless, due to the population growth observed in those years, the absolute number of people in extreme poverty remained almost constant, whereas the number of those in moderate poverty rose by almost five million.

In the previous period (1984-89), inequality had increased considerably and the number of people living in poverty increased. Nonetheless, despite increasingly favourable macroeconomic conditions during 1989-2004, the degree of poverty was limited, and, indeed, deceiving. The 23 per cent increase in real GDP per-capita that was achieved during the period could not prevent an increase in the absolute number of poor.

These results can be explained by the fact that instead of experiencing sustained and stable growth, the economy remained highly volatile and, during the downturns, this instability had a more adverse effect on the poor (Ortega and Székely, 2006). These negative effects were not fully offset during the upturns either through income growth or higher social spending.

The high economic volatility and instability that Mexico experienced during 1984-96 was detrimental for progress towards the MDGs. In contrast, the greater economic stability and growth from 1996 until 2008 has allowed for greater progress, as shown below. If these conditions can be maintained, achieving most of the MDGs by 2015 would seem feasible.

Progress towards the MDGs

Mexico has made significant progress towards the MDGs. This has been insufficient in some areas, though, in particular with respect to the targets for reducing child and maternal mortality.

According to the available information, Mexico prematurely achieved the goal of reducing extreme poverty by half (MDG 1). The percentage of the population that lives on less than one dollar a day at purchasing power parity (PPP) fell from 10.8 per cent in 1989 to 4.1 per cent in 2004. However, the international yardstick for measuring extreme poverty is of little relevance to Mexico, as the given poverty line would not be sufficient to cover even basic food needs in the country. When using the official national threshold for food poverty, the target would be to reduce extreme poverty from 22.7 per cent in 1989 to 11.4 per cent by 2015. Using a linear projection towards this target, food poverty should have been brought down to 16.3 per cent by 2004. According to the official estimates, food poverty incidence had fallen to 17.3 per cent by that point in time; one percentage point short of the target.

Poverty and economic growth are strongly correlated. Between 1982 and 1995, real GDP growth averaged only 1.3 per cent per year, implying negative growth in per capita terms. In this period, the incidence of moderate poverty increased from 59.6 per cent in 1989 to 69.6 per cent in 1995, with most of the increase attributable to the crisis of 1995. In the subsequent period from 1997 to 2004, GDP growth averaged 3.4 per cent, contributing to the reduction of the moderate poverty rate to 41.1 per cent by 2004. If the economic policies are successful in maintaining growth stable at this pace, Mexico should be able to meet the food poverty target by 2015.

In education, the biggest challenge is ensuring that all students enrolled in primary school also complete the cycle on time; in other words, to achieve a 100 per cent completion rate. The goal of universal coverage in primary education was practically attained by the end of the 2003-04 school year, when the net enrolment rate reached 99.6 per cent. By 1990, coverage was already over 95 per cent. It will be difficult to increase school enrolment further, given that the remaining 0.4 per cent of the population in primary school age is found in remote and difficult-to-reach localities.[6] The officially recorded rate of primary school completion was close to 90 per cent in 2003-04.[7] Nonetheless, according to the projections by the Ministry of Public Education, Mexico would not reach the target of 100 per cent by 2015.

Achieving the target of bringing the child mortality rate down to 14.7 per 1,000 live births (MDG 4) and that of maternal mortality to 22 per 100,000 live births (MDG 5) by 2015 are probably the greatest challenges for Mexico's MDG agenda. In 1990, there were 44.2 deaths among children under the age of five per 1,000 live births, and though the rate had fallen to 25 in 2003, this progress is well short of the target. By 2003, the child mortality rate should have been reduced to 28 if a gradual and linearly declining trend towards the target was followed. However, the rate of reduction has slowed since 1995 and progress in the 2000-03 period was less than that of earlier trends. As Ortega and Székely (2006) show, the same applies for the pace of reduction of infant mortality (mortality of children under one year), which accounts for most of the under-five child mortality.

There are also shortfalls in the degree of reduction in the maternal mortality rate. This is largely explained by inequalities in access to health services and other unmet social needs affecting some regions of Mexico, mainly those in the south of the country. Maternal mortality fell by 26.7 per cent between 1990 and 2003, reaching 65.2 deaths per 100,000 live births. The delays observed are the result of limited progress during the 1990s. Indeed, maternal mortality fell by 1.2 deaths per year between 1990 and 1995, while it increased by 2.08 deaths per year during 1995-2000. Between 2000 and 2003, maternal mortality resumed its decline, now at a pace of 2.5 fewer deaths per 100,000 live births per year, yet short of the reduction of 2.7 per year required to meet the 2015 target.

MDG 7, which reflects the aspiration of ensuring environmental sustainability, includes a large number of targets. For this study, however, we restrict ourselves to assessing the progress made towards the targets to half both the percentage of the population without access to drinking water (7a) and that without access to basic sanitation (7b) between 1990 and 2015. Coverage of the population with access to drinking water increased from 75.4 per cent in 1990 to 89.4 per cent in 2003, thus reducing the proportion of the population without this service to 10.6 per cent.[8] The coverage of the population with access to basic sanitation also increased in recent years, although it continues to be substantially less than that of drinking water. Total sanitation coverage was 77.3 per cent in 2003, which is 15.8 percentage points more than in 1990 and benefitting 31 million more people who gained access to the service. These gains show that achieving both targets by 2015 is within reach. Nonetheless, this progress does not mean that sustainable management of water resources is guaranteed. It is endangered by the overexploitation of aquifers and the pollution of rivers and lakes caused by the discharge of urban and industrial waste. Therefore, the most important challenge is to attain those goals without degrading the aquatic ecosystems and their environmental services.[9]

Scenario simulation methodology

A few important conclusions can be drawn from the two preceding sections. While there has been satisfactory progress towards some of the MDGs, more recent trends suggest that there is no guarantee that all of them can be attained by 2015. Any deviation from the relatively stable macroeconomic context of the late 1990s and early 2000s would mean not only a slowdown, but could even imply a backtracking on earlier progress. Attaining the targets for reducing child and maternal mortality, however, will be a challenge even if stable economic growth can be sustained.

In order to identify the conditions under which the goals considered above could be achieved, various policy scenarios were simulated using the computable general equilibrium model known as MAMS. The methodological aspects of this model are discussed at length in Chapter 3. The model-based analysis should facilitate an improved public debate in Mexico as to the trajectory the country could follow in the future and how this would translate into progress towards the MDGs, going beyond assessments based on mere linear projections from past trends.

The empirical estimation of MAMS for Mexico draws mainly on information organized in a Social Accounting Matrix (SAM), though in addition to this values for a range of other key parameters and elasticities need to be obtained. The SAM was constructed using 2003 as the base year, based on information from the System of National Accounts and economic censuses provided by the national statistical office, INEGI, as well as data from the Ministry of Education, the Ministry of Public Health, Banco de México, the Ministry of Finance (SHCP), and estimates from Székely (2005a), among others. The information was systematized to construct the SAM in accordance with the accounting structure of MAMS, and also drawing on the methodology described in Lee-Harris (2002) to reconcile data sources and achieve accounting balances.[10] As required by MAMS, those sectors directly related to the MDGs were identified based on their service provider (public and private).[11]

The macroeconomic aggregates used in the model are obtained from the System of National Accounts of Mexico for the 1990-2003 period and from a series of other sources identified in Ortega and Székely (2006). These authors also report on the procedures they followed to compile and estimate the key elasticities of the model. Ortega and Székely estimated income elasticities of consumption demand using the theoretical specification of the linear expenditure system (LES) proposed by Stone (1954). A SURE model specification was used to calculate the elasticities empirically. Elasticities for the substitution in the demand for domestically-produced goods and imports in response to changes in relative prices were obtained econometrically following specifications as in Kapuscinski and Warr (1996) and using the ordinary least squares estimation procedure.

Constant elasticities of transformation determining shifts in the shares of production destined to exports and the domestic market in response to changes in relative prices were estimated using an error correction model, which provided the better fit. Most of the elasticities associated with the determinants of the MDGs were estimated using information from INEGI and the ministries of health and education. The values for some elasticities were defined on the basis of ad-hoc assumptions, because of data constraints, but with the magnitudes all within the range consistent with a feasible model solution that enabled the generation of plausible trends for the MDG indicators.[12] Finally, the elasticity of private savings with respect to per-capita household income was taken from Attanasio and Székely (2001).

Policy scenarios for attaining the MDGs

For the baseline scenario, key exogenous variables are set in line with recent observed trends. Subsequently, 12 policy scenarios were run to assess the requirements of public spending for attaining the MDGs. These scenarios were simulated for achieving either one or two MDG targets at a time and for all of the targets to be achieved simultaneously, all under alternative financing options. In the baseline scenario, the default macroeconomic closure rules set for MAMS were used (see Chapter 3). Accordingly, any government financing gap is assumed to be covered by raising direct-tax rates. This closure rule is changed under the alternative financing scenarios whereby increased public spending is financed through either domestic or external public borrowing. In these scenarios, the direct-tax rate is kept fixed.

Prospects for increasing completion rates in primary education

Substantial progress has been made in improving access to primary schooling, with enrolment rates reaching near 100 per cent in 2003-04. Considerable room exists, however, for improving completion rates in primary education, which averaged 90 per cent in 2003-04. In the scenarios simulated with MAMS, the target for primary education is to reach a completion rate of 100 per cent by 2015.

As shown in Figure 10.3, this target is not quite met under the baseline scenario assumptions. These results are consistent with 'business-as-usual' projections of the *Secretaría de Educación Pública* (SEP), though the results generated in the MAMS baseline scenario are somewhat better after 2010.[13]

Policy options for reducing child and maternal mortality

To reduce under-five child mortality by two-thirds, the target for MDG 4, an additional effort is needed as the target would not be met at the rate of reduction of the observed trend and that of the baseline scenario (Figure 10.4). According to the scenario in which only MDG 4 is targeted, public spending on health services would need to increase by 61 per cent from 2003 to 2015 (or by 5.1 per cent per year). The additional spending would also contribute towards meeting the target set for reducing maternal mortality (Figure 10.5). The maternal mortality target would be reached ahead of the child mortality, as improved health services have a greater impact on reducing the risk of maternal mortality relative to that on child mortality (see Ortega and Székely, 2006).

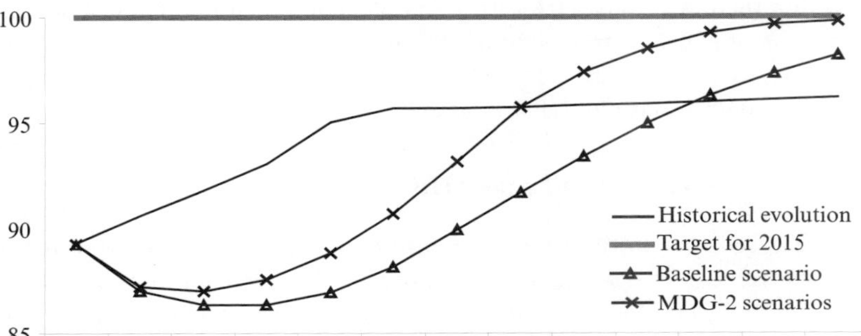

Figure 10.3 Mexico: Historical and simulated evolution of completion rates in primary education, 2003-20151[a]

Source: MAMS for Mexico and SEP.

[a] From 2004 the official trend represents a projection made by the SEP. The MAMS-based trends are the results for the baseline scenario and the MDG scenarios that target only the attainment of MDG 2. The trend of the primary completion rate in primary education is the same in the MDG-2 scenarios, independent of the financing strategy.

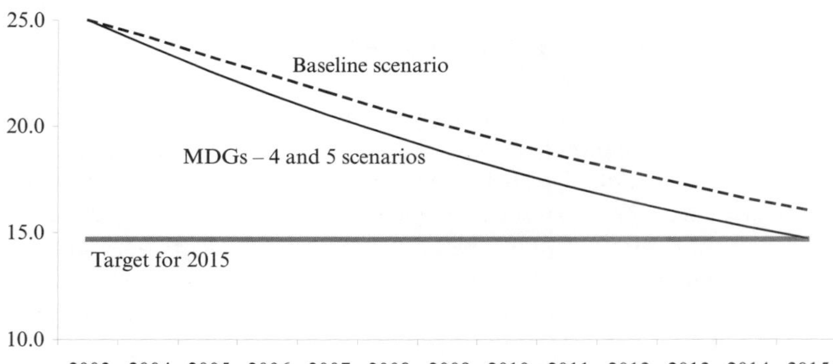

Figure 10.4 Mexico: Simulated evolution of child mortality per 1,000 live births, 2003-2015[a]

Source: MAMS for Mexico.

[a] The simulated trends refer to the baseline scenario and the MDG scenarios in which only the targets for child and maternal mortality are achieved. In these latter cases, the trend of the indicator is the same, independent of the financing strategy.

Policy options to increase access to drinking water and sanitation

The official target for the MDG for improving access to drinking water was reached by Mexico in 2003. A more ambitious and relevant goal would be to extend this service to 95 per cent of the population by 2015. Figure 10.6 shows that sustaining existing growth of public spending on water and sanitation would suffice to meet this more ambitious target for drinking water supply coverage.

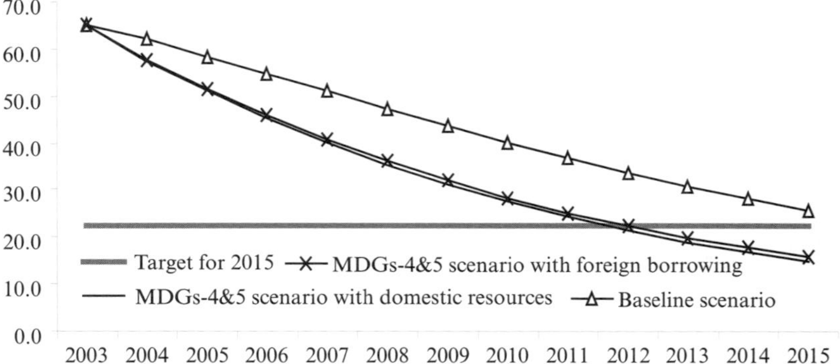

Figure 10.5 Mexico: Simulated evolution of maternal mortality per 100,000 live births, 2003-2015[a]

Source: MAMS for Mexico.

[a] The simulated trends refer to the baseline scenario and the MDG scenarios in which only the targets for child and maternal mortality are achieved. In these latter cases, the trend of the indicator is the same, independent of the financing strategy.

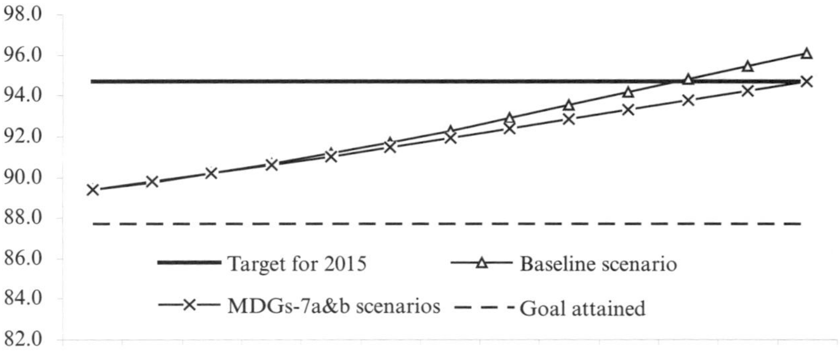

Figure 10.6 Mexico: Simulated evolution of the percentage of the population with access to drinking water, 2003-2015[a]

Source: MAMS for Mexico.

[a] The simulated trends refer to the baseline scenario and the MDG scenarios in which only the targets for drinking water and sanitation are achieved. In these latter cases, the trend of the indicator is the same, independent of the financing strategy.

Such a scenario would involve a 30 per cent increase in spending on drinking water and sewerage services between 2003 and 2015. With somewhat less spending on drinking water supply, the target would also be met, but not until 2015.

As in the case of drinking water services, the pace of expansion of sewerage services has been greater than what would be needed to achieve the international target for 2015. Even though the target of 79.1 per cent was not yet met by 2008, the target could be reached ahead of time by 2013 at the baseline rate of improvement (Figure 10.7).

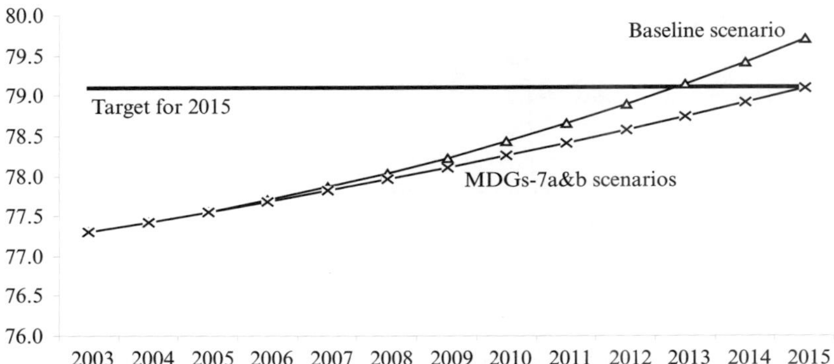

Figure 10.7 Mexico: Simulated evolution of the percentage of the population with access to basic sanitation, 2003-2015[a]

Source: MAMS for Mexico.

[a] The simulated trends refer to the baseline scenario and the MDG scenarios in which only the targets for drinking water and sanitation are achieved. In these latter cases, the trend of the indicator is the same, independent of the financing strategy.

Public spending and economic feasibility of achieving the MDGs

The feasibility of achieving the MDGs will depend on the rate of economic growth and adequacy of government revenues. According to the simulations with MAMS for Mexico, an annual rate of GDP growth of 3.5 per cent on average between 2003 and 2015 would not be sufficient to reach all MDGs, while increased government revenues would be needed in order to finance the additional public spending required to meet the MDGs.

Table 10.4 shows the public spending requirements as a percentage of GDP. Only the results of the baseline scenario and of the scenario in which the MDGs of reducing under-five child mortality and maternal mortality—which are those most in need of resources—are presented. One can deduce that, on average, public spending would have to increase approximately 5 per cent of GDP per year with respect to the baseline scenario in order to achieve MDGs 4 and 5. This holds in the cases when the additional spending is financed through direct taxes or domestic borrowing.[14] As can be observed, it is secondary care

Table 10.4   Mexico: Required government spending in the baseline scenario and the MDGs 4&5 scenarios with domestic resource mobilization, 2003-2015 (percentage of GDP)

	2003	2003-2005	2005-2010	2010-2015	2003-2015	2015
Baseline scenario						
Current spending on education	3.52	3.51	3.52	3.47	3.50	3.40
Current spending on health	2.23	2.22	2.23	2.20	2.21	2.20
- Type 1 health service[a]	0.20	0.20	0.20	0.19	0.20	0.19
- Type 2 health service[b]	0.72	0.71	0.72	0.71	0.71	0.69
- Type 3 health service[c]	1.32	1.31	1.32	1.30	1.31	1.28
Current spending on water and sanitation	0.03	0.03	0.03	0.03	0.03	0.0
Current spending on other public infrastructure	0.38	0.38	0.38	0.37	0.38	0.40
Current spending on other government services	5.41	5.40	5.41	5.33	5.37	5.30
Investment in education	0.01	0.01	0.01	0.01	0.01	0.00
Investment in health	0.00	0.00	0.00	0.00	0.00	0.00
Investment in water and sanitation	0.23	0.24	0.27	0.32	0.29	0.30
Investment in other public infrastructure	9.92	9.26	7.93	4.10	6.49	0.60
Investment in other government services	0.01	0.01	0.01	0.01	0.01	0.00
MDGs-4&5 scenarios with domestic resource mobilization[d]						
Current spending on education	3.52	3.50	3.47	3.34	3.42	3.30
Current spending on health	2.23	3.11	5.98	10.61	7.45	13.40
- Type 1 health service[a]	0.20	0.30	0.53	0.94	0.66	1.18
- Type 2 health service[b]	0.72	1.00	1.92	3.41	2.39	4.31
- Type 3 health service[c]	1.32	1.80	3.53	6.26	4.40	7.91
Current spending on water and sanitation	0.03	0.03	0.03	0.03	0.03	0.0
Current spending on other public infrastructure	0.38	0.38	0.37	0.36	0.37	0.40
Current spending on other government services	5.41	5.38	5.32	5.13	5.25	5.00
Investment in education	0.01	0.01	0.01	0.01	0.01	0.00
Investment in health	0.00	0.00	0.01	0.00	0.00	0.00
Investment in water and sanitation	0.23	0.23	0.27	0.31	0.28	0.30
Investment in other public infrastructure	9.92	9.22	7.81	3.99	6.39	0.60
Investment in other government services	0.01	0.01	0.01	0.01	0.01	0.00

Source: MAMS for Mexico.

[a] Primary health services, including those provided through social welfare programmes.

[b] Intermediate health services, including medical and dental clinics, as well as nursing and obstetric services.

[c] Specialized health services, including hospitals, sanatoria, clinics, maternity clinics, and blood banks.

[d] Domestic resource mobilization refers to raising direct taxes or borrowing domestically.

(hospitalization) and tertiary care (specialty care) that put the most pressure on public spending.

To increase the likelihood of attaining the mortality targets it will be necessary to implement a fiscal reform that increases government revenues such that the capacity for investment in public health services goes up by 60 per cent over the next 12 years. Figure 10.8 shows that in the scenarios in which the mortality targets are attained, in isolation or accompanied by increased public spending towards the attainment of the goals for primary education and water and sanitation, the income tax burden would need to climb from 5.5 per cent to just over 22 per cent of GDP. This is a rather tall order and alternatives to the raising income taxes must be considered.

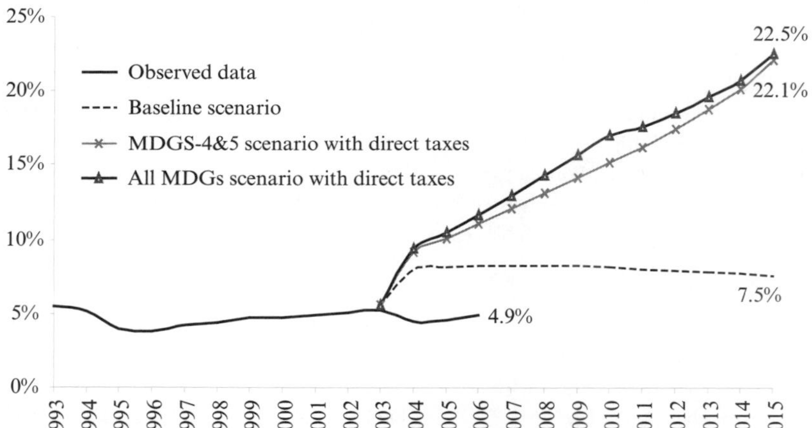

Figure 10.8 Mexico: Observed and simulated income-tax rate, 1993-2015 (percentage of GDP)

Source: Based on observed data of the SHCP and simulations results of MAMS for Mexico.

Prospects for reducing poverty

As explained in the second section of this chapter, Mexico is a country that has achieved the goal of reducing extreme poverty early, if one takes the international definition of a poverty line of one dollar a day at purchasing power parity (PPP). It is therefore more relevant for Mexico to analyse progress towards poverty reduction according to national definitions. By construction, MAMS does not specify any particular policy instrument for income poverty reduction, as was done for all the other goals being examined. In addition, while MAMS does provide results for macroeconomic conditions that influence poverty outcomes, it lacks sufficient detail about the household income distribution to reliably measure the evolution of poverty and inequality in all simulated scenarios.

Therefore, the microsimulations methodology described in Appendix A2.1 of Chapter 2 is used to make up for this methodological limitation. The methodology links the changes in the labour market simulated with MAMS to microeconomic household income distribution data and makes it possible to estimate the sequential and cumulative effects of shifts in employment and labour incomes on poverty and inequality.

Information on the economically active population as recorded by the 2002 household income and expenditure survey (ENIGH) was used to apply the microsimulation exercise. Monetary incomes were adjusted in order to link these to the CGE model results and official poverty lines were used to calculate poverty indicators according to the national definitions, differentiating between urban and rural areas.[15]

Figure 10.9 presents the results of the cumulative effects of the labour market changes of the baseline scenario of MAMS on international extreme poverty, measured by the line of one dollar a day PPP, as well as on food poverty as defined by the national food-sufficiency threshold. In the case of international extreme poverty, results indicate that increases in the average real wage (W2 effect), stemming mainly from maintaining the current economic context, would not only ensure staying on target for meeting the MDG for poverty reduction

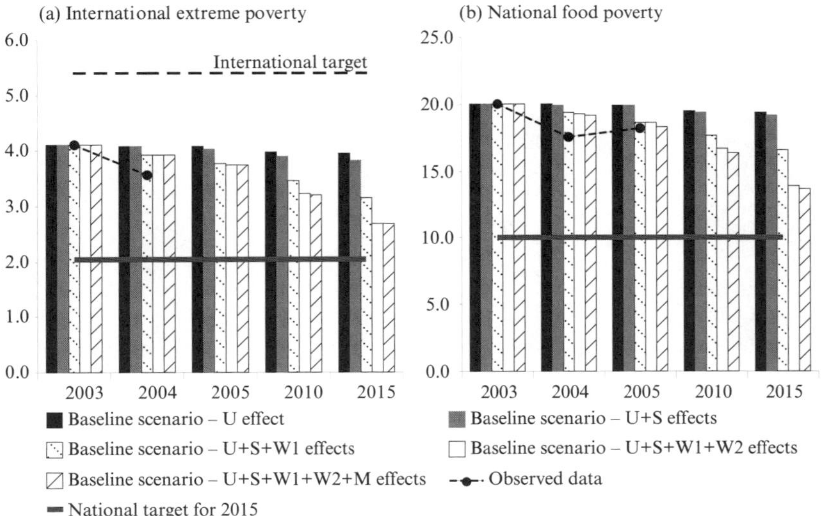

Figure 10.9 Mexico: Evolution of international extreme poverty and national food poverty, 2003-2015[a]

Source: MAMS for Mexico and microsimulations based on the 2002 ENIGH.

[a] The cumulative effects of the labour market in the baseline scenario are due to the sequential changes in the unemployment rate (U), the structure of employment and remuneration by sector (S and W1, respectively), average labour income (W2), and the structure of employment by skill level (M).

between 1990 and 2015, but would also achieve a 50 per cent reduction between 2002 and 2015. This would almost make it possible to achieve a more ambitious target of reducing extreme poverty, according to which less than 2.1 per cent of the population would have incomes of less than one dollar a day at PPP by 2015. Changes in the sector structure of employment (S effect) and remuneration structure across labour categories and sectors (W1 effect) also have a favourable impact in terms of reducing extreme poverty. These occur to the extent that the workers in the agricultural sector move towards the services sector; that is, the labour factor is reallocated, moving from lower-wage to higher-wage sectors.

The level of poverty does not change substantially with the simulated changes in the structure of employment, but its reduction is closely tied to the increases in the average level of real wages, which in turn depends on maintaining a sufficient rate of labour productivity growth.[16] These baseline results do not change much under the MDG scenarios. This is mainly due to the fact that Mexico is already close to meeting the education target. As a consequence, the MDG scenarios produce only minor few additional impacts on the labour market.

Labour income inequality (as measured by the Gini coefficient) falls in the baseline scenario and is part of the explanation of falling poverty (see Figure 10.10). Increases in the relative supply of skilled labour (M effect) partially roll

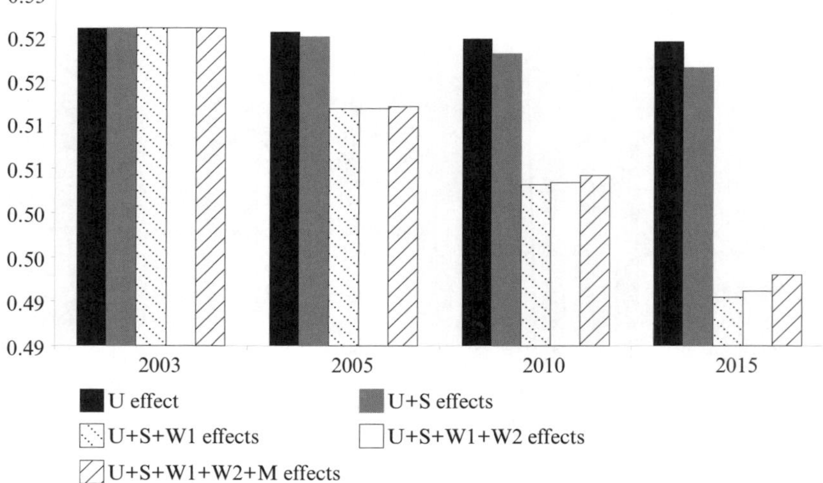

Figure 10.10 Mexico: Evolution of the Gini coefficient for labour income in the baseline scenario, 2003-2015[a]

Source: MAMS for Mexico and microsimulations applied to 2002 ENIGH (income and expenditure household survey).

[a] The cumulative effects of the labor market on the baseline scenario are due to the sequential changes in the unemployment rate (U), the structure of employment, and remuneration by sector (S and W1, respectively), average labor income (W2), and the structure of employment by skill level (M).

back the positive effect of the higher average real wage (W2) on poverty reduction. Based on these results, one can infer that in order to maintain a constant degree of inequality until 2015 or to decrease inequality to achieve additional poverty reduction, it is necessary to change the sectoral structure of employment. This is so for two reasons. First, the baseline and MDG scenarios only have a very small effect on the Gini coefficient. Second, as could be foreseen, improved educational performance enhances the skill-intensity of overall employment (M effect) causing a rise in inequality.

Conclusions and policy recommendations

Prior to the 2008-09 global economic crisis, Mexico's prospects of achieving the MDGs were good. According to the various scenarios simulated by applying MAMS for Mexico, and supplementing this model with a series of microsimulations, two key requirements for the favourable prospects to materialize were identified. The first would be to ensure a continuation of the macroeconomic climate of economic stability, growth, and expansion of social spending observed between 1998 and 2006 in Mexico. The economic crises of the 1980s and 1990s have made it clear that progress in education, health, and poverty reduction can easily be halted or reversed in a context of macroeconomic volatility, recession, and contraction of social spending. Specifically, a stable and favourable macroeconomic environment will allow for real wage growth which, as shown through simulated scenarios, is central for poverty reduction.

The second requirement is to step up efforts towards meeting the targets for reducing maternal and child mortality. The results suggest that fiscal revenues should increase substantially in order to finance the required increase in spending on health services of over 5 per cent of GDP per year up to 2015. This in turn would require a drastic fiscal reform. Whether it is possible to obtain sufficient political support for such a reform will depend on a variety of factors whose consideration goes beyond this analysis.

Acknowledgements

The authors would like to express gratitude to María Fernanda Arce, Emiliano Díaz and especially Elizabeth Monroy for their excellent research assistance, as well as to Martín Cicowiez, Enrique Ganuza, Marco V. Sánchez and Rob Vos for their valuable comments, suggestions and guidance. The opinions expressed in this chapter are the sole responsibility of the authors and are not necessarily attributable to the institutions with which they are affiliated.

Notes

1   Some aspects developed in the research have been omitted due to space considerations. These may be found in Ortega and Székely (2006), which is a lengthier version of this study.

2   The initial reference year of the MDGs is 1990, but due to lack of information for that year, 1989 is taken as the baseline year for evaluating progress in the goal of reducing extreme poverty by half by 2015.

3   According to the Presidencia de la República Mexicana (2006), federal public spending for reducing poverty increased by 5 per cent of GDP from 1995 to 2006, to the point of accounting for 16 per cent of GDP in 2006.

4   For more detail, see Ortega (2006).

5   For a detailed discussion of these reforms for the Mexican case, see Clavijo and Valdivieso (2000).

6   In addition, there are remaining gender gaps. The ratio of girls to boys enrolled in primary education was 95.4 per cent in 2003. The gap is smaller in lower-secondary and tertiary education, while at the level of higher-secondary education more girls than boys are enrolled.

7   The primary school completion rate is also targeted in the general equilibrium analysis presented below.

8   Drinking water coverage refers to the proportion of persons living in private housing with piped water reaching the property or the home.

9   For more detail on this, see UNDP and Secretaría de Desarrollo (2004).

10   An exhaustive description of the construction of the SAM and the structure of its accounts can be found in Ortega and Székely (2006).

11   The education and health sectors are subdivided by levels of specialization. Infrastructure is divided into activities that provide services for capture, treatment and supply of water by the public sector, and of construction and infrastructure services such as gas, electricity, communication and transportation.

12   These are the elasticities of the determinants of education outcomes and those related to the production functions of the model.

13   The SEP defines the completion rate as the percentage of students that complete primary school, whether they have repeated a grade or not. The MAMS model, on the other hand, defines it as the percentage of students in the cohort who begin primary and complete it on time, that is, without repeating any grade. To correct for this definitional difference, an adjustment was made by rescaling the simulated results, such that these are compatible with the observed trends. This adjustment explains the slight reduction in the completion rate in the model-based outcomes for 2003 to 2006, as shown in Figure 10.3.

14   In the foreign borrowing scenario, the required additional spending would be just under 3 per cent of annual GDP.

15   Monetary incomes were expressed in constant pesos of August 2002. Differences in the timing of data collection from households for different types of income were taken into account, ensuring all income data effectively reflect constant pesos for August 2002. The FIX exchange rate of August 2002 of 9.9109 pesos, published by the Banco de México, was used to estimate incomes in US dollars and calculate poverty indicators according to the international definitions of one and two dollars a day at PPP.

16   This conclusion coincides with that of Hernández Licona and Székely (2005), who show that the historical evolution of poverty in Mexico has been closely linked to the evolution of labour productivity.

References

Attanasio, Orazio, and Miguel Székely, eds. (2001). *Portrait of the Poor. An Asset-based Approach,* Johns Hopkins University Press (for the Inter-American Development Bank), Washington, D.C.

Clavijo, F., and S. Valdivieso (2000). "Reformas Estructurales y Política Macroeconómica: El Caso de México, 1982-1999", *Serie de Reformas Económicas*, No. 67, ECLAC: Santiago, Chile.

Hernández Licona, G., and M. Székely (2005). "Labor Productivity: the link between economic growth and poverty in Mexico", in Bane, M. J. and R. Zenteno (eds.), *Poverty and Poverty Reduction Strategies: Lessons from Mexican and International Experience*, Cambridge, Massachusetts: Harvard University Press.

Kapuscinski, Cezary A., and Meter G., Warr (1996). "Estimation of Armington Elasticities: an Application to the Philippines", Australian National University, Department of Economics.

Lee-Harris, Rebecca (2002). "Estimation of a Regionalized Mexican Social Account Matrix: Using Entropy Techniques to Reconcile Disparate Data Sources", TMD Discussion Paper No. 97, International Food Policy Research Institute (IFPRI), Washington D.C.: IFPRI.

Lora, Eduardo (2001). "Structural Reforms in Latin America: What has been reformed and how to measure it", Washington, D.C.: Inter-American Development Bank.

————, and F. Barrera (1997). "A decade of structural reforms in Latin America: Growth, productivity and investment are not what they used to be", Research Department Working Paper 352, Washington, D.C.: Inter-American Development Bank, Research Department.

Ortega, Araceli (2006). "Assessment of the Relationship between Economic Growth and Income Distribution. (Panel Data Analysis for the 32 Federal Entities of México 1960-2002)", in Badi H. Baltagi (ed.), *Panel Data Econometrics, Volume 274: Theoretical Contributions and Empirical Applications (Contributions to Economic Analysis)*, Amsterdam: North Holland.

————, and Miguel Székely (2006). "Retos y Perspectivas para Alcanzar Los Objetivos del Milenio en México: Aspectos Metodológicos y Aplicación Empírica", Research report prepared for the project "Public Policies for MDGs in Latin America and the Caribbean", United Nations Development Programme, Mexico City.

PNUD and Secretaría de Desarrollo Social (2004). *Más Allá de las Metas del Milenio*, Mexico City, D.F.

Presidencia de la República Mexicana (2004). *Cuarto Informe de Gobierno*, Mexico City, D.F.

Stone, R. (1954). 'Linear Expenditure System and Demand Analysis: An Application to the Pattern of British Demand', *The Economic Journal* 64: 511-27.

Székely, Miguel (2005a). "Es Posible un México con Menor Pobreza y Desigualdad", in J. A. Aguilar (ed.), *México, Crónicas de un País Posible*, Mexico City, D.F.: Conaculta-Fondo de Cultura Económica.

———— (2005b). "Pobreza y Desigualdad en México entre 1950 y el 2004", *El Trimestre Económico*, No. 288, Vol. LXXII (4), October-December.

11
Nicaragua

Marco V. Sánchez and Rob Vos

Introduction

For several decades, Nicaragua lagged far behind most of the countries of Latin America and the Caribbean (LAC) in terms of economic and social development. It suffered significant setbacks in the 1980s as a consequence of the armed conflict and the suspension of commercial and financial relations with the United States and the main international financial institutions (IFIs). From 1985 to 1989, per capita income dropped 7.4 per cent annually in a context of hyperinflation. This situation turned around markedly in the early 1990s once the peacemaking process was underway and commercial and financial relations resumed.

A massive influx of external aid backed an economic stabilization programme characterized by restrictive monetary policy and strong fiscal discipline. Once the economy showed signs of stability, a series of fiscal reforms and reforms of the state apparatus were undertaken, along with a far-reaching liberalization of the country's trade, foreign-exchange and financial regimes. Controls on foreign direct investment (FDI) were also removed. As a result, during the 1990s, public finances were put in order, inflation was brought down, and international trade recovered. Nonetheless, the economic recovery was neither swift nor sustained. Rather, growth slowed in the second half of the 1990s, discouraged by unfavourable internal and external factors. In the first half of the 2000s, volatile terms of trade were a source of unstable economic growth, reflecting the economy's continued external vulnerability.

In addition, the level of external public indebtedness still averaged near 150 per cent of GDP between 2000 and 2005. Because of its low income and debt problems, Nicaragua was able to benefit from the relief offered by the Heavily Indebted Poor Countries (HIPC) initiative and the Multilateral Debt Reduction Initiative (MDRI). The economy is excessively dependent on external financing and grants, including the mentioned debt-relief programmes, to pay for the cost of its social programmes. Mounting trade deficits following import liberalization and the heavy debt-service burden have led to chronic current account deficits and continued demand for vast amounts of external financing.

In the late 1990s and during the first half of the 2000s, several programmes and strategies were formulated with support of the IFIs and aimed at reducing the high level of poverty. In 2000, Nicaragua undertook to achieve the Millennium Development Goals (MDGs) with specific targets to be met by 2015, including reducing extreme poverty. The MDGs were incorporated into the Strengthened Growth and Poverty Reduction Strategy (ERCERP: *Estrategia Reforzada de Crecimiento Económico y Reducción de la Pobreza*). This is equivalent to Nicaragua's Poverty Reduction Strategy Paper (PRSP), drawn up initially in the context of the HIPC initiative. In 2003, the goals were made part of the National Development Plan (PND) which succeeded the ERCERP.[1]

While Nicaragua's population has seen major social gains since 1990, considerable challenges remain in order to achieve the MDGs. Extreme poverty has fallen, but far from enough. Much remains to be done for all children who enter primary education to complete it on time by 2015. Increases in the access to health services have helped reduce under-five child mortality, yet similar results have not been seen in maternal mortality. The coverage of drinking water and sanitation services has expanded, yet shortcomings persist in infrastructure and water quality, and there has been too little progress towards attaining the MDG for sanitation. Consequently, public policy efforts will need to be stepped up in order to increase the likelihood of achieving the MDGs in Nicaragua.

This chapter has three purposes: first, to quantify the additional public spending that would be needed to meet the MDGs in primary education, health, and water and sanitation in Nicaragua; second, to identify viable financing strategies to cover the cost of increased public spending; and third, to assess the macroeconomic trade-offs and social impact of the additional public spending for the MDGs. The core methodology is a dynamic computable general equilibrium model, called MAMS (see Chapter 3), in which the MDGs respond to a series of determinants. The feasibility of meeting the target for reducing extreme poverty is assessed through a complementary method of microsimulations (see Chapter 2).

The rest of the chapter includes six sections. The next section highlights the main reforms implemented since 1990 and the subsequent economic performance in Nicaragua. The subsequent section addresses aspects of social policy and the progress made towards the MDGs. An analysis of the main determinants of the MDGs is presented in the fourth section. The steps taken to adapt the modelling methodology to Nicaragua's context are summarized in the following section, while the results of the simulated policy scenarios are analyzed in section six. Finally, the last section provides some final considerations and policy recommendations.

Main reforms and economic performance in Nicaragua

The 1990s represented a turning point in Nicaragua's economic and social development, as illustrated by the data in Table 11.1. The peacemaking process ushered in renewed lending from the IFIs and the resumption of commercial ties with the United States. Official assistance (grants and non-concessional loans from abroad) came to represent more than 35 per cent of GDP per year from 1990 to 1994 and, even though it fell significantly and suffered important fluctuations during 1995-2005, aid remained high on average at approximately 14 per cent of GDP per year. The external assistance supported the effective implementation of a macroeconomic stabilization programme based on tight monetary policy and strong fiscal discipline. It also supported economic performance while subsequent fiscal and other public-sector reforms and economic liberalization policies were undertaken. Nonetheless, the foreign resources did relatively little to enhance the government's space for discretionary spending, as more than 85 per cent of the official assistance is project-specific. According to preliminary estimates by Guimarães and Avendaño (2007), however, the share of aid granted in the form of budget support increased after 2006, consistent with agreements with donors in the context of the poverty reduction strategy and the Paris Declaration on Aid Effectiveness by the Development Assistance Committee (DAC).

The reform of the state apparatus included the privatization of some public enterprises. With the 1997 fiscal reform, the tax system was simplified, a land-tenure tax was introduced, and the tax base was expanded. The tax base expanded further after 2002 with the implementation of the Law on Fiscal Equity. In May 2003 all the laws related to Nicaragua's tax administration were consolidated into a single law, some tax rates were changed, mainly for luxury goods, and the income-tax rate was increased and made more progressive.

The stabilization programme and economic reforms helped consolidate public finances and substantially lower inflation. Tax revenues mounted and the non-financial public sector generated savings of over 3.6 per cent of GDP per year on average between 1995 and 2005. Nonetheless, the tax burden continued to be relatively low at around 15 per cent of GDP, while the deficit of the non-financial public sector increased to 6.5 per cent of GDP on average between 2000 and 2005, up from 5.4 per cent of GDP per year during 1995-99. Grants from abroad helped reduce the deficit, bringing it to 1 per cent of GDP in 2005; without this assistance, the deficit would have reached 4.5 per cent of GDP. Revenues from privatizations and the access to external financing reduced dependence on domestic financing. Reducing the domestic public debt was a priority during the 1990s, but the banking crises of 2000 and 2001 drove it up considerably, with maturities concentrated in the 2002 to 2004 period. The external debt, which in 1990 peaked at 1,062 per cent of GDP, was slashed drastically falling to 110 per cent of GDP in 2005.

Table 11.1   Nicaragua: Macroeconomic indicators, 1990-2005 (annual averages)

Indicator	1990-1994	1995-1999	2000-2005
External sector and foreign investment			
Exports of goods and services (% of GDP)	20.0	21.4	24.8
Imports of goods and services (% of GDP)	46.4	44.6	51.8
Trade balance (% of GDP)	-26.4	-23.2	-27.0
Current account balance (% of GDP)	-31.2	-23.3	-17.6
Remittances of emigrant workers (% of GDP)[a]	1.2	4.7	10.0
Foreign direct investment (% of GDP)	1.5	5.5	5.1
Public finances, public debt, and external assistance			
Tax burden (% of GDP)[b]	n.a.	14.1	15.4
Government savings (% of GDP)[b]	n.a.	4.4	3.6
Actual fiscal deficit before grants from abroad (% of GDP)[b,c]	n.a.	-5.4	-6.5
Actual fiscal deficit after grants from abroad (% of GDP)[b,c]	n.a.	-1.2	-2.9
Domestic public debt (% of GDP)[b]	n.a.	17.8	31.3
External public debt (% of GDP)[b]	674.9	206.6	145.7
Official external assistance (% of GDP)[d]	36.1	15.8	12.5
Concessional loans (% of GDP)	18.3	8.9	6.2
Grants (% of GDP)	17.8	6.9	6.3
Prices			
Annual inflation (%)	2.096.3	11.2	7.7
Index of real effective exchange rate (2000 = 100)	69.5	98.8	94.2
Terms of trade (2000 = 100)[e]	120.4	114.2	91.7
Production, employment and wages			
Real GDP (rate of growth)	0.6	5.4	3.2
Real per capita GDP (rate of growth)	-1.8	3.3	2.2
Employment (rate of growth)	2.1	5.6	3.7
Real wage per employed worker (rate of growth)[f]	-19.2	2.3	3.1

Source: World Bank (World Development Indicators), except for the data on public finances, public debt, and external debt, which are from the Central Bank of Nicaragua.

[a] The data for the first period exclude 1990 and 1991.

[b] Non-financial public sector.

[c] Grants from abroad include part of the project-specific external cash grants as well as interim relief in the context of the HIPC initiative.

[d] Budget support and project aid.

[e] Data for the last period exclude 2005.

[f] Data for the first period exclude 1990.

n.a.: no data available.

From 1991 to 1993, the United States Agency for International Development (USAID) and the governments of France, the Netherlands, and Finland cancelled debts owed by Nicaragua which together came to US$ 366 million (Vos and Johansson, 1998). In 1996, the former Soviet Union and other bilateral donors that are not members of the Donor Assistance Committee (DAC) (including Mexico and the other Central American countries) cancelled most of their outstanding loans to Nicaragua. The debt cancellation totalled US$ 4 million, accounting for nearly 40 per cent of Nicaragua's external debt (Dijkstra and Evans, 2003). In the context of the HIPC initiative, which came about in October 1996, before reaching the completion point in the 1997-2003 period, the country benefited from additional debt cancellation to the tune of US$ 1.3 billion. In 2004, when reaching the completion point of HIPC-II, further debt reduction was granted for US$ 4.5 billion covering the period up until 2023. In addition, US$ 896 million of Nicaragua's debt with the IFIs will be cancelled in the framework of the MDRI. The debt relief thus obtained should allow Nicaragua to allocate more budgetary resources to programmes aimed at attaining the MDGs.

The trade regime was radically reformed as of the early 1990s. The State's monopoly over trade was eliminated, and quantitative restrictions on international trade were lifted. Export taxes were eliminated in 1993, and taxes on imports dropped precipitously as a result of unilateral measures as Nicaragua joined the World Trade Organization in 1995 and subsequently entered into various free trade agreements. Special mention should be made of the treaty signed by Central American countries and the Dominican Republic with the United States (DR-CAFTA).

The trade opening was accompanied by liberalization of the exchange and financial markets, and restrictions on the FDI regime were eliminated. There was no move to a flexible exchange-rate regime, however. In February 1991, the Córdoba Oro was introduced with a fixed exchange rate tied to the U.S. dollar, and in 1993 a system of pre-announced mini-devaluations was adopted. This exchange-rate policy resulted in a marked depreciation of the real exchange rate in the early 1990s. The real exchange rate appreciated during 1993 and 1997, as the economy stabilized. From 1997 to 2001, however, the system of mini-devaluations succeeded in improving the competitiveness of the real exchange rate, which depreciated during that period. From 2001 to 2005, there was a clear and renewed trend towards exchange-rate appreciation as the pace of the mini-devaluations was slowed.

The importance of international trade for the economy increased significantly. Liberalization cheapened imports, while export promotion policies, including the system of mini-devaluations, made sales abroad more competitive. Exports have not diversified much, however. Imports grew much more than exports from 1995 to 2005. The resulting wider trade deficit was covered by rising inflows of worker remittances from Nicaraguans abroad and high levels of foreign grants. The current account deficit of the balance of payments has declined steadily as a result since the mid 1990s. Even so, external deficits have remained relatively large, especially on account of the persistent heavy external debt-service burden. Next to concessional loans, rising FDI helped cover the wide current account deficits. FDI recovered notably in the second half of the 1990s, stabilizing at just over 5 per cent of GDP in the period from 1995 to 2005.

The economic gains from controlling inflation and the reforms were felt in the 1990s, but did not translate into a swift and sustained economic recovery. The rate of growth of real per- capita GDP fluctuated in the 1990s (see Figure 11.1) and, in general, fell, on average, from 3.3 per cent per year in the second half of the 1990s to 2.2 per cent per year in the period 2000-05. By and large, the economy showed major volatility as a result of its high degree of external vulnerability.

Based on a decomposition of GDP growth, Sánchez and Vos (2006) determined that the contraction in spending and tax reform limited growth in the 1990-2003 period. They also determined that trade liberalization stimulated the propensity to import and that exports became the engine of the economy's modest growth. During part of the second half of the 1990s, output growth was also supported by expanding investment, especially for the reconstruction of infrastructure following Hurricane Mitch in the late 1990s. The abrupt slowdown in 1999, which endured until 2002, is explained by the end of the reconstruction process, the slowdown in the world economy, falling world prices of main export products (coffee and sugar), and rising oil prices.[2] Later,

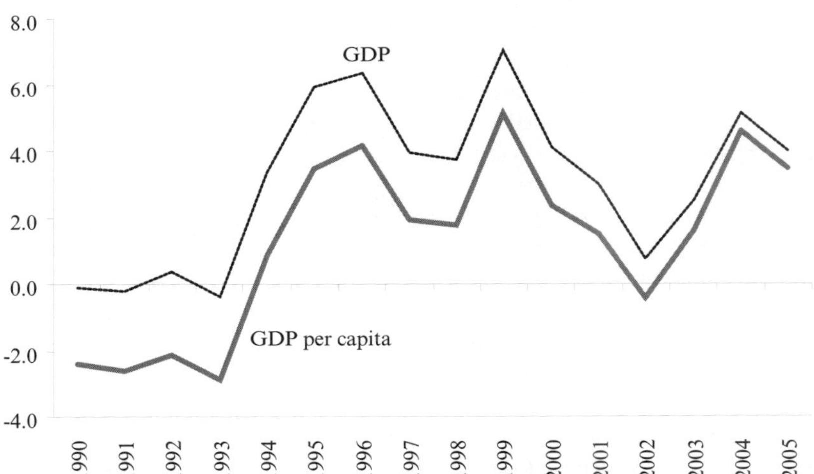

Figure 11.1 Nicaragua: Growth of real GDP and per capita GDP, 1990-2005
Source: World Bank. World Development Indicators.

the recovery of the world economy and export prices helped spur economic growth again during much of 2003-08, but given the country's external vulnerability growth remained volatile.

Employment has fluctuated with the swings in output. During 1990 and 1994, employment increased, but with much of the growth reflecting higher levels of underemployment and increased informal sector activity. As a result and with inflation still very high, real wages fell almost 20 per cent per year on average during that period. Output recovery and falling inflation allowed for a rise in real wages from the mid-1990s. Output volatility led to inadequate employment growth, however, resulting in sustained high levels of unemployment. Consequently, rising average real wages did not translate into systematic reductions in poverty.

Social policies and progress towards the MDGs in Nicaragua

Amidst slowing economic growth, a beginning was made with the process of defining the poverty reduction strategy in the framework of the HIPC initiative at the turn of the new century. The strategy puts priority on maximizing growth as well as achievement of the MDGs. The initiative made Nicaragua eligible for substantial debt relief and for obtaining resources from the Poverty Reduction and Growth Facility (PRGF) granted by the IMF in January 2004 when the country reached the completion point in complying with the HIPC conditions. The resources freed up by the debt relief and the additional donor resources granted through the HIPC initiative should be allocated for the poverty reduction strategy as laid down initially in the ERCERP and subsequently in the PND.

In this context, public social spending could be increased, though apparently not enough to make further progress towards the MDG targets. According to ECLAC (2006), public social spending as a percentage of GDP increased from 6.6 per cent in 1990-91 to 7.6 per cent in 1998-99 and further to 8.8 per cent in 2002-03. At these levels, social spending was among the lowest in Latin America. After introduction of the poverty reduction strategy, the share rose to 9.1 per cent of GDP in 2002, 12.1 per cent in 2006 and, based on the approved budget, to 13.2 per cent in 2007 (see Table 11.2).[3] This upward trend has little to do, however, with increases in spending on MDG-related services, which experienced little change between 2002 and 2006, remaining around 6 per cent of GDP and increasing slightly to 7 per cent of GDP in 2007. Given the enormous social challenges which Nicaragua faces and given the vast amounts of external aid the country has absorbed, the modest increase in public social spending is of concern. Although per capita expenditure for poverty reduction increased from US$68.3 to US$110.2 between 2002 and 2006, it remains among the lowest in the region.

During 2003-05, only one third of the spending associated with the poverty reduction strategy was financed from domestic resources, mainly taxes, while the rest was financed through foreign aid and debt relief (see Table 11.2). Only part of the debt relief has been earmarked to poverty reduction programmes. In 2005, only 53 per cent was earmarked as such. The remaining 47 per cent was allocated to repayment of domestic central government debt (Guimarães and Avendaño, 2007). In 2006 and 2007, there was a sharp increase in subsidies on the consumption of drinking water, electricity, and public transport in response to rising food and energy prices. Education and health spending has continued to rely heavily on external financing and to the donor conditionality associated with it.

Insufficient poverty reduction

Nicaragua has committed to meeting the international targets for MDG 1 of halving both the percentage of persons living on less than one dollar a day and the percentage of persons suffering hunger between 1993 and 2015.[4] The government aims to achieve a similar reduction in the percentage of the population with per-capita consumption below the national thresholds for moderate and

Table 11.2   Nicaragua: Public spending earmarked to the poverty reduction strategy (PRS) and its financing, 2002-2007[a]

	2002	2003	2004	2005	2006	2007
Public spending on MDG services (% of GDP)	9.1	11.1	11.9	13.0	12.1	13.2
Education	2.6	2.9	2.8	3.2	3.0	3.4
Health	2.9	3.3	2.9	3.1	3.2	3.5
Water and maintenance	0.1	0.0	0.1	0.0	0.1	0.0
Others	3.5	4.9	6.1	6.7	5.8	6.2
Per-capita public spending on MDG services (US$)	68.3	82.7	94.9	105.1	110.2	131.6
Total public spending on MDG services (millions of US$)	364.6	453.5	533.9	606.9	651.3	796.7
Financing of public spending on MDGs (percentage shares)						
Fiscal resources[b]	54.8	33.2	28.3	38.7	52.0	59.8
External development cooperation[c]	36.5	45.5	48.5	42.3	33.4	24.4
External debt relief[d]	8.67	21.3	23.2	19.0	14.6	15.9

Source: Ministry of Finance (spending data) and BCN (average exchange rate).
[a] Public spending accrued in 2002-2006 and public spending budgeted for 2007. For 2002-2006, the public spending accrued represents on average approximately 90 per cent of public spending budgeted.
[b] Includes mainly tax revenues, as well as earmarked revenues. The latter account on average for 2.3 per cent of budget financing during 2002-2007.
[c] Includes grants and loans.
[d] Includes debt relief under the HIPC initiative and cancellation of Paris Club debt.

extreme poverty.[5] Poverty fell between 1993 and 2005, mainly in the rural areas. This reduction was the result of the economic recovery, the increase in real wages and social programmes (see Table 11.3). Also, relative prices for the main products of the basic consumption basket (rice and beans) fell in the late 1990s (World Bank, 2003).[6] Increasing remittances from emigrant workers helped reduce poverty further, as in other Central American countries (see, for example, Sánchez, 2005). Nonetheless, the rate of poverty reduction has been insufficient to be on track towards the 2015 target (see Table 11.3).

The volatility of economic growth has attenuated poverty reduction. In fact, the population living on less than one dollar a day increased slightly during the economic slowdown between 1998 and 2001. In addition, in this period an important part of social spending was used to address demands for emergency relief brought on by natural disasters. Poverty, as measured by the national poverty lines, also increased during other recent episodes of economic slowdown (2001-02 and 2004-05), especially in rural areas. Extreme poverty as measured by the one-dollar-a-day threshold did not fall, however, as a result of targeted social programmes.

The government redefined some priorities in the PND for 2006-10 in order to reach sustained economic growth with the expectation that this would trickle

Table 11.3 Nicaragua: Poverty indicators, 1993-2005 and target for 2015

Indicator	Percentage of the population					Reduction observed 1993-2005[c]	Reduction needed 2005-2015[c]
	1993	1998	2001	2005	Target for 2015		
Percentage of the population living on less than 1 dollar a day (MDG 1)	44.0	42.2	43.0	39.4	22.0	-4.6	-17.4
Urban	26.0	24.9	27.5	22.3	13.0	-3.7	-9.3
Rural	69.2	62.8	64.7	60.7	34.6	-8.5	-26.1
National moderate poverty[a]	50.3	47.9	45.8	48.3	25.2	-2.0	-23.2
Urban	31.9	30.5	30.1	30.9	16.0	-1.0	-15.0
Rural	76.1	68.5	67.8	70.3	38.1	-5.8	-32.3
National extreme poverty[b]	19.4	17.3	15.1	17.2	9.7	-2.2	-7.5
Urban	7.3	7.6	6.2	6.7	3.7	-0.6	-3.1
Rural	36.3	28.9	27.4	30.5	18.2	-5.8	-12.4

Source: Living Standards Measurement Study (LSMS) survey, National Institute of Statistics and Census (INEC).

[a] Percentage of the population with per-capita consumption below the official poverty line.
[b] Percentage of the population with per-capita consumption below the official extreme poverty line.
[c] In percentage points.

down and help reduce poverty. Increased social spending is less dominant in the new plan.

Nicaragua not only needs higher economic growth, but also less inequality. According to INEC's household survey data, the Gini coefficient of per-capita consumption fell from 0.49 in 1993 to 0.43 in 2001. Various food subsidies and poverty reduction programmes may have influenced this outcome. Income inequality, however, does not seem to have decreased. According to ECLAC (2006), the Gini coefficient of per-capita income increased slightly between 1993 (0.582) and 1998 (0.584) and fell only marginally thereafter (to 0.579 in 2001). According to ECLAC-IPEA-UNDP (2003), Nicaragua would have to increase per-capita GDP by 2.7 per cent per year if it aspires to reach the MDG for reducing extreme poverty, assuming that it is able to reduce inequality (measured by the Gini coefficient) by 3.6 per cent. Using this redistributive scenario as a benchmark, both the rate of growth of per-capita GDP observed from 2000 to 2005 and the degree of income redistribution were insufficient for the country to be on track in attaining the poverty reduction target.

Universal primary education: A feasible but costly target

Primary education indicators have improved significantly (see Table 11.4). Gender inequalities in primary education have been eliminated (MDG 3). Net enrolment rates and the proportion of students who begin first grade and reach fifth have increased as a result of lower drop-out and higher retention rates, permitting progress towards the MDG 2 target of making it possible for all children able to complete primary education by 2015. The proportion of students who begin primary school and complete it increased almost 29 points in 13 years, from 1991 to 2003. At a continued linear trend, the target can be met by 2015. This would require substantial further increases in public spending considering the remaining educational gaps. Improved performance in education was helped by increased spending on school infrastructure and school meal programmes and by improvements in the quality of education following the modernizing of the sector. In addition, it is likely that lower child mortality and growing average incomes of the population have had a positive impact on primary school outcomes.

The public resources required to attain the primary education target would have to be allocated efficiently to priority areas. The schooling infrastructure capacity (schools and teaching materials) and the number of teachers are still insufficient.[7] In rural areas, for example, many schools do not offer the complete primary cycle. In addition, new resources will need to be earmarked to improve the quality of teaching, relevance of curriculums, and administration of education, including through hiring better-trained and better-paid teachers.[8] As explained below, the quality of education is an important determinant for primary school enrolment. In addition, income constraints, migratory flows,

Table 11.4   Nicaragua: MDG indicators, 1990-2004 and target for 2015

Indicator	1990	2000	2004	Target for 2015
Percentage of students who begin and complete primary (MDG 2)	44.3[a]	66.0	73.1[b]	100.0
Percentage of students who begin first grade and reach fifth grade	44.1[a]	54.2	73.5	
Net enrolment rate (%)	72.6[a]	80.5	87.9	
Net enrolment rate for girls with respect to boys (%) (MDG 3)	1.1[a]	1.0	1.0	1.0
Under-five child mortality, per 1,000 live births (MDG 4)	68.0	43.0	38.0	22.7
Infant mortality, per 1,000 live births	52.0	34.0	31.0	
Maternal mortality, per 100,000 live births (MDG 5)	160.0	230.0	n.a.	40.0
Percentage of the population with access to an improved water supply (MDG 7a)[c]	70.0	n.a.	79.0	85.0
Urban area	91.0	n.a.	90.0	95.5
Rural area	46.0	n.a.	63.0	73.0
Percentage of the population with access to improved sanitation (MDG 7b)[d]	45.0	n.a.	47.0	72.5
Urban area	91.0	n.a.	90.0	95.5
Rural area	46.0	n.a.	63.0	73.0

Source: United Nations Statistics Division (http://mdgs.un.org/unsd/mdg/Default.aspx).
[a] Data from 1991.
[b] Data from 2003.
[c] Includes access to: connection to a water supply system, public pipe, natural or protected well, protected spring, and the supply of collected rainwater.
[d] Includes the connection to a public sewage system or a septic system, or access to a latrine with a particular technology (for example, dry compost latrines, pit latrines, or improved ventilated pit latrines).
n.a.: no data available.

and the cost of education affect demand for schooling among low-income groups. These factors also influence drop-out rates, especially in rural areas where opportunity costs are also high as reflected in widespread child labour.[9] The area of residence also influences the probability of primary school attendance. Because of easier access to schools and higher mean incomes of parents, this likelihood is much higher in urban than rural areas. Accordingly, a large part of the new resources should be earmarked to subsidizing households that cannot cover the private cost and opportunity cost of education, mainly in rural areas.

Opposite trends in child mortality and maternal mortality

Comprehensive care for children under 6 years with nutritional and educational vulnerability has been a social policy priority. As a result, under-five child mortality was reduced by 30 deaths per 1,000 live births from 1990 to 2004 (see Table 11.4). Child mortality is due almost entirely to deaths during the first year of life (infant mortality). According to the United Nations (Sistema de las Naciones Unidas, 2003), the drop in infant mortality in Nicaragua is associated with the expansion of the coverage (now more than 80 per cent) of the Expanded Programme on Immunization, as well as the promotion of breast-feeding, a greater use of oral rehydration therapy and control of infections, increased public investment in basic services in the rural areas, and comprehensive social protection programmes geared at serving children under six years of age in extreme poverty. Greater access to an improved water source in rural areas may also have helped reduce child mortality, as explained below.

Public spending on health care in Nicaragua is relatively low by Latin American standards. Even so, and despite the fact it has not increased as a share of GDP, health spending has been effective in reducing child mortality. At continued trends, it would be possible to meet the MDG target of reducing child mortality by two-thirds between 1990 and 2015. If this is accomplished, 15 more child deaths per 1,000 live births would have been prevented each year by 2015, as compared with the situation in 2004. This may well be feasible, given that during 1990-2004, twice as many deaths were prevented in a shorter period of time. While feasible, it would require a larger share of public spending on health being earmarked to further reduce the prevalence of diarrheal diseases and acute respiratory infections, premature births, and the problems of low birth-weight, asphyxia, and sepsis.

The outlook is less encouraging for maternal mortality, which increased from 160 per 100,000 live births in 1990 to 230 in 2000 (see Table 11.4).[10] Complications during childbirth were the main cause of the deaths of women of reproductive age in the period from 1990 to 2000. Reducing maternal mortality would contribute to reducing infant mortality since, according to the official statistics, two-thirds of maternal deaths are caused by direct obstetric complications, such as haemorrhage, hypertension during pregnancy, sepsis and unsafe induced abortion (MINSA, 2000). The programmes of integrated child care for those at risk of nutritional and educational vulnerability may have helped to offset the negative impact of rising maternal deaths on infant mortality.

Achieving the target of reducing maternal mortality by three fourths between 1990 and 2015 will require higher and more sustained growth of public health spending. The priority areas are to improve the quality and coverage of pre-natal care, childbirth, puerperium and care for preventing complications in pregnancy. According to the United Nations (Sistema de las Naciones Unidas, 2003), the efficiency of health services must improve. This will require greater coverage and improvements in health infrastructure, especially at the primary and secondary levels of care, as well as better preventive care and health promotion for households and communities, especially in rural areas.

Increasing coverage of drinking water, but lags in sanitation

Nicaragua also intends to reduce by half the number of persons without access to drinking water and improved sanitation services from 1990 to 2015. The coverage of both services has expanded, albeit to a limited extent, given existing infrastructure deficiencies and very slight increases in public spending on water and sanitation (see Tables 11.2 and 11.4). The proportion of the population with access to an improved water source increased to 79 per cent in 2004, up by 9 percentage points from 1990. This progress is largely due to enhanced supply in rural areas and in the neighbourhoods of Managua through the investment programme of the water and sewage company, *Empresa Nicaragüense de Acueductos y Alcantarillados Sanitarios* (ENACAL).[11] To attain this target, there should be a 6 per cent increase in the population with access to an improved water source by 2015. This is less than the progress made in 15 years during 1990-2004. Achieving the target would thus require additional public spending efforts, including the effective implementation of the investment programmes agreed upon in the PND.

Increased household incomes will further help improve access to water and sanitation, as suggested by the econometric estimates analyzed in the next section. With respect to sanitation, the sewerage programmes of ENACAL and the rural latrine promotion projects of the Emergency Social Investment Fund (FISE) have benefited thousands of households in recent years. Nonetheless, the percentage of the population with access to improved sanitation increased by a meagre 2 per cent between 1990 and 2004, reaching coverage of only half of the total population (see Table 11.4). Coverage improved in rural areas, but fell in urban areas. It will be hard for the country to meet the sanitation target of increasing coverage by 25 percent by 2015, unless there is a more sustained increase in public spending to expand and improve the sewerage and rural latrines infrastructure.

Determinants of primary school completion, maternal and child mortality, and access to water and sanitation

The CGE model (MAMS), discussed below, includes a module defining the determinants of the MDGs presented in Table 11.4. Hammill (2006) has estimated the related functional relationships and the corresponding elasticities for Nicaragua. These estimates have been used for the application of MAMS for Nicaragua.

The probability of students completing the full cycle of primary schooling is hypothesized to increase with improved public infrastructure (excluding water and sanitation), better health status of children (as measure through lower child mortality), higher quality of education, a larger wage premium on education, and a higher level of per-capita household consumption. To determine the statistical significance of these determinants, Hammill (2006) applies a standard logit model, as well as a proportions model, merging data on schooling from the 2001 LSMS with data on the quality and availability of school infrastructure by level of education and municipality from the Ministry of Education.[12] He finds that the last three of the mentioned determinants are statistically significant in the case of Nicaragua. The coefficient for public infrastructure has the expected sign, but is not significant, possibly because its influence is estimated with variations at the municipal level only.[13] In addition, due to data constraints, the impact of lower child mortality had to be measured on the basis of averages at the municipal level. Possibly as a result of this limitation, the health status variable was not found to be statistically significant either.

Hammill's estimates have two salient results (2006). First, primary schooling outcomes are most responsive to changes in the wage premium. Consequently, improved labour market conditions would significantly increase the likelihood of children attending primary school, offsetting the opportunity cost involved. Second, other determinants not taken into account in MAMS, but found to be statistically significant in explaining primary schooling performance include geographic area (urban and rural) and the proportion of students who benefit from the school meals programme. These findings confirm the recommendation suggested above: that more public spending should be allocated to programmes aimed at reducing the large number of children who are now outside the school system and who have dropped out, especially in rural areas, and at targeting the integrated early childhood and school meal programmes at those in extreme poverty.

Other studies show findings consistent with Hammill's. For example, to evaluate the impact of the "Education for All" programme, Arcia (2003) projects the levels of schooling and spending on education from 2001 to 2015, using transition matrices for education and employment of children, as well as population projections. The author concludes that due to the shortcomings in the quality of education, it will be extremely difficult to increase the proportion of students who complete primary schooling to more than 80 per cent by 2015. In addition, he estimates that by providing an annual cash transfer of US$145 per student in the first four grades of primary education, school attendance of children aged 7 to 13 years could increase by 21.7 per cent, the net enrolment rate by 30.1 per cent, and the number of students who continue attending school beyond the fourth grade by 8 per cent. According to these findings, the enrolment rates and the number of students who complete primary school would depend mainly on the cost of education. In addition, the opportunity cost of attending school for children aged 10 to 15 is approximately US$108 per year per family. The cash transfer would compensate for this opportunity cost. Other social assistance programmes for schoolchildren will also help reduce child labour and school dropout and improve economic conditions for poor households. Hammill's estimates confirm these findings by showing the significant and positive effect of household consumption on primary school outcomes and of the wage premium on education.

Differences in the importance of these determinants by specific population groups were found by Ponce (2005). Using a probit model, Ponce found that the likelihood that a child (mainly poor) will attend primary school in rural areas is statistically correlated to public social spending, travel time to school (infrastructure variable), and the number of students per class and of children with only one teacher (quality-of-education variables). Other determinants of schooling in primary education – though relatively less elastic – are school meal programmes and provision of a school bag, but only for the group of poor children from rural areas, in the first case, and poor children in urban areas in the second. In addition, the author finds that to reduce the number of students per classroom or of children with just one teacher to international standards (that is, from 34 to 30 and from 40 to 36, respectively), education spending should be increased by 1.4 per cent of GDP from 2003 to 2015, after adjusting for population growth and inflation. Even so, the author finds that the primary education target would not be met, since this would also require an improvement in quality of education, especially in rural areas. Increasing public spending by a similar amount to expand the cash transfer programme, reduce the number of students per classroom, and expand the school bag programme, however, would also be insufficient to attain the goal, since in that scenario the primary school attendance rate would increase to 89 per cent by 2015.

Less empirical evidence is available in the area of health, lacking especially for determinants of maternal mortality. In MAMS, under-five child mortality and maternal mortality are assumed to depend on changes in per-capita health spending, per-capita household consumption, public infrastructure (excluding water and sanitation), and access to improved water sources and sanitation. Hammill (2006) tests these relationships econometrically. Using data from the 2001 LSMS, his study finds that higher per-capita household consumption and greater access to adequate water and sanitation services indeed reduce the likelihood of child death, but only the first determinant is statistically significant at the highest confidence level. Data limitations impede testing the impact of improved public infrastructure on child mortality.[14]

In its 2001 study on poverty in Nicaragua, the World Bank estimated a probabilistic model of survival at five years, using data from the 1993-98 demographic and health surveys (World Bank, 2001). The Bank finds that the maternal and child health care services are the most significant determinant, whereas other important factors are maternal education and access to a safe water source (both with a positive sign), as well as the number of pregnancies at young ages (with a negative sign).

Using population projections based on a model that projects cohorts and multiple socio-demographic conditions, Andersen (2004) estimates that public spending on health should increase steadily until almost doubling the level observed in 2000 if one wishes to meet the MDGs.

MAMS considers a relatively smaller number of determinants of access to improved water sources and sanitation. These encompass: per-capita spending on both services, per-capita consumption of households, and availability of general public infrastructure (excluding water and sanitation). Using a pooled logit model based on panel data from the LSMS for 1998 and 2001, Hammill (2006) estimates that these determinants correlate positively with improved coverage of water and sanitation services. Nonetheless, only the first two determinants listed are found statistically significant. Once again, as was the case for the microeconometric analysis of the health and education determinants, the lack of information makes it hard to measure the effect of infrastructure with greater precision. According to the estimates cited, the likelihood that a household will have access to improved water and sanitation services is also greater in urban areas, which is to be expected to the extent that there are marked lags in rural areas. The study by Andersen (2004) also highlights the importance of public spending on water and sanitation systems. In order to achieve the MDGs for water and sanitation, the study concludes that spending would need to increase to levels that are, respectively, 1.2 and 3.4 times greater in 2015 as compared with those of 2000.

Modelling methodology

Definition of scenarios and main assumptions

The main conclusions of this study stem from an analysis of scenarios simulated using the CGE model that is described in Chapter 3 (that is, MAMS). The model captures the dynamic impact on the economy of attaining the MDGs (for example, through changes in the composition of labour supply), and the repercussions that the public social spending needed to achieve them and its financing could have on productive activities.

First, a baseline scenario was defined for the period 2000-15, which by and large reproduces the observed trajectory of the economy during the first years of the period. The baseline also projects growth of spending for final government consumption at the pace of the first years of the 2000s. This growth of public spending is not sufficient to meet the MDGs. The baseline is subsequently used as the reference for policy scenarios that simulate achievement of the MDGs for education, health, and water and sanitation by scaling up the corresponding public expenditures sufficiently to meet the established targets. These policy scenarios are run for each MDG separately, as well as for the case where all these MDGs would be achieved simultaneously. The model simulations yield outcomes under four alternative sources of financing of the increased public spending: foreign grants, external borrowing, taxation, or domestic borrowing.

The following macroeconomic closure rules are assumed for the baseline scenario. First, income taxes are adjusted to balance the government budget. Levels of public borrowing are assumed to be fixed. As explained above, fiscal reforms over the past decade allowed for a broadening of the tax base and significant increases in government revenue in Nicaragua. Second, adjustments in the real exchange rate are assumed to balance the external account as the level of capital inflows is kept fixed in the baseline. This external closure rule is not an entirely adequate representation of exchange-rate adjustments through the system of mini-devaluations, with implications for the interpretation of the model results as discussed below. Third, having determined government investment spending, realized private investment is assumed to adjust to the level of total investment that matches total savings in the economy. The first closure rule is changed in accordance with the alternative financing scenarios for achieving the MDGs, in the cases where increased public spending is not met by raising tax rates, but by, respectively, domestic borrowing, foreign grants or external borrowing. In these three cases, one of the mechanisms of financing becomes a flexible variable, while the income tax rates are kept fixed.

Three types of workers compete in the labour market: unskilled workers (those who have not completed secondary education), semi-skilled workers (with completed secondary education or incomplete tertiary education) and skilled workers (with completed tertiary education). Depending on the state of the economy, equilibrium in each segment of the labour market is reached either through adjustments in the level of unemployment or real wages. If the unemployment rate by type of worker is higher than a pre-established minimum rate, the real wage remains fixed at a so-called "reserve wage" level and supply and demand for labour balances through adjustments in the level of employment (and hence the degree of unemployment). Alternatively, if the rate of unemployment drops to the minimum, the labour market reaches equilibrium through adjustments in the real wage. The capital market, in turn, reaches equilibrium through adjustments in the return to capital under the assumption of full utilization of the production factor capital.

Calibrating MAMS for Nicaragua

To calibrate MAMS empirically to the conditions of the Nicaraguan economy, first a Social Accounting Matrix (SAM) was constructed for the year 2000 based on the SAM elaborated by Sánchez and Vos (2006). The steps taken to adapt this SAM for MAMS are described in Annex 1 of Sánchez and Vos (2007). Next, the elasticities associated with the MDG determinants were estimated as discussed above. Those used in MAMS for Nicaragua are presented in Table A11.1. Original estimates were in some cases adjusted to achieve model consistency. Those adjustments were made after conducting a sensitivity analysis testing for a feasible range (upper and lower bounds) within which the values of those elasticities should fall for the model to find a consistent solution. Most of the elasticities estimated by Hammill (2006) fell within feasible ranges, except the elasticities for achievements in primary education which were too low for the model to converge to a solution. These elasticities were adjusted upwards to reach the lower bound of the range of feasibility. Other exceptions are for some of the elasticities for which Hammill (2006) did not obtain statistically significant results or did not obtain any result at all for lack of data, as in the case of maternal mortality. To overcome these limitations, ad-hoc values, falling within the range of feasibility, were assumed in these cases. In the case of the determinants of maternal mortality, the same elasticities were assumed as those for child mortality, on grounds that several of the causes of maternal mortality are closely related to those of infant mortality and that in MAMS both types of mortality are assumed to depend on the same determinants.

Other key elasticities of the model define the degree of substitution in production and consumption in response to changes in relative prices and the responsiveness of household spending to changes in income. These elasticities were taken from the study by Sánchez and Vos (2006) who estimated these econometrically for Nicaragua. In the cases where the sector disaggregation of MAMS differed from the CGE model developed by Sánchez and Vos (2006), the elasticities were adjusted by reweighting these in function of sector size (see Sánchez and Vos, 2007, for this procedure). Values of most elasticities are low, reflecting relatively low degrees of substitutability in production and consumption in the Nicaraguan economy.

The MDG indicators used in MAMS are those presented in Table 11.4. The population data come from ECLAC/CELADE (2002) and employment data are derived from INEC's Labour Force Survey for November 2000. Student performance in education (entering school, passing a grade, graduating from a cycle, repeating a grade, and dropping out) was measured using data from the 2001 LSMS and the Ministry of Education and the National Council of Universities (CNU). Andersen's projections for public spending (Andersen 2004) were valuable to calibrate the parameters associated with the logistic functions through which MAMS determines the degree of effectiveness over time of the MDG determinants in reaching the given targets. Generally, the functions show diminishing marginal returns to interventions working on the determinants the closer one gets to the targets.

Sánchez and Vos (2007, Annex 2) give a full account of all other relevant data and data sources used to calibrate MAMS.

Microsimulation methodology to estimate impact on poverty

As is the case with any typical general equilibrium model, MAMS lacks sufficient income distribution detail in order to make robust estimates of the impact on poverty of simulated scenarios. To overcome this limitation, the microsimulations methodology explained in Appendix A2 of Chapter 2 is applied. Each of the scenarios simulated with MAMS generates a new structure of the labour market for each year of the simulation period. These new labour market structures were imputed to the full household income distribution as derived from the 2001 LSMS. To obtain initial poverty estimates comparable with official estimates, two adjustments had to be made. First, per-capita incomes of non-poor households were adjusted to the level of their per-capita consumption if by the original estimates the former was higher than the latter. A similar adjustment was made to the incomes of a number of poor households whose per-capita income was greater than their per-capita consumption according to the original survey estimates.[15] Second, the original survey recorded some families as having higher labour income than their total income. In these cases, total household income was adjusted to the sum of labour incomes of household members. With these adjustments, the official estimates of poverty as calculated by INEC could be reproduced using income data, even though INEC measures poverty on the basis of per-capita household consumption.

Analysis of the simulated scenarios

Baseline scenario

The main results of the baseline or 'business-as-usual' scenario are presented in Table A11.2 in the Appendix. Real GDP grows on average by 3.2 per cent per year, close to the rate observed for the 2000-05 period. The actual observed rate of growth was slightly higher, however, since MAMS for Nicaragua underestimates export growth given that the external closure rule does not properly capture the positive influence of the system of mini-devaluations on competitiveness. The baseline, in contrast, shows a steady appreciation of the real exchange rate.[16] As a result, imports increase gradually, while exports fall as a share of output. The rising imports and expanding supply of non-tradable goods resulting from the currency appreciation are mirrored in increasing domestic demand.

Employment moves hand-in-hand with production, though at a more modest pace (2.7 per cent per year), though somewhat lower than that observed (see Table 11.1). This is so for two reasons. First, in the baseline scenario it is assumed that an increasing number of children in primary-school age enter the education system, while fewer enter the labour market. As a consequence, the supply of unskilled workers in MAMS is less than observed. In parallel, education outcomes improve, leading to lower growth in both the supply and employment of unskilled workers (1.9 per cent per year) compared with that of semi-skilled and skilled workers (5.5 per cent per year). Second, the appreciation in the exchange rate leads to a contraction of employment in export sectors. Owing to these changes in employment, semi-skilled and skilled workers see their average real wage decline by 1.2 per cent and 0.4 per cent per year, respectively. By contrast, unskilled workers see their average real wage grow at 2 per cent per year. As unskilled workers are predominant in the labour force, the average real wage in the economy increases by 1.4 per cent per year.

These changes in the labour market translate into lower poverty and less income inequality in the baseline scenario (see Table A11.3). As shown in Figure 11.2, poverty falls considerably, but the target of halving extreme poverty between 1990 and 2015 is not met in the business-as-usual scenario.

In the baseline scenario, government spending on final consumption grows at 6.8 per cent per year, following the observed trend for 2000-04. Public investment falls 3.6 per cent per year in the first five years, then returns to growth at a pace of 0.1 per cent per year. It is important to note that in practice, public investment showed marked fluctuations in Nicaragua in the 1990s and into the new millennium, but it dropped at an average rate of 3.7 per cent per year during 2002-06. The growth in overall public spending facilitates important progress towards attaining the MDGs for education, health, and drinking water and sanitation. Yet, none of the targets for these MDGs is attained, as shown in Figure 11.3. In other words, current growth in public spending is insufficient to reach the MDGs in Nicaragua.

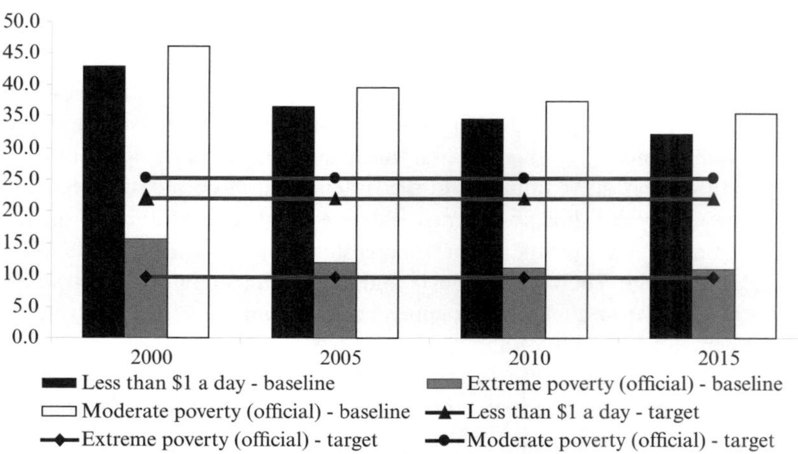

Figure 11.2 Nicaragua: Poverty indicators in the baseline scenario, 2000-2015 (Percentages)

Source: MAMS for Nicaragua and microsimulation results based on the 2001 LSMS.

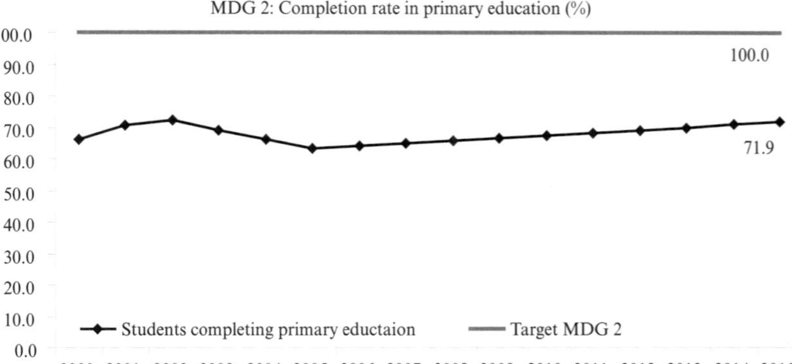

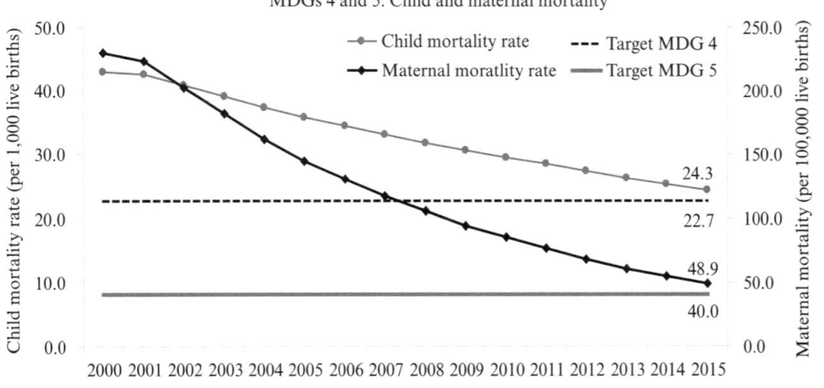

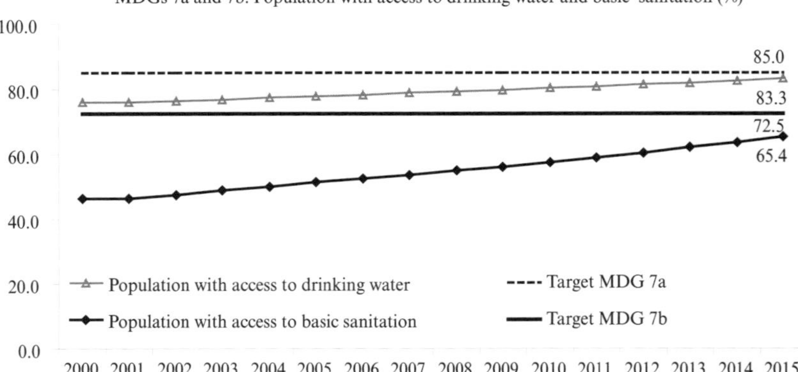

Figure 11.3 MDG indicators in the baseline scenario, 2000-2015
Source: MAMS for Nicaragua.

The fiscal deficit as a percentage of GDP increases with the strong increase in final government consumption. At the same time, the falling wages of semi-skilled and skilled workers affects the collection of income taxes. Income tax revenue falls as a percentage of GDP from the base year (2000) level, only to recover in the last five years of the simulation period. With no new domestic public borrowing, internal domestic debt falls with respect to GDP. External debt, in contrast, increases by almost 8 percentage points of GDP between 2000 and 2015 in the baseline scenario, as external borrowing continues to grow at (fixed) historical rates and the baseline only consider the cancellation of Nicaragua's external debt that took place during 2000-2006.

Scenarios for attaining the MDGs

Detailed results of the scenarios in which the MDGs are attained simultaneously under alternative strategies to finance the scaled-up public spending are presented in Tables A11.2-A11.3.[17] The results show that public spending on MDG related services would need to increase substantially to meet the targets (see Table 11.5). Average annual public spending would need to increase by 3.6 per cent of GDP as compared with the baseline in the scenarios where the additional expenditures are financed from abroad, by 4.4 per cent of GDP if financed through domestic borrowing and by 4.7 per cent of GDP if the costs of the MDG strategy are covered by increasing income taxes. Attaining universal primary education would be most expensive, requiring additional public spending of 2 per cent of GDP per year.[18] Reaching the targets for reducing child and maternal mortality would also be significant, costing an additional 1.1-1.7 per cent of GDP in public spending per year.

Financing the MDG strategy through domestic resource mobilization is more costly as shown in Table 11.5. Increased domestic public borrowing reduces savings available for financing of private investment. Higher income taxes limit disposable household income reducing private consumption compared with the baseline. Tax financing also crowds out private investment to some extent, but this effect is less significant than the compression of private consumption. In both cases, private spending on MDG-related services declines compared with the baseline, such that government spending has to increase by more in order to meet the MDG targets. In the case of Nicaragua, tax financing turns out to be the costliest option owing to the impact on private consumption.

It is less onerous for the treasury to finance all the goals simultaneously, due to the synergies among them (see Table 11.5). The sum of additional public spending in the scenarios in which only one or two MDGs are reached at the same time exceeds that required for attaining them simultaneously. The synergy effects amount to 0.8 per cent, 0.5 per cent, and 0.3 per cent of GDP per year, respectively, when using external financing, domestic borrowing, or higher income taxes.

Table 11.5   Nicaragua: Additional public spending per year required to attain the MDGs simultaneously or individually under alternative financing strategies, 2000-2015 (Percentage of GDP)

	Average spending in baseline scenario	Foreign grants	Taxes	Public borrowing		Foreign grants	Taxes	Public borrowing	
				External	Internal			External	Internal
		All MDGs simultaneously				*Only the primary education MDG*			
Primary education	2.0	1.9	2.0	1.9	2.1	2.1	2.2	2.1	2.2
Final consumption	1.7	1.5	1.5	1.5	1.6	1.6	1.7	1.6	1.7
Investment	0.3	0.4	0.4	0.4	0.4	0.5	0.5	0.5	0.5
Health	3.4	1.1	1.7	1.1	1.6	0.0	0.0	0.0	0.0
Final consumption	2.9	0.7	1.1	0.7	1.1	0.0	0.0	0.0	0.0
Investment	0.5	0.4	0.6	0.4	0.5	0.0	0.0	0.0	0.0
Water and sanitation	0.3	0.6	1.0	0.6	0.8	0.0	0.0	0.0	0.0
Final consumption	0.2	0.6	1.0	0.6	0.8	0.0	0.0	0.0	0.0
Investment	0.1	0.0	0.0	0.0	0.0	0.0	0.0	0.0	0.0
Total	5.7	3.6	4.7	3.6	4.4	2.0	2.1	2.0	2.2
Final consumption	4.8	2.8	3.7	2.8	3.5	1.6	1.7	1.6	1.8
Investment	0.9	0.8	1.0	0.8	0.9	0.4	0.5	0.4	0.5
		Only the health MDGs				*Only the MDGs for water and sanitation*			
Primary education	2.0	0.0	0.0	0.0	0.0	0.0	0.0	0.0	0.0
Final consumption	1.7	0.0	0.0	0.0	0.0	0.0	0.0	0.0	0.0
Investment	0.3	0.0	0.0	0.0	0.0	0.0	0.0	0.0	0.0
Health	3.4	1.6	2.1	1.6	1.9	0.0	0.0	0.0	0.0
Final consumption	2.9	1.1	1.4	1.1	1.3	0.0	0.0	0.0	0.0
Investment	0.5	0.5	0.7	0.5	0.6	0.0	0.0	0.0	0.0
Water and sanitation	0.3	0.0	0.0	0.0	0.0	0.8	0.9	0.8	0.8
Final consumption	0.2	0.0	0.0	0.0	0.0	0.8	0.9	0.8	0.8
Investment	0.1	0.0	0.0	0.0	0.0	0.0	0.0	0.0	0.0
Total	5.7	1.6	2.1	1.6	1.9	0.8	0.8	0.8	0.8
Final consumption	4.8	1.1	1.4	1.1	1.3	0.8	0.8	0.8	0.8
Investment	0.9	0.5	0.7	0.5	0.6	0.0	0.0	0.0	0.0

Source: MAMS for Nicaragua.

New public spending makes it possible to expand public services associated with the MDGs. As a result, the demand for inputs in health, education, and other services increases as does the demand for, mostly, skilled workers (doctors, nurses, teachers, and so on). The costs of these inputs and workers increase as these are not unlimited in supply. The rising costs of producing public services translate into a higher relative price of non-tradable goods and services with respect to the price of tradable goods. This is consistent with the appreciation of the real exchange rate by 1 point or more per year with respect to the baseline scenario, except in the case of tax-financing of the strategy (see Table A11.2).

The exchange-rate appreciation discourages exports and stimulates imports. Private investment contracts slightly with respect to the baseline to the extent that export sectors are affected. The impact is stronger in the scenarios with domestic resource mobilization. Nonetheless, average output growth does not fall with respect to the baseline scenario since increased government spending compensates for this fall in aggregate demand (see Table A11.2). In the domestic borrowing scenario, however, output does fall below the baseline level after 2010 as a result of the "crowding out effect" on private investment. This is not the case in the scenario when income taxes are raised, since the drop in private consumption has a stronger effect on reducing the import leakage, and rising public consumption otherwise offsets the drop in private spending on aggregate demand. Because of the drop in the demand for imported consumer goods in the tax-financing scenario, the trade gap narrows reducing the pressure on the exchange rate to appreciate.

The MDG scenarios do not produce any great impact on average labour market indicators (see Table A11.2). In the scenario with domestic borrowing, employment falls slightly with respect to the baseline scenario (0.1 per cent per year), owing to the crowding out of private investment. Average real wages remain practically unchanged when the additional spending is covered by taxation but increase by 0.2 per cent per year when the strategy is financed by external funds and drop by 0.2 per cent per year when relying on domestic borrowing. There are a number of reasons for this limited impact. First, the changes in total output with respect to the baseline scenario are equally modest. Second, the small changes in employment and remuneration are also a result of the fact that a larger number of children enrol in primary education and finish it on time in the MDG scenario, thereby generating a relative scarcity of unskilled workers with respect to the baseline scenario. As a result, employment for these workers tends to fall, while their remuneration rises. In the aggregate, these changes are partially offset by a decline in the average real wage of semi-skilled and skilled workers and the demand for these workers increases. Third, some of the children that are now encouraged to enter the primary school system were in the labour market thus further limiting the positive employment effects of the strategy. Finally, the children entering for the first time in the educational system take at least 12 to 16 years to complete secondary and tertiary studies and thus would remain in the schooling system, rather than entering the labour market for most if not all of the simulation period to 2015.

Because of the small impact of the MDG scenarios on the labour market, inequality in per-capita household income also changes only marginally with respect to the baseline scenario (see Table A11.3). In the baseline, income inequality falls slightly over the simulation period. This decline is less pronounced in the MDG scenarios, explained mainly by the stronger increase in the demand for skilled workers. The impact on poverty is equally small. The MDG strategy generates slightly more poverty reduction, as compared with the baseline, when financed through foreign grants or external borrowing. When financed through domestic resource mobilization, the degree of poverty reduction is slightly less. These differences are mainly due to the differences in the outcomes for employment and real wages. In the MDG scenarios with external financing, aggregate employment falls slightly but its impact on poverty is more than offset by rising real wages. In the domestic borrowing scenario, both employment and real wages fall with respect to the baseline. In the case of the tax-financing scenario, the impact on poverty of the decline in employment for unskilled workers and the drop in real wages for unskilled workers with respect to the baseline is not made up by the slight increase in the real wage for unskilled workers. For all MDG scenarios it holds that poverty reduction remains insufficient, as in the baseline, to meet the target for MDG 1.

The macroeconomic viability of increasing public spending to meet the goals depends on the source of financing. External borrowing would not seem very viable given the high initial level of external indebtedness, even after considering the debt relief received under the HIPC initiative until 2006. According to the simulations with MAMS, the MDG strategy would lift external public debt to 158.3 per cent of GDP in 2015 (see Table A11.2). Financing through domestic borrowing would yield an even more explosive debt situation: domestic public debt would increase by 57.3 percentage points between 2000 and 2015, reaching 192.7 per cent of GDP at the end of the period. In this scenario, the fiscal deficit practically doubles with respect to the baseline scenario, while financing through domestic borrowing has added costs in terms of lower growth and less poverty reduction as compared with the baseline. This scenario is also less viable, as the capacity of the government to borrow on the domestic capital market is rather limited in practice given the lack of a developed domestic bond market in Nicaragua.

Increasing taxes could be a better alternative, requiring that revenue from income taxes increase by 4.2 per cent of GDP between 2000 and 2015, in order to reach 6.5 per cent of GDP at the end of the period (see Table A11.2). This is a substantial increase, but may be feasible to achieve considering the already seen increase in tax collection as a result of the fiscal reform of the 1990s. Total tax income increased by 4.7 per cent of GDP between 1995 and 2005. In addition, even with this increase the current tax burden remains relatively low at around 15 per cent of GDP (see Table 11.1). Further increasing the tax base would also help lower the public debt overhang. On the downside, however, tax financing makes the MDG strategy more costly in terms of the required additional public spending, as indicated.

These macroeconomic trade-offs can be avoided by and large if the strategy is financed through increasing foreign grants. Nicaragua would need approximately 3.5 per cent of GDP per year in additional resources from foreign donors. While substantial, such an increase is not out of reach considering historical levels of official development assistance for Nicaragua (see Table 11.1). A different matter is how much and for how long Nicaragua wishes to remain aid dependent, but the macroeconomic trade-offs associated with this form of financing are of lesser concern than those of the alternative financing options.

Conclusions and policy recommendations

Nicaragua faces enormous challenges to reach the MDGs by 2015. Poverty is widespread and income distribution is highly skewed. Domestic economic constraints and external vulnerability have made the economy highly dependent on foreign aid and other sources of external financing. This dependence has led to high levels of external indebtedness, making the debt relief obtained through the HIPC initiative essential to enable the country to free up more resources for poverty reduction and expansion of social programmes. Progress made towards the MDGs has been insufficient, especially with regard to poverty reduction, increasing access to basic sanitation, and reducing maternal mortality. Progress towards the MDG targets for universalizing primary education, reducing child mortality, and enhancing access to drinking water has been more satisfactory, such that Nicaragua should be able to meet these targets without major difficulty by 2015.

The model-based analysis shows that with continued trends in public spending, Nicaragua would make further, yet insufficient, progress towards timely achievement of the MDGs for primary education, health, and water and sanitation. The analysis indicates further that trying to achieve all MDGs simultaneously would be less costly given the synergy effects among the MDGs. Even so, public social spending would need to be scaled up substantially to achieve the targets. The precise increase that is required depends on the financing strategy. When financed through foreign grants or external borrowing, government spending would have to increase by 3.6 per cent of GDP per year compared with the simulated baseline scenario. When financed through domestic borrowing, the required increase would be 4.4 per cent of GDP per annum, and the increase would have to be 4.7 per cent in the case of tax financing. About half of the additional resources would be needed to achieve 100 per cent primary completion rates.

Increasing public spending to such an extent would adversely affect investment in export sectors as it causes an appreciation of the real exchange rate. Nonetheless, overall economic growth would not be affected as aggregate demand is kept up by the increase in public social spending. Since the aggregate output effects are modest at best, labour market outcomes of the MDG strategy do not differ greatly from the baseline scenario. Consequently, the impact on poverty and inequality are minor and the target for reducing extreme poverty is not met even as the other MDGs are being met.

Financing the strategy through external borrowing would be undesirable. It would lead to an unsustainable level of public debt with the external debt-to-GDP ratio increasing to 158.3 per cent of GDP in 2015. It should be noted that this rise in indebtedness does not account for the debt relief the country received after 2007. Debt relief in the framework of the HIPC initiative would thus be critical for keeping the degree of external debt overhang below 100 per cent of GDP, but even then the debt burden would be too high for comfort.

Financing the MDG strategy through domestic borrowing appears to be even more prohibitive. Not only would public debt inflate to almost 200 per cent of GDP by 2015, but it would entail losses in terms of economic growth and poverty reduction. Given this, the recommended alternative would seem to be to finance the increased public spending by raising income taxes. In the model simulations the tax increase is applied uniformly to all households and direct tax revenue would need to be increased by 4.2 per cent of GDP, reaching 6.5 per cent of GDP in 2015. Such an increase, while substantial, may be feasible. During 1995 and 2005, the government managed to increase tax revenue by a wider margin and the existing total tax burden is still relatively low by international standards. Moreover, increasing the tax base would help improve public finances and reduce indebtedness. It would make the MDG strategy more costly, however, since the government would need to step in with more resources to compensate for lower private spending on the MDGs as disposable incomes would be affected by the tax increase. The scenarios considered here do not include a possible fiscal reform which would put most of the additional tax burden on high-income households. Such a progressive tax reform could avoid affecting the consumption of low-income households, thereby avoiding one of the downsides to this financing option.

For the short to medium run, Nicaragua will need to continue relying on foreign development assistance to complement domestic resources in financing spending towards the achievement of the MDGs. With additional aid several of the trade offs of the alternative financing options could be avoided. When fully financed through grants, Nicaragua would need an additional 3.5 per cent of GDP in development assistance per year to finance the MDG strategy. This would entail an increase by about 50 per cent from the level of aid received during 2000-05. This may be a preferable option in the short run, but in order to reduce aid dependence, the country should consider further fiscal reforms such that it can gradually replace aid financing with tax revenue. A progressive fiscal reform could also help reduce inequality and, in this way, enhance the impact of economic growth on poverty reduction.

The target for MDG 1 is not met under any of the scenarios simulated, including also when public spending is increased to meet the other MDGs. Apart from what might be achieved through redistributive taxation, perhaps more important for meeting the poverty reduction target will be for the government to engage in more active production sector and labour market policies in order to raise productivity growth and create more jobs in the economy. In this regard, successive governments have placed high hopes on free trade agreements, including the DR-CAFTA agreement with the United States and the agreement being negotiated with the European Union. Nonetheless, as Sánchez and Vos (2006) concluded, free trade agreements such as DR-CAFTA are anything but a panacea for Nicaraguan economic development and will not yield sufficient poverty reduction without complementary policies aimed at improving production capacity and encouraging the creation of employment.

Table A11.1   Nicaragua: Elasticities of the MDGs module of the MAMS model

| | Determinants in the MAMS model | | | | | |
(a) MDGs 4, 5 and 7	Per-capita spending on water and sanitation	Infrastructure (except water and sanitation)	Access to drinking water (MDG 7a)	Access to sanitation (MDG 7b)	Per-capita household consumption	Per-capita health consumption
MDG 4: child mortality		-0.2000[c]	-0.3268[a]	-0.1315[a]	-0.6133[a]	-0.5000[c]
MDG 5: maternal mortality		-0.2000[c]	-0.3268[a]	-0.1315[a]	-0.6133[a]	-0.5000[c]
MDG 7a: access to water	0.0360[a]	0.0020[a]			0.1120[a]	
MDG 7b: access to sanitation	0.1600[a]	0.0840[a]			0.2650[a]	

| | Child mortality rate (MDG 4) | Infrastructure (except water and sanitation) | Wage premium: complete vs incomplete secondary | Wage premium tertiary vs complete secondary | Per-capita household consumption | Quality of education |
(b) MDG 2 (education)						
Percentage of students at the age for entering primary school who enrol in the cycle	-0.6300[b]	0.3815[b]	1.3650[a]		0.3063[b]	1.0000[c]
Percentage of students who passed their grade in primary school.	-0.6300[b]	0.1715[b]	0.5167[a]		0.1187[b]	1.0000[c]
Percentage of students who passed their grade in secondary school	-0.0046[a]	0.1059[a]	1.5874[a]		0.4269[a]	0.2881
Percentage of students who passed their grade in tertiary education.	-0.0046[a]	0.1059[a]		2.3849[a]	1.9724[a]	0.2881
Percentage of primary school graduates who go on to secondary education.	-0.0046[a]	0.1059[a]	1.5874[a]		0.4269[a]	0.2881
Percentage of secondary school graduates who go on to tertiary education.	-0.0046[a]	0.1059[a]		2.3849[a]	1.9724[a]	0.2881

Source: Econometric estimates taken from Hammill (2006) and own imputations.

[a] Econometric estimates from Hammill (2006).

[b] Econometric estimates adjusted proportionally to make them fall within the range of feasibility of the MAMS model for the elasticity in question.

[c] Value assumed ad-hoc, but falling in the range of feasibility to obtain a consistent model solution for MAMS.

Table A11.2   Nicaragua: Main results of the scenarios simulated using the MAMS model, 2000-2015

	Values of the baseline scenario			Deviation with respect to baseline values for MDG scenarios financed with:							
				foreign grants		external borrowing		domestic borrowing		income taxes	
	2000	2015	2000-2015	2015	2000-2015	2015	2000-2015	2015	2000-2015	2015	2000-2015
Exchange rate (index 2000 = 100)	100.0	76.0	91.2	-1.4	-1.8	-1.4	-1.8	-3.5	-1.6	-0.2	-0.1
Real GDP growth (%)		2.7	3.2	0.1	0.2	0.1	0.2	-0.6	-0.3	0.0	0.2
Composition of GDP (% of GDP)											
Private final consumption	76.8	105.0	85.3	-1.0	-0.4	-1.0	-0.4	4.5	1.3	-4.8	-4.2
Government final consumption	17.3	29.6	24.0	4.1	2.8	4.1	2.8	5.7	3.5	5.0	3.7
Private gross fixed capital formation	25.2	36.3	28.8	-0.3	-0.2	-0.3	-0.2	-8.7	-6.0	-1.6	-1.4
Public gross fixed capital formation	7.6	4.7	5.2	0.2	0.8	0.2	0.8	0.4	0.9	0.2	1.0
Exports of goods and services	27.2	12.4	20.4	-0.8	-1.2	-0.8	-1.2	-1.9	-1.4	-0.5	-0.5
Imports of goods and services	54.0	88.0	63.7	1.3	1.5	1.2	1.5	1.4	-0.8	-2.5	-1.5
Public finances (% of GDP)											
Income taxes	2.3	2.6	1.5	-0.1	0.0	-0.1	0.0	0.0	0.0	3.9	4.5
Government savings	-2.6	-9.8	-7.5	-2.3	-2.1	-3.0	-2.4	-7.7	-4.7	0.5	1.3
Foreign savings	23.4	24.8	21.4	3.2	3.3	4.1	3.7	0.6	0.1	-0.6	-0.5
Foreign grants	4.5	4.5	4.5	3.1	3.5	0.0	0.0	0.0	0.0	0.0	0.0
Domestic government debt	17.9	7.3	12.3	-0.3	-0.4	-0.3	-0.4	67.9	27.5	-0.2	-0.3
External government debt	112.6	120.5	97.6	-7.1	-5.1	30.8	12.6	-3.0	-1.4	-3.1	-2.2

Table A11.2 (cont'd)

| | Values of the baseline scenario | | | Deviation with respect to baseline values for MDG scenarios financed with: | | | | | | | |
| | | | | foreign grant | | external borrowing | | domestic borrowing | | income taxes | |
	2000	2015	2000-2015	2015	2000-2015	2015	2000-2015	2015	2000-2015	2015	2000-2015
Labour market											
Employment											
(thousands of persons employed)	1,808	2,712	2,215	-17	-8	-17	-8	-43	-31	-8	-11
Unskilled workers	1,466	1,953	1,694	-46	-20	-46	-20	-47	-31	-27	-17
Semi-skilled workers	241	537	370	23	9	23	9	5	904	17	5
Skilled workers	101	222	152	6	3	6	3	-1	-467	2	340
Real wage per worker											
(*córdobas* per year)	1,477.3	1,826.8	1,621.0	55.6	36.0	55.6	36.0	-50.6	-16.3	1.2	4.9
Unskilled workers	1,157.7	1,553.4	1,316.3	78.4	39.7	78.4	39.7	-55.0	-20.2	18.3	10.5
Semi-skilled workers	2,007.4	1,682.3	1,815.4	-32.3	-0.8	-32.3	-0.8	-59.0	-22.9	-54.5	-19.8
Skilled workers	4,845.0	4,551.7	4,702.8	-32.9	18.9	-32.9	18.9	-37.0	-11.8	-56.7	-19.2

Source: MAMS for Nicaragua.

Table A11.3   Nicaragua: Results of the microsimulations in simulated scenarios, 2000-2015[a]

	Moderate poverty[b]				Extreme poverty[b]				Population living on less than one dollar a day (%)				Gini coefficient for per-capita household income			
	2000	2005	2010	2015	2000	2005	2010	2015	2000	2005	2010	2015	2000	2005	2010	2015
Baseline scenario																
(1) U	46.2	43.3	42.5	43.6	15.8	13.3	13.4	14.4	43.0	39.5	39.0	40.0	0.540	0.520	0.510	0.470
(2) U + S	46.2	43.3	41.9	43.5	15.8	13.4	13.1	14.2	43.0	39.9	38.7	39.9	0.540	0.520	0.510	0.470
(3) U + S + W1	46.1	43.5	43.1	44.2	15.7	14.6	15.6	16.6	43.0	40.7	40.5	41.1	0.540	0.530	0.530	0.480
(4) U + S + W1 + W2	46.1	39.9	37.8	36.1	15.7	12.0	11.2	11.0	43.0	37.1	35.2	33.1	0.540	0.530	0.530	0.480
(5) U + S + W1 + W2 + M	46.1	39.6	37.4	35.4	15.7	12.0	11.2	10.8	43.0	36.6	34.6	32.3	0.540	0.530	0.530	0.480
MDG scenarios financed with:																
Foreign grants or external borrowing																
(1) U	46.1	44.0	42.5	43.8	15.9	13.5	13.1	13.7	43.0	40.7	39.0	40.5	0.540	0.530	0.510	0.490
(2) U + S	46.1	43.7	42.6	43.6	15.9	13.6	13.3	14.0	43.1	40.2	39.0	40.1	0.540	0.520	0.520	0.490
(3) U + S + W1	45.0	44.2	43.4	44.8	15.1	15.2	17.1	17.1	42.1	41.3	40.5	41.8	0.530	0.540	0.530	0.510
(4) U + S + W1 + W2	45.0	40.2	35.8	34.6	15.1	12.2	11.0	9.8	42.1	37.2	33.2	31.6	0.530	0.540	0.530	0.510
(5) U + S + W1 + W2 + M	45.0	39.7	35.2	34.2	15.1	12.4	10.7	9.9	42.1	36.8	32.5	30.7	0.530	0.540	0.540	0.520
Incomes taxes																
(1) U	46.4	43.0	42.9	43.7	15.9	13.2	13.5	14.2	43.2	39.7	39.2	40.5	0.540	0.510	0.490	0.500
(2) U + S	46.4	43.3	42.4	43.3	15.9	13.3	13.2	14.2	43.2	39.7	39.3	39.9	0.540	0.520	0.490	0.500
(3) U + S + W1	46.3	43.0	43.2	45.0	15.8	14.2	16.8	18.2	43.2	40.2	40.5	42.5	0.540	0.520	0.500	0.520
(4) U + S + W1 + W2	46.3	38.2	37.9	37.6	15.8	11.3	11.8	12.4	43.2	35.1	34.7	34.9	0.540	0.520	0.500	0.520
(5) U + S + W1 + W2 + M	46.3	37.8	37.3	36.5	15.7	11.3	12.0	12.2	43.1	34.9	34.4	33.8	0.540	0.520	0.510	0.530

Table A11.3 (cont'd)

	Moderate poverty[b]				Extreme poverty[b]				Population living on less than one dollar a day (%)				Gini coefficient for per-capita household income			
	2000	2005	2010	2015	2000	2005	2010	2015	2000	2005	2010	2015	2000	2005	2010	2015
Domestic borrowing																
(1) U	46.5	44.1	47.2	48.7	15.8	13.9	16.1	17.2	43.4	40.8	44.0	45.6	0.540	0.530	0.510	0.510
(2) U + S	46.5	43.8	47.1	48.7	15.8	14.2	16.2	17.2	43.4	40.4	43.9	45.5	0.540	0.530	0.510	0.510
(3) U + S + W1	46.2	44.0	47.4	49.8	15.7	16.1	19.0	21.0	43.3	41.5	45.0	46.9	0.540	0.540	0.520	0.540
(4) U + S + W1 + W2	46.2	40.5	40.7	41.2	15.7	13.2	13.3	13.6	43.3	37.7	37.9	38.5	0.540	0.540	0.520	0.530
(5) U + S + W1 + W2 + M	46.2	39.8	39.4	40.7	15.7	13.2	13.1	13.8	43.3	37.2	36.7	37.9	0.540	0.540	0.520	0.540

Source: MAMS for Nicaragua and microsimulations based on the 2001 LSMS.

[a] Showing the cumulative effects of: U, changes in the structure of unemployment by level of skill of the worker; S, changes in the structure of employment by sector of activity, according to the level of skill of the worker in the different segments of the labour market; W1, changes in the structure of labour incomes by sector of activity, according to the level of skill of the worker in the different segments of the labour market; W2, changes in average labour income; M, changes in the skills structure of the employed labour force. The final result on poverty and inequality is given by the cumulative effect of the sequence of all the changes simulated in the labour market in the fifth step.

[b] Percentage of the population with incomes less than the corresponding official poverty line for 2001.

Acknowledgements

The authors would like to thank María Rosa Renzi and Octavio Zeledón for their valuable comments on a preliminary version of this chapter. They also thank Ana María Torres, Luz Elena Sequeira, Octavio Zeledón, Luis Alaniz, Janet Ramírez and Leonel Pérez Lainez for all the information and support they have offered. Matthew Hammill of ECLAC's Subregional Office in Mexico City is acknowledged for his valuable contribution in the form of the econometric estimates of the MDG determinants. The opinions expressed are the sole responsibility of the authors and do not necessarily represent the view of the United Nations or its member States

Notes

1   The National Development Plan (PND) is also known as the second document that defines Nicaragua's Poverty Reduction Strategy Paper (or PRSP-II).
2   Nicaragua's production could have been greater had oil prices not increased from 2002 to 2006 (United Nations, 2007, Box I.4).
3   Uses the definition of public social spending introduced in 2005, according to which it is specified in relation to its association with poverty reduction.
4   Due to the lack of comparative surveys for 1990, the baseline year established internationally for evaluating the MDGs, 1993 is taken as the baseline year for establishing the MDG for extreme poverty in Nicaragua.
5   National extreme poverty indirectly quantifies the scourge of hunger, as the extreme poverty line considers only the cost of basic food items.
6   Reducing the cost of these basic foods is due to the *pound-for-pound* programme for rice as well as to the incentives for bean production as part of the reconstruction programmes after Hurricane Mitch.
7   According to the Ministry of Education, investment in school infrastructure diminished steadily from 2000 to 2003, falling from US\$ 35.3 million to US\$ 8.7 million, 67 per cent lower than in 1997.
8   Data from the Ministry of Education indicate that the salary of teachers in the basic and middle education system remained far below the cost of the basic market basket from 1998 to 2003.
9   The Survey of Child and Adolescent Labour in Nicaragua (ENTIA: *Encuesta de Trabajo Infantil y de Adolescentes de Nicaragua*) for 2000 indicates that there were 314,000 child and adolescent workers aged 5 to 17, just over 54 per cent of whom did not go to school; 18 per cent of those who attended school said that working had a negative impact on their regular school attendance. Of these, 22.3 per cent were illiterate and only 20.5 per cent had reached the last grade of primary school (United Nations System, 2003: 26).
10   Data on maternal mortality in Nicaragua vary, depending on the source. According to the PND, maternal mortality per 100,000 live births rose from 106 in 1998 to 201 in 2001, and dropped to 96 in 2004 (Gobierno de Nicaragua, 2005). The first report monitoring the MDGs in Nicaragua indicates that the rate first decreased after 1993, but subsequently increased between 1998 and 2001, as reported by the previous source (Sistema de las Naciones Unidas, 2003). The data compiled by the Ministry of Health based on reported death cases by health centres differ from those mentioned above.

According to this source, maternal mortality increased from 98 to 125 per 100,000 live births between 1993 and 1996, falling thereafter to 89.6 in 2005. Those data also show two major spikes in maternal mortality: one from 1998 to 1999 when the rate jumps from 106 to 118 and one from 2000 to 2001 when it is up from 87 to 115 deaths per 100,000 live births. The causes of the volatility in these estimates are not clear, but are likely to be a result of weaknesses in the administrative records of health centres. For this reason, Ministry of Health data are not used in this study.

11　The percentage of the population with access to drinking water also increased notably, from 45.8 per cent in 1990 to 70.5 per cent in 2001, though with significant lags in rural areas (United Nations System, 2003).

12　The model of proportions is estimated by means of the "quasi-maximum likelihood method" suggested in Papke and Wooldridge (1996).

13　In Hammill (2006), the quality of education is also measured indirectly by the average number of teachers per school, in some cases, and the average number of students per teacher, in others.

14　Greater density and quality of the road system, for example, would improve access to health centers, and better communications and energy infrastructure would facilitate the operation of such centers.

15　Deficiencies in reporting of income sources explain most of these cases where consumption levels exceed household income.

16　It should be noted, however, that in reality the real exchange rate appreciated during 2001-05, as the pace of devaluation was diminished. Yet, MAMS for Nicaragua shows a somewhat stronger exchange-rate appreciation than that observed.

17　The results of the scenarios in which only one or two MDGs are attained at the same time are reported in Sánchez and Vos (2007).

18　It should be noted that these cost estimates consider economy-wide effects, including endogenous effects on changing teacher salaries as well as the impact of changes in household incomes, in wage premiums, and in children's health status on education performance. Considering these feedback effects leads to lower estimates of the additional public spending required to achieve the MDG for primary education than likely would have been obtained when using sector analysis or a partial equilibrium approach. For example, ECLAC and UNESCO (2005) estimate that the cost of universalizing primary education and of ensuring that all students complete at least five grades of primary schooling by 2015 would be more than 3 per cent of GDP per year in Nicaragua.

References

Andersen, Lykke E. (2004). "Population, poverty and social spending projections for Nicaragua 2000-2015," Final Consulting Report prepared for the United Nations System in Nicaragua, Managua.

Arcia, Gustavo (2003). "The incidence of public education spending in Nicaragua: The impact of the Education for All-fast track initiative", Consulting Report prepared for the World Bank.

ECLAC (Economic Commission for Latin America and the Caribbean) (2006). *Panorama social de América Latina 2006*, ECLAC: Santiago, Chile.

__________, and UNESCO (Economic Commission for Latin America and the Caribbean - United Nations Educational, Scientific and Cultural Organization) (2005). "Invertir mejor para invertir más. Financiamiento y gestión de la educación en América Latina y el Caribe", *Serie Seminarios y Conferencias No. 43*, ECLAC, Santiago, Chile.

ECLAC-IPEA-UNDP (2003). "Hacia el objetivo del milenio de reducir la pobreza en América Latina y el Caribe", *Libros de la CEPAL No. 70*, Santiago, Chile.

Dijkstra, Geske, and Trevor Evans (2003). "Results of international debt relief in Nicaragua", IOB Working Paper (Office of the Comptroller of Netherlands External Cooperation), The Hague, Directorate General for International Co-operation (DGIS/IOB) (January).

ECLAC/CELADE (2002). "Latin America and the Caribbean: Population estimates and projections 1950-2050", *ECLAC Population Division Demographic Bulletin No. 69*, Santiago, Chile.

Gobierno de Nicaragua (2005). *Plan Nacional de Desarrollo*, Managua.

Guimarães, João, and Nestor Avendaño (2007). "Nicaragua: Pobreza, problema postergado. Informe país Nicaragua - 2006", Evaluation of Poverty Reduction Strategies in Latin America, Sida Informes, The Hague, Institute of Social Studies (for SIDA, Sweden).

Hammill, Matt (2006). "Determinants of selected MDGs in the framework of the MAMS model for Nicaragua", Background paper for the country study of Nicaragua in the framework of the project *Public Policies for MDGs in Latin America and the Caribbean*, ECLAC Subregional Office in Mexico, United Nations.

MINSA (Ministry of Health of Nicaragua) (2000). "Boletín Epidemiológico de Vigilancia de la Mortalidad Materna", Managua: MINSA.

Papke, Leslie E., and Jeffrey M. Wooldridge (1996). "Econometric methods for fractional response variables with an application to 401(k) plan participation rates", *Journal of Applied Econometrics* 11(6): 619-32.

Ponce, Juan (2005). "Cómo Mejorar el Gasto Educativo en Nicaragua: Un Análisis Costo-Efectividad", Research report prepared for the Swedish International Development Cooperation Agency (SIDA).

Sánchez, Marco V. (2005). "Reformas Económicas, régimen cambiario y choques externos: Efectos en el desarrollo económico, la desigualdad y la pobreza en Costa Rica, El Salvador y Honduras", *Serie Estudios y Perspectivas*, No. 36, ECLAC Subregional Headquarters in Mexico.

__________, and Rob Vos (2006). "Impacto del CAFTA en el crecimiento, la pobreza y la desigualdad en Nicaragua", Managua: Ministry of Development of Industry and Commerce (MIFIC) and United Nations Development Programme (UNDP).

__________, and Rob Vos (2007). "¿Cómo financiar el gasto público para alcanzar las metas de desarrollo del milenio en Nicaragua? Opciones y disyuntivas", Project *Public Policies for MDGs in Latin America and the Caribbean*, UNDP/UN-DESA/World Bank, August (mimeo.).

Sistema de las Naciones Unidas (2003). *Metas de Desarrollo. Seguimiento a la Cumbre del Milenio. Nicaragua. Primer Informe*, Managua.

United Nations (2007). *World Economic Situation and Prospects 2007*, New York: United Nations.

Vos, Rob, and Sara Johanssen (1998). "Nicaragua", in Howard White (ed.) *Aid and Macroeconomic Performance. Theory, Empirical Evidence and Four Country Cases*, London and New York, Macmillan, pp. 139-194.

World Bank (2001). *Nicaragua Poverty Assessment: Challenges and Opportunities for Poverty Reduction*, Report No. 20488-NI, Washington, D.C.: The World Bank.

__________ (2003). Nicaragua Poverty Assessment: Raising Welfare and Reducing Vulnerability, Washington, D.C.: The World Bank.

12
Peru

Juan F. Castro and Gustavo Yamada

Introduction

In recent years, successive Peruvian governments have given importance to achieving the Millennium Development Goals (MDGs). But the necessary conditions to reach the related targets still need to be put it place. Those conditions would include high and sustained economic growth, significant income redistribution, and better targeted social policies.

This chapter provides an assessment of the costs associated with the MDG targets for poverty reduction, primary education, health, and access to water and basic sanitation by the year 2015 in Peru. The study is based on a scenario analysis using the computable general equilibrium model called MAMS, as described in Chapter 3, and adapted to Peru's socio-economic structure and conditions. The policy simulation analysis with MAMS for Peru was combined with cost-effectiveness analyses of delivery of education, health, and water and sanitation services and with the application of a microsimulation methodology that enables assessment of outcomes for poverty reduction and income inequality (see Appendix A2.1 of Chapter 2).

This chapter is organized as follows. The next section briefly summarizes the main macroeconomic trends in Peru as well as changes in the MDG indicators between the early 1990s and 2005. The following section summarizes the results of econometric estimations that were conducted to determine the likely impact of different socio-economic and demographic determinants of progress towards the MDGs for education, health, and drinking water and sanitation and further identifies the effectiveness of relevant public policy variables in achieving the targets. The fourth section briefly explains the calibration of MAMS using Peruvian data. The fifth section discusses the main results of the policy simulations with MAMS. It first discusses the macroeconomic results and progress towards the MDGs under a baseline scenario with "business-as-usual" assumptions. These are compared with outcomes of scenarios that scale up public spending to the level required to achieve pre-set MDG targets for education, health, and water and sanitation under alternative financing strategies. The subsequent section presents the main results obtained from the application of the microsimulation methodology, assessing how much progress would be made towards the target for reducing income poverty, while scaling up public spending for achieving the goals for education, health and basic sanitation. The main conclusions and policy recommendations are summarized in the final section.

Recent social and economic development trends in Peru

Peru's economy showed a robust performance over the past decade and a half. Economic growth averaged 4.1 per cent per year between 2000 and 2005, similar to the 4 per cent per year achieved during the 1990s and above the historic average of 3 per cent per year during 1960-2005. Since 2002, inflation stabilized at around 2.5 per cent, around the pre-set inflation target. The fiscal deficit did not surpass the ceiling of 1 per cent of GDP during 2004-05, in compliance with that stipulated by the Fiscal Transparency and Responsibility Law. The fiscal deficit stood at 0.3 per cent of GDP in 2005 and was financed by mobilizing domestic resources. Public external debt was reduced from over 40 per cent of GDP in 2000 to 35.2 per cent in 2005. The public domestic debt ratio has been relatively stable, averaging 9.4 per cent of GDP in the late 1990s to only slightly increase to 9.8 per cent in 2005. The current account deficit of the balance of payments has narrowed and shifted into a surplus of 1.3 per cent of GDP in 2005, while maintaining a managed floating exchange-rate regime.

The main financial constraint to increase social spending is the ceiling for the budget deficit imposed by the Fiscal Transparency and Responsibility Law of 2000. Peru's tax burden remains low by international standards even though it increased to 13.6 per cent of GDP in 2005, only slightly above the historic average of 13.1 per cent and well below the average for Latin America (17.5 per cent). The low tax burden is the result of several factors, including the high degree of informality in the economy, pervasive tax evasion, and legislation that provides multiple tax exemptions.

In all of the public opinion surveys, Peruvians name the lack of job opportunities as the biggest problem affecting the country. Open unemployment is not the main issue, though. The unemployment rate in the metropolitan area of Lima is at single-digit levels—ranging between 7 per cent and 9 per cent—and is practically non-existent in the rural areas of Peru. The main problem is the high degree of underemployment, affecting more than half of the economically active population. Workers are considered underemployed if they have full-time jobs with wages insufficient to cover the cost of a basic basket of consumption goods or if they involuntarily have had to take part-time jobs. Because most workers are engaged in informal sector activities, much of the adjustment in the Peruvian takes place through prices (labour incomes) rather than through quantity (unemployment). The low and volatile income levels in the large informal segment of the labour market are clear manifestations of this. It has also been shown that the rate of open unemployment is not very sensitive to the short-term business cycle in Peru (Yamada, 2004).

During the first half of the 2000s, Peru's economy suffered few adverse shocks unlike in the past.[1] This has supported the strong overall economic performance. Public spending, however, tends to be strongly pro-cyclical. This applies in particular also to social expenditures by the government which follow the ups and downs of the economy in an amplified way. This pro-cyclical spending behaviour complicates the implementation of poverty reduction programmes. In addition, those programmes suffer from problems of inadequate targeting and inefficiencies. In order to achieve the MDGs, public policies would need to become better targeted and more predictable and to avoid pro-cyclical swings so as to ensure sustained progress towards the targets.

An earlier study about the feasibility of achieving the MDGs in Peru showed uneven paths towards the targets (Beltran and others, 2004). While some MDGs (universal access to primary education, for example) could be achieved without major changes in macroeconomic variables or in public policies, others (like greater access to water and basic sanitation) are only expected to be achieved following major policy changes. Large disparities also exist in the progress towards the MDGs across geographic regions.

Table 12.1 shows that progress in reducing moderate and extreme poverty as measured by national poverty lines has been insufficient.[2] Progress also seems insufficient to meet poverty reduction targets by international measures for moderate poverty defined as the share of the population living on less than two dollars per person per day at purchasing power parity (PPP). At given trends, only the target for reducing extreme poverty measured by the international poverty line of one dollar per day at PPP could be achieved by 2015.

While the net enrolment rate for primary education is close to 90 per cent, the rate of completion of primary school at the normative age was only 56.8 per cent in 2004, as a consequence of many children entering school late and high rates of grade repetition and dropout. The poor quality of education in Peru is also well documented.[3] Real per capita social spending began to recover in the 1990s after significant declines during the period of hyperinflation. The share of spending on education in total social spending declined, however, in favour of more spending on social protection, especially food and nutritional support programmes which serve mainly as a palliative measure to counteract the lack of progress made towards reducing income poverty (Yamada and Castro, 2007). The gender gap in primary and secondary education has narrowed since 1990 and the country will most likely achieve full parity in access to education for boys and girls in the next years (see Table 12.1).

Table 12.1   Peru: Indicators for evaluating the MDGs (1991 and 2004) and targets for 2015

MDG and associated indicator	1991	2004[a]	Target for 2015
MDG 1: Poverty incidence–1dollar a day line at PPP (% of population)	6.6	3.7	3.3
MDG 1: Poverty incidence–2 dollar a day line at PPP (% of population)	26.1	17.4	13.0
MDG 1: Incidence of moderate poverty–national line (% of population)	54.5	53.6	27.3
MDG 1: Incidence of extreme poverty–national line (% of population)	23.0	26.8	11.5
MDG 2: Primary school completion rate (% of students between 11and 17 years who completed 6th grade of primary school)	75.1	89.5	100.0
MDG 2: Rate for completion of primary school at normative age (% of students who completed primary school at 12 years of age)	22.7	56.8	71.4[b]
MDG 3: Gender equality in primary education (proportion of girls to boys enrolled in education system in per cent)	98.5	95.0	100.0
MDG 3: Gender equality in secondary education (proportion of girls to boys enrolled in education system in per cent)	94.5	92.0	100.0
MDG 4: Under-five mortality rate (per 1.000 live births)	81.0	34.0[c]	27.0
MDG 7a: Sustainable access to drinking water (% of population)	63.0	75.0	88.0
MDG 7b: Access to basic sanitation services (% of population)	54.0	56.0	78.0

Source: 2004 National Household Survey (ENAHO), 1991 National Household Living Standards Survey (ENNIV), and 2000 Demographic and Health Survey (ENDES).
[a] Corresponds to the base year of scenarios simulated through the general equilibrium model.
[b] As explained in the text, this is considered to be the feasible target given the "natural" rate of school grade repetition.
[c] Data are for 2000.

The child mortality rate dropped significantly during the 1990s, reaching 34 deaths per 1,000 live births in the early 2000s, down from 81 in 1990. The priority given to public spending on preventative and primary health care during the 1990s likely was an important factor in achieving this progress (Cotlear, 2006). With continued trends one could be moderately optimistic about achieving the MDG target for reducing child mortality in 2015 (see Table 12.1). However, national averages mask the critical situation of much higher probability of mortality of children born to parents belonging to low-income groups, possessing low levels of education, and living in rural areas. For example, in the period between 1986 and 1996, the under-five mortality rate averaged 114 per 1,000 live births among children born to mothers without education and 100 among those born in rural areas.

Coverage of drinking water and basic sanitation services is low in Peru. This is of great concern as international comparative studies as well as evidence for Peru suggest that access to better water sources and basic sanitation services has a positive impact on progress towards other goals in the areas of health, nutrition, and possibly also education (Beltran and others, 2004). Access to drinking water increased from 63 per cent around 1990 to 75 per cent in 2004, but this is not sufficient for achieving the pre-set MDG target by 2015 (see Table 12.1). Moreover, progress stagnated during the 2000s. The situation regarding access to basic sanitation services is even more worrisome as coverage increased only slightly from 54 per cent to 56 per cent during this same time period, putting Peru well off track towards the target set for 2015. The Government of Alan Garcia is giving priority to improving access to drinking water. It was a key issue in his presidential election campaign during which he promised to implement a "Water for All" plan. The plan targets to provide at least one million Peruvians living in poor urban areas with access to drinking water over a number of years.

Determinants of MDG progress: A partial equilibrium analysis

The elasticities of the determinants of progress towards the MDGs were estimated using microeconometric techniques. Determinants included socio-economic characteristics of individuals, household income and expenditures, and public spending on different services.

Available information only permits the estimation of microeconomic models for probabilities associated with determinants of education (MDG 2) and for under-five child mortality (MDG 4). Data on maternal mortality are deficient. Only national aggregates are available, but there are no consistent time series and neither is there information to link maternal mortality with detailed information at the household level in order to study its determinants.[4] Because of these limitations, MDG 5 was not included in the macro and micro modelling analysis presented in this study. Moreover, the lack of information about spending on infrastructure for water and sanitation at the local level impedes full estimation of a behavioural model of the demand for these two services. In this case, point elasticities that quantify the impact of changes in the determinants of access to drinking water supply and sanitation on actual access were derived from past trends in coverage for these services and per-capita public investment spending on water and sanitation during 1999-2004.[5]

Table A12.1 (Appendix A12) shows the estimated values of all relevant elasticities used in the MDG module of MAMS. Most estimated elasticity values for the determinants of progress towards the MDGs turned out to be statistically significant. A detailed description of the estimation procedures used, as well as a detailed analysis and presentation of the results can be found in Castro and Yamada (2006).

Calibration of MAMS to Peruvian data

MAMS was calibrated using parameter values that adequately define the main behavioural relationships of the Peruvian economy and impose a number of constraints required for obtaining a feasible model solution. Three basic data inputs were required: a Social Accounting Matrix (SAM) that defines the structure of the economy and provides accounting consistency for the flows of incomes and payments between different sectors and institutions in the base year; elasticities that characterize the behavioural relationship determining demand and supply at the level of production sectors and commodities, spending and saving decisions, and MDG achievement; and projected growth rates and levels of exogenous variables between the base year and 2015. It was also necessary to define the type of closure rules that determine adjustment towards equilibrium in factor markets and those determining macroeconomic adjustment (see also Chapter 3).

A new SAM was constructed for the present study using data for 2004, the base year chosen for the calibration and simulation exercise of the model. The SAM distinguishes 3 institutions, 16 types of production sectors and commodities, and 5 production factors. A detailed description of the compilation of the 2004 SAM for Peru can be found in Castro and Yamada (2006).

As in the case of the elasticities of the MDG determinants, an effort was made to also estimate all other elasticities econometrically. Due to data limitations, however, plausible estimates were obtained only for those associated with the behavioural functions for demand, supply (in particular, decisions relating to selling on domestic and world markets), and savings. In general, elasticities were derived from multivariate time-series regression models specifying behavioural relationships as also captured in MAMS and following procedures suggested by Sánchez (2004). Elasticities that could not be estimated econometrically were derived as point elasticities using data from the Ministry of Economy and Finance (MEF) (2004). Table A12.2 (Appendix A12) presents the values of the key elasticities as applied to solve MAMS with Peruvian data. Further details on how these were estimated and which data sources were used can be found in Castro and Yamada (2006).

Analysis of simulated scenarios

After calibrating MAMS the model was solved for a baseline scenario for the 2004-15 period. The baseline assumes continued trends for key exogenous variables and continuation of existing policies, including fixed growth of government spending at a rate similar to that observed in years prior to 2004. In other words, the baseline may be seen to represent "business as usual". This scenario is used as the reference to assess various MDG scenarios under which public expenditures are scaled up to the level required to achieve the MDG targets for education, child mortality, and water and sanitation by the year 2015. The model uses these scenarios to facilitate the analysis of how higher public spending would affect the rest of the economy under different assumptions about how the increase in government spending is financed.

Baseline scenario

GDP increases at an annual average rate of 4.8 per cent in the baseline scenario (Table 12.2). This rate is somewhat above the performance of the 1990s and early 2000s, though 0.5 percentage points below the official projection of the Multi-annual Macroeconomic Framework for 2007-09 (MEF, 2006). It would not be prudent to assume a much more optimistic scenario for economic growth, given the likely unrealistic assumption of continued favourable international economic conditions for the whole simulation period.

The level of external savings would increase slightly in the baseline, reaching 0.32 per cent of GDP towards the end of the projected period and averaging 0.30 per cent per year during the entire period (see Table 12.2). Most of the increase in foreign savings is to make up for a slight drop in private savings in financing private sector investment. The fiscal deficit remains more or less stable in the baseline at around 1 per cent.

Table 12.2   Peru: Real GDP, primary components of spending and savings-investment gaps in the baseline scenario, 2004-2015

	Initial value (2004)	**Average value (2004-2015)**
	Billions of new soles	*Growth rate*
GDP	230.34	4.83
Consumption	160.60	4.89
Investment	42.61	4.60
Government spending	20.65	2.68
Exports	49.72	5.13
Imports	43.24	4.21
	Percentage of GDP	*Percentage of GDP*
Private savings	16.77	16.57
Private investment	15.79	15.78
Private gap	0.97	0.79
Government savings	1.69	1.09
Government investment	2.71	2.19
Fiscal deficit	-1.01	-1.10
External savings	0.01	0.30

Source: MAMS for Peru.

Government final consumption spending—including that on goods and services related to education, health, and sanitation—is assumed to grow on average at 2.68 per cent per year, while public investment increases at an annual pace of 2.81 per cent. This rate of expansion of government services is insufficient to make adequate progress towards the four non-poverty MDG targets analyzed in this study (see Figure 12.1). For instance, between 2004 and 2015, the percentage of children who complete primary education on time would increase from 56.8 per cent to 65.6 per cent, well short of the target of 100 per cent. Most of this increase would be on account of increased school enrolment of children in primary school age. The percentage of children graduating, however, would remain practically unchanged (at around 94 per cent) throughout the simulation period.[6]

The 100 per cent target for primary school completion (that is, ensuring that all children enter the schooling system at the mandated age and that no child repeats a grade in any of the six years of the primary school cycle), is extremely challenging for Peru. Once enrolled, the probability of completing primary school was already quite high in the base year (93.5 per cent) and the elasticity of this indicator with respect to the provision of educational goods and services is too low to expect much improvement can be achieved through supply-side measures. The interpretation of these results is based on the premise that, while scaling up the public spending aimed at improving access to and quality of primary education can ensure that most families decide to enrol their children in school, further measures need to be considered should repetition be reduced.[7] This premise is taken into account in the analysis of the remaining scenarios.

Consequently, for the present analysis, the decision was made to work with the following two targets for MDG 2: (1) primary school completion on time, using the contemporaneous probability of a child (of six) enrolling in the first grade of primary school and that of a child (of six to twelve years old) completing a grade of primary, as shown in Figure 12.1; and (2) primary school completion one year after what is established as the normative year (at 13 years of age), also using the contemporaneous values of the two previously mentioned probabilities ("MDG2, 13 years" in Figure 12.1).[8] In this sense, the results reported in Figure 12.1 allow us to reach two conclusions. First, using the contemporaneous values mentioned has only a marginal effect on the percentage of children who finish primary school on time. Second, nearly 93 per cent of the children would be able to complete primary school by the year 2015, without any specific policy measures being taken, under the assumption that each one might repeat one of the six grades of primary school. These considerations lead to adjusting the target for MDG 2 to 71.4 per cent, as indicated in Table 12.1.

In terms of under-five child mortality, while the indicator is relatively close to its goal in the base year, the baseline scenario predicts a drop of only 2 units (from 34 to 32 deaths per 1,000 live births), possibly due to strongly decreasing

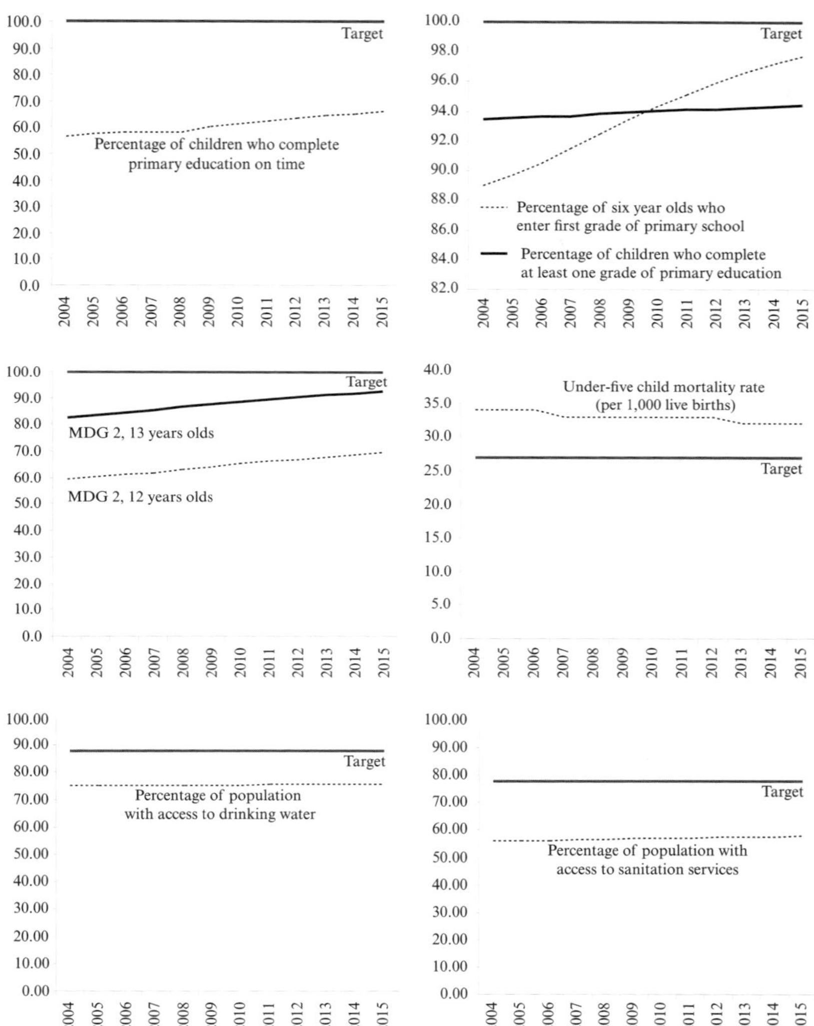

Figure 12.1   Peru: Progress towards MDG-related indicators in the baseline scenario, 2004-2015

Source: MAMS for Peru.

marginal returns from policy interventions in this area. Finally, and in line with the insignificant improvements observed in the baseline scenario, the percentage of households with access to adequate water and sanitation services (75 per cent and 56 per cent, respectively) remains practically unchanged during the entire period in projection.

MDG scenarios

Table 12.3 summarizes the results of the simulated progress towards the MDGs in the baseline scenario and in the scenarios in which MDGs 2, 4, and 7a/b are targeted separately. Public spending in each MDG scenario is assumed to be financed through increased taxation. In the scenario where only the primary education goal is met, the percentage of children who complete primary education at the normative age increases more than in the baseline scenario, but the target of 100 per cent is far from achieved and only the adjusted target of 71.4 per cent is approximated.

In terms of the additional public spending required to reach one or two of the goals separately, the goal for primary education is the one that demands the

Table 12.3   Peru: MDG indicators in baseline scenarios and scenarios targeting one or two MDGs at a time only, 2004-2015[a]

| | | | Simulated values in 2015 by scenario: | | | |
MDG and related indicator	2004	Target for 2015	Baseline	MDG2	MDG4	MDGs 7a and 7b
MDG 2: Proportion of children who complete primary school on time (%)	56,80	100,00	65,64	70,68	66,63	67,44
MDG 2: Proportion of children of 6 years of age enrolled in first grade of primary school (%)	89,00	--	97,82	99,41	97,44	98,01
MDG 2: Proportion of children who passed at least one grade of primary education (%)	93,50	--	94,48	95,00	94,79	94,90
MDG 2, 12 years[b]	59,46	--	69,56	73,09	70,70	71,59
MDG 2, 13 years[c]	82,66	--	92,61	95,01	92,79	93,50
MDG 4: Under-five child mortality rate (per 1,000 live births)	34,00	27,00	32,00	32,05	26,91	29,03
MDG 7a: Share of population with access to drinking water (%)	75,00	88,00	75,84	75,84	75,84	88,00
MDG 7b: Share of population with access to basic sanitation (%)	56,00	78,00	57,77	57,77	57,77	78,00

Source: MAMS for Peru.

[a] In the MDG scenarios, public spending is scaled up as required to meet the corresponding target and the spending increase is assume to be financed through increased direct taxes.

[b] Probability that a child enrols in primary education at age six and passes at least one grade until reaching age twelve.

[c] Probability that a child graduates from primary school one year after the mandated age of twelve (that is, at age 13).

most fiscal effort to achieve. With respect to the baseline scenario, additional public spending required for reaching just the primary education goal is, on average, around 0.5 per cent of GDP per year.[9] Additional public spending in the scenarios for the under-five child mortality goals and two goals of water and sanitation is about 0.46 per cent and 0.33 per cent of GDP respectively. Because of synergies between better access to water and sanitation and health, on the one hand, and between health and education outcomes, on the other, the sum of these additional expenditures surpasses the additional public spending shown in the scenario in which all of the goals are achieved simultaneously, but primarily because of the impact that the achievement of the water and sanitation goals has on the reducing under-five child mortality. If the required increase in public spending is financed through direct taxes, for example, the savings resulting from these synergies would be about 0.38 per cent of GDP per year.

Table 12.4 provides some detail on the required additional public spending to reach the goals for education, health, and water and sanitation simultaneously.

Table 12.4 Peru: Required public spending to achieve the MDGs under alternative financing scenarios, 2004-2015 (percentage of GDP)

	Public spending per year		Annual average additional spending per year (2004-2015)[a] in scenarios where MDGs are financed through:			
	Base year (2004)	Baseline scenario (2004-2015)	direct taxes	foreign aid	external borrowing	domestic borrowing
Total spending	2.18	2.03	0.95	0.88	0.88	0.93
Current spending						
Primary education	0.56	0.50	0.49	0.43	0.43	0.47
Secondary education	0.48	0.43	0.00	0.00	0.00	0.00
Tertiary education	0.30	0.27	0.00	0.00	0.00	0.00
Primary healthcare	0.30	0.27	0.05	0.05	0.05	0.05
Higher levels of healthcare	0.22	0.20	0.03	0.03	0.03	0.03
Water and sanitation	0.06	0.05	0.11	0.10	0.10	0.11
Capital spending						
Primary education	0.02	0.02	0.03	0.02	0.02	0.03
Secondary education	0.04	0.06	0.00	0.00	0.00	0.00
Tertiary education	0.09	0.10	0.00	0.00	0.00	0.00
Primary healthcare	0.05	0.05	0.01	0.01	0.01	0.01
Higher levels of healthcare	0.01	0.01	0.00	0.00	0.00	0.00
Water and sanitation	0.05	0.07	0.23	0.23	0.23	0.23

Source: MAMS for Peru.
[a] With respect to baseline scenario.

Meeting the target for education would demand the most resources and current spending would have to increase the most. In line with what was found in other country cases, the costs of achieving the MDGs tend to be higher when these are covered through the mobilization of domestic resources (ranging between 0.93 per cent and 0.95 per cent of GDP per year) as compared with financing through external resources (0.88 per cent of GDP per year). Financing through increasing direct taxes would be the most onerous option for Peru in terms of the required additional public spending to achieve the MDGs.

In the scenario where all of the goals are achieved simultaneously and the government uses tax revenues to finance the new spending, the direct tax burden should increase to 5.6 per cent of GDP in 2015—2.4 percentage points more than in the baseline scenario. The fiscal deficit would be kept at around 1 per cent of GDP. As a result, private savings and investment fall moderately as a percentage of GDP and growth in real GDP falls to a rate slightly below the baseline (see Table 12.5).

For Peru to be able to finance the new public spending through foreign grants, the required aid transfers would need to be 2.7 per cent of GDP or 248 soles per person in 2015—2 percentage points of GDP and 233 soles per person more than in the baseline scenario. In the MDG scenario with external borrowing, the flow of foreign loans would need to increase from 0.01 per cent of GDP in the baseline scenario to 2.6 per cent of GDP by 2015. The external debt-to-GDP ratio would increase in this scenario to 34.2 per cent of GDP in 2015, up from 23.2 per cent in the baseline. Finally, under the domestic borrowing scenario, the government would need to mobilize 4.2 per cent of GDP from domestic capital markets by 2015, up from 1 per cent of GDP in the baseline scenario. The domestic public debt would increase to 27.6 per cent of GDP by 2015 in this scenario, as compared with 14.5 per cent of GDP in the baseline. As Table 12.5 shows, the fiscal deficit would increase substantially in these three alternative financing scenarios.

Two additional comments must be made with respect to the fiscal deficit. First, the injection of public spending that is allocated to non-tradable sectors of the economy exercises pressure on the exchange rate, which tends to appreciate in all scenarios. This effect tends to intensify when external resources are used to finance the additional public spending and, consequently, export sectors are also affected more strongly.[10] As a further result, export-tax revenue and taxes levied on export production are lower than in the scenarios with domestic financing. Nonetheless, the fiscal deficit (as a share of GDP) is larger under the scenario where domestic borrowing is used, as can be seen in Table 12.5. This outcome is caused by the "crowding-out" effect on private investment of this source of funding. Private investment drops by around 3 percentage points of GDP towards the end of the projected period with consequences in the form of a lower rate of output growth and less overall tax revenue as compared with the baseline and the other financing scenarios.

Table 12.5   Peru: Summary of macroeconomic results in selected simulated scenarios

	Baseline scenario	**Scenario where MDGs are financed through:**			
		direct taxes	**foreign assistance**	**external borrowing**	**internal borrowing**
Government revenue (% GDP, 2015)					
Direct tax revenue	3.20	5.60	3.20	3.20	3.20
Total tax revenue	11.90	14.30	11.90	11.90	11.90
Transfers from the rest of the world	0.70	0.70	2.70	0.60	0.70
Domestic borrowing	1.00	1.00	1.00	1.00	4.20
External borrowing	0.01	0.01	0.01	2.61	0.01
Savings and investment (% GDP, 2015)					
Private savings	16.57	16.25	16.64	16.64	16.76
Private investment	15.78	15.45	15.84	15.84	12.90
Public savings	1.08	1.74	-0.28	-0.79	-1.26
Public investment	2.19	2.86	2.83	2.83	2.93
Fiscal deficit	-1.10	-1.12	-3.12	-3.62	-4.19
External savings	0.30	0.31	2.26	2.75	0.32
Foreign aid (soles per person)	14.51	14.51	248.22	14.51	14.51
Annual average growth rate (%, 2004 – 2015)					
GDP	4.83	4.65	4.72	4.72	4.39
Consumption	4.89	4.50	4.82	4.82	4.53
Investment	4.60	4.59	4.85	4.85	2.99
Government spending	2.68	4.05	3.90	3.90	4.03
Exports	5.13	4.84	4.11	4.11	4.56
Imports	4.21	3.92	4.14	4.14	3.64

Source: MAMS for Peru.

Given the restrictions on public finances imposed by the Fiscal Transparency and Responsibility Law and the macroeconomic trade-offs generated by the alternative financing scenarios, increasing tax revenue would seem the preferred financing strategy for achieving the MDGs, despite the fact that in this case the required additional public spending would be slightly higher as a share of GDP than in the case of the other financing options. This finding is consistent with the Multi-annual Macroeconomic Framework (2007-09), as defined prior to the 2008 global economic crisis. The Framework specifies measures aimed at expanding the tax base and envisages the possibility of increasing the tax burden to near 14 per cent of GDP. This tax burden is, in fact, quite close to what is required for the year 2015 in the tax-financed MDG scenario (see Table 12.5).

Microsimulations

Like most computable general equilibrium models, MAMS does not measure intra-household income distribution. The SAM for Peru only has one representative household and even with more groups the model would still not provide enough detail about changes in the income distribution in order to be able to to estimate the implications for poverty with any precision. To overcome this limitation, the microsimulation methodology described in Appendix A2.1 of Chapter 2 was applied to study the changes in income poverty for each of the scenarios discussed in the previous section. Using this methodology, the labour market outcomes of each scenario simulated with MAMS were linked to household survey data with information about the complete income distribution. The survey used was the 2004 ENAHO.[11]

The main results for the tax-financed MDG scenarios are shown in Table 12.[12] Poverty as measured through the one-dollar-per-day poverty line (at PPP) would fall from 3.98 per cent in 2004 to 3.33 per cent in 2015. Consequently, the target for MDG 1 would be achievable. Extreme poverty as measured through the international poverty line was 6.6 per cent in 1990, leading to a target of 3.3 per cent for 2015. The target for halving poverty as measured by the line of two dollars per person per day (at PPP) would also be achieved. In this case, the indicator would fall from 26.1 per cent around 1990 to about 11.6 per cent in 2015 under the tax-financed MDG scenario. However, indicators for moderate and extreme poverty, as measured by national poverty lines (which would be more relevant for national discussion), fall by less than 50 per cent between 1990 and 2015, as shown in Table 12.6.

The decomposition of the microsimulation results by sequential effects of the simulated changes in the labour market helps to provide more insight into which effect has the largest impact on poverty and inequality. The MDG strategy would lead to a change in the employment structure by sector (the S effect) towards non-tradable activities including those with lower average labour incomes. Taken in isolation, this effect would lead to an increase in poverty. Changes in the relative labour income across sectors (the W1 effect) enhance this impact, especially as average earnings of unskilled and semi-skilled workers fall relative to the mean (Table 12.6). This is so because the supply of these two types of worker increases faster than that of skilled workers during the simulation period.13 Furthermore, the demand grows faster than the supply for skilled workers as more teachers and medical personnel are being hired for the implementation of the MDG strategy.

In contrast, growth of average real labour income (at 2.6 per cent per year) and per capita household income (at 4.3 per cent per year) help reduce poverty. The rate of real wage growth (W2 effect) is similar to that of GDP in the tax-financed MDG scenario (4.65 per cent per year) and higher than growth of the

Table 12.6   Peru: Summary of microsimulation results in base year and tax-financed MDG scenarios

Indicator	Base year (2004)	Sum of sequential effects (2015)[a]			
		S	S+W1	S+W1+W2	S+W1+W2+M
Poverty incidence (% of population):					
1 dollar a day poverty line (at PPP)	3.98	5.53	6.03	2.91	3.33
2 dollars a day poverty line (at PPP)	17.38	19.00	20.66	11.13	11.60
National moderate poverty line	53.63	54.17	56.11	37.05	37.59
National extreme poverty line	26.79	28.29	30.37	16.81	17.31
Gini coefficient					
Per capita household income	0.51	0.52	0.54	0.54	0.54
Labour income	0.56	0.56	0.57	0.57	0.57
Average income (new soles)					
Per capita household income	331	328	328	537	525
Labour income per worker	1,385	1,376	1,376	1,869	1,839

Source: MAMS for Peru and microsimulations based on 2004 ENAHO data.

[a] Sequential effects in the structure of employment by sector (S), the structure of remunerations by sector (W1), average labour income (W2), and the employment structure by skill level (M). The last step of the sequence of cumulative effects measures the final impact on the quantification of poverty and inequality.

total labour force (about 2 per cent per year). As indicated above, the change in the composition of the labour force by skill level (M effect) would have a mild poverty-increasing effect, but on balance the poverty incidence would fall between 2004 and 2015 owing to the real wage increase.

Yet, as analyzed in greater detail in Castro and Yamada (2006), the decline in the incidence of extreme poverty as measured by the one-dollar-per-day poverty line would be somewhat weaker in the MDG strategy than in the baseline scenario. In the baseline scenario the extreme poverty incidence would fall to 3.02 per cent (as opposed to 3.33 per cent in the tax-financed MDG scenario). This outcome is the result of the much weaker employment shift in favour of jobs in the non-tradable sector and remuneration shift in favour of skilled workers (S+W1) in the baseline.

These findings suggest that more active policies are needed to achieve MDG 1 alongside the other MDGs. One option would be to introduce measures that would accelerate the rate of growth of the economy. A further analysis using MAMS for Peru and the microsimulation methodology suggests that the economy would need to expand by 7 per cent per year through the year 2015 in order to meet the poverty reduction targets when measuring poverty through the national income thresholds. In such a scenario of fast growth, the incidence of extreme poverty would fall to 11.83 per cent in 2015 and that for moderate poverty to 26.98 per cent. The faster growth would facilitate stronger real labour income growth which in turn would foster the indicated poverty reduction. Higher economic growth would also have a positive impact on the probability of enrolment in higher education. This would lead over time to an accelerated increase in the supply of skilled workers. At the same time, higher incomes would allow families to invest more themselves in education, which in turn reduces the fiscal effort that would be required to reach the target for primary education. As a result, the additional annual average public spending required to meet the MDGs would decrease to 0.49 per cent of GDP, almost half of the amount required in the scenarios where the economy grows at near 5 per cent per year (see Table 12.4).

Conclusions and policy recommendations

The analysis carried out in this chapter, based on the scenarios simulated through MAMS, indicates that in the case of Peru, it would be possible to achieve the MDGs of primary education, child mortality, and water and sanitation at affordable cost through further expansion of the provision of social services. In a scenario where the economy grows at a pace of 4.7 per cent per year, the additional public spending required for reaching the goals in those areas would be around 0.95 per cent of GDP per year when financed through an increase in direct taxes. This cost would be 40 per cent higher if the MDGs are not pursued simultaneously but sequentially, showing that there are important synergies between improvements in education, health, and water and sanitation.

At the same time, however, the findings also show that it would not be possible to ensure that all children begin and complete primary school on time by the year 2015, primarily because of the difficulties in introducing additional improvements to the probability of graduating from primary school, which already has quite a high level in the base year for the model (2004), and whose natural limit may be below 100 per cent. Results also show, however, that an expansion in education services would permit a considerable increase in the percentage of children who enrol in primary school at the mandatory age and that this would ensure that the percentage of children who complete primary school by 13 years of age (with a one year delay) could increase to close to 96 per cent in 2015. For all practical purposes, we consider this as a more realistic target for MDG 2 in the case of Peru.

Given the commitment of the Peruvian government to fiscal discipline and macroeconomic stability, the required increase in public spending may best be financed through an increase in the tax burden. The model simulations show that this burden would need to increase by close to 1.3 percentage points of GDP on average between 2004 and 2015. However, since the marginal returns of the interventions would diminish when getting closer to the MDG targets towards the end of the period (2015), the cost would be higher and the tax burden would need to be increased by around 2.4 percentage points of GDP.

The analysis further shows that MDG 1 would be achieved if the poverty incidence is measured through the international poverty lines of one or two dollars per day, though the degree of poverty reduction would be less than in the baseline because of the employment and remuneration shifts in favour of non-traded sectors and skilled workers under the MDG strategy. When using the national poverty lines, however, the poverty reduction target would not be met; neither in the baseline nor in the MDG scenarios. In other words, achieving the goals for education, health, water and sanitation by themselves does not contribute to poverty reduction within the given simulation period. In fact, the indicated shift in the labour market leads to higher income inequality thereby limiting the impact of overall economic growth on poverty reduction.

The economy would need to grow at an average rate of 7 per cent per year between 2004 and 2015 in order to halve both moderate and extreme poverty (measured by the national poverty lines) by 2015 (from 1990 levels). However, sustained economic growth at a pace of 7 per cent per year seems rather ambitious by historic standards. Peru's economic history has not seen any decade during which growth rates of more than 5.5 per cent on average per year could be sustained. In fact, such rates of growth were achieved only during the 1950s and 1960s.

Therefore, in addition to short-term policies of income transfers for the most vulnerable groups, Peru would have to consider more aggressive long-term policies aiming at a redistribution of incomes and assets. Accelerated progress in education at all levels for the poorer segments of the population would be one element of such policies. The results of the present analysis suggest that progress towards MDG 2 could be poverty enhancing in the short run. In the medium to long run, however, a greater supply of skilled labour will not only contribute to reducing existing wage gaps, and thereby income poverty, but would also contribute to productivity increases through increased availability and quality of human capital. This increase in human capital would, in turn, increase the capacity of families to generate wealth and underpin faster economic growth.

Appendix A12

Table A12.1　Elasticities of MDG determinants as used in MAMS for Peru

	Determinants								
	QES[a]	WGS	WGT	MDG4	PCS	PCH	MDG 7a	MDG 7b	PCW
MDG 2: Probability that a child (6 years old) will enrol in first grade of primary school[a]	0.0661	0.0000	0.0000	0.0000	0.2211	--	0.0431	--	--
Probability of completing (passing) a grade of primary school	0.0057	0.0221	0.0000	-0.0206	0.0157	--	0.0075	0.0054	--
Probability of completing (passing) a grade of secondary school	0.0057	0.0221	0.0000	-0.0206	0.0157	--	0.0075	0.0054	--
Probability of completing (passing) a grade of higher education[a]	0.0057	0.0221	0.0000	-0.0206	0.0157	--	0.0075	0.0054	--
Probability of graduating from the last grade of primary school and continuing on to secondary school[a]	0.1399	0.0000	0.0000	0.0000	0.0000	--	--	--	--
Probability of completing the last year secondary school and continuing on to higher education.	0.0366	0.0000	0.0000	0.0000	0.8861	--	--	--	--
MDG 4: Probability of child death before reaching 5 years of age.	--	--	--	--	-0.0777	-0.1681	0.0000	-0.3219	--
MDG 7a: Percentage of the population with sustainable access to drinking water	--	--	--	--	0.0000	--	--	--	0.0030
MDG 7b: Percentage of population with access to basic sanitation services	--	--	--	--	0.0000	--	--	--	0.0086

Source: Authors' estimates.

Abbreviations: QES: Quality of education services; WGS: Wage gap: Secondary vs. no education; WGT: Wage gap: Tertiary vs. secondary; MDG4: Under-five child mortality; PCS: Per capita household spending; PCH: Per capita supply of aggregate health goods and services; PCW: Per capita supply of water and sanitation services.

Table A12.2　Elasticities of demand and supply behaviour used in MAMS for Peru

Description	Value	Source
Demand		
Armington elasticity	0.454	Econometric estimates
Supply		
Constant elasticity of transformation of supply for domestic and export markets	0.933	Econometric estimates
Output aggregation elasticity by commodity	4.000	MEF (2004)
Production functions		
Substitution between factors for each activity		
Agriculture	0.750	MEF (2004)
Mining	0.500	MEF (2004)
Manufacturing	1.000	MEF (2004)
Other activities	1.250	MEF (2004)
Substitution between value added and intermediate inputs for each activity.	0.600	MEF (2004)
Consumption and savings		
Elasticities of consumer demand with respect to total expenditures (LES)		
Minerals and manufactured products	1.000	MEF (2004)
Other private goods.	0.850	MEF (2004)
Elasticity of private savings with respect to per capita income	0.943	Econometric estimates

Sources: Authors' calculations and MEF (2004).

Acknowledgements

The authors would like to thank Carlos Gallardo, Edgar Salgado, and Lucciano Villacorta for their excellent work as research assistants. They would also like to recognize the important contributions of Eugenia Mujica (UNDP) and Juan Manuel García (MEF) in the initial stages of the research and the valuable comments of Marco V. Sánchez, Rob Vos, Miguel Gutiérrez and others. All errors and omissions are the exclusive responsibility of the authors.

Notes

1   Shocks that have affected the Peruvian economy in the past on a regular basis include the El Niño and La Niña climate phenomena, deteriorating terms of trade, international financial crises, and internal institutional and political crises.

2   This study used the database from the 2004 National Household Survey (ENAHO) made available in the first half of 2006.

3   Peru ranked next to last in Latin America on the 2001 international reading comprehension tests (PISA) with grades 20 per cent below the average for the region (Cotlear, 2006).

4   According to United Nations data, there were approximately 410 maternal deaths per 100,000 live births in Peru in the year 2000. However, there is no reliable comparable information to assess how the indicator has changed over time.

5   Data on service coverage were derived from the ENAHO surveys for 1999-2004. Access to water and sanitation services for urban households was defined as adequate where people reported having a connection to the public system inside their house. For rural households, adequate water and sanitation services was considered having access to a well (or something better) and a latrine (or better), respectively. The public investment figures for water and sanitation services are those reported by the Integrated System for Public Financial Management (SIAF-SP). The elasticities estimated for access to water and sanitation with respect to units of per capita investment in these services are 0.003 and 0.00857, respectively.

6   Given the way in which the indicator for MDG 2 (percentage of children who complete primary school on time) is conceived in the model, an increase in the probability of primary school enrolment has an impact on the percentage of children who complete primary school on time after six years (the length of the primary school cycle). At the same time, it is worth emphasizing that the final value of the indicator is particularly sensitive to changes in the probability of completing each year of primary school. In fact, this probability must be quite close to one starting in 2010 for the percentage of children who complete school on time to approach the goal of 100 per cent in 2015.

7   At high values for the probability of completing each year of primary school, it can be expected that the students' performance will be a function of a set of family characteristics that are difficult to quantify (such as the level of motivation and discipline) and which lie outside the sphere of influence of public policy. Therefore, it is not very realistic to expect that 100 per cent of the children enrolled in a particular grade of primary school will complete that grade successfully on the first try. While the drop-out rate may approach zero as a result of improvements in educational services and household income, the same is not true for the rate of grade repetition. The reduced elasticity of the probability of completing each year of primary school with respect to the provision of these services (validated through the econometric analysis) reflects this reality.

8 The use of these contemporaneous values is the equivalent of projecting the percentage of children who would complete primary school at 12 and 13 years of age, under the assumption that the probability of completion would stay constant during the next six and seven years, respectively. Given that the probability of dropping out is quite low in the base year (0.5 per cent), the probability (Pr) of completing primary school at 13 years of age (since the child enrolled on time) was approximated using the following procedure: Pr(enrolling on time) *[Pr(completing primary school in six tries) + Pr(completing primary school in seven tries, after not completing in six)].

9 Additional public spending, with respect to the baseline scenario, corresponds to the average of the four scenarios in which the sources of financing are, respectively, direct taxes, foreign assistance, public external borrowing, and public internal borrowing.

10 For more details on the exchange-rate adjustment created by public spending associated with the MDGs, see Chapter 2.

11 As explained in the Appendix to Chapter 2, MAMS simulates various changes in labour market parameters, which will impact on income inequality and poverty at the household level. Changes in the unemployment rate were not included, because, as indicated in the second section of this chapter, open unemployment is not the main source of employment problems in Peru.

12 We only assess the results for the tax-financing scenarios here since, as indicated in the previous section, raising taxes would appear to be the preferred MDG financing strategy. Nonetheless, it should be noted that the poverty and inequality outcomes of this scenario are quite similar to those of the alternative financing scenarios for the other financing options.

13 The supply of unskilled, semi-skilled and skilled labour increases, respectively, by 1.99 per cent, 2 per cent and 1.64 per cent per year, between 2004 and 2015.

References

Beltrán, Arlette, Juan F. Castro, Enrique Vásquez and Gustavo Yamada (2004). "Objetivos de Desarrollo del Milenio en el Perú: Alcanzando las Metas," United Nations Development Programme (UNDP) and the Research Centre of the University of the Pacific.

Castro, Juan F., and Gustavo Yamada (2006). "Evaluación de estrategias de desarrollo para alcanzar los MDG. El caso del Perú," Research Centre of the University of the Pacific, Discussion Document 06/11.

Cotlear, Daniel (ed.) (2006). "Un nuevo contrato social para el Perú ¿Cómo lograr un país más educado, saludable y solidario?" Washington, D.C.: World Bank.

MEF (2004). "Implementación de un Modelo Macroeconométrico Social para determinar los efectos del crecimiento económico en los niveles de pobreza y distribución del ingreso," Ministry of Economy and Finance of Peru, General Office of Social and Economic Affairs.

__________ (2006). "Marco Macroeconómico Multianual 2007-2009," Ministry of Economy and Finance of Peru.

Sánchez, Marco V. (2004). *Rising inequality and falling poverty in Costa Rica's agriculture during trade reform. A macro-micro general equilibrium analysis*, Maastricht: Shaker.

Yamada, Gustavo (2004). "Economía Laboral en el Perú: Avances recientes y agenda pendiente," Working Document 63, Research Centre of the University of the Pacific, Lima.

__________, and Juan F. Castro (2007). "Poverty, Inequality and Social Policies in Peru: As Poor as It Gets," Draft chapter for Harvard/CAF Project "The Peruvian Growth Puzzle," Research Centre of the University of the Pacific, Discussion Document 07/06.

Index